TURBOJET

HISTORY AND DEVELOPMENT
1930–1960

This book
is dedicated to the Memory
of our Son, David

TURBOJET
HISTORY AND DEVELOPMENT
1930–1960
VOLUME 2
USSR, USA, JAPAN, FRANCE, CANADA, SWEDEN,
SWITZERLAND, ITALY, CZECHOSLOVAKIA AND HUNGARY

Antony L. Kay MRAeS

THE CROWOOD PRESS

First published in 2007 by
The Crowood Press Ltd
Ramsbury, Marlborough
Wiltshire SN8 2HR

www.crowood.com

British Library Cataloguing-in-Publication Data
A catalogue record for this book is available from the British Library.

ISBN 978 1 86126 939 3

Picture Acknowledgements.
The majority of illustrations in both volumes of Turbojet have been acknowledged but a
few have not. In these cases, efforts to trace the provenance have failed. The author and
publisher will, of course, welcome any opportunity to correct such omissions.

Typeset by Florence Production Ltd, Stoodleigh, Devon
Printed and bound in Great Britain by TJ International Ltd, Padstow

Contents

Introduction

This second volume covers the work on aeronautical gas turbine engines and their application carried out in the Soviet Union, the USA, Japan, France, Canada, Sweden, Switzerland, Italy, Czechoslovakia and Hungary. These countries had their own pioneers and many capable engineers and physicists who made valuable contributions to the early development of the turbojet and its derivatives, notably Arkip Lyul'ka (Soviet Union), Nathan Price (USA), Osamu Nagano (Japan), Sensaud de Lavaud (France), Alfred Lysholm (Sweden), Jakob Ackeret (Switzerland) and György Jendrassik (Hungary). Their work

was often inspired by that pioneered in Great Britain and Germany during and just after the Second World War, as narrated in the previous volume. A generalization would be to say that the new, fast jet aircraft owed a great deal to British turbojets and German cutting-edge aerodynamics, the best examples of this being the famous MiG-15 and F-86 Sabre jet fighters, which met each other in combat during the Korean War. As far as is feasible, the history has been told chronologically, first by countries and then by companies and events.

As in the first volume, turboprop and turboshaft engines are covered as well as

the turbojet, and their applications in the fields of research, military and civilian aircraft are described. The range of types of aircraft powered by these new engines was great, as designers all over the world sought the best ways, often novel, to utilize them.

An example of an aircraft, novel in 1955, is illustrated in the photograph below showing the Martin XP6M-1 Seamaster high performance, multi-role flying boat, seen on its removable wheels. This large aircraft was powered by four turbojets and was one of the fastest flying boats ever built.

The Russian MiG-15 jet fighter came as a shock to the West when first encountered in the Korean War and was produced in large numbers in the Soviet Union and other countries. The bottom photo illustrates a flight of Polish-built machines in that country's air force. Top: Russian Aviation Research Trust. Bottom: Philip Jarrett

PART III

The Soviet Union

Soviet indigenous development of the turbojet engine got off to a slow start but, following a period of work experience with German and then British engines in the early years after the Second World War, Soviet scientists and engineers were soon producing some remarkable engines. This is not to say, however, that they were slow in grasping the potential of the new form of powerplant but, as we shall see, the war, red tape and stifling bureaucracy held back earlier progress by a few years. Another impediment was the political persecution prevalent in dictator Joseph Stalin's Soviet system, which could be visited on anyone, however talented they might be and however useful to their country. Imprisonment, deportation and even death could be the sentence, whether deserved or not, often at the whim of the all-powerful Stalin. Quite often, lack of initial success in a project was not tolerated, promising developments were scrapped and personnel were not given a second chance. Examples of persecution and imprisonment of important people at different times (concerned with this history only) are Nivikov (wartime commander of the Air Force), Shakhurin (minister of the Aircraft Industry, responsible for R&D (research and development)), the engine designers Stechkin and Mikulin and the aircraft designer Tupolev. At the end of the 1930s an 'engineers' prison' allowed a number of detainees, such as Tupolev, to go on working for the State.

On the technological front, the main barrier to Soviet progress in turbojet development was the lack of indigenous, suitable heat-resisting steels, even though plenty of the alloying metals were available. However, analysis of British Nimonic alloys pointed their metallurgists in the right direction after the end of the Second World War.

Perhaps the earliest Russian study for a jet-propelled aircraft was in 1912, when the engineer A. Gorokhov designed an aircraft to be driven by a piston engine driving a compressor that supplied a combustion chamber with air. The first Soviet experiments with reaction propulsion were carried out between 1928 and 1930 by the engineer Fridrikh Tsander from Avia Trest, who built and successfully tested his OR-1 liquid-fuelled rocket engines. By 1931 Tsander was presiding over the Group for Exploration of Reaction Propulsion (GIRD), which was established in Moscow. A Scientific Test Institute (NII) was founded in 1933 and this became the basis for subsequent work with liquid-fuelled rockets, although, owing to their dangerous nature and excessive fuel consumption, these were not seen as practical for powering aircraft. Neither did intensive work with ramjets point the way forward at that time. Already, however, studies were being made of a gas turbine turbojet engine to power aircraft and to take over at speeds where the piston engine and airscrew were becoming inefficient. The turbine was already well known as a means of extracting power from steam. An early example was the low-pressure steam turbine designed around 1910 by the young Aleksandr Mikulin, who was later to excel in turbojet design: the turbine was used to lift water buckets from a well but, following an attempt to boost its power, the boiler exploded, inflicting minor injuries.

In 1924 the engineer Vladimir I. Bazarov, who later became a leading designer at Mikulin's design bureau, proposed the construction of a reaction engine in which the airflow was divided into two upon leaving the combustion chamber. Boris S. Stechkin, another engineer who was later to play a pivotal role in Mikulin turbojet design and development, was developing the theory of the turbojet engine by 1929. The rocket pioneer K.E. Tsiolkovskii projected jet engines in 1932, including one with the bypass concept (apparently before Whittle). On 27 August 1936 (exactly three years before Heinkel's He 178 made the world's first turbojet aircraft flight), a research programme was authorized by the Council of Labour and Defence (STO) of the Council of People's Commissars (SNK) and this was to include reaction engines, the gas turbine and aircraft powered by such means.

At least three separate groups embraced the turbine part of this programme, but initially they worked on a steam turbine system to drive an aircraft's airscrew. These groups included S.A. Aksyutin's at the NII of the Civil Air Fleet (GVF or Aeroflot), Moscow, and I.M. Sinyev's group at the Kirov works in Leningrad. There was also Prof. V.T. Tsvetkov's group at the aero-engine department of the Kharkov Aviation Institute (KhAI) in the Ukraine. Tsvetkov's group was working on a closed-circuit steam turbine system originally intended to power the eight-engined giant ANT-20 Maxim Gorkii aircraft.

At about this time research on the turboprop engine was being undertaken by Prof. V.V. Uvarov and a group at the Moscow Higher Technical School (MVTU), but it is uncertain if this was also in the STO SNK programme.

CHAPTER ONE

Lyul'ka's Early Pioneering Work

Arkip Mikhaylovich Lyul'ka was born on 23 March 1908 into a peasant family living in Savarka, a village near Kiev. He later graduated at the Kiev Polytechnic Institute and acquired work experience at the turbo-generator factory in Kharkov, where he became involved in an aeronautical steam turbine project as part of his postgraduate work.

Lyul'ka was given the most difficult task of developing the steam condenser, which was an essential component of the closed-circuit system. Estimates soon showed, however, that at the designed speed of 400km/h (248mph), the drag of the condenser system would absorb some 40 per cent of the available power, resulting in a fuel consumption double that of a typical piston engine. Before the end of 1936 Lyul'ka had concluded that the steam turbine as a power unit for aircraft was a non-starter.

During the steam turbine research programme at the Kharkov Aviation Institute (KhAI), Lyul'ka began investigating ideas for a gas turbine engine. Together with other young Institute engineers, he was ready in 1937 to present a joint project for an aircraft gas turbine engine of 500kp (1,103lb) thrust with a centrifugal compressor and a single-stage turbine. Various designs of annular combustion chamber were suggested. Designated the RTD-1 (rocket turbojet engine), this was the first

Arkip Mikhaylovich Lyul'ka, pioneer of early Soviet turbojet engines.

turbojet engine to be designed in the Soviet Union. A projected straightforward fighter was also designed at the Institute to demonstrate the engine. This fighter, designated KhAI-2, featured an under-fuselage air intake and was planned for a maximum speed of 900km/h (559mph).

The whole project was put before the KhAI Scientific Council, which found little merit in it. G.F. Proskura, the head of its aerodynamics department, however, recommended sending Lyul'ka and the project to the NKOP Inventions Department in Moscow to obtain their views and so a meeting of top-level technical people was held on 13 December 1938.

This committee then passed Lyul'ka's project on to the Chief Administration of the Aviation Industry (GUAP), which in turn sent it to Prof. V.V. Uvarov of MVTU for his opinions. Uvarov, who was researching a turboprop project, rated Lyul'ka's project very highly and this eventually led to GUAP allocating some 160,000 roubles for the realization of the turbojet and for the project to be introduced into the plans of the NII V-VS (Scientific Test Institute of the Air Force).

A base for the development of the turbojet engine was found at one of the works of the KhAI, but unfortunately these works lacked the facilities to pursue the work. Lyul'ka attended various reviews (all unfavourable) and meetings, one of which was with GUAP chief M. Kaganovich in 1938. The outcome was that he was posted to I.M. Sinyev's SKB-1 (Special Design Bureau 1) at the Kirov works in Leningrad, where Lyul'ka oversaw the evolution of the centrifugal compressor RTD-1 turbojet design into the RD-1 engine design with an axial-flow compressor. Included in the team were the established piston-engine designers P.S. Shyevchenko and I.F. Kozlov. The team appears to have been undaunted by the task of developing an axial compressor and anticipated that it would produce a higher efficiency and greater compression ratio than the centrifugal type.

Although the Kirov works specialized in the development and manufacture of steam and gas turbines, conditions were far from ideal for the prosecution of Lyul'ka's project and the promised official support was not received. On 29 February 1939 he was visited by Shibayev from the Scientific Test Institute of the Soviet Air Force (NII V-VS), who promised that the funds and contract for the work would be in place by 10 March 1939. Two months later, nothing official had happened, even though Lyul'ka had taken steps to organize a team, obtain materials and had begun work. Lyul'ka sensed an inexplicably frosty attitude from NII V-VS and so, on 29 April 1939, he appealed to higher authority, writing to V.M. Molotov, chairman of the Defence Committee of SNK, and asking for help in breaking the deadlock. This letter apparently had the desired effect because resources were being released for the project by the end of 1939.

Help with preparing a complete set of engineering drawings for the RD-1 engine was provided by an SKB (Special Design Bureau) of the Central Boiler-Turbine Institute. In 1940 this SKB was joined with the aero-engine Experimental Construction Bureau (OKB) of the Kirov works at Leningrad to form a subsidiary organization (known as no.1 SKB) with technical independence and its own development programme. The ambitious aims of this programme included building a prototype of the RD-1, the development and testing of its components and the establishment of an experimental production site. Within a year, after starting with virtually nothing, Lyul'ka's SKB had amazingly completed much of the experimentation, completed 70 per cent of the RD-1 construction and established the experimental production site. Studies included comparisons of different engine layouts, engine regulation with altitude and a project for a 1,300kp (2,977lb) thrust turbojet.

The RD-1 was designed for a thrust of 525kp (1,158lb) with a weight of about 500kg (1,103lb). It had a six-stage axial

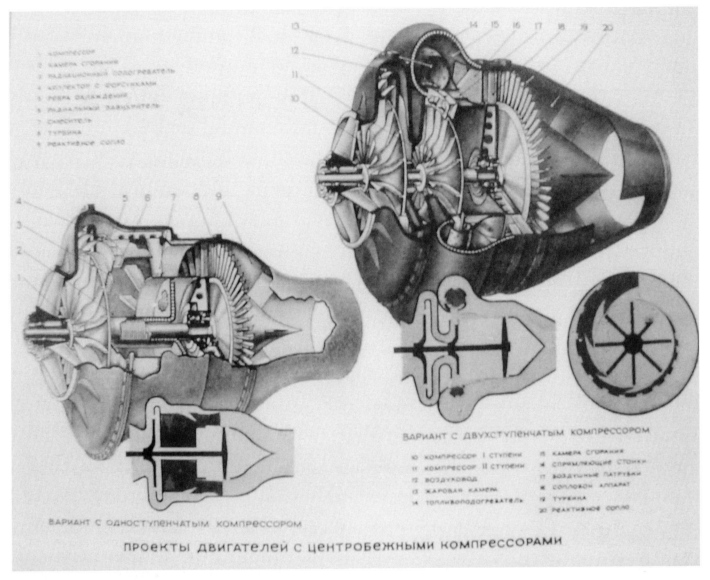

The first turbojet designs in the Soviet Union, Lyul'ka's RTD-1 of 1937. Here it is shown in two forms: one with a single centrifugal compressor, and a larger engine with two centrifugal compressors in series. The aim to use lightweight construction is notable.

compressor and a single-stage axial turbine, the latter running in a temperature of 700°C. Anti-friction bearings supported both the compressor and turbine shafts at each end and the two were connected by a flexible coupling. Can-type combustion chambers were mounted inside an annular space leading to the turbine and the exhaust nozzle was of fixed area. It appeared to be an elegant enough design but was yet to be tested in 1941. During that time, Lyul'ka also proposed the bypass engine (already suggested by Frank Whittle in 1936) and considered the idea of afterburning applied to the turbojet. In April 1941 he obtained a Soviet inventor's certificate for his bypass scheme.

The invasion of the Soviet Union by German forces on 22 June 1941 signalled the start of the Great Patriotic War and the interruption of Soviet work on the turbojet. On 12 July 1941 orders came from V.K. Kuznyetsov, deputy to the chief of the State Commissariat for Aviation Industry (NKAP), to stop RD-1 development, so closing down the country's most promising turbojet programme. This, combined with earlier bureaucracy, bungling officialdom and an official enchantment with rocket engine programmes, cost the country some two-and-a-half years towards the realization of the turbojet engine and robbed it of the chance to use it during the Great Patriotic War.

Some 1,500 major factories and 10 million workers, as well as smaller facilities, from the Leningrad area were moved lock, stock and barrel back to the Urals or other areas out of reach of the advancing Germans. Anything that was left was burned. The Kirov works, together with Lyul'ka and his team, were evacuated to Chelyabinsk (south of Sverdlovsk, now Yekaterinburg, in the Urals). Much of the RD-1 project, including sub-assemblies, was hidden in Leningrad and never found by the Germans. Meanwhile, work at Chelyabinsk concentrated on the development of diesel engines for tanks, since the turbojet programme was not considered important or urgent for the defence of the country.

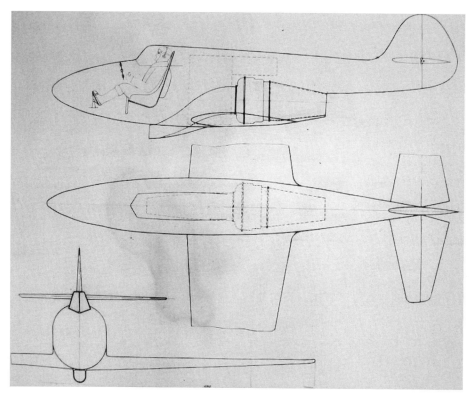

A projected fighter, designed at the Kharkov Aviation Institute and designated KhAI-2, was to be powered by an RTD-1 centrifugal turbojet.

In September 1941 there was an NKAP meeting in Moscow to review reaction propulsion development but Lyul'ka was not invited to attend. By the end of February 1942, however, the aero-engine department of the NII V-VS was reviewing the possibility of restarting development of the RD-1, which was seen as a stepping stone towards a more powerful engine. However, what followed was a miasma of bureaucracy with a complete lack of urgency. Even the location of Lyul'ka and his team, hidden away in the Ural mountains, came about by accident. Following a chance meeting between Maj. Sorokin, a leading NII V-VS engineer, and two former associates of Lyul'ka, Sorokin tracked down Lyul'ka and his team at Chelyabinsk through a maze of postboxes, the normal means of contact between organizations at that time. It was the wish of the Air Force that Lyul'ka's turbojet engine should be developed in conjunction with an aircraft designed by V.F. Bolkhovitinov, the work to be carried out at the latter's OKB at no.293 GAZ (State Aviation Factory) in

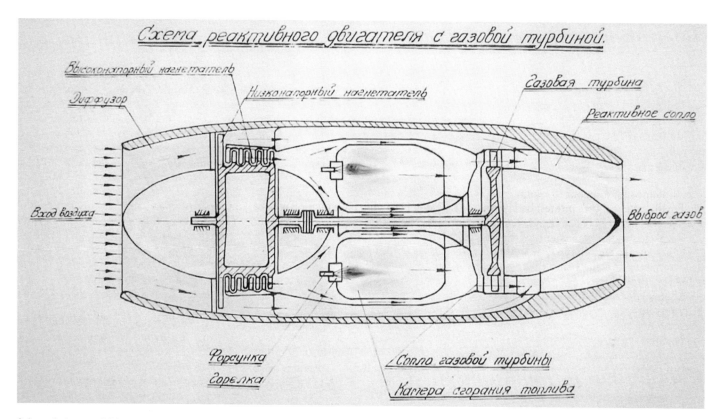

Schematic for an axial bypass turbojet submitted for patent by A.M. Lyul'ka in 1941. The bypassed airflow joined the hot gas exhaust just after the turbine.

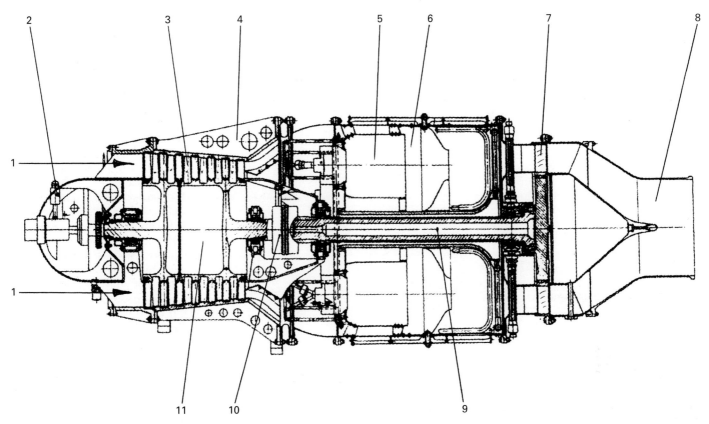

Lyul'ka's RD-1 axial turbojet of 1941, based on his RTD-1, the Soviet Union's first turbojet engine design of 1937: (1) air inlet; (2) starter shaft; (3) six-stage axial compressor; (4) bracing struts; (5) can-type combustion chambers; (6) annular space for combustion chambers; (7) single-stage turbine; (8) fixed-area exhaust nozzle; (9) hollow shaft, with anti-friction bearings at each end; (10) flexible coupling; (11) compressor hollow drum rotor, with anti-friction bearings at each end.

Sverdlovsk. Early in March 1942 Lyul'ka and Bolkhovitinov met at Sverdlovsk but, despite memos sent to the NKAP, two months later still nothing had been ordered officially.

Therefore, on 19 May 1942, Lyul'ka went straight to the top and took the bold step of addressing a memo to Stalin himself. Finally, after Stalin's interest had been passed down the chain of command, Lyul'ka and a fifteen-strong team were transferred to Bolkhovitinov's OKB on 1 July 1942. Unfortunately the facilities there were suited to airframe work and not to engine work, especially the manufacture of compressor and turbine blades, and the NKAP provided almost no technical facilities or equipment.

At this time, Lyul'ka was planning an axial turbojet to give a thrust of 1,500kp (3,308lb) for a weight of 700kg (1,544lb), with a diameter of 0.90m (2ft 11½in) and a length of 2.10m (6ft 10¼in). Chief designer Mikhail I. Gudkov enthusiastically designed a fighter around such an engine

by early April 1943. Gudkov eschewed the rockets and ramjets then popular as auxiliary power units, seeing that the way ahead for fast, sustained flight was with the turbojet. The layout of his projected fighter, designated Gu-VRD, was not unlike the earlier project for the KhAI-2 fighter. The Gu-VRD fighter was to have a wing area of 11.0sq m (118.36sq ft), a take-off weight of 2,250kg (4,961lb), and have a maximum speed of 1,000km/h (621mph) at 6,000m (19,700ft) altitude. It was to be armed with a cannon and a machine gun and have one Lyul'ka turbojet mounted beneath the nose with a short air intake and exhaust nozzles. Gudkov was also working on a twin-jet fast bomber project with a take-off weight of 6,500kg (14,333lb) and a maximum speed of 800km/h (497mph) at 6,000m (19,700ft). It was to be armed with 1,200kg (2,646lb) of bombs, and would also have a cannon and machine gun.

Although some merit was seen in these aircraft projects, no official sanctions were given to proceed further because the engine

work had not progressed very far. On 20 May 1943 an NKAP commission reviewed Lyul'ka's project but, even though Lyul'ka attended the meeting, the subsequent reports were unfavourable: despite his high praise for Lyul'ka's work back in 1939, V.V. Uvarov, who was still working on his own gas turbine project, downgraded Lyul'ka's turbojet to a recent invention that 'should be further evaluated'. Another report, from G.M. Abramovich of the Central Aerodynamics and Hydrodynamics Institute (CAHI), took a similar line and so the outcome was that nothing was recommended that would advance Lyul'ka's work.

Following the crash, on 12 June 1943, of his prototype fighter, which was similar to the American Bell Airacobra, Gudkov was accused of incompetence and his bureau was disbanded. Things finally took a turn for the better, although without any official urgency, when Lyul'ka and his team were moved to Moscow in August 1943. There they were organized into a research laboratory for turbojet engines, attached to the

Central Institute of Aviation Motors (CIAM). Other scientific institutes, including that headed by Uvarov, were ordered to participate in this research programme to complete a turbojet engine up to 50 per cent power and have its sub-assemblies tested by 1 May 1944. This engine was not intended for flight testing.

Meanwhile, at no.21 GAZ at Gorki, chief designer Semyon M. Alexeyev designed the La-VRD fighter under S.A. Lavochkin. This was to be powered by a 1,250kp (2,756lb) thrust Lyul'ka turbojet and was to have a twin boom layout and an all-metal wing with a CAHI laminar-flow aerofoil section. Apart from the turbojet, advanced features included a retractable tricycle undercarriage and a pressurized cockpit with an armoured backrest. Its armament was to consist of two NS23 23mm cannon inside the tailbooms.

La-VRD fighter project			
Wing area		15.50sq m	(166.78sq ft)
Aspect ratio		5.85:1	
Take-off weight		3,300kg	(7,277lb)
Useful load		910kg	(2,007lb)
Maximum speeds	at sea level	890km/h	(553mph)
	at 5,000m (16,500ft) altitude	850km/h	(528mph)
Landing speed		140km/h	(87mph)
Time	to 5,000m (16,400ft)	2.5 minutes	
Service ceiling		15,000m	(49,200ft)
Endurance	at 80% max. speed	20 minutes	

CHAPTER TWO

Stopgap Measures
to Boost Speed

From about 1942, a team under K.V. Kholshchyevniko at the Central Institute of Aviation Motors (CIAM) began development of a jet augmentation system for application to airscrew-driven aircraft. This system consisted of a 1,400hp Klimov VK-107 piston engine driving an airscrew in the conventional way, but with a rearwards extension shaft from the engine that connected, via step-up gearing of 13:21 and a clutch, to a compressor. This compressor drew air through the engine's radiator and fed it to a combustion chamber having seven fuel burners, the resulting jet thrust adding speed to the aircraft. Compressed air was tapped off immediately behind the

compressor and ducted to supercharge the piston engine. When a boost of speed was required, the clutch to the compressor was engaged and the fuel burners were lit by sparking plugs. It was estimated that the thrust from the jet would be equivalent to adding up to 90 per cent extra power to the piston engine, and yet it is reported that the thrust was only 300kp (661lb) at low level, which would be equivalent to an extra power of about 20 per cent. This system was known as Kholshchyevniko's Accelerator and the compressor/combustion component was designated VRDK (Vozdushno-Reaktivnyi Dvigatyel Kompressornyi or air-reaction engine compressor).

In spring 1944, following news of German jet aircraft activities, Stalin flew into a fury because the Red Air Force had no jet aircraft to match the Luftwaffe. He therefore ordered a crash programme to obtain high-speed aircraft at all costs. Stalin, of course, already knew of Lyul'ka's work and that the turbojet was not yet ready for deployment. Stopgap measures to obtain more speed were therefore taken. Tests were made with ramjets under the wings of conventional piston-engined fighters, such as the Yak-7PVRD, and a boost in speed of up to 100km/h (62mph) was demonstrated. Pulsejets were also tried in a similar manner, but with detrimental acoustical

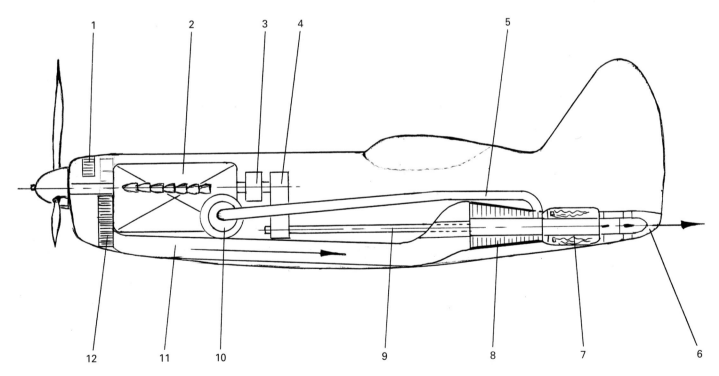

Schematic of Kholshchyevniko's Accelerator: (1) oil cooler; (2) Klimov VK-107R 1,400hp piston engine; (3) variable clutch; (4) step-up gears; (5) air tap-off for supercharger; (6) variable-area exhaust nozzle (faired over when cruising); (7) combustion chambers with seven fuel burners; (8) compressor; (9) compressor drive shaft; (10) supercharger; (11) air intake duct; (12) radiator. Author

15

effects on the airframe. Little use was made of these schemes. Now was the time to try Kholshchyevniko's Accelerator and experimental fighters to test it were ordered from the Sukhoi and MiG design bureaux.

For both, their designs were all-metal aircraft of conventional, if rather chunky, layout using a VK-107 piston engine to drive an airscrew in the nose, but with the compressor at about the centre of the fuselage and the jet exhaust outlet below the tail empennage. For both aircraft, the exhaust nozzle area could be varied by hydraulic actuation. N1, the first prototype of MiG's I-250, as it was designated, first flew on 3 March 1945, the pilot being A.P. Dyeyev. In distinctive MiG style, the cockpit was very far aft. On the third flight of the armed I-250 N1, the jet drive was turned on and an increase in speed of about 100m/h (62mph) was achieved. Unfortunately Dyeyev was killed on 19 May 1945 when the aircraft broke up under high-G. The second, unarmed prototype, the N-2, had a larger fin but was destroyed in a forced landing. The maximum speed given for the MiG I-250 was 620km/h (385mph) at sea level and 825km/h (512mph) at 7,000 m (23,000ft).

Sukhoi's aircraft was of similar layout to the MiG, but with the cockpit over the wing, and was designated the I-107 or Su-5. The chunkiness of both types was due to the air ducting. The I-107 first flew in

A MiG-13 fighter with Kolshchyevniko Accelerator, an emergency jet propulsion scheme to boost speed to combat German jets that was also used on the Sukhoi Su-5. Although an emergency scheme, pending the introduction of Soviet jet aircraft, fighters of this type continued in service after the war, until 1948, and so it must have worked satisfactorily. Russian Aviation Research Trust

April 1945 with G. Komarov at the controls. Like the MiG, it was armed with three guns. Although it proved to be a satisfactory aircraft, it did not fly again after 15 June 1945. Its maximum speed was 645km/h (400mph) at sea level or 768km/h (477mph) at 5,000m (16,400ft). Although

another nine MiG I-250s were built in time for the 7 November 1945 flypast, which was cancelled due to fog, this type of jet-boosted aircraft was not put into production owing to the obvious superiority of the forthcoming turbojets.

CHAPTER THREE

Lyul'ka and the First Soviet Turbojets

The capture of a German engineer, Franz Wanbrünn, on 1 January 1944 on the road between Vitebsk and Orsha road brought further news of German work because Warnbrünn had worked in von Ohain's team at the Heinkel works and he also knew of Messerschmitt's jet aircraft activities. The result was the announcement of Articles 5945 and 5946 from the State Defence Committee (GKO) on 22 May 1944. Article 5945 instructed P.F. Fyodorov (chief of no.1 Scientific Test Institute, or NII, in Moscow) and Lyul'ka (now no.1 designer at NII) to proceed with the development and construction of a turbojet of 1,250kp (2,756lb) static thrust. This engine was to be ready for test runs by 1 March 1945, or in just over nine months' time. Article 5946 instructed S.A. Lavochkin to proceed with the development and construction of an experimental fighter proto-

type. To facilitate this, Lavochkin was to be furnished with a mock-up of Lyul'ka's projected turbojet.

Lyul'ka's brief was that his turbojet was to achieve the designated thrust with a dry weight of not more than 900kg (1,985lb) and a maximum diameter of 0.95m (3ft 1⅜in). Furthermore, the second and third examples of the TR-1, as the engine was designated, were to be ready by 1 November and 1 December 1945, respectively. To realize this, work began in autumn 1944 on developmental prototypes, known as the S-18, with an eight-stage axial compressor and a single-stage axial turbine. The combustion chamber was long and of exceptionally large volume, this apparently having the aim of keeping the temperature of the combustion gases relatively low at the turbine. It was air-cooled around the outside and had two rows of inner and outer hollow

fingers that introduced the air for combustion. The exhaust nozzle was of the fixed type with a central cone and the outer casing of the engine consisted of castings, ribbed for strength with lightness, bolted together. A starter motor and gearing was enclosed in the streamlined central fairing of the air intake, all other auxiliaries being clustered below the compressor section. Multiple vanes were used as supports between the outer casing and the compressor and turbine rotor bearings.

Once again Lyul'ka found himself without suitable facilities to produce engines and so another GKO resolution ordered his team from no.1 NII to no.165 GAZ in Moscow, where stamping dies were being made. A design and production facility for the turbojet prototypes was set up there and by the start of 1945 it had produced the first running S-18 prototype. This and

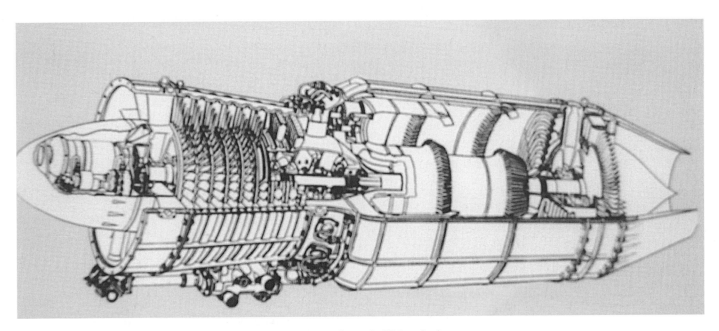

Cutaway of Lyul'ka's 1944 turbojet, the axial S-18 developmental engine leading to the TR-1 production engine. The S-18 had an eight-stage compressor, a very large volume combustion chamber and a single-stage turbine. In comparative tests this turbojet outperformed captured German Junkers 109-004B engines.

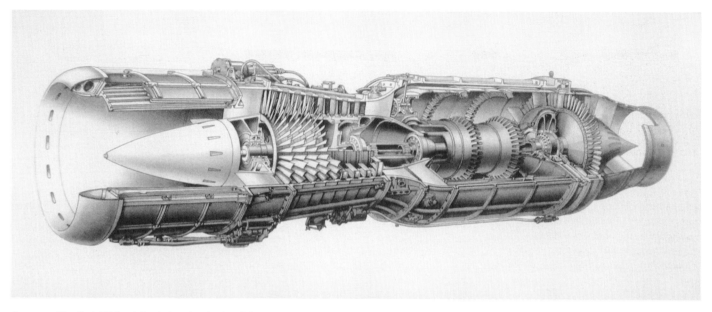

Cutaway of Lyul'ka's TR-1 axial turbojet, showing its eight-stage compressor, large-volume annular combustion chamber, single-stage turbine and fixed-area exhaust nozzle. It was a four-bearing engine with a flexible coupling between compressor and turbine shafts.

the second prototype were used for heat-resisting tests; the third prototype was used to optimize subassemblies; and the fourth and fifth prototypes were used to measure performance. During this development phase the compressor stages of the S-18 were reduced from eight to seven.

During 1946 comparative tests were made between Lyul'ka's S-18 and captured German Junkers 109-004 turbojets. The satisfying result was that, with less weight, the S-18 produced more thrust and was more economical to operate. Due to the highly satisfactory course that the devel-

opment was taking, Lyul'ka was appointed the chief designer and technical director of no.165 GAZ and he was ordered to proceed with the development of the S-18 into the flight-cleared TR-1 turbojet. To this end, flight tests were performed by mounting a TR-1 engine on a pylon beneath the

Lyul'ka's TR-1A axial turbojet. This was the Soviet Union's first indigenous production turbojet and powered some of the country's first jet aircraft.

A 1947 Sukhoi Su-11 fighter, powered by two Lyul'ka TR-1A axial turbojets and one of the first aircraft to be powered by Soviet turbojets.
Russian Aviation Research Trust

The Ilyushin Il-22 bomber of 1947, powered by four TR-1A turbojets:
RIGHT: artist's impression;
BELOW: under construction with the fuselage on its starboard side and the curve of the vertical fin at the top left-hand corner. Russian Aviation Research Trust

Sukhoi's first jet aircraft, the Su-9 fighter shown here, was originally flown with two RD-10 turbojets in 1946. However, an improved version, the Su-11, was powered by two TR-1 engines.
Russian Aviation Research Trust

fuselage of a North American B-25 Mitchell bomber. The TR-1, with an eight-stage compressor, passed its acceptance tests in December 1946.

Production and further testing was to take place at no.45 GAZ, in Moscow, which was an aero-engine factory that grew into a giant engine plant. It was run by director Komarov and its chief engineer was Kiundzhi. By the end of 1946 this factory had produced thirty-six TR-1s. The State Acceptance evaluation programme was ordered on 10 February 1947 and was completed by 27 November 1947 with better than projected results. With a dry weight of 840kg (1,852lb), the S-18 produced a static thrust of 1,300kp (2,867lb) and had a specific fuel consumption of 1.27.

Thus came about the creation of the Soviet Union's first indigenous turbojet engine, the TR-1, and Lyul'ka's achievement was recognized with the award of the Order of Lenin and a Stalin Prize. With hindsight it would appear that he would soon have given the USSR outstanding turbojets without any help from German technology.

During 1946 Lyul'ka's OKB proceeded with further development of the TR-1: in the TR-1A the static thrust was increased to 1,500kp (3,308lb). TR-1 engines were test flown from 28 May 1947 in the prototype of the twin-engined Sukhoi Su-11

fighter and, from 24 July 1947, four of them powered the Ilyushin Il-22 bomber. These were the first jet aircraft to be powered by Soviet-made turbojets. These two aircraft flew at the Tushino air show of August 1947 but they did not go into production. The TR-1 was also intended to power the Il-30 bomber, a swept-wing development of the Il-28 that was later intended to be powered by two TR-3 engines, but never flew.

By 17 July 1947 the static thrust of the TR-1A had been increased to 1,600kp (3,528lb) and its time between overhauls (TBO) to 50 hours, but the engine was not produced in large numbers since the order was given to concentrate on developing more powerful engines.

The first flight of the all-red prototype I-211, which was a twin-jet aircraft using TR-1A engines, took place on 13 October 1947. Fighter, heavily armed and bomber variants were proposed. It had un-swept flying surfaces and was designed by the OKB of S.M. Alekseyev, who had previously designed for Lavochkin. It was planned for a maximum speed of 950km/h (590mph) at sea level and to have a service ceiling of 13,600m (44,600ft) but was cancelled in order to concentrate on more powerful aircraft.

At about this time Sukhoi produced the Su-10, a large bomber fitted with four

TR-1 engines, one mounted above the other and projecting forward from the leading edge of the wing at each side. This was not unlike the engine arrangement of the British Short SA-4 Sperrin bomber. Only the fin was swept back, the wings and tailplane having approximately equi-taper planform. The Su-10 featured a glazed nose and rear gunner's position, a tricycle undercarriage and hydraulically boosted controls. It was expected to carry a 4-tonne bomb load and achieve a maximum speed of 810km/h (503mph) at sea level, a ceiling of 12,000m (39,360ft) and a range of 1,500km (932 miles). However, the sole prototype never flew and the programme was abandoned in 1948.

Sukhoi's first jet, the Su-9 twin-jet fighter, had already flown in 1946 using two RD-10 engines but an improved version, the Su-11, was built using two TR-1 (later TR-1A) turbojets. This fighter, which was very similar in layout to the Messerschmitt Me 262 (but with straight wings) and the Gloster Meteor, first flew on 28 May 1947. A.S. Yakovlev did his best to undermine Sukhoi's offering by telling Stalin that the Su-11 was merely a copy of the Me 262, which was not true, and that it was dangerous to fly. At this point in the Soviet story, we will return to the dark days of 1945.

CHAPTER FOUR

Building on German Achievements

Reports of German V1 (Fi 103) flying bomb attacks on London reached Moscow in June 1944. The first German jet aircraft appeared over the German-Soviet front early in 1945 and the situation appeared critical since the Red Air Force (V-VS) had no such machines. Soviet forces, however, were soon pushing deep into Germany, culminating in the Battle of Berlin and the end of the Second World War in Europe in early May. Even before this battle had ended and the Red flag had been raised above the Reichstag and the now dead Hitler's bunker, a commission was formed to 'utilize the German reaction propulsion technology'. This commission, headed by A.S. Yakovlev, included many important people such as Lyul'ka and Mikoyan, the CAHI chief Shishkin, Kishkin and Fadeyev from CIAM, the test pilots Petrov and Fyodrovi, I.A. Serov, the deputy head of the People's Commissariat for Internal Affairs (NKVD), and various scientists and engineers. Their brief was to assess German progress and report on its usefulness.

Soviet study of German research

Prior to this, the remains of two V1 flying bombs had been sent by Britain to the Soviet Union and the pulsejet engine of one was examined by a team under B.S. Stechkin at no.300 GAZ, Moscow. By March 1945 the first pieces of Junkers 109-004 turbojets had reached the Central Institute of Aviation Motors (CIAM). The following month crates of new BMW 109-003 turbojets were found by Soviet forces at Rostock and, soon after, Junkers 109-004 engines and Me 262 jet fighter spares were discovered at Warnemünde airfield. Luftwaffe jet aircraft, ranging from partially destroyed to brand new, were also captured and soon whole factories were overrun.

On 28 April 1945, before the war had ended and Yakovlev's commission had begun its work, the State Commissariat for Aviation Industry (NKAP) ordered the experiment of making a small batch of Junkers 109-004B turbojets, as the RD-10, at no.26 GAZ at Ufa. The works director there was S.S. Balandin, who later worked from 1946 to 1953 at no.500 GAZ, Moscow, on a compound engine that used a reciprocating engine as a gas generator supplying a turbine geared to an airscrew. Chief designer V.Ya. Klimov and his deputy N.D. Kuznyetsov, both of whom were to become famous in Soviet turbojet development, were tasked with producing to Soviet standards the detailed drawings for the Junkers 109-004B turbojet and for its assembly at no.1 Scientific Test Institute (NII) by 1 July 1945.

In the summer of 1945 the State Defence Committee (GKO) issued a decree entitled 'On measures of studying and familiarization with German jet equipment', which required the evaluation of the results of scientific research works on turbojets in Germany, testing of captured jet aircraft and the copying and production of Junkers 109-004 and BMW 109-003 engines. The first flight of a German Messerschmitt Me 262 jet fighter with a Soviet pilot took place on 15 August 1945, the pilot being A.G. Kochetkov of NII V-VS. This institute had repaired the fighter after its forced landing and capture in East Prussia in April 1945. Kochetkov made eighteen flights in this Me 262 (probably c/n: 170063) up to November 1945, and various other Soviet pilots flew it from October. On 17 September 1946, however, this aircraft crashed, killing the test pilot F.F. Demida. The cause was said to be a faulty trim control relay, but Kochetkov had also previously got into difficulties with this aircraft and the Me 262 was said to be difficult to fly. Yakovlev was an implacable opponent of it.

From August 1945 no.1 NII and CIAM were bench-testing captured Junkers, BMW and Heinkel-Hirth 109-001 (HeS 8A) turbojets. To assist Klimov in his task of producing 109-004B engines, the prominent designer and ex-technical director of the Junkers engine plant in Dessau, Ferdinand Brandner, was released from a PoW camp and brought into Klimov's team. Difficulties in adapting German designs to Soviet standards slowed the work and it was not until the beginning of 1946 that a few RD-10 engines had been built at no.26 GAZ, Ufa. In the construction of these first engines, many captured components from Germany were used. Assembly of 109-004 turbojets was also continued at a captured underground factory near Dessau, probably at Muldenstein, using available stocks of components.

Faster progress was made in the copying of the BMW 109-003A turbojet under the leadership of Kolosov at no.16 GAZ in Kazan'. The Soviet copy of this engine was designated RD-20 and several examples had been built by the end of 1945. Although much of the BMW material had been removed by the Americans, the Soviets were able to manage with a few captured engines and drawings brought together from various places. During the war, German development and production was dispersed over many sites and so there were many opportunities for finding useful material.

German projects under Soviet control

The Soviets immediately put into effect a plan to enlist the help of German specialists in the turbojet programme and, indeed, in many other fields as well. Some were found in their homes or the ruined establishments, while others were found in PoW camps. Although some were compelled to cooperate, in those dark days just after the end of

An RD-10A axial turbojet, the Soviet version of the Junkers 109-004B. Jan Hoffmann

the war, when all of Germany lay in ruins, food rations and even a salary from the Soviets were most welcome and some specialists voluntarily applied to the Soviet authorities for work. Some of the finance for this actually came from the coffers of the captured German establishments.

In any event, by March 1946 the organization of the German-staffed Special Technical Bureaux (OTBs), later renamed as Special Design Bureaux (OKBs), was complete and the following month they were allotted their specific development tasks. Since the organization of these OKBs in Germany was in contravention of agreements between the victorious Allies, their work was carried out in great secrecy and any German breaking this secrecy could expect to see his whole family shot. Interestingly, when the Soviet press made a big fuss about US Navy encouragement of post-war Heinkel-Hirth manufacture of the 109-011 turbojet in 1946, the Heinkel programme was very quickly shut down.

OKB-1, in the former Junkers plant in Dessau, was to develop by May 1946 the Junkers 109-004E turbojet, which was an afterburning version of the engine planned for a static thrust of 1,200kp (2,646lb). Junkers had already tried extra fuel injection both at the turbine inlet nozzles and upstream behind the turbine, the latter method being preferred. OKB-1 was also ordered to have the projected Junkers 109-012 turbojet of 2,780kp (6,130lb) static thrust running on the bench by August 1946. The chief designer at OKB-1 was the ex-Junkers Dr Scheibe.

OKB-2, in the former BMW plant in Stassfurt, was to develop the BMW 109-003 turbojet (one source mentions an 003S) up to 1,050kp (2,315lb) static thrust by June 1946, and it was to have the projected BMW 109-018 turbojet running at 3,400kp (7,497lb) static thrust on the bench by October. The chief designer at OKB-2 was the ex-BMW engineer K. Prestel.

By May 1946 the first Junkers 109-004E was ready at OKB-1, but a disappointing thrust of only 1,050kp (2,315lb) was obtained on the bench and a service life of only 25 hours was possible. In September this engine was cancelled in order to concentrate on the more powerful projected Junkers 109-012 turbojet. After overcoming a shortage of drawings, the first 109-012 was built and ready for testing on 23 September 1946. However, using this and two others in bench tests, it was found that the engine suffered from excessive turbine blade creep and there was plenty of scope for general development.

OKB-2's first BMW 109-003(S) was being readied for testing by 14 June 1946 and six more engines were built by October that year. However, even with development, the service life of this engine was only extended to 35 hours. By 18 October 1946 the first of the very much larger BMW 109-018 turbojets was ready, but this was not tested in Germany, since in April 1946 the Soviets had decided that, owing to the need for secrecy, the German OKBs were to be moved bodily to the Soviet Union.

German work in the USSR

At 3.00 am on 22 October 1946 Soviet troops armed with sub-machine guns arrived in a coordinated operation at the homes of about 530 selected aircraft and engine specialists in Germany. They were being abducted in order not to compromise their secret work helping their Soviet conquerors, and were allowed a mere four hours to collect their belongings and pile into trucks waiting in the streets. In some cases they were allowed to take their families and furniture, but for others these would have to follow later. The troops were accompanied by Soviet specialists who explained the reasons for the sudden move, guaranteeing the Germans' safety and that they would work in their own specialization. The troops assisted with the loading, with design documentation being loaded separately with the luggage.

They had come from the engine factories of Junkers, BMW and Heinkel-Hirth, and from the aircraft factories of Arado, Dornier, Heinkel, Henschel, Junkers, Messerschmitt and Siebel, all in the Eastern zone of Germany, which was under Soviet control. After an arduous train journey across Eastern Europe the aircraft specialists were taken to Podberez'ye, a small village 120km (75 miles) north of Moscow. The engine specialists, about 250 people, were transported to Upravlencheskiy village near Kuibyshev (now Samara), some 180km (110 miles) south of Kazan'. Also delivered to this village were about 100 Germans specializing in instrumentation and other equipment. Unfortunately it was discovered that, during the reloading of the train at Brest-Litovsk, necessary because of the change in the track gauge, the safe containing the design documentation had been lost!

The engine specialists at Upravlencheskiy village, which was to become known as no.2 experimental GAZ, fared better than the aircraft specialists at Podberez'hye, where initially there were only unheated barracks. It is noteworthy that the winter of 1946/7 was especially bad all over Europe: in Russia temperatures dropped to as low as −40°C at night. For the engine specialists, however, the village was cleared and in its place were erected more than a hundred well-insulated Finnish-style houses. In due course, the Germans received good wages and their children attended a school where the German women also worked.

As a training exercise for the Soviet engineers, the first task for the Germans was to continue development of their BMW 109-003A and Junkers 109-004B axial turbojets, and to get these into production as the RD-20 and RD-10 respectively.

Further refinement of the RD-20 was carried out only by Soviet engineers. The engine at first had the same static thrust as the original BMW engine at 800kp (1,764lb) but, by allowing it to run hotter in the RD-20F version, a static thrust of 1,000kp (2,205lb) was reached. Research work in Kazan' improved the annular combustion chamber, turbine inlet nozzles and the turbine itself, and this resulted in a redesigned version known as the RD-21. However, its life was never raised much above 35 hours.

The static thrust of the RD-10 was initially the same as the Junkers engine at 900kp (1,985lb), but was raised to 1,000kp (2,205lb) in the RD-10A version and then to 1,100kp (2,426lb) in the RD-10F with an early form of afterburning. Its service life was also very low, at about 25 hours; the RD-10F was cancelled in September 1946.

Orders for production of these Soviet derivatives of the German engines came from NKAP in summer 1945 for the RD-20 at no.16 GAZ in Kazan' (and, from 1947, at no.466 GAZ 'Krasnyi Oktyabr') and for the RD-10 at no.26 GAZ, Ufa, and no.10 GAZ in Kazan'. Once they were in production (on 30 September 1945, in the case of the RD-10), the Germans were directed to develop the 3,400kp (7,497lb) static thrust BMW 109-018 and the 2,780kp (6,130lb) static thrust Junkers 109-012 axial turbojets, which were the most powerful engines projected at that time. The first BMW 109-018 was actually ready in Germany by 18 October 1946 but testing was carried out in the Soviet Union. By the beginning of 1948, despite problems including blade creep, the Junkers 109-012 had been improved into the B version and a service life of 100 hours had been achieved. However, by then work on original German turbojets had stopped since they were surpassed by British and Soviet engines, particularly with regard to fuel consumption and weight. Also, the air-cooling methods used on German engines were no longer necessary thanks to the availability of heat-resisting steels.

While the RD-20 engine appears to have remained largely as a production training exercise and to have been utilized very little, the RD-10 went on to power many of the Soviet Union's first turbojet aircraft in service. This resulted from a February 1945 meeting at the Kremlin when Stalin instructed the fighter design bureaux of Sukhoi, Lavochkin and Yakovlev to each produce three prototypes of a fighter using BMW and Junkers turbojets. The MiG bureau had apparently already decided on this approach to produce its first jet aircraft, a fighter designated Aircraft F, which was designed by A.T. Karyev to use two Lyul'ka TR-1 engines; it was then redesigned as the I-300 to use two captured BMW 109-003A engines that had been allocated to the bureau. The I-300 was a straightforward design in which the engines were in the lower fuselage and fed from a nose intake. It had straight wings, a tricycle undercarriage, bubble cockpit canopy and three nose-mounted cannon. The first I-300 was sent to the NII flight test centre at Chaklovskaya to be tested at the same time as Yakovlev's first turbojet aircraft, the Yak-15 fighter.

MiG I-300 with two BMW 003A engines			
Span		10.0m	(32ft 9⅝in)
Length		9.75m	(31ft 11¾in)
Wing area		18.2sq m	(195.83sq ft)
Empty weight		3,283kg	(7,239lb)
Loaded weight		4,860kg	(10,716lb)
Maximum speed	at sea level	864km/h	(537mph)
	at 4,500m (14,800ft)	910km/h	(565mph)
Service ceiling		13,000m	(42,600ft)
Range		800km	(497 miles)

Three examples of early Soviet fighters using German turbojets or Soviet copies of same; TOP: MiG I-300 (two BMW 109-003As); CENTRE: Yakovlev Yak-15 (one RD-10); BOTTOM: Lavochkin La-150 (one RD-10).
Russian Aviation Research Trust

The Yak-15 prototype was derived from the successful Yak-3 piston-engined fighter and utilized a captured Junkers 109-004B turbojet, but subsequent examples were to employ the Soviet-built RD-10 engine. Of similar layout to MiG's I-300, the Yak-15 differed in having a single engine and a tailwheel undercarriage. Simplicity was its keynote and it derived as much as possible from the Yak-3. It was, in fact, the Soviet Union's first completed turbojet aircraft and was ready for wind-tunnel testing in October 1945. (It was actually tested, with 109-004 engines, in CAHI's T-104 full-size wind tunnel in 1946.) On the toss of a coin on 24 April 1946, however, the rival I-300 was flown first, followed three hours later by the Yak-15. A.N. Grinchik piloted the I-300 on the Soviet Union's first turbojet flight, followed by M.I. Ivanov, who piloted the Yak-15 on its first flight. On 11 July 1946 the Yak-15 and the I-300, together with a captured German Heinkel He 162 Volksjäger jet fighter, were demonstrated before the minister of Aircraft Production, M.V. Krunishev, other officials and the aircraft designers Yakovlev and Mikoyan. Grinchik and Ivanov again flew the Soviet jets, while the He 162 was piloted by Georgi M. Shiyanov of the Flight Research Institute (LII). Unfortunately the I-300 crashed during this demonstration, killing Grinchik.

The first public appearance of the Yak-15 and MiG I-300 was on 18 August 1946 at the Tushino Aviation Day, following which Stalin ordered that twelve of each type should be ready for the Red Square parade on 22 October! Prodigious efforts by both bureaux, involving much work by hand, produced the aircraft in time only to have the fly-past cancelled due to fog!

The MiG I-300 was developed into the MiG-9 'Fargo', still with BMW 109-003A engines; by the end of 1948 some 500 of these had been built and put into service. The MiG-9 was the first Soviet jet with an ejection seat and about 950 of all versions were built. The Yak-15 entered V-VS service on 24 April 1946 and its improved successor, the Yak-17, in 1948, although most of these were two-seat trainers designated as Yak-17UTI.

Lavochkin's first turbojet aircraft, the La-150 fighter, was similar in layout to the Yak-15 but employed a straight, shoulder-mounted wing and tricycle undercarriage. A nose intake fed the RD-10 engine in the lower fuselage. The first of five prototypes was completed in September 1946 and

Yak-15 with one RD-10 engine			
Span		9.20m	(30ft 2⅛in)
Length		8.70m	(28ft 6½in)
Wing area		14.85sq m	(159.79sq ft)
Empty weight		1,918kg	(4,229lb)
Loaded weight		2,634kg	(5,808lb)
Maximum speed	at sea level	700km/h	(435mph)
	at 5,000m (16,400ft)	805km/h	(500mph)
Service ceiling		13,350m	(43,800ft)
Range		510km	(317 miles)

MiG-9 with two RD-20 engines		
Span	10.0m	(32ft 9⅝in)
Length	9.83m	(32ft 2⅛in)
Wing area	18.20sq m	(195.83sq ft)
Empty weight	3,420kg	(7,541lb)
Loaded weight	4,963kg	(10,943lb)
Performance very similar to I-300 (see page 23)		

flown by A.A. Popov. The type was not successful owing to poor stability and inadequate tail section stiffness, while a high airframe weight contributed to poor acceleration. Nevertheless, the La-150F type is noteworthy as one of the first aircraft to use an afterburning engine in the form of the RD-10F. Further developments were the La-152 and 156, which each used an RD-10 or 10F engine, but these projects were virtually stillborn because of their unswept wings. (The La-154 was to use a TR-1 engine but was not completed.) Finally, using the same basic layout and an RD-10F engine, Lavochkin produced the La-160 with swept-back wings, the Soviet Union's first. It first flew on 24 June 1947 and eventually reached Mach 0.92, but it remained a research aircraft owing to its low power.

Sukhoi's first turbojet aircraft, designated Aircraft K and then Su-9, also employed the RD-10 engine. As a competitor to the MiG I-300, it used two such engines in a layout very similar to the Me 262. The Su-9 featured a pressurized cockpit with a bubble canopy, tricycle undercarriage and all-hydraulic controls, including flaps and dive brakes, an ejection seat and a landing drag chute. Its armament consisted of three nose-mounted cannon and it could

also be fitted with a solid ATO rocket at each side of the rear fuselage. Piloted by G. Komarov, the Su-9 made its first flight in August 1946; subsequent flights confirmed that its handling was as good as

that of the Me 262, and even better at low speeds and on one engine. Despite its wing-mounted engines, its rate of roll was higher than that of the MiG I-300. The Su-9 was an obvious candidate for production, which was officially recommended, but curiously it was said that there was no production capacity available. Therefore the Su-9 prototype's flight in the Tushino fly-past on 3 August 1947 was also the type's swansong.

As with all these early turbojet aircraft, take-off runs were long (up to 1,000m) unless assisted take-off (ATO) was used; because the engines would take up to 15 seconds to spool up, a landing overshoot was not possible. Also, on the I-300 for example, the high idling thrust of a BMW 109-003A led to the practice of shutting down one engine upon touchdown.

Kuznyetsov

During 1946 Lt Col Nikolay Dimitriyevich Kuznyetsov (1911–1995), later to be a famous name in Soviet engines, was appointed to the post of chief designer at no.26 GAZ in Ufa. At the same time, most of the Soviet designers there left to join V.Ya. Klimov at his OKB in Leningrad (see Chapter 7). Kuznyetsov was therefore kept very busy. He had trained in the aero-engine department of the Moscow Aviation Technical

A MiG-9 'Fargo' fighter, here preserved at Monino, used two RD-20 turbojets – Soviet versions of the BMW 109-003A. Author

La-150 with one RD-10 engine			
Span		8.20m	(26ft 10¾in)
Length		9.42m	(30ft 10¾in)
Wing area		12.15sq m	(130.73sq ft)
Empty weight		2,059kg	(4,540lb)
Loaded weight		2,961kg	(6,529lb)
Maximum speed	at sea level	840km/h	(522mph)
	at 5,000m (16,400ft)	850km/h	(528mph)
Service ceiling		12,500m	(41,000ft)
Range		700km	(435 miles)

Su-9 with two RD-10 engines			
Span		11.20m	(36ft 8⅞in)
Length		10.55m	(34ft 7¼in)
Wing area		20.20sq m	(217.35sq ft)
Empty weight		4,060kg	(8,952lb)
Maximum loaded weight		6,380kg	(14,068lb)
Maximum speed	at 5,000m (16,400ft)	885km/h	(550mph)
Service ceiling		12,800m	(42,000ft)
Range		1,200km	(745 miles)

College in 1930 and was then a fitter at no.24 aero-engine GAZ until being enrolled into the aviation technical department of the VVA Zhukovskii. His later creative and original engine work was put to good use solving problems on many M-type piston engines at Klimov's OKB.

Kuznyetsov was a modest but very hard-working man with exceptional scientific and technical talents. He was also an outstanding organizer and his persistence and insights were ideally suited to solving difficult engine developmental problems.

At no.26 GAZ Kuznyetsov proceeded to develop a turbojet designated the RD-12, planned for a static thrust of 3,000kp (6,615lb). Unlike the RD-10, the RD-12 had a compressor of the centrifugal type. The blades of this new compressor unfortunately failed during testing, injuring Kuznyetsov and another engineer. This accident delayed the development of not only the RD-12 but also a less powerful RD-14 version, which was intended for a three-engined fighter. Strangely, no.26 GAZ was disbanded at the end of 1948. Kuznyetsov found himself unemployed until taking up a new post in 1949 at no.2 experimental GAZ, where the work of the German engineers continued to be valued, in particular that of Dipl.-Ing. Ferdinand Brandner, who commanded the highest salary.

Kuznyetsov strove to get the best out of no.2 experimental GAZ. He eliminated the long-standing competition between former BMW and Junkers personnel and reorganized them into new teams for greater cooperation. Later, he organized a technical education programme in which Germans gave lectures: Dr R. Scheinost, for example, lectured on structural calculations and Dr H. Heinrich on thermodynamics. Those Soviet specialists who passed the German language examination received a 20 per cent bonus. Finally, Kuznyetsov opened up employment in his design bureau to graduates from the Kuibyshev Aviation Institute. In the summer of 1950 the order came to stop the development of several turbojet types at no.2 GAZ in order to concentrate on a new turboprop engine (see Chapter 6).

CHAPTER FIVE

More from Lyul'ka: The AL-5 and AL-7

During 1947 the development of Lyul'ka's TR series of axial-flow turbojets continued and three TR-2 engines of 2,000kp (4,410lb) static thrust were built at no. 165 GAZ in Moscow during the spring. The start of 1947 also saw work begin on the design of the 4,000kp (8,820lb) static thrust TR-3; the first example was on the test rig by 7 September 1947. Before the year's end another TR-3 had been built and, during its testing, it was decided to halt work on the TR-1 and TR-2 and concentrate on the redesign and refinement of the TR-3. The result of this concentration was that the TR-3 had passed its fifty-hour State Acceptance Test run by November 1948. Its evaluation report proclaimed that it was the 'most powerful turbojet engine of indigenous design, with increased compression ratio and temperature at the turbine disc'.

The TR-3 used a seven-stage axial compressor, an annular combustion chamber with 24 nozzles and a single-stage axial turbine. It used a fixed exhaust nozzle and was started pneumatically by an SV-3 unit using the airfield source of compressed air. All indigenous materials were employed in its construction and altogether the engine was a remarkable early achievement for Lyul'ka and his team. The TR-3 developed a static thrust of 4,600kp (10,143lb), had a dry weight of 1,700kg (3,749lb) and gave a specific fuel consumption of 1.1.

Continued development of the TR-3 endowed it with increased reliability and engine life. Nearly all its components were strengthened, resulting in an increase of dry weight to 1,900kg (4,190lb) but the specific fuel consumption was slightly improved while retaining the same thrust. A problem of flame-out when suddenly throttling back was thought to be cured by stabilizing the combustion process. Between February and April 1949 a turbine starting unit was developed so that the TR-3 could be started anywhere and this became a standard feature of Lyul'ka engines.

Lyul'ka TR-3 axial turbojet in the spring of 1947.

27

The Ilyushin Il-30 swept-wing aircraft of 1949 was powered by two Lyul'ka TR-3 turbojets and was a developmental prototype for a frontal bomber.
Russian Aviation Research Trust

AL-5 turbojet

By September 1950 the TR-3 had achieved a 100-hour TBO and begun its State Acceptance evaluation programme. Soon the TR-3A, with a static thrust of 5,000kp (11,025lb), was produced; this engine was redesignated as the AL-5 in recognition of A. Lyul'ka as a General Constructor.

The AL-5 was then one of the world's most powerful turbojets and Lyul'ka's design bureau received a Stalin Prize for its work. Flight testing of the AL-5 was carried out in the MiG I-350 fighter prototype, intended to be a supersonic version of the MiG-17 family. On its first flight on 16 June 1951, however, soon after climbing to 2,000m (6,560ft), the AL-5 flamed out

when it was throttled back. The pilot, G.A. Sedov, despite the heavy manual control resulting from the loss of hydraulic power, performed miracles in making a safe landing, extending the landing gear using the emergency air bottle just before touching the runway. Only five more short flights were made with the I-350 prototype.

In autumn 1949 it was decided to stop work on the TR-1 and TR-2 turbojet series and concentrate on refining the TR-3. Illustrated is the TR-3B, later redesignated the AL-5 in recognition of Arkip Lyul'ka's achievements. It delivered around 5,000kp (11,025lb) of static thrust by 1950 and was one of the world's most powerful turbojets at that time.

The Lavochkin La-190 was designed to use the AL-5 turbojet and reached Mach 1.03 early in 1951. Russian Aviation Research Trust

Mention should be made of two remarkable experimental aircraft that employed the AL-5 engine. By autumn 1948 the demand for a truly transonic fighter was being felt. To meet this the Lavochkin bureau designed the La-190, powered by the AL-5. Its wing was swept back at 55 degrees and it had a delta planform tailplane mounted on a swept-back fin. Provision was made for a radar housing inside the circular nose intake and there was a tandem undercarriage with small stabilizing wheels at the wingtips. Starting in February 1951, the aircraft made only eight flights, its maximum speed being Mach 1.03. The other aircraft, Yakovlev's Yak-1000, was very dramatic in appearance, with a long, cigar-shaped fuselage of minimum cross-section to fit the AL-5 engine. All its flying surfaces were of approximate delta shape, the wing having a tiny span of only 4.52m (14ft 9⅞in). A low-drag cockpit canopy was positioned close to the nose intake (the pilot semi-reclining) and there was a tandem undercarriage. The design speed of the Yak-1000 was Mach 1.65, but it never flew since taxiing tests in 1951 showed dangerous instability.

Contrary to previous development, it seemed that the AL-5's combustion at lower powers was still unstable. Following modifications of the combustion chamber, the AL-5 was again flight-tested, this time using

The dramatic Yakovlev Yak-1000 of 1951 was intended to reach Mach 1.65, using an AL-5 turbojet, but was never flown as taxiing tests showed dangerous instability. Russian Aviation Research Trust

This Junkers EF 150A was a German project built in the USSR in 1951, powered by two Lyul'ka AL-5 turbojets. The sole prototype was abandoned in favour of Tupolev's Tu-16.
Russian Aviation Research Trust

Prototype of the Ilyushin Il-46 bomber with two AL-5 engines. Although an excellent aircraft, it could not compete with the Tupolev Tu-88.
Russian Aviation Research Trust

The sole prototype of Tupolev's Tu-98 supersonic tactical bomber was powered by two Lyul'ka AL-7F afterburning turbojets. Russian Aviation Research Trust

two of them in the Ilyushin Il-46 straight-wing bomber prototype. Its first flight was made on 3 March 1952: V.K. Kokkinaki, at the controls, reported that the AL-5s worked reliably at all flight modes. However, although the Il-46 was an excellent aircraft, it could not rival Tupolev's Tu-88. Furthermore, the mishap with the I-350 fighter had sealed the fate of the AL-5 engine (and the I-350) in official circles and it was not to go into production. This was despite the fact that, by 1952, the AL-5 was producing a static thrust of 5,200kp (11,466lb) and had passed a 200-hour test run.

AL-7 turbojet

Undaunted by the small use made of the AL-5 but encouraged by its performance, Lyul'ka went on to develop the type into the outstanding AL-7 series, which became his first mass-produced turbojets. The AL-7 had a nine-stage axial compressor with supersonic flow through the first two, widely spaced stages. This compressor handled 114kg (251.37lb) of air per second and had a pressure ratio of 9.0:1. The AL-7 passed its first acceptance test in 1954 and gave a static thrust of 6,500kp (14,333lb). This thrust rose to a maximum of 9,000kp

(19,845lb) with the advent of the after-burning AL-7F; gradual development led to the 9,900kp (21,830lb) AL-7F-1 (6,900kp or 15,215lb without afterburning), the 10,100kp (22,271lb) AL-7F-2 and the 10,700kp (25,594lb) AL-7F-4.

A considerable number of experimental aircraft types were powered by the AL-7 engine. Prototypes of supersonic tactical bombers were ordered in 1952 and resulted in the Ilyushin Il-54 and Tupolev Tu-98, both with swept-back wings and using two AL-7s. (The Tu-98 actually used the after-burning AL-7F engine.) The sole prototype of the Il-54 first flew on 3 April 1955 and

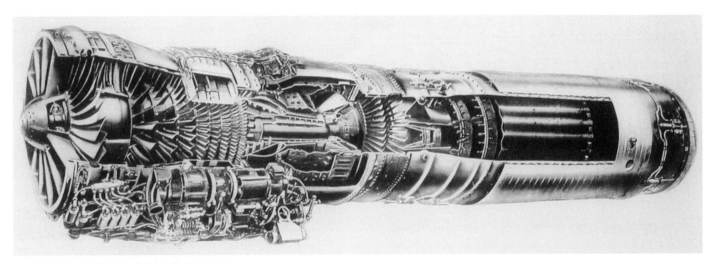

The outstanding AL-7 axial turbojet became Lyul'ka's first mass-produced engine; TOP: AL-7F-2 in section and; BOTTOM: the AL-7F-1, both with afterburner.

The Sukhoi S-1 interceptor prototype first flew in 1956. Powered by a Lyul'ka
AL-7F turbojet, it could reach speeds of up to Mach 2.0 at altitude and utilized a
conical centre body in its intake. This aircraft led to the Su-7 frontal fighters and
a long association between Sukhoi and Lyul'ka. Russian Aviation Research Trust

Sukhoi S-1 interceptor			
Span		9.309m	(30ft 6_in)
Length	excluding pitot tube	15.70m	(51ft 6in)
Wing area		34.0sq m	(365.8sq ft)
Empty weight		7,890kg	(17,397lb)
Maximum loaded weight		10,859kg	(23,944lb)
Maximum speed	at sea level	1,140km/h or Mach 0.932	(708mph)
Ceiling		19,100m	(62,648ft)
Range		1,370km	(851 miles)

the sole prototype of the Tu-98 flew early in 1956. A four-engined version of Tupolev's famous Tu-104 jet airliner using AL-7 engines was first flown on 11 March 1957 and a stretched version followed in April 1959, but again the design was not put into production. This aircraft, designated Tu-110, used AL-7P engines.

A maritime version of the AL-7, designated AL-7PB, was produced for flying boat use. It was smaller and lighter than other AL-7s, had no afterburning and was derated to give greater reliability on long flights over water. The AL-7PB was used to power the impressive Beriev Be-10 maritime reconnaissance and attack flying boat, which

replaced the piston-engined Be-6. The Be-10 featured all-swept flying surfaces and two AL-7PB engines mounted below and forward of the wing leading edges, close to the fuselage sides. First flown on 20 July 1956, the Be-10 equipped two units of the Black Sea Fleet. Although they had a short operational career, four Be-10s, designated as M-10s, gained world records in 1961 including carrying a 10-tonne payload to 12,733m (41,764ft) and a speed of 875.86 km/h (543.9mph) carrying a 5-tonne payload over a 1,000km (621 mile) circuit.

Following a period of assignment to the Tupolev OKB, Sukhoi's OKB was re-established in May 1953. (Confusingly, its

aircraft designations were begun again from '1': Sukhoi designations were S, swept wing, or T, delta, for prototypes and Su when an aircraft entered production, e.g. S-1 became Su-7.) The S-1 was a sleek, all-swept interceptor designed around an AL-7F engine. Its wing was swept back at 62 degrees, the tailplane was of the all-flying type and the nose air intake had a conical centre body to generate shock waves for pressure recovery at supersonic speeds. (The concept of using several shock waves for this purpose was fundamental for supersonic intakes and derived from the work of Dr Klaus Oswatisch and his assistant, H. Böhm, who worked on the problem from 1941 under Prof. L. Prandtl at the Kaiser-Wilhelm-Institut in Germany.) The S-1 first flew in September 1955 and had achieved a speed of 2,170km/h (1,348mph) in a test by April 1956. Despite the crash of an S-1 on 21 November 1956, the type was accepted for production and thus started the long association between Sukhoi aircraft and Lyul'ka turbojet engines.

Production developments of this interceptor included the Su-7 interceptor, with area-ruled fuselage, the Su-7B fighter-bomber and Su-11 delta-winged interceptor, each of which used a single AL-7F turbojet. The maximum speed of 2,120km/h (1,316mph) at 10,000m (33,000ft) or Mach 2.00 of the Su-7 was increased to 2,340km/h (1,453mph) at 11,000m (36,000ft) or Mach 2.20 with the Su-11.

Lavochkin used two AL-7F engines to power the large La-250 delta-winged, long-range, two-seat interceptor, which was first flown on 16 July 1956. Much development was needed to sort out the control system, and prototype crashes had to be endured. Intended to attain a speed of Mach 1.50, the unreliability of its engines was an inexplicable reason given for the cancellation of the La-250 in 1959.

Development of Sukhoi aircraft and Lyul'ka engines continued long after the scope of this history and Lyul'ka was bestowed with many honours. For the AL-7F engine alone, which was made in large quantities at a number of factories, he was made a Hero of Socialist Labour. Beginning with the significantly advanced AL-21 family of engines, other engines were developed from the AL-7 and today Lyul'ka's bureau is known as Lyul'ka Saturn, Inc.

CHAPTER SIX

Turboprop Development

With its great need for a strategic bomber, by 1947 the Soviet Union had introduced into service the Tupolev Tu-4 version of the excellent American B-29. The intensification of the Cold War brought a need for an intercontinental bomber to rival the American's B-36 and B-52, which was under development. Tupolev decided that such an aircraft should be of about 200,000kg (441,000lb) take-off weight and, to obtain the required performance and range, four turboprops of between 12,000 and 15,000hp were deemed necessary. Turbojets were ruled out since they were, at that time, too thirsty and, of course, no piston engines could provide the power needed.

In 1949 Stalin demanded a bomber that could fly to the USA and back. Vladimir Myasischchyev, Tupolev's son-in-law, took up this challenge and, with Stalin's approval, was permitted to reopen a large factory and to obtain resources and poach workers as necessary from other design bureaux. Beginning as Project 25 and continuing with various versions known in the West as the Bison, the Myasischchyev offering of 1953 was the Soviet Union's first strategic jet bomber. However, with its high aspect ratio swept wings and four AM-3 turbojets mounted in the wing roots, this bomber was a failure. The turbojets could not provide the power to carry a useful payload and they were too thirsty to give more than half of the intended 15,000km (9,300 miles) range. This and other failures later caused Myasischchyev to lose his design bureau.

German origins and the 2 TV-2F

The German teams at Upravlencheskiy had brought with them the projected turboprops from BMW (109-028) and Junkers (109-022), which had their basis in the 109-018 and 109-012 turbojets respectively. Pooling of ideas, which were quite fluid at that time, especially those of BMW, brought about the

first turboprop project at no.276 OKB, under the direction of N.D. Kuznyetsov, an engineer of high intelligence and wide technical knowledge, who had been ordered to concentrate on the turboprop at the expense of turbojet projects. The chief member of his team was the Austrian engineer Dipl.-Ing, Ferdinand Brandner, formerly of Junkers. This first turboprop engine, known as the TVD TV-022, was based mainly on the Junkers 109-022 and had a fourteen-stage axial compressor and a three-stage turbine. This drove two AV-41 contra-rotating airscrews through internal reduction gears, and it was the task of producing a reliable but compact gearing and airscrew assembly that was the cause of so many headaches. Brandner tells us that, in 1949, a Soviet deputy minister said to him:

You [the German team] will all go home when you have finished your work and the engine is in production somewhere. You can then talk about everything, we don't mind. You certainly will not want to copy the engine. We all cook with the same ingredients. But you will never find out how many engines we build, and that is the only thing that interests the West.

Little did the Germans realize what arduous technical tasks lay ahead of them.

In November 1950 the TV-022 completed its acceptance tests, in the light of which it was modified as the TV-2 and began flight tests in May 1951. For these tests a TV-2 replaced the starboard inner engine on a Tu-4 (c/n: 225402) and tests continued until October. During 1951 the TV-2 qualified with a power of 5,000shp; although it eventually reached 6,000shp, this was not enough for Tupolev's intercontinental bomber.

Following these first successes, notwithstanding an engine fire on the Tu-4, Tupolev and Kuznyetsov decided on a scheme to obtain enough power for each airscrew group by coupling together, via a common gearbox, two TV-2F engines to produce the 2 TV-2F turboprop. This was

The very talented N.D. Kuznyetsov concentrated on the development of large turboprop engines.

preferable to a scheme in which Tupolev was considering an eight-engine bomber, perhaps with four pushing and four pulling airscrews. Instead of internal gears, the common gearbox to which the two engines were connected was a separate, large, external unit and from it led the coaxial shafts for the contra-rotating airscrews. This coupled engine was seen as an interim measure and, as a concurrent development, work was to proceed on the TV-12 turboprop to give power equal to the coupled 2 TV-2F engine or at least 12,000shp.

Flight testing of the 2 TV-2F engine began on 12 November 1952 with four of them fitted to Tupolev's mighty Tu-95/I bomber prototype. This bomber had all flying surfaces swept back, the wing being swept back at 37 degrees. Its wingspan was 49.80m (163ft 4⅛in), length 44.35m (145ft 5⅜in) and loaded weight was 140,000kg

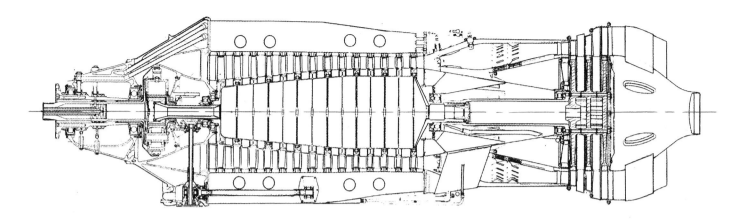

Kuznyetsov's first turboprop, the TVD TV-022, was based on the Junkers 109-022 engine. It had a fourteen-stage axial compressor and a three-stage turbine and drove contra-rotating airscrews.

(459,200lb), considerably less than Tupolev's first estimates but, nevertheless, a large machine.

Each 2 TV-2F installation was inside a wide cowling, had its centre line below the wing leading edge (unlike later Tu-95s) and was fed from chin inlets directing air to the left and right engine. The engines fed power to the common, external gearbox and the left engine drove the front airscrew and the right engine drove the rear airscrew of an AV-60 contra-rotating unit. Each airscrew was four-bladed and of 5.60m (18ft 4½in) diameter. Flights of the Tu-95/I proceeded without mishap until the

seventeenth flight on 11 May 1953, when the intermediate gearbox failed and the no.3 engine caught fire. The aircraft was written off in the ensuing crash and four of the crew, including the pilot A.D. Perelyot, were killed.

Failure of the gearbox had been caused by fractures of the reduction gears that could happen after thirty or forty hours of running, as was discovered by running the 2 TV-2F in static tests. It was found that set procedures for the gear manufacture had not been followed and the person responsible was sentenced. Unjustly, Kuznyetsov himself was also in big trouble

and faced a jail sentence, but he was saved by Tupolev's pleading at the enquiry in a desire to save the world's most powerful engine and the Tu-95 bomber. More help was given to Kuznyetsov, but he was now working under suspicion and more pressure. It was decided to abandon the 2 TV-2F coupled engine, after only seven had been built, and instead concentrate all efforts on developing the TV-12 turboprop. This must have been a courageous decision. Even so, the TV-12 was always under threat of cancellation and it was only the concern of Tupolev, who sent his engineers on regular visits to report on how the work was

This is the best picture known of the Kuznyetsov TV-2 turboprop, flight tested in 1951 and eventually achieving 6,000shp.

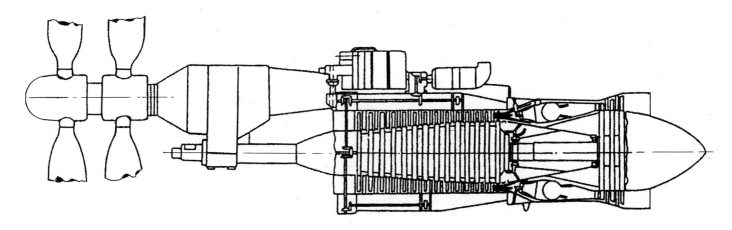

Schematic of the Kuznyetsov TVD 2 TV-2F turboprop, in which two TV-2F engines were coupled to a common gearbox to deliver 12,000shp to the contra-rotating airscrews.

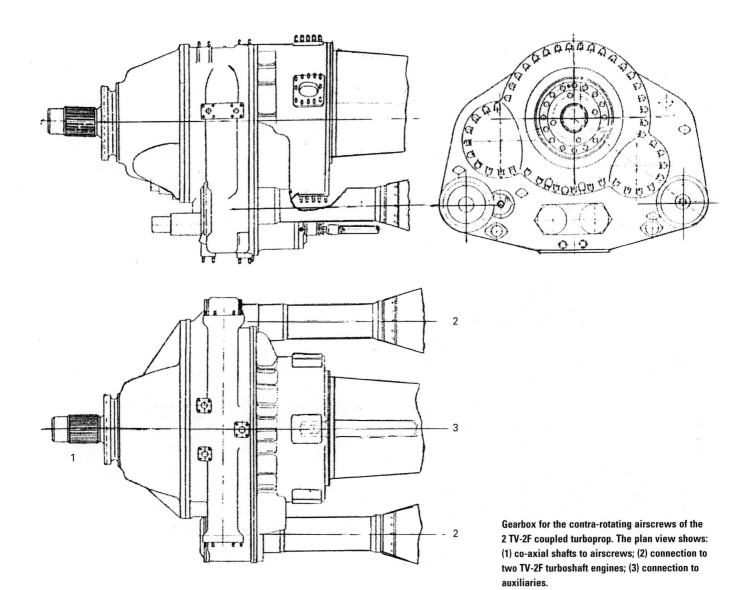

Gearbox for the contra-rotating airscrews of the 2 TV-2F coupled turboprop. The plan view shows: (1) co-axial shafts to airscrews; (2) connection to two TV-2F turboshaft engines; (3) connection to auxiliaries.

Kuznyetsov 2 TV-2F coupled turboprop with its massive gearbox. This, the world's most powerful aero-engine, was abandoned after only seven examples were built in order to concentrate on development of the TV-12 turboprop.

progressing, that gained time for the project. Altogether, it was an unenviable atmosphere in which to carry out a difficult development.

NK-12 turboprop

After the debacle with the 2 TV-2F gearbox, exceptional care was taken over the design and development of the internal gearing, drives and airscrews for the TV-12. These items were the responsibility of K. Zhdanov and an extremely fine, compact design, using planetary gears, was evolved. By June 1954 the airframe of the second prototype of the Tu-95 was completed, but TV-12 engines were not ready for installation until December that year. By then the TV-12 had completed its 100-hour State Acceptance test run and was giving 11,000shp. Further engine testing delayed the first flight until 16 February 1955, by which time the engines were designated NK-12, indicating that Kuznyetsov had redeemed himself in official eyes. The pilots for this maiden flight were M. Nyukhtikov and I. Sukhomlin.

The NK-12 turboprop engine, which was in a world class of its own for size, had an annular, conical magnesium alloy air intake casting with six radial, streamlined struts to support the compact gearbox and the front main bearing. The annular inlet to the compressor had variable incidence steel guide vanes and the fourteen-stage axial compressor had a four-piece welded sheet steel casing. The casing was welded from 2mm (0.079in) steel sheet stiffened by U-section steel rings. These rings also supported the rotor blade casing rings and the stator blade outer rings. The stator blades were inserted in and welded to their rings. At the inner end of the stator blades were other U-section support rings. This complicated stator assembly was annealed as a whole after welding and then separated longitudinally into two halves. A five-stepped aluminium alloy drum was used for the compressor rotor blades and a pressure ratio of 9.5:1 (one source states 13:1 at 11,000m/36,000ft), at an efficiency of 86 per cent, was achieved. Twelve cannular combustion chambers were employed, each with a conical flame tube, duplex fuel burners and a two-piece outer shell. The combustion system had an efficiency of 98 per cent and a life of between 300 and 500 hours.

A five-stage turbine was used which, helped by small clearances, achieved an efficiency of 93 per cent. The turbine rotor blade shroud rings were lined with graphite or sintered metal to avoid damage should the blade tips rub on them. For the prototype engines, the turbine rotor blades and discs were milled out of austenitic chrome-nickel-manganese-vanadium steel, and then polished to a mirror finish and nickel plated. The turbine stator blades were cast in cobalt alloy and supported by U-section inner and outer rings, all welded together in the manner of the compressor stator construction. Hollow steel turbine inlet nozzle vanes were used, the inlet temperature at the turbine being only 657°C. A fixed-area exhaust nozzle was used, the inner cone being supported on six radial struts.

The two coaxial, counter-rotating airscrew shafts were driven through compound gears from the front of the compressor shaft. Despite careful design and development, the airscrew and gearbox life was initially very short. On the ground it was possible to move one airscrew by hand easily without the other moving. Control of the NK-12 was by means of a hydromechanical unit with automatic starting and acceleration, integrated fuel and airscrew control and exhaust gas temperature control. A single-lever master control was used. The chief Soviet designer of automatic control systems for turbojet and turboprop engines was Fyodor Amosovich Korotov (1908–1988), who was the recipient of many awards. His design bureau for this work was no.33 OKB.

Because of the sweep-back of the Tu-95's great wings, it was necessary to position the

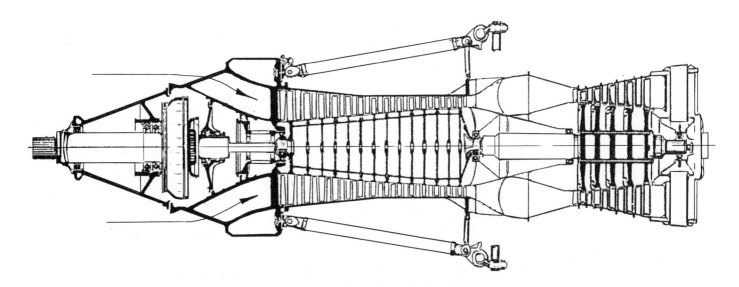

ABOVE: A schematic of Kuznyetsov's 12,000shp NK-12 turboprop, which was in a world class of its own for size. It featured a fourteen-stage axial compressor, twelve cannular combustion chambers and a five-stage turbine. It drove contra-rotating airscrews. The light compressor casing was braced by the external mounting struts.

RIGHT: The coupling and massive planetary and spur reduction gears of the Kuznyetsov NK-12 turboprop.

BELOW: Kuznyetsov NK-12MV turboprop.

Three shots of the huge Tupolev Tu-95 'Bear', the only turboprop bomber to enter service, which it did in the late 1950s. Powered by four Kuznyetsov NK-12 turboprops, this long-range bomber had a maximum speed of 910km/h (565mph) if necessary, making it the fastest airscrew-driven aircraft ever built. It was in service in many forms, the last being for maritime reconnaissance. Russian Aviation Research Trust

A Tupolev Tu-95 'Bear' at Monino. Author

AV-60N contra-rotating airscrews far ahead of the leading edges. Consequently, each NK-12 engine was mounted on long steel tube trusses that led from the rear of the gearbox casing back to the wing. Careful design and development avoided the transmission of powerful low-frequency vibrations from the airscrews to the airframe as the aircraft cruised at Mach 0.835. To limit the problem to one set of factors, the turboprop engines were run at a constant 8,300rpm and the airscrews at a constant 750rpm, power being varied by control of the fuel flow and airscrew pitch. The tip speed of the airscrews was 792km/h (492 mph). Each engine had a jet exhaust outlet at each side of its nacelle, the gases passing through heat exchangers to provide hot air for de-icing the flying surfaces. The NK-12 was spooled up for starting by a specially designed TS-12 65hp turbo-starter, which ran at 36,000rpm and drove the engine through differential gears. The starter had a radial compressor, spiral combustion chamber and a single-stage turbine. To facilitate starting, the turboprop's compressor had adjustable first-stage stator blades and blow-off valves.

The NK-12 developed 11,834shp at 8,250rpm at sea level (7,890shp at 11,000m) plus some 1,198kp (2,640lb) of thrust.

Kuznyetsov's NK-12M turboprop was developed in 1957 to produce 15,000shp and had auto-feather with manual back-up.

A preserved Antonov An-22M cargo transporter (CCCP-09334) of Aeroflot, with NK-12MA turboprops. The airscrews are 6.2m (20ft 4in) in diameter. In the background is a derelict VVA-14 Ekranoplan wing-in-ground effect aircraft (CCCP-10687). Author

BELOW: Maintenance being carried out on a Kuznyetsov NK-12MV 15,000shp turboprop in the No.3 position of a Tupolev Tu-114 airliner. Note the support rings for the two halves of the contra-rotating spinner.

Its specific fuel consumption was as low as 0.57 at sea level and 0.35 when cruising at 11,000m. Dimensions were an overall diameter of 1.15m (3ft 9¼in) and a length of 6.0m (19ft 8in), and the weight was 2,300kg (5,070lb) without the airscrews.

In the course of developing the Tu-95, Tupolev decided that engines of 15,000shp were needed. These were eventually provided in 1957 in the shape of the NK-12M turboprop, which had auto-feather backed up by manual feather capabilities. The Tu-95, known by its NATO designation as 'Bear', went on to be very successful and was produced in a number of versions. Its range was typically 13,000km (8,073 miles) with 76,000kg (167,580lb) of fuel, a service ceiling of 12,500m (41,000ft) and a bomb-load of 5,000kg (11,000lb).

The Tu-95 Bear was the only turboprop bomber in the world to enter front-line service, which it did in the late 1950s. It was a unique achievement and its maximum speed of 910km/h (565mph) was some 200km/h (124mph) faster than most experts thought possible for an airscrew-driven aircraft of such a size. As a dedicated long-range bomber, its range allowed it to reach the USA over the North Pole, the threat causing the Americans to erect three lines of early-warning radar and to institute their Air Defence Command (ADC). Another job for the Bear was to fly along the coast of Cuba to photograph the USA. Regular interceptions of the dramatic Tu-95 were carried out by F-106 interceptors and, around Britain's shores, RAF Lightnings. Some pilots commented on the discomfort to their ears caused by the Tu-95's airscrews, since it was one of the loudest

aircraft ever built. The Tu-95 Bear had one of the most modified airframes in history and was adapted and upgraded to carry various stand-off missiles and even a MiG-19 fighter. Its production ended in 1992 after forty years, making it one of the most successful and lengthy aircraft programmes ever.

Other aircraft using the NK-12 turbo-prop were the Tu-114 airliner, the Tu126 AWACS early-warning aircraft and the Tu-142 ASW aircraft. The Tu-114 entered service with Aeroflot in 1961 and soon

became the backbone of Soviet inter-national travel, making, for example, daily non-stop flights on the Moscow–Cuba route. The NK-12MA version of the engine was developed for the An-22 cargo aircraft and drove AV-90 airscrews of increased diameter (6.20m). The NK-12MK was produced for marine use, employing more corrosion-resistant materials and with a more thorough anti-corrosion surface treatment. The NK-12MK of 13,270shp was used in the Orlyonok wing-in-ground effect vehicles (Ekranoplans). The NK-12MP version was produced with improved economy in the early 1980s and was used to power the Tu-142M anti-submarine warfare (ASW) aircraft types and the Tu-95MS strategic missile launcher. Total production of the NK-12 turboprop was 1,672 engines: 848 of the NK-12 and NK-12M (1954–9), plus 824 of the NK-12MV (1960–62).

NK-4 and AI-20 turboprops

In 1955, following the early success of the NK-12 turboprop, Kuznyetsov was given the job of developing a much less powerful engine for use by the Antonov An-10 and Ilyushin Il-18 medium-haul airliners and the An-12 cargo aircraft. At the same time the A.G. Ivchenko OKB was also tasked with developing such a turboprop. After the difficulties of developing the NK-12 engine, Kuznyetsov was much more relaxed about this job, which he considered relatively easy: the NK-4 was ready in only seven months. Its development was made all the easier since it was to drive a single four-bladed airscrew and so there was no need to develop contra-rotating gearing. A power of 4,000shp plus about 450kp (993lb) of exhaust thrust was required.

The NK-4 had an annular magnesium alloy air intake casting with four radial struts supporting the front main bearing and enclosing the airscrew gearbox. Variable incidence steel guide vanes directed airflow into the axial compressor, which had only six stages but included for the first time supersonic stages. All compressor blades were of steel and enclosed by a two-piece aluminium alloy casing. Aluminium alloy discs were bolted between stub shafts to make up the compressor rotor. Twelve cannular-type combustion chambers were used, each having a conical flame tube and duplex burner. A tubular shaft led from the compressor to the three-stage turbine, which had solid blades. The fixed-area exhaust nozzle had an inner cone supported by four radial struts. Control of the NK-4 was similar to the NK-12 with constant speed operation.

In 1957 the NK-4 turboprop passed its State Acceptance evaluation programme and no.24 GAZ in Moscow started its series production. It was light (only 1,050kg or 2,315lb), easily produced and simple. The NK-4 and NK-4A were fitted to early production examples of the four-engined An-10 Ukraina and Il-18 airliners. Unfortunately, misfortune from the past came

Two views of the Tupolev Tu-114 airliner with NK-12 turboprops.
Bottom: Russian Aviation Research Trust

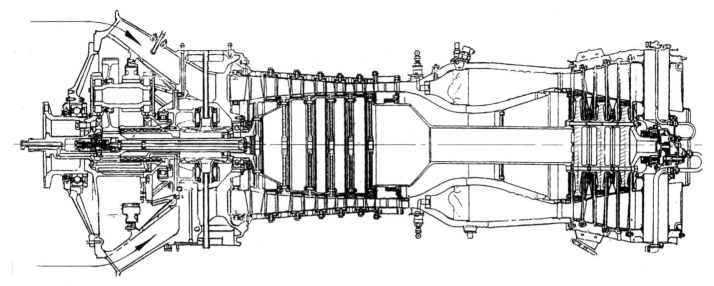

Kuznyetsov NK-4 axial turboprop engine, designed to drive a single airscrew.

Kuznyetsov NK-4 turboprop. This 4,000eshp engine was relatively light and easily produced.

back to haunt Kuznyetsov when the gearbox shaft of an Il-18 failed and the airscrew flew off, striking the adjoining engine nacelle. A more serious event with an Il-18 occurred in 1958 when one crashed, killing a number of high-ranking officers. The cause was cited as the absence of an airscrew feathering system so that, when one engine failed, it seized up and the excessive drag could not be countered.

Kuznyetsov very quickly introduced an automatic feathering system, as had already been provided for the NK-12M, but this could not save the NK-4 from cancellation at the end of 1958, only 222 examples having been made. Ivchyenko's competing AI-20 turboprop was therefore adopted as the only other choice for the An-10 and An-12 aircraft; both the engine and the aircraft were made in the Ukraine. It was

said, in vain, that the NK-4 was the better and more economical of the two engines.

At Zaporozh'ye the AI-20 turboprop was worked on by designer-general A. Ivchyenko (1903–1968), chief designer Lotarev and head of design bureau A.N. Zlenko. This engine was of similar size and performance to the NK-4 but of different design. It had a ten-stage axial compressor with a slightly lower compression ratio but ran at a higher speed; also, the combustion chamber was of the annular type. As with the NK-4, a three-stage turbine was used. By 1956 the AI-20 was undergoing bench tests and, once in production, it went from strength to strength. By 1963, for example, its TBO was up to 1,000 hours and then 4,000 hours (1966) and, finally, 6,000 hours.

Ivchyenko was succeeded at Zaporozh'ye by Vladimir Lotarev, the first engine from the new design team being the D-36, which was a three-shaft turbofan engine with a static thrust of 5,600kp (12,348lb) and which became the basis for various engines going beyond the time scale of this history, under the company name of ZMKB Progress.

Another turboprop that lost out to the AI-20 was the VK-2 developed at no.117 GAZ in Leningrad under V.Ya. Klimov from 1947 until its cancellation in 1952. The VK-2 had an eight-stage axial compressor and developed between 4,500 and 4,800shp at 9,000rpm. State Acceptance tests of the VK-2 were held in March 1951 when its rating was given as 4,800ehp, but it did not go into serial production.

The designer A. Ivchyenko.

An Ilyushin Il-18, powered by Ivchyenko AI-20 turboprops and carrying a multi-sensor reconnaissance pod. Author

Two views of the very successful Ivchyenko AI-20M turboprop.

CHAPTER SEVEN

Assimilation of British Turbojet Technology

Before the German turbojet and aircraft teams were set up in the Soviet Union, a meeting was held at the Kremlin on 6 April 1946 to assess Soviet progress in jet aircraft development. Progress was considered to be unsatisfactory, despite the promise of Lyul'ka's S-18 turbojet, and so it was decided to try to buy some technology from Great Britain in order to speed matters up. A sceptical Stalin thought the British would be unlikely to sell any of their secrets, but it was agreed to make the approach anyway.

This was soon after the end of the Second World War when, despite the beginnings of the Cold War between East and West, it was still possible for a Soviet delegation

to make a friendly visit to its wartime British ally. Arrangements were therefore made and a Soviet commission visited England between 3 December and 22 December 1946. This consisted of A.I. Mikoyan (aircraft designer), S.T. Kishkin (metallurgist) and V.Ya. Klimov (engine designer), the latter staying on in England until 1 February 1947.

On 10 January 1947 Mikoyan and Kishkin submitted to the Chief Administration of the Aviation Industry (GUAP) a report covering their visits to the factories of Bristol, De Havilland, English Electric, Gloster, Metropolitan-Vickers, Rolls-Royce and Vickers-Armstrong. The essence of this report was as follows. All British companies

were concentrating on the turbojet and the most successful of their engines were the Rolls-Royce Nene 1 and Derwent 5. British turbojets were, at that time, rightly considered the best in the world and highlighted the lag in Soviet developments. The British engines far outstripped German engines at the end of the war, especially regarding efficiency, reliability, ruggedness and service life. Largely this was attributed to the use of Nimonic 80, a secret heat- and creep-resisting steel alloy used for turbine blades and other parts. The copying of the Rolls-Royce engines as soon as possible was recommended, irrespective of work on indigenous Soviet engines.

A prime motive for obtaining British technology was to learn the secrets of Nimonic 80 and turbine blade manufacture, about which the British had not been very forthcoming. To this end, Kishkin pocketed a turbine blade during one visit! Klimov, on the other hand, wore soft-soled shoes under which he carefully collected some swarf from a machining process in one of the factories. These samples were sent to Moscow for analysis.

After negotiations with the Soviet Commission, Rolls-Royce agreed to supply ten Nene and ten Derwent engines, and a letter from GUAP confirmed the deal on 11 March 1947. Ten days later the first Derwent left for Murmansk aboard the merchant ship *Feodosia* and all twenty engines had been delivered by June 1947. Another batch, consisting of twenty Derwents and fifteen Nenes, was delivered by November of that year.

In view of the fact that, as we shall see, the sale of these engines gave the Soviets a technological leap forward that led to the excellent MiG-15 fighters used in the Korean War, it seems a strange move for the British to have made. However, early in 1946 Rolls-Royce had made a deal with China for licensed production of turbojets (which was not taken up) and also sold a

In December 1946 a Soviet commission visited aircraft and engine factories in England. The engine designer V.Ya. Klimov (LEFT) and the aircraft designer A.I. Mikoyan (CENTER) are seen here on an airfield.

licence to Hispano in France for turbojet manufacture. By one means or another, the Soviets could obtain information from other sources such as these. In any case, the engines sold were centrifugal types and the official British view was that axial types were the way forward. Besides, an almost bankrupt post-war Britain badly needed to sell manufactured goods, one of its many burdens being the need to pay for loans and the supply of war matériel from the USA. Nevertheless, as we shall see, the Nene was copied and built with its derivatives in huge quantities by the Soviets. Strangely, the sale of De Havilland Vampire and Gloster Meteor jet fighters to the Soviet Union did not take place even though these aircraft

were sold and could be inspected all over the world.

Inspection and copying

Altogether the Soviet Union received fifty-five turbojet engines from Britain: thirty Derwent 5s, twenty Nene 1s and five Nene 2s. For testing, measuring and back-engineering into the RD-500 engine, five Derwents went to no.500 GAZ in Tushino, Moscow, where four were dismantled and the fifth was kept complete for comparison purposes. For installation into experimental aircraft, a total of twenty Derwents went to six aircraft factories. For studying and

testing, one Derwent went to CIAM. Three Derwents went to no.45 GAZ as a reserve and one is unaccounted for.

Regarding the Nene engines, some eight examples went to no.45 GAZ, a giant engine factory in Moscow. These were for testing, measuring and back-engineering into the RD-45 engine. For installation into experimental aircraft, a total of sixteen Nenes went to five aircraft factories and, for studying and testing, one Nene went to CIAM. Test results for the Derwent and Nene at CIAM were close to those given by Rolls-Royce, but thrust was down slightly due to the greater density of Soviet fuel affecting the maximum rpm limiting device. The tested Nene (c/n: 1007), for

An RD-500, the Soviet copy of the Rolls-Royce Derwent centrifugal turbojet. Jan Hoffmann

example, gave a maximum static thrust of 2,055kp (4,531lb) at 11,850rpm compared with 2,218kp (4,891lb) at 12,000rpm when checked by Rolls-Royce before despatch.

At no.500 GAZ chief designer V.M. Yakovlev received the order to copy the Derwent in March 1947. Metric drawings to Soviet standards were produced and the various materials were analysed to find indigenous substitutes. Only the British high-temperature Nimonic 80 alloy presented a problem. Eventually, after much work by various research institutes, a Soviet substitute alloy know as KhN 80T (or EI. 437) was produced; as was later found when put into production and use, however, it had the heat-resisting properties required but not the creep-resisting properties. According to Ferdinand Brandner, British-type Nimonic alloys were not (generally) available in the Soviet Union until 1953.

The first Derwent copy, designated RD-500, was running under test on 31 December 1947 and others followed in 1948. All was not well, however, since various faults were revealed, such as uneven combustion and cracked combustion chambers. Differences from the Derwent included modified fuel, speed control and starting systems. Nevertheless, the RD-500 closely matched the Derwent's performance and passed its 100-hour State Acceptance test in September 1948. It gave a static thrust of 1,590kp (3,506lb), as for the Derwent, but was heavier at 580.7kg (1,280lb) compared to 567kg (1,250lb) for the Derwent. In 1948 ninety-seven RD-500s were built at no.500 GAZ, which then produced another 462 in 1949. No.16 GAZ in Kazan' also produced 300 engines in 1949.

At the special Design Bureau in no.45 GAZ the task of copying the Nene largely fell to N.G. Motskhvarishvili under the direction of the head, V.Ya. Klimov, who was also Chief Designer at OKB-117 in Leningrad. New drawings were produced at OKB-117 but difficulties in manufacture were similar to those for the Derwent. The first copies of the Nene 1, designated RD-45, were available for testing in 1948 and passed the 100-hour State Acceptance test that August, a month before the Derwent copies. The RD-45 gave a similar thrust to that of the Nene but, at 800kg (1,782lb), it was slightly heavier. This was strange since initially any modification of the Nene during the copying process was forbidden.

Much reconstruction of the plant took place at no.500 GAZ and two new workshops were added. However, despite the

Yakovlev Yak-23 fighter powered by an RD-500 turbojet. Russian Aviation Research Trust

high priority in supplying equipment, personnel and funds, manufacture of the copied British engines brought great difficulties that were reflected in the high wastage rate and excessive man-hours spent on each engine: during 1947 the man-hours required to build each RD-500 engine was a colossal 20,000, but this had been reduced by 1 November 1948 to 7,900 man-hours per engine. By 1 March 1949 the man-hours per engine had been further reduced to 4,734, which approached the planned figure of 4,000 man-hours and reflected the great progress made in overcoming the severe difficulties. The most serious problems with early RD-500s concerned the turbine blades, 30 per cent of which were rejected due to recrystallization after casting. Also, up to 40 per cent of early RD-500s had to be stripped down before delivery for readjustment. In particular, poor creep resistance of the KhN 80T alloy resulted in dangerous elongation of the turbine blades. Despite earlier State tests, a life of 100 hours could not be obtained in service.

Vast funds and resources were also used to build up the factory at no.45 GAZ to produce RD-45 copies of the Derwent 5 engine. Difficulties in production were attributable largely to supply shortages and waiting for the Soviet KhN 80T alloy to be improved. Finally, on 31 July 1948, the first quantities of the improved alloy were received and the first RD-45 passed its State Acceptance tests on 19 August 1948. Even then a problem of fluctuating fuel pressure had to be solved. The man-hours required to manufacture an RD-45 were very much less than those initially required for the RD-

500, presumably because lessons learned in the manufacture were passed on. By 1 March 1949 the man-hours required to build an RD-45 totalled 3,557, as opposed to the planned number of 2,500. No.26 GAZ in Rybinsk (previously disbanded in Ufa) was brought in to help boost production in 1948, but got off to a slow start and does not seem to have built any engines by the end of the year. In the meantime, production of the RD-45F with afterburner was planned.

Because of all the difficulties, the production of British turbojet copies in 1948 fell far short of that planned. The shortfalls were 53.5 per cent for the RD-500 and 70 per cent for the RD-45. About 400 RD-500s were built, but by the time production of the RD-45, a close copy of the Nene 1, finished in 1950, a total of 3,281 RD-45s had been built. A total of 6,132 RD-45F and RD-45FA engines, the latter being a slightly modified version with a shorter afterburner. Service life was eventually increased to 250 hours.

VK-1 turbojet and other Klimov engines

On 9 April 1946, seven months before the Commission visited Britain, the Soviet Council of Ministers ordered the development of an indigenous turbojet of 2,700kp (5,954lb) static thrust. This centrifugal engine, designated VK-1, was to become the most important in early Soviet development. The job was entrusted to Vladimir Yakovlyevich Klimov (1892–1962), who

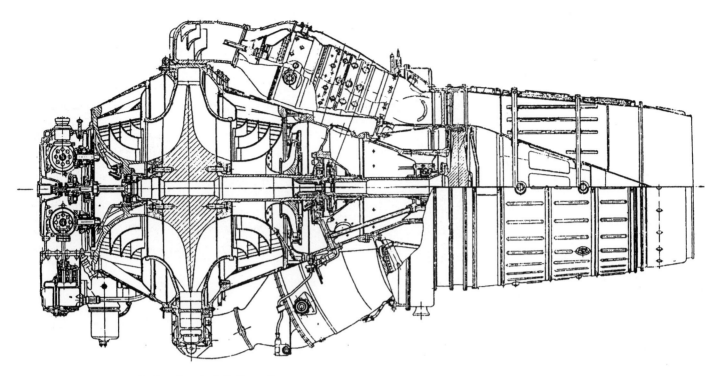

Klimov VK-1 centrifugal turbojet, based on the Rolls-Royce Nene.

A Klimov VK-1A centrifugal turbojet at an exhibition in Moscow in 1997.

headed the design bureau OKB-117 in Leningrad. As a basis for the design he used the British Nene engine, scaled up slightly to give greater thrust, because this was known to be very reliable. However, no example of the Nene was available in the USSR at the time and all that Klimov had to guide him were articles in Western magazines and some photographs, including a cross-section of the general assembly. This latter was, of course, most useful for indicating the layout and the all-important general proportions.

Development of the VK-1 began around June 1946, but some modifications to the design were made following Klimov's visit to England, when he first saw a Nene, and after the first Nenes arrived in the USSR. In general, the use of indigenous materials and Soviet-designed auxiliaries and sub-assemblies was continued. The weight of the VK-1 prototype came out at 870kg (1,918lb) and less than 10 per cent of its 1,431 parts had any commonality with the RD-45 copy of the Nene. Heat-resisting alloys for the VK-1s turbine and other parts were initially based on the German Tinidur (titanium-nickel-chromium-steel), probably with an increased nickel content to improve creep resistance, which normally fell off at about 580°C. However, it was only after the introduction of a Soviet version of the British Nimonic 80 heat-resisting alloy that the VK-1 was able to pass its 100-hour test. Thus, the VK-1 would not have gone very far without the introduction of the superior British Nimonic steels.

In October 1947, even before the RD-45, the first of Klimov's VK-1s was ready for bench testing and a further five engines were completed by the end of that year.

These engines incorporated modifications made in the light of testing, which revealed faults such as oil leaks, fluctuating fuel pressure and, most worrying, an unstable airflow. The VK-1 finally passed its 100-hour State Acceptance Test in November 1949. Production was initiated at no.45 GAZ, the giant engine factory in Moscow, and the first eleven engines appeared before the end of 1949. During 1950 and 1951 the plants of no.16 GAZ (Kazan'), no.24 GAZ (Kuibyshev), no.26 GAZ (Rybinsk) and No.500 GAZ (Moscow) were also brought into the production programme. Because the VK-1 was designed specifically for Soviet manufacturing methods, production soon outstripped the RD-45 and RD-500 direct British engine copies, and the trend was that these latter were used in experimental and training aircraft while the VK-1 engines and its derivatives were used in front-line aircraft.

Improvements made to the VK-1 during its production included modified compressor diffuser blades, the use of new alloys, better protective coatings and more reliable sealing. The VK-1 was phased out of production in 1952 after some 12,018 had been manufactured. It was replaced in production by the VK-1A and, later, the afterburning VK-1F. New and better features of the VK-1A included solid-drawn sections for the combustion chamber casings, reinforced turbine inlet nozzle blades, new burners, seals and electrical systems, and new fuel system components. Of particular importance was the introduction of better heat-resisting alloys for the turbine blades, which, while the thrust remained unchanged, brought the VK-1A's service life up to 200 hours. Four versions of the engine were produced, differing in the length of the jet pipe, the accessories and the accessories gearbox, depending on the aircraft being fitted. The four versions were: VK-1A for the Il-28, VK-1B for the Tu-14, VK-1S for the MiG-17 and VK-1V for the MiG-15bis. The VK-1V was the lightest at 881kg (1,943lb). The VK-1A series was the most prolific of Soviet turbojets, 34,605 being made before phase-out in 1960.

Less prolific, but nevertheless important, was the VK-1F, which began production in 1953 at no.45 GAZ in Moscow. This version had an afterburner and was first flight-tested in the MiG-17 (c/n: 850) on 29 September 1951, the pilot being A.N. Chernoburovi. The VK-1F turbojet had a large six-petal exhaust nozzle that varied the outlet diameter from 540mm to 624mm (1ft 9in – 2ft 0½in) and its thrust was rated at 2,650kp (5,843lb) dry and 3,380kp (7,453lb) with afterburning on. Initially afterburning was limited to 3 minutes at 7,000m (23,000ft) altitude or 10 minutes above this height. Later, a modified plenum chamber, better cooling of the jet pipe (to ensure structural integrity) and an improved fuel supply system for all heights relaxed the limitations. A total of 3,978 VK-1Fs were made and the type was phased out in 1959.

Soon after production of the VK-1F began, a new hydraulic actuation system for the exhaust petals was introduced and the turbine seals were changed. Feedback from Korean War operations brought about the reinforcement of the afterburner section and, later, the compressor discs also. Production of the VK-1 peaked in 1953 during the Korean War: 50,601 VK-1s of all types were made altogether.

As well as the VK-2 turboprop (see Chapter 6), other engines were also developed under Klimov at no.117 GAZ.

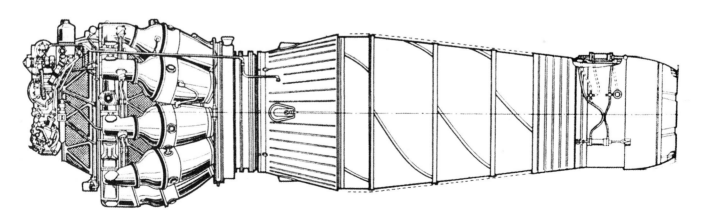

Klimov VK-1F with afterburner.

The VK-3, designed by S.V. Lyunevich, was a pioneering two-shaft turbojet with two low-pressure stages and eight high-pressure stages. Its airflow was 98.4kg/sec (216.97lb/sec) and the pressure ratio 12.7 to 1. The VK-3 was designed for a static thrust of 5,730kp (12,635lb) dry and 8,440 kp (18,610lb) with afterburning. It was run in 1952 but the project was abandoned in 1956.

The centrifugal VK-5 turbojet was a further development of the VK-1 and designed by A.S. Mevius. With airflow increased to 52.0kg/sec (114.66lb/sec) and higher fuel consumption, the VK-5 had a take-off thrust of 3,100kp (6,836lb) and was tested in 1952, but remained in prototype form only. The VK-5F, which had a variable-area exhaust nozzle and electronic control of the temperature in the afterburner, had a take-off thrust of 3,850kp (8,489lb) and was tested in June 1952 in the MiG-17R reconnaissance version of the fighter.

Also in 1952, the VK-7 turbojet was created. This represented the last centrifugal type in the Soviet Union and was essentially an enlarged Nene, but with a greater airflow and a pressure ratio of 6.3:1 that was produced with a new two-stage centrifugal compressor of complex form. There were also modified combustion chambers and many minor changes, including new seals. The resultant take-off thrust was 4,200kp (9,261lb) dry or 6,270kp (13,825lb) with afterburning. The VK-7 did not go into production and so the further stretching of the Nene design was halted. With Klimov's VK-2 turboprop also cancelled in 1952, he ended his career on a low note. When he was succeeded by Sergei P. Isotov, the bureau concentrated on turboshaft engines for helicopters and is now known as the Isotov Corporation.

Based on Junkers projects, this I 40-R reconnaissance aircraft, with swept-forward wings, was powered by two VK-1 turbojets. Built in 1949 only as a back-up in case Tupolev, Ilyushin and other Soviet design bureaux failed, it was later abandoned. Russian Aviation Research Trust

A Klimov VK-7 two-stage centrifugal turbojet. This was the last centrifugal engine developed in the Soviet Union.

CHAPTER EIGHT

Utilization of the British Engines, Their Copies and the VK-1

The reason why the Soviets ordered a second batch of Nene and Derwent engines (bringing the total to fifty-five) was that their copies were not ready for the various experimental jet aircraft that were waiting for engines.

Interceptors

During 1947 the design bureau of S.M. Alexeyev worked on designs for a night and all-weather interceptor to be powered by two Nene engines. Especially demanding was the requirement for a range of 2,300km (1,428 miles), or 3,100km (1,925 miles), with drop tanks. Alekseyev offered the I-212 with all-swept flying surfaces, the wing at 45 degrees, and a tricycle undercarriage. The wings mounted two nacelles, each enclosing a Nene (later an RD-45) mounted ahead of the wing spar box, the exhaust pipe passing through structural rings. A bubble canopy was mounted on a streamlined fuselage. Construction of the I-212 was started but not completed.

MiG also offered a swept-wing day and night interceptor powered by two RD-45F engines, but the engines were fuselage mounted, in an unusual way, with a large nose air intake. One engine was in the lower fuselage, exhausting from a short tailpipe, while the other was in the rear fuselage, exhausting from below the fin. This aircraft, designated the MiG I-320, had a cockpit canopy enclosing side-by-side seats and a tricycle undercarriage. It had what was to become typically MiG, a large swept-back fin with a tailplane mounted halfway up it. Starting with the first flight on 16 April 1949, three prototypes were flown but the type lost out to the Yak-25 (second use of that number). MiG also flew its I-310, prototype of one of the most famous aircraft of all time, the MiG-15 fighter (see below), on the power of a Nene 2 engine.

The first jet fighter to use the Soviet-built RD-500 engine was the Yak-23 with straight flying surfaces and an underslung engine with nose intake and a short jet pipe. Its development was rapid since it was based on the similar, but RD-10A-powered, Yak-17. First flown on 17 June 1947, the Yak-23 went into production but was soon superseded by the MiG-15, which it could out-climb, and so saw most of its service in Poland, Czechoslovakia and Bulgaria. The Polish test pilot Ablamovicz set an international record for climb performance on 21 November 1957 when a Yak-23 attained 6,000m (19,680ft) in 3 minutes 17 seconds. Because its cockpit was not pressurized, its service ceiling was limited to 13,000m (42,600ft), although it was capable of reaching 14,800 m (48,500ft).

Yakovlev followed this fighter in October 1947 with the greatly improved Yak-25 (first use of that number), again with an RD-500 engine but this time with a pressurized cockpit, the bureau's first. This enabled a service ceiling of 14,000m (46,000ft) to be attained. Its maximum speed was 982km/h (610mph) at sea level and it excelled among straight-winged fighters but, again, could not compete with the MiG-15. The bureau turned next to a swept-wing version of the Yak-25, the Yak-30, again with a single RD-500 engine. It first flew on 4 September 1948 but was out-flown by the MiG-15 and the bureau was never to gain ascendancy over MiG in the fighter field.

Yakovlev's last use of a straight wing on a jet fighter was on the La-174TK, albeit the thinnest fighter wing in the world at that time, its thickness/chord ratio being only 6 per cent. (The American Douglas X-3 had a wing of only 4.5 per cent thickness/chord ratio, but that, of course, was an experimental aircraft.) The TK stood for Tonkoye Krylo ('thin wing'). First flown in January 1948, the La-174TK was powered by an imported Derwent engine. Despite its

thin wings, it was slower (970km/h at sea level) than the less powerful but swept-wing La-160 and so was abandoned. A small production batch of the La-15 fighter, with a single RD-500 engine and all-swept surfaces, including a shoulder-mounted wing and a tall fin carrying the tailplane, was built in 1949. The La-15 achieved a maximum speed of 1,026km/h (637mph) at 3,000m (9,840ft).

Continuing the theme of the Su-9, Sukhoi produced the Su-11 and then, early in 1948, proposed the Su-13. Despite the use of two wing-mounted RD-500 engines, the estimated performance of the straight-wing Su-13 was still considered inadequate and so it was not built. Swept surfaces then appeared on Sukhoi's Su-15, which was powered by two RD-45 engines and was a radar-equipped interceptor first flown on 11 January 1949. This time the engines were mounted inside the fuselage and fed from a bifurcated nose intake, one engine exhausting below the fuselage and the other beneath the tail. All went well at first, but then severe flutter was experienced at high speed, forcing the pilot Anokhin to eject. The maximum speed of the Su-15 was 1,050km/h (652mph) at sea level.

Bombers

On the bomber scene, Tupolev produced the Type 73, which aimed to carry a 3-tonne bomb load at 800km/h (497mph) by utilizing the power of two wing-mounted Nene I engines and one fuselage-installed Derwent 5 engine. The air intake for the Derwent was in a forward dorsal extension from the base of the vertical fin. Apart from the tailplane, all flying surfaces were unswept. A similar layout was tried in the Type 78, but with two RD-45 engines and one RD-500 engine. Only prototypes were built, the Type 73 first flying on 20 December 1947, and a maximum speed of

TOP: Tupolev's 1947 Type 73 bomber was powered by two wing-mounted Rolls-Royce Nene turbojets and a tail-mounted Rolls-Royce Derwent V turbojet. The air intake for the Derwent is in the dorsal fairing of the vertical fin.

BOTTOM: The type was then redesigned as the Tu-14 with two VK-1 engines only. Russian Aviation Research Trust

872km/h (542mph) at 5,000m (16,400ft) was achieved.

The Ilyushin bureau was destined to have considerable early success with the jet bomber. Following its four-engined Il-22, an improved version, the Il-24, was projected in 1947 with four RD-500 engines. Having cut its teeth on these experimental aircraft, the bureau began work in December 1947 on the famous Il-28 tactical bomber. The Il-28 was a straight-wing aircraft but had swept tail surfaces. Taper on the wing's trailing edge only, plus the long engine nacelles projecting well forward of the wing, gave this bomber its distinctive shape. Although the Il-28 was powered by only two engines, these were all-Soviet VK-1 turbojets of 2,700kp (5,954lb) static thrust and the aircraft was relatively small. To assist take-off, a pair of solid-fuelled rockets could be fitted underwing, inboard of each engine. Of all-metal construction, the design was handicapped by the requirement to carry a manned tail gun and considerable armouring. Nevertheless, the Il-28, which first flew on 8 July 1948 with V.K. Kokkinaki at the controls, proved to be superior to its competitor, the Tupolev

Type 78, after a fly-off in October 1948. With a crew of four, the Il-28 could carry 1 tonne of bombs or even, in overload condition, a nuclear bomb. Following its public appearance over Moscow on May Day 1950, the Il-28 became known in the West as the 'Beagle' and it went into production at no.53 GAZ and, later, no.125 GAZ in Irkutsk. By 1955 some 1,959 Il-28s had been built: it was made in various versions including the Il-28T torpedo bomber for the A-VMF (Naval aviation), the Il-28U trainer, the Il-28 reconnaissance version and the Il-28D nuclear bomber, which had the nose and tail guns removed. Typical performance included a maximum speed of 900km/h (559mph) at 4,500m (14,760ft), a service ceiling of 12,300m (40,300ft) and a maximum range (Il-28R) of 2,780km (1,726 miles). From January 1955, Aeroflot used demilitarized Il-28s, designated Il-20, as jet crew trainers and also for carrying urgent cargo.

So successful was the Il-28 that more than a thousand were exported to many countries. In addition, China put it into production as the H-5 and also exported several hundred. The Il-28 was very long-

lived and was often the flying test-bed of choice for the development of engines and much other equipment.

Tupolev, having lost out to the Il-28, had slightly more success with its Tu-14 (developed from the Type 78), which used a similar formula to the Il-28 in that it featured two VK-1 engines and a straight wing. Although popular in service, only a hundred or so Tu-14s were built. A swept-wing version of the Tu-14, designated Tu-22 (first use of that number), was proposed in 1949 but was not built.

MiG-15 fighter

From the end of 1949 increasing numbers of aircraft were powered by the VK-1 turbojet and its derivatives. By far the most important was the MiG-15 fighter, destined to become one of the most famous aircraft of all time. Initially it was designated as the I-310, which had its origins in an October 1946 meeting at the Kremlin. In February 1947 the MiG bureau received accurate details of the VK-1PO turbojet (PO indicating 'first consignment') and the fighter project went ahead with all possible speed under deputy general constructor A.G. Brunov and chief engineer A.A. Andreyev. The aircraft was of traditional all-metal, stressed-skin construction and generally used many simplifications. The barrel-like fuselage, of circular cross-section, had the very smallest diameter that could accommodate the centrifugal engine and all flying surfaces were boldly swept back, the wing at 35 degrees at the quarter-chord position. The simple nose air intake bifurcated around the cockpit and then again, but vertically, around the unbroken wing centre section. From the start, the cockpit was pressurized and had an ejector seat. Altogether the airframe was extremely rugged, including the tricycle undercarriage. Armament was to be formidable as well and consisted of one 37mm and two 23mm cannon installed as a removable gunpack under the nose.

Three views of Ilyushin's famous tactical bomber, the Il-28 'Beagle', which was powered by two Klimov VK-1 turbojets. The bottom two photos show the same Il-28 at Monino, the centre picture being of much earlier days. In the bottom picture, the nose of the giant Myasishchyev M-50 'Bounder' is seen behind the Il-28. Top two photos: Russian Aviation Research Trust. Bottom: Author

The first prototype of the MiG-15, the S-01, made its maiden flight on 30 December 1947 with Victor N. Yuganov at the controls. This aircraft was actually powered by an imported 2,235kp (4,928lb) thrust Nene 1 engine. Easy access to the engine was afforded by removal of the rear half of the fuselage, an excellent idea already employed by Lockheed for its P-80 fighter. The slightly more powerful Nene 2 engine was used to power the second prototype, the S-02, which first flew on 27 May 1948, piloted by G. Sedov of the Air Force. By March 1948 the S-03 prototype, also with a Nene 2, was ready and was first flown on 17 June. It incorporated desirable but relatively minor modifications, chiefly the strengthening of the wing and the rear fuselage and the addition of dive brakes to the sides of the rear fuselage. What could not be readily cured was the tendency to spin off a high-G turn. Also, despite a fin of generous area, the aircraft snaked at high speed so that a service limit of Mach 0.92 was imposed. Nevertheless, despite its shortcomings, the fighter was an outstanding success that beat all its rivals and so it was ordered into production as the MiG-15 in August 1948. In production there were wide variations in quality and performance, and the same thing happened with the production of its later rival, the F-86 Sabre.

The first production MiG-15s, and the two-seat MiG-15UTI trainers, used the RD-45 and, later, the RD-45F engines. Initial production was at no. 1 GAZ at Khodinka, Moscow, and delivery to V-VS units commenced on 8 October 1948, with combat readiness achieved by mid 1950. From May

The MiG-15 fighter, powered by the Klimov VK-1 turbojet, is one of the most famous aircraft of all time. The centre picture is of a MiG-15P with radar gun laying. Russian Aviation Research Trust

1949, various other factories joined in the production, including plants in Poland and Czechoslovakia. MiG-15s appeared in public for the first time when forty-five flew over Moscow on 1 May 1949 and then on 17 July that year at the Tushino Air Show. At the 1950 May Day parade, no fewer than 139 MiG-15s flew over Red Square. Soon given the reporting name of Fagot by the West, it did not at that time ring the alarm bells that it warranted.

Pilots loved the MiG-15. The pilot V. Bondarenko said that 'Conditions in the MiG-15 were wonderful. It was designed with love and the view was fantastic. Flying it was like gliding over a precipice.' The MiG test pilot A. Scherbakov said that there was no vibration or noise and that he 'seemed to be standing still when flying it'. The heads of the design bureau, Artem I. Mikoyan and Mikhail I. Gurevich (MiG), were awarded the Stalin Prize in recognition of the achievement of the MiG-15.

Yakovlev's response to the MiG-15 was the Yak-50, which, with a VK-1 engine, began flying on 15 July 1949. It soon proved to be an excellent fighter and in some regimes, such as at high altitude, could out-perform the MiG-15 and even the later MiG-17. However, the Yak-50 failed to go into production because the huge MiG-15 programme had already been set in motion.

In September 1949 the prototype of the improved MiG-15bis first flew and this became the production model in September 1952. It was powered by the VK-1 engine, which was designed to fit onto the previous mountings and with the same connections as the RD-45 engine, but it had the greater thrust of 2,700 kp (5,954 lb). The new airframe was reinforced in various places and improvements were made to the control surfaces and dive brakes. On the other hand, Lavochkin's La-200 two-seat, all-weather interceptor, which was powered by two VK-1 engines, failed because of numerous deficiencies.

The MiG-15s' baptism of fire came in China when they were flown by Soviet pilots of the 29th GvIAP. Their purpose was to protect Shanghai from air raids being made by Chiang Kai-shek's Nationalist aircraft operating out of the island of Taiwan against Mao Zedong's Communist forces on the mainland. The Nationalists had retreated to Taiwan following one of the greatest land battles of all time with the Communists. On 28 April 1950, the MiG-15s shot down a Taiwanese P-38 Lightning and this was followed by the downing of a B-24 Liberator bomber on 12 May. Two Mig-15s then shot down a Tupolev Tu-2 bomber on 12 May 1950, mistaking it for a B-25. These victories were, of course, against airscrew aircraft and the first jet-versus-jet combat was not until the Korean War. Although no MiGs were shot down in the conflict in China, a MiG-15 fatally crashed on 29 March 1950, cause unknown.

At 4am on 25 June 1950, North Korean forces invaded the South of the country, driving the lightly-armed US and South Korean forces before them as far as the southern city of Pusan. Later, UN forces made an amphibious landing on the port of Inchon in North Korea and succeeded in pushing the enemy North again. So began a see-saw war, which involved the USSR and China assisting the North and the USA and many other nations in the UN and British Commonwealth assisting the South. The Korean war, largely fought on the ground, eventually ended in stalemate and an uneasy truce. However, as always, air power was important and Stalin soon sanctioned the clandestine intervention of Soviet units flying MiG-15s to bolster the weak North Korean Air Force (NKAF), which was using Second World War airscrew aircraft. UN forces also had largely airscrew aircraft at first, plus a few F-80 Shooting Star and F-84 Thunderjet jet fighters. The main job of these fighters, together with F-51 Mustangs and F-82 Twin Mustangs, was to protect B-26 and B-29 bombers pounding the North's bridges and power stations along the Yalu River.

The first six MiG-15s swept across the Yalu from the Antung base in China on 1 November 1950 and attacked F-51s

(shooting one down), but little attention was paid to the reports of these jets, especially as a short war was expected. On 8 November 1950, according to the USAF, an F-80C Shooting Star, flown by 1st Lt R.J. Brown of the 26th FIS, succeeded in shooting down one MiG-15 from a flight of six, making this history's first jet-versus-jet victory. However, Soviet sources dispute this. Their version of events is that five out of six of Lt Brown's machine guns jammed, giving him little firepower. When he fired at the MiG, at low level, its drop tanks were jettisoned, streaming fuel, and the subsequent dust and fuel spray as these tanks hit the ground looked as though the MiG had gone in. However, the Soviets claim that their fighter made it back to base.

According to the Soviets, the first jet-versus-jet combat took place earlier, on 1 November 1950, when three MiG-15s, led by Maj. Bordoon, intercepted ten F-80s flying at about 4,500m (14,760ft) near the MiG's Antung base. Lt Khominich attacked the F-80s by diving out of the sun and from behind. A three-second burst shot down one F-80. Maj. Bordoon's pair then attacked four F-80s bringing up the rear, which, in turn, were attacking Lt Khominich as he completed his firing pass. The F-80s then broke up their formations and left the area. However, according to the USAF, an F-80 was lost that day, but the cause was anti-aircraft fire during an attack on Sinûiju airbase.

The first agreed and confirmed jet-versus-jet kill occurred on 9 November 1950 when MiG-15s attacked F4U-4 Corsairs and AD-1 Skyraiders that were bombing a bridge over the Yalu near Sinûiju. The MiGs, in turn, were bounced by US Navy Grumman F9F-2 Panthers from VF-111. In this battle, the MiGs shot down six airscrew

aircraft, but Lt Cdr William T. Amen brought down a MiG-15, killing its pilot, Capt. Mikhail Grachov. On this eventful day, MiG-15s shot down two B-29s and damaged an RB-29.

The Korean War was the first occasion on which jet aircraft opposed each other and, because many nations were involved, so were most of the world's jet combat aircraft. Although, in November 1950, US Navy F9F-2 Panthers claimed further MiG-15 kills, it soon became apparent that the MiG-15 was better than any other UN jet in the theatre. By destroying B-26s, B-29s, F-80s, F-84s, Meteors and others virtually at will, the MiG-15 was soon poised to dominate the North Korean skies in what became known as 'MiG Alley', south of the Yalu. By December 1950, Soviet pilots were sent to Xingdao base to train North Korean and Chinese pilots to fly jet fighters, and these pilots began operating MiG-15s in MiG Alley in the summer of 1951. Many of these new pilots, in what was designated the Joint Chinese/Korean Air Army, later complained that they were taught little beyond how to take off in a MiG-15.

In any event, now was the time that the USAF's F-86 Sabre, based only in the USA, was desperately needed. It was the only fighter of the day that had a hope of matching the MiG-15, both aircraft having benefited from German Second World War swept-wing research and British turbojet technology. Hastily, F-86As of the 336th FIS moved to an unprepared base at Kimpo in bad winter weather. Their first sortie took place on 17 December 1950, when the first aerial victory of an F-86 (flown by Lt Col B. Hinton) over a MiG-15 occurred. The MiG's pilot, Maj. Yakov Yefromeyenko, was killed. On 21 December 1950, Capt. Ivan Yourkevich became the

MiG-15bis			
Span		10.085m	(33ft 1in)
Length		10.11m	(33ft 2in)
Wing area		20.6sq m	(222sq ft)
Empty weight		3,681kg	(8,117lb)
Loaded weight		5,055kg	(11,146lb)
Maximum speed	at sea level	1,076km/h	(668mph)
	at 5,000m (16,400ft)	1,045km/h	(649mph)
Landing speed		178km/h	(111mph)
Climb rate at sea level		2,760m/min	(9,053ft/min)
Service ceiling		15,500m	(50,840ft)
Range		1,200km	(745 miles)

first MiG-15 pilot to shoot down an F-86. Such victories, it soon became clear, were rarely easily won.

The MiG-15 could climb faster than the F-86, with a better than 760m/minute (2,492ft/minute) advantage overall. Also, it could out-accelerate (and decelerate) and fly higher than the F-86, so that its pilot usually chose the time and place to attack at the start of a battle. In addition, it usually took a great many hits to bring down a MiG-15, with its good cockpit armouring, self-sealing tanks and generally tough airframe and engine. It was estimated by the USAF that some 1,400 rounds of 0.5 calibre machine gun ammunition from an F-86 were typically needed to bring down a MiG-15, which routinely arrived back at base after taking forty or fifty hits. On the other hand, if one or two explosive cannon shells from a MiG-15 hit an F-86, it would probably be going down.

Claims of kill rates were originally exaggerated by both sides. Second World War aces from both sides were involved in combat, but the quality of the North's pilots was often diluted by the undertrained Korean and Chinese pilots and by the complete rotation of Soviet units without leaving behind experienced pilots to lead the way. In the end, the outcome of any

A MiG-17 fighter, powered by the Klimov VK-1F turbojet with afterburner.
Russian Aviation Research Trust

combat usually depends on the quality of the pilots involved, and the MiG-15 and F-86 were fairly evenly matched. This was proved by Chuck Yeager, who first flew an F-86 and then a captured MiG-15 in a mock combat between the two aircraft, and Yeager came out on top in both cases. Over 13,000 MiG-15s were built.

MiG-17

On 13 January 1950 the prototype of the MiG-17 was flown by I.T. Ivashchyenko.

Using the VK-1A engine, the MiG-17 had aerodynamic improvements that enabled it to reach Mach 1.03. It was followed by the MiG-17F with the afterburning VK-1F engine, which could, with afterburner on, reach a maximum speed of 1,154km/h (717mph) at 3,000m (9,840ft). About 8,900 MiG-17s were built, plus more in Poland. In the years that followed, MiG jet fighters and Il-28 jet bombers were seen in the air forces of many nations and flew the flag for Communism.

Klimov VK-5F turbojet with afterburner.

CHAPTER NINE

Mikulin and Tumanskii Turbojets

Aleksandr Aleksandrovich Mikulin (1895–1985) was to become a brilliant engineer. He was one of the first to work at NAMI, the scientific auto motor institute, and from 1916 he worked on engine design. By the late 1920s he was specializing in the design and development of piston engines for aircraft. In April 1934, while concentrating on the largest engines feasible for the time, he became the chief designer at no.24 GAZ in Moscow. He was 'demoted' to a leading designer in January 1938 in order to allow him to concentrate on developing his AM-34 engine up to 1,000hp, and then the AM-35 up to 1,400hp; these engines were of the V12 form, which was the choice for aeronautical use all over the world.

Team building

With the start of the Great Patriotic War, no.24 GAZ was evacuated to Kuibyshev. Working through the exceptionally hard winter of 1941/2, it was ready to concentrate on development of the AM-38F piston engine by January 1942. In order to avoid disruption to other research work, Mikulin formed a special team at no.19 GAZ in Molotov (now Perm'), far to the east, where the OKB was headed by A.D. Shvetsov. Various so-called design brigades were set up there, including one under P.F. Zubets that worked on a new type of centrifugal supercharger and another under V.N. Sorokin that worked on gas turbines, turbochargers and reaction exhaust nozzles. Another design brigade was headed by Vladimir I. Bazarov, who had obtained a patent in 1923 for a turbojet engine with a multi-stage compressor. Mikulin's team, which continued to work on AM piston engines, was moved from Molotov to Kuibyshev in May 1942.

February 1943 saw the beginning of the reconstruction of a site on the outskirts of Moscow that was to become no.300 GAZ, its main purpose being to develop AM engines up to 3,000hp and ready them for production elsewhere. As his deputy there, Mikulin appointed Sergei Konstantinovich Tumanskii (1901–1973), who had previously been chief designer at no.29 GAZ aero-engine plant in Zaporozh'ye. Tumanskii was already famed for his work on superchargers for high-altitude piston fighters during the war and had a good relationship with the MiG bureau. Mikulin also secured Stechkin's release from a Kazan' prison (see below) and established a Reaction Engine Theory Department at no.300 GAZ.

Already, in 1943, the development of the TK-3, the USSR's first turbocharger for high-altitude flight, had been completed by Zubets's team at no.300 GAZ. Series production of the TK-3 commenced in March 1943. Mikulin's AMTK-1 turbocharger and others were also developed. In July 1945 a MiG I-224 (4A) high-altitude interceptor with an AM-39B-1 piston engine and AMTK-1 turbocharger reached 13,700m (44,936ft) and, later, 14,200m (46,576ft). By 1946 the AMTK-2 turbocharger had been developed for piston engines of up to 3,000hp.

Although Mikulin's main interest was in piston engines and a compound piston engine turbine unit, as we have seen, he was already looking forward and making preparations for the development of turbojet engines. Accordingly he encouraged the expansion of departments that could handle such development work. Vitali N. Sorokin (1914–1996), who directed the gas turbine department, was one of Mikulin's youngest pupils but was very talented; in 1956, he was to become chief designer of no.26 OKB in Ufa (today GNPP 'Motor').

In March 1943, under conditions of great secrecy, a small team was established at no.300 GAZ under the control of Boris Sergeyevich Stechkin (1891–1969).

Stechkin, together with N.Ye. Zhukovskii, had taken part in establishing the famous CAHI, where he worked between 1918 and 1930. He was a major scientific specialist in the fields of thermal physics and the mechanics of fluids and air. The purpose of Stechkin's team at no.300 GAZ was to develop the mechanics and mathematics connected with turbine units and jet propulsion so that later, when the construction of gas turbine engines was begun, there were to be no problems with methods of calculation. Information from the specialists in the production departments, especially those concerned with turbochargers, was useful. The talented M.G. Dubinsky headed this team.

In August 1944 Mikulin received the remains of an Argus 109-014 pulsejet from a German V1 flying bomb sent over from England. He studied them with interest and was ordered in September 1944 to produce five similar pulsejets for flight testing by the end of that year. These were test flown mounted above a Petlyakov Pe-2 and a Tupolev Tu-2. (Indigenous Soviet pulsejet work had already begun in 1942 under Vladimir N. Chelomey. These smaller pulsejets, designated D-10 or RD-13, were flown under the wings of Lavochkin La-7 fighters in 1947.)

In order to further the research into components for turbine machinery, Mikulin formed a strong team of designers, mathematicians and test specialists. This team included M.S. Vladimirov, S.B. Tapel'zon, V.Ye. Kuzmin and Stechkin, under whose guidance a large gas dynamics laboratory was later built to investigate turbine machines. A great many centrifugal and axial compressor stages and stator grids were tested, electric motors being used to drive the compressors up to speed. A 2,000hp AM-42 piston engine was also used to drive a compressor to supply the air flow for combustion chambers and turbines under test. Kuzmin was in charge of the

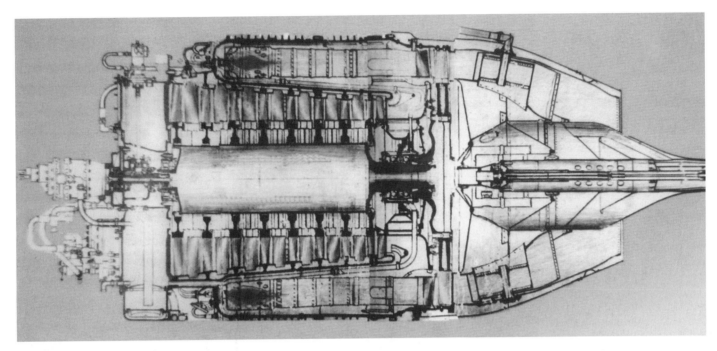

The **AMTKRD-02** axial turbojet, with reverse-flow cannular combustion chambers, was produced in 1949.

Combustion Laboratory and Tapel'zon was in charge of the Gas Dynamics Laboratory. Their work was also valuable to others working on turbojets. In April 1945 Mikulin and Balandin were ordered to produce detailed drawings for, and arrange the engineering for, the production of the German Junkers 109-004 turbojet at no.1 NII by 1 July 1945. Klimov, whose view of the 109-004 engine was that it was primitive but had a complex control system, was further ordered to prepare drawings and documentation for the experimental production of the RD-10 turbojet based on the 109-004. To assist in this work, he made N.D. Kuznyetsov a deputy. With the end of the war in May 1945, no.300 GAZ was allocated the former Junkers plant at Tausch, near Leipzig, and more than 550 items of equipment were transferred from Germany. By then Mikulin's power was well established and, with Tumanskii still as his deputy, he opened a giant turbojet KB; as was the way in those difficult times, however, he was not powerful enough to save himself from future trouble, as we shall see.

AM and RD series turbojets

The first experimental turbojet produced by the design team headed by Stechkin was the AMTKRD-01 in 1947. This had an eight-stage axial compressor, a large annular combustion chamber and a single-stage turbine. Its weight was 1,720kg (3,793lb) and its diameter was 1.365m (4ft 5¾in). It developed a remarkable static thrust of 3,000kp (6,615lb), later raised to 3,300kp (7,277lb). The experimental turbojet AMTKRD-02, produced in 1949, had an eight-stage axial compressor, a single-stage turbine and reverse flow into cannular combustion chambers arranged around the outside of the compressor casing. This arrangement gave the engine a short, fat appearance, the diameter being 1.380m (4ft 6½in) and the length 3.60m (11ft 9¾in). For a weight of 1,675kg (3,693lb), the 02 developed a static thrust of 3,850kp (8,489lb) and was eventually brought up to 4,250kp (9,371lb)

thrust. Although these engines were not meant for production, Mikulin was clearly thinking big.

The first attempt at a production engine was the AM-2 turbojet of 4,600kp (10,143lb) thrust, but it did not go beyond the test stage. Then, in 1950, Zubets's team designed the first important Mikulin turbojet for his KB. The AM-3 was a large turbojet designed for reliability, performance being secondary, and it was therefore kept as simple as possible. With a diameter of 1.40m (4ft 7in), it had an eight-stage axial compressor with a pressure ratio of 6.4:1 and delivering 135kg/sec (297.6lb/sec) of air at 6,500rpm. It had a two-stage turbine and an annular combustion chamber. Beginning with a static thrust of 6,750kp (14,884lb), the AM-3A was giving 8,690kp

The best picture known of the **AMTKRD-01** axial turbojet, designed by Boris Stechkin's team.

(19,161lb) by 1952 and 9,500kp (20,948lb) by 1957 (AM-3M-500), such was its development potential. It was flight-tested under a Tu-4LL bomber. The AM-3M was rated for civil use and was noted for its reliability and robustness. During development, its TBO was gradually raised from the original 300 hours to 2,000 hours. More

than 9,000 AM-3s were produced, its service designation being RD-3. It was also built in China as the WP-8.

In 1953 a very much slimmer axial engine, the AM-5, was produced, its diameter being only 0.670m (2ft 2in) and its length 2.770m (9ft 1in). For a weight of only 445kg (981lb), it produced a static

thrust of 2,000kp (4,410lb), but it was not successful enough to go into production. Instead, in 1954 the team concentrated on the equally slim (0.660m/2ft 2in) AM-9 turbojet, which, for a weight of 700kg (1,544lb), was producing a static thrust of 2,150kp (4,741lb) dry or 3,300kp (7,277lb) with afterburner on. These remarkable results were being seen by 1955. The AM-9 had a nine-stage axial compressor giving a pressure ratio of 6.3:1 (in later versions 7.5:1). There was an annular combustion chamber and a two-stage turbine. With the afterburner, the AM-9 was exceptionally long (for its diameter) at 5.560m (18ft 3in).

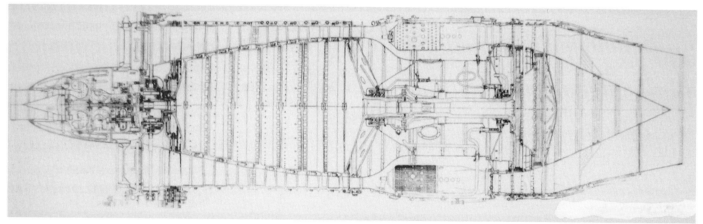

Drawing and photograph of the Mikulin AM-3 axial turbojet, noted for its reliability and robustness. Note that the intake is on the left in the drawing, but on the right in the photo.

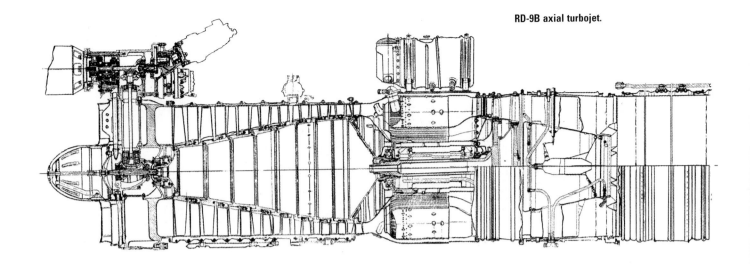

RD-9B axial turbojet.

The AM-9 went into production, but in 1956 Mikulin was blacklisted and removed from his post, to be replaced by his deputy Tumanskii. This came about because, some years previously, the aviation minister Krunichyev came under the suspicion of Stalin and he was imprisoned, pending investigation. Mikulin, for reasons best known to himself, did what he could to incriminate Krunichyev, who could have faced execution but was released after Stalin's death on 5 March 1953. Krunichyev then set about sealing Mikulin's fate.

With Mikulin removed, Tumanskii was in charge as a General Constructor of the KB, which was renamed. From then on, all its engines were known by the service designation 'RD': the AM-9, therefore,

became known as the RD-9. Seven major variants of the RD-9 were produced until 1959, while the RD-9BF-811 continued in production in China until 1990 as the Shenyang-built WP-6A of 4,050kp (8,930lb) static thrust.

The R-11 turbojet (known as the AM-11 until Mikulin's departure) was first run in 1953. It was based on experience with the RD-9, but was considerably larger and also a two-shaft engine. Relatively simple, it had two single-stage turbines. One turbine drove a three-stage low-pressure compressor and the other turbine drove, via a coaxial shaft, a five-stage high-pressure compressor. An innovation at the time was that the first, large-diameter stage of the low-pressure compressor was overhung in front of the

front bearing and was devoid of any inlet guide vanes, giving it a fan-like appearance. Total pressure ratio of the compressor system was 8.9:1. The combustion chamber was of the annular type and there was a multi-flap, variable-area exhaust nozzle.

The R-11 went into production and became the most numerous type from the KB under Tumanskii. For a weight of 1,040kg (2,293lb) it was giving a static thrust of 4,000kp (8,820lb) by 1956 and 5,100kp (11,246lb) with afterburner by 1958. The R-11-300 of 1959, with an enlarged afterburner and a new exhaust nozzle, gave an increased afterburning thrust of 5,950kp (13,120lb). Also in 1959, the R-11F-300A gave an increased dry thrust of 4,300kp (9,482lb) and an afterburning thrust of 5,750kp (12,679lb) by running at a higher speed and temperature but with the afterburner unchanged. Other versions, designated R-11FS-300 and R-11F2S-300, could bleed off large volumes of air to supply the blown flaps of an aircraft such as the MiG-21. The R-11F2S-300 was the final version in production and gave a maximum thrust of 6,200kp (13,671lb). In total some 20,900 R-11s of all types were made in the USSR. It was also made under licence as the WP-7 at Chengdu in China and by Hindustan Aeronautics (HAL) at Koraput in India. Its relative simplicity made it very suitable for production by emerging industries. A small turbojet, the RU-19, was designed at the Tumanskii KB for the Yak-30 straight-wing jet trainer built in 1959 to meet V-VS requirements. Many thousands of turbojets were made under Tumanskii, who died in 1973, and the KB continues under the name of Soyuz.

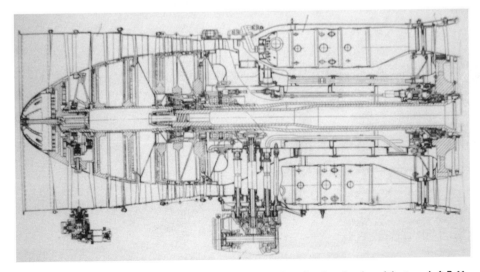

The low- and high-pressure stages of the axial compressor and combustion chamber of the two-shaft **R-11** (previously **AM-11**) turbojet. Innovative at the time was the first, large-diameter stage of the **LP** compressor, which was overhung, before the front bearing.

CHAPTER TEN

Mikulin and Tumanskii Turbojets in Service

The first of the Mikulin KB's engines to be utilized was the AM-3 of 6,750kp (14,884lb) static thrust, which was the sort of turbojet that Tupolev was seeking for a new strategic bomber to carry a 5,000kg (11,025lb) bomb load over 5,000km (3,100 miles). This was the origin of the Tu-88, later given the service designation of Tu-16, which was to become an outstanding twin-jet bomber known by its

NATO designation as 'Badger'. A sleek design resulted, with a wing swept back 41 degrees on the leading edge and all-swept tail surfaces. The wing had a distinctive anhedral of –3 degrees and a pod at each trailing edge into which the main undercarriage bogies retracted. Also distinctive was the engine installation, each of the two nacelles nestling against the fuselage with the air ducts curving inwards

and the jet exhaust ducts curving outwards. This gave a waisted shape to the nacelles, which were positioned to conform to area rule with the wing.

The first Tu-16 prototype made its maiden flight on 27 April 1952, the pilot being N.S. Rybko. It went into production late in 1953 and 1,520 of all types were built in the USSR. The Tu-16 was also built in China as the H-6, which first flew in December 1968.

Tu-104 airliner

An immediate development of the Tu-16, again with two AM-3 turbojets, was the Tu-104 airliner, which consisted primarily of a new passenger fuselage married to the Tu-16's flying surfaces. The prototype (L-5400) first flew on 17 June 1955, piloted by Yu.T. Alasheyev. Crew training began that summer using the Tu-104G, which was actually a demilitarized Tu-16. Having completed its test programme in the winter of 1955/6, the prototype Tu-104 was flown into London's Heathrow airport on 22 March 1956, a day of rain and low cloud. The sudden appearance of this Soviet jet airliner caused a sensation in the West, even though it had flown some years after Western jet airliners such as the Comet, 707 and Caravelle.

Although the Tu-104 was offered to Western airlines at a very good price, no orders were forthcoming due to its uneconomic operation. Nevertheless, beginning with proving flights with forty-eight passengers on the Moscow–Irkutsk route (with stops) on 15 September 1956, the Tu-104 provided sterling service within the vast

TOP: The Tupolev Tu-88, powered by two Mikulin AM-3 axial turbojets, went into service as the outstanding Tu-16 'Badger' bomber (BOTTOM), here seen refuelling. Russian Aviation Research Trust

60

Tu-16 bomber 'Badger'		
Span	35.5m	(116ft 5¼in)
Length	34.80m	(114ft 1¾in)
Wing area	164.65sq m	(1,771.6sq ft)
Empty weight	36,600kg	(80,703lb)
Maximum weight	72,000kg	(158,760lb)
Maximum speed	1,010km/h or Mach 0.95	(627mph)
Service ceiling	15,000m	(49,200ft)
Range with 3,000kg (6,615lb) bomb load	5,760km	(3,577 miles)

USSR and to certain European capitals, cutting flight times dramatically. Aeroflot took delivery of at least 200 aircraft, including the Tu-104B with a slightly longer fuselage to carry 100 passengers. Uneconomic by Western standards, the Tu-104 was also somewhat primitive with, for example, sudden painful cabin pressure changes among its faults. Also, the TBO of the AM-3 engines was not considered very long. Despite its shortcomings, the Tu-104 did set some twenty-two FAI records for speed and load. In a parallel development with the Tu-104, the Tu-110 was created with a new wing and four Lyul'ka AL-7 turbojets in the wing roots, but only four were built.

Tupolev Tu-104 jet airliners of Aeroflot. Airborne is CCCP-42385 and, being towed, is CCCP-42471. Developed from the Tu-16 bomber, the Tu-104 was also powered by two Mikulin AM-3 turbojets. For a while, following the Comet disasters, the Tu-104 was the only jet airliner in service in Europe.

Russian Aviation Research Trust

3M strategic bomber 'Bison'

In 1956 it was found that utilization of Myasishchyev's 3M Bison strategic bomber was poor, due to the low TBO of its four Dobrynin VD-7 turbojets. This economical engine was the most powerful then in production, at 11,000kp (24,255lb) thrust, and had only just been introduced, but it proved to be troublesome. Consequently, the Bisons were fitted with less-powerful but reliable RD-3M-500As (developed AM-3s) as a temporary measure. With the lower thrust of 9,500kp (20,948lb), however, this measure greatly reduced the bomber's range. In fact, the Bison was a complete failure, having the range for only a one-way trip to the USA. Since only about thirty-five of them were built, it became necessary to trick the USA into thinking that hundreds of Bisons existed.

Vladimir A. Dobrynin (1895–1978) was the head of a design section at CIAM in 1931 and designed aero-engines from 1934. From 1943 until 1960 he was the chief designer of the aero-engine KB in Rybinsk (RKBM). The first turbojet of note produced under him was the VD-5, which, at 13,000kp (28,665lb) thrust, was the most powerful engine of 1954, while the smaller VD-7 was the most powerful in production. First run in 1954, it went into production for the 3M Bison in 1956. Dobrynin's successor, P.A. Koliesov (1915–), went on to develop the VD-7M for supersonic aircraft, the engine giving a thrust of 16,000kp (35,280lb) with afterburner on. The VD-7M powered the Tupolev Tu-105 and M-50 prototypes. Much later, the RD-7M-2 of 16,500kp (36,383lb) thrust was used to power the Tu-22 Backfire supersonic bomber.

Tu-104A airliner			
Span		34.50m	(113ft 3½ in)
Length		38.85m	(127ft 5in)
Wing area		174.40sq m	(1,876.5sq ft)
Empty weight		41,600kg	(91,728lb)
Loaded weight		75,500kg	(166,478lb)
Maximum speed	at 10,000m (32,800ft)	950km/h	(590mph)
Service ceiling		11,500m	(37,720ft)
Range		2,650km	(1,646 miles)

Myasishchyev 3M 'Bison' strategic bombers were converted to use four RD-3M-500A turbojets (developed AM-3s). Russian Aviation Research Trust

A Yakovlev Yak-25RV 'Mandrake' with two R-11V-300 turbojets. Russian Aviation Research Trust

Yak-25M with AM-9A engines			
Span		11.0m	(36ft 1in)
Length		15.665m	(51ft 4½in)
Wing area		28.94sq m	(311sq ft)
Empty weight		6,350kg	(14,002lb)
Loaded weight		10,045kg	(22,149lb)
Maximum speed	at 9,000m (29,500ft)	1,040km/h or Mach 0.954	(646mph)
Service ceiling		13,900m	(45,592ft)
Range		2,730km	(1,695miles)

Yakovlev

Design work began at the Yakovlev bureau early in 1951 on a new radar-equipped interceptor for which two under-wing AM-5A turbojets were chosen. This left the nose free for a large di-electric nose to house the radar. All flying surfaces were swept, the wing at 45 degrees, and a long canopy covered the pilot and radar operator. First flown on 19 June 1952, some 480 Yak-25s, as the type was designated, were built in 1957 and it was in front-line service until 1965; in the West it was known as 'Flashlight'. AM-5B and then AM-9A engines were later fitted. In 1959 the Yak-25RV ('Mandrake') was produced as a single-seat, ultra-high-altitude photographic reconnaissance aircraft powered by two R-11V-300 engines and with a new long-span wing without sweepback, similar to the wing of Lockheed's U-2. The engines required long nacelles, which projected far forward of the wing, and there was an in-line main undercarriage with outriggers at the wingtips. Records were set with the Yak-25RV in July 1963, including reaching an altitude of 20,456m (67,096ft) with a 1,000kg (2,205lb) payload. A total of 165 of all versions were built, but it is said to have not been very successful.

The supersonic (Mach 1.16) Yak-26 with RD-9AK engines was not accepted into service. The Yak-27R ('Mangrove'), of which 180 were delivered, was an improvement and had very long RD-9AF afterburning engines beneath swept-back wings.

The final development of this type of aircraft was the supersonic (Mach 1.79) Yak-28, powered by R-11AF2-300 engines and produced in both bomber and interceptor versions. Because of the supersonic speed, the air intakes now had sharp lips and translating conical centre bodies to provide shock-wave pressure recovery. This type served until long after the time-scale of this history, but an interesting incident in 1966, albeit a small one in the big picture of the Cold War, is worth recording. On 6 April 1966 a Yak-28PM (Firebar) interceptor crashed into the Havelsee, a lake that straddled the British- and Soviet-controlled sectors of Berlin in those days. The pilot tried desperately to stay within the Soviet side of the lake, but failed, and both crew perished. The British immediately mounted a salvage operation, promising to return the airmen's bodies, which they did the next day. Working underwater, however, the British also removed the engines and the

Yak-25RV with R-11V-300 engines		
Span	23.4m	(76ft 9in)
Length	18.45m	(60ft 6in)
Wing area	51.5sq m	(554sq ft)
Maximum loaded weight	9,950kg	(21,940lb)
Maximum speed above 11,000m (36,000ft)	870km/h	(540mph)
Service ceiling	21,000m	(68,880ft)
Range	3,500km	(2,174 miles)
Endurance	6 hours	

secret Skipspin radar from the Yak-28. These were towed underwater to the lake bank, flown to RAE Farnborough for examination and then returned to the wreck site, all within 48 hours. Finally, amid much clamouring from the Soviets, most of the wreckage was returned to the Soviets at midnight on 13 April. Nothing

was said about the fact that the tips of some of the turbine blades had been sawn off! Perhaps someone on the Soviet side recalled the fact that S.T. Kishkin had purloined a turbine blade from a British factory some twenty years before! About 2,000 of all types from the Yak-25 to Yak-28 were built.

Mention should also be made of the use of a single RD-3 engine to power the VTOL experimental test rig known as the Turbolyet. Inspired by the Rolls-Royce 'Flying Bedstead' VTOL test rig, the Turbolyet was designed at LII and first flown with tethers early in 1957. Later it was flown free and helped develop the control systems for Yakovlev VTOL aircraft. The RD-3 engine, which was installed vertically, was modified with a bell-mouth air intake, special bearings and oil system and air bleed pipes leading to four reaction control jets on long outrigger arms.

Replacements for the MiG-15

In January 1949 the MiG OKB began planning a replacement for the MiG-15 fighter. Designated the I-330, it was to become the MiG-17 ('Fresco') and incorporated aerodynamic improvements but

The supersonic Yakovlev Yak-26 with RD-9AK turbojets. Russian Aviation Research Trust

RD-9F axial turbojet with afterburner. Jan Hoffmann

The Yakovlev Yak-27R 'Mangrove' had very long RD-9AF afterburning engines beneath its swept-back wings. Russian Aviation Research Trust

A single RD-3 (AM-3) powered this VTOL flying test rig, known as the Turbolyet. On the left is a high-altitude balloon gondola. Preserved at Monino. Author

Yak-28B with R-11AF-300 engines			
Span		11.70m	(38ft 4½in)
Length		21.52m	(70ft 7in)
Wing area		35.25sq m	(379sq ft)
Empty weight		7,220kg	(15,920lb)
Loaded weight		13,630kg	(30,054lb)
Maximum speed	at 12,000m (39,360ft)	1,900km/h or Mach 1.79	(1,180mph)
Service ceiling		16,200m	(53,136ft)
Range with drop tanks		2,630km	(1,633 miles)

still used the VK-1 or VK-1F engine until 1952, when the MiG SM-1 or I-340 version appeared with two AM-5A engines. The fitting of two engines was possible due to the smaller diameter of the axial AM-5 engines (compared with the centrifugal VK-1 engine), although almost the full width of the rear fuselage was maintained back to the width of the twin exhaust nozzles. More than 10,000 MiG-17s of all versions were built in the USSR, plus many more in Poland (as the LIM-5), Czechoslovakia (S-104) and China (J-5).

While the MiG-17 was just about supersonic, the MiG-19 ('Farmer'), a new design using twin AM-9B (or RD-9B) engines, was readily supersonic. The prototype first flew on 5 January 1954 as the SM-9/1 with Sedov as pilot and was soon able to demonstrate a phenomenal climb rate for the time of 10,800m/minute (35,424ft/min) and, although not perfect, was ordered into production only six weeks later. This was even before official tests were carried out. The MiG-19S was in service by March 1955. About 7,000 were built in the USSR plus some in Poland (LIM-7) and many more in China (J-6).

During 1957 experiments to increase the speed of the MiG-19 were made by modifying the nose intake. This modification consisted of a sharp lip to the intake and a two-position (horizontally) conical centre body that was supported from the bifurcation of the duct inside the intake. Once the speed of sound was passed, the new intake gave improved pressure recovery to the air flow as it passed through the shock waves produced by the sharp lip and the cone. This was all based on the work pioneered by Dr Klaus Oswatisch. This arrangement was tried by MiG on the prototype SM-12/1 early in 1957 and a speed of Mach 1.817 was achieved using two RD-9BF-2 turbojets. Many other prototypes and developments followed, leading eventually to one of the most famous and prolific Soviet aircraft of all time, the MiG-21.

The MiG-21 finished up as a quite small interceptor with the new Tumanskii R-11 turbojet (giving 5,100kp or 11,246lb of thrust with afterburner on), a small delta wing and swept tail surfaces. The conical centre body was there in the intake, to suit its Mach 2.0 performance. Many MiG-21s were built, stretching into the 1970s, but the only versions dating from the 1950s that went into service were the MiG-21F and the MiG-21PF.

MiG-19S 'Farmer'			
Span		9.0m	(29ft 6¼in)
Length	(without pitot boom)	12.54m	(41ft 1½in)
Wing area		25.16sq m	(271sq ft)
Empty weight		5,172kg	(11,404lb)
Maximum loaded weight		8,832kg	(19,475lb)
Maximum speed	at 10,000m (32,800ft)	1,454km/h or Mach 1.367	(903mph)
Service ceiling		17,500m	(57,400ft)
Range	without drop tanks	1,390km	(863 miles)

The MiG-21 interceptor, powered by the R-11 turbojet, became the most famous and prolific Soviet aircraft of all time. Russian Aviation Research Trust

MiG-21F 'Fishbed-C'			
Span		7.154m	(23ft 5½in)
Length	(without pitot boom)	14.90m	(48ft 10½in)
Wing area		23.13sq m	(249sq ft)
Empty weight		approx. 5,675kg	(12,513lb)
Maximum loaded weight		8,200kg	(18,081lb)
Maximum speed	at 12,000m (39,400ft)	2,230km/h or Mach 2.10	(1,385lb)
Service ceiling		20,000m	(65,600ft)
Range	with drop tank	885km	(550 miles)

CHAPTER ELEVEN

Soloviev's Turbojets

The design bureau of Pavel A. Soloviev (1917–1997) seems to have been a relatively new one or, at least, appears to have been unknown until the late 1950s. Soloviev, however, was a highly decorated engineer who, after graduating at the Rybinsk Aviation Establishment, had worked on engine design from 1940. He became a chief designer in 1953 and was still in an advisory capacity until 1988. His D-15 turbojet, probably of the two-shaft type, appeared in 1957, when it was rated at 13,000kp (28,665lb) static thrust and between 15,000 and 17,500kp (33,075 and 38,588lb) with afterburner on.

Four D-15s were fitted to the Myasishchyev 201-M (a version of the M-4 Bison) for record-breaking purposes in 1959. Its FAI records included carrying 10,000kg (32,800lb) to an altitude of 15,317m (50,240ft) and 55,220kg (121,760lb) up to 2,000m (6,560ft).

Later came the D-20P, the Soviet Union's first two-shaft turbofan engine, which had a three-stage fan and an eight-stage high-pressure compressor, the bypass ratio being 1:1. The fan was driven by a two-stage (low pressure) turbine and the compressor by a single-stage (high pressure) turbine. The airflow was 113kg/second (249lb/sec) and the pressure ratio 13:1 at 8,550rpm. The first stage of the fan had supersonic tips, while the third and fourth stages of the compressor had automatic air bleeds to avoid stalling of the blades. For a weight of 1,468kg (3,237lb) this turbofan gave a static thrust of 5,400kp (11,907lb). Twelve cannular combustion chambers

were used. The D-20P was the USSR's first turbofan engine to go into series production. Soloviev went on to develop the huge D-30 turbofan engine of 12,000kp (26,460lb) static thrust. The D-30F6 was the Soviet Union's first turbofan with an afterburner, and various other D-30s were of high-economy performance.

This bureau's engines were particularly used to power airliners, such as the Tu-134 and Tu-154, but it also branched into helicopter turboshaft engines. With the USSR's penchant for large and powerful helicopters, such engines were the only answer. As an example, early in 1954 the large D-25V turboshaft engine was designed to power the Mil Mi-6 heavy transport helicopter, which first flew in September 1957 and went on to achieve many records. Two D-25V engines were used, each of 5,500hp output. The D-25V, which was the first Soviet helicopter gas turbine, had a nine-stage compressor, twelve cannular combustion chambers and a single-stage turbine to drive the compressor. A further, two-stage free turbine drove a shaft at the rear of the engine, this shaft passing through a left- or right-handed exhaust outlet to connect with the power gearbox. The weight of each D-25V was 1,325kg (2,922lb), but the Mi-6 gearbox weighed another 3,200kg (7,056lb)! The Mi-6 ('Hook') was very successful, some 800 being built, and it was in service with the V-VS and Aeroflot in addition to being exported.

By far the largest helicopter ever built, the Mil V12 was powered by two pairs of Soloviev D-25V engines, each pair driving a giant rotor. Only two, unsuccessful, prototypes of this 100-tonne giant were built.

Soloviev's turbojets were especially used to power Tupolev's airliners, like the Tu-134 (CCCP-65610) shown here. Russian Aviation Research Trust

Two Soloviev D-25V turboshaft engines were used to power the Mil Mi-6 heavy transport helicopter, CCCP-58647 being shown. Large, single main rotors became a Soviet speciality. Russian Aviation Research Trust

The largest helicopter ever built was the Mil V12. The port nacelle, housing two of the four Soloviev D-25V turboshaft engines that drove the two giant rotors, is seen here. Author

This assembly of American research aircraft epitomizes the enormous amount that had to be learned about high-speed jet flight in the 1950s.

All but the X-1A were powered by the turbojet. Research from foreign countries, notably Great Britain and Germany, was utilized in the design work.

(Centre) The Douglas X-3 Stiletto was built to explore kinetic heating at high Mach numbers but was underpowered.

(Clockwise, starting from bottom left)

• The Bell X-1A rocket plane, flown to Mach 2.44 on 12 December 1953.
• The straight-wing Douglas D-558-1 Skystreak, which explored transonic flight.
• The Convair XF-92A, built to explore the delta wing.
• The Bell X-5, which explored wing sweep variable in flight.
• The swept-wing Douglas D-558-2 Skyrocket, powered by turbojet and rocket and the first to exceed Mach 2.0.
• The Northrop X-4 Bantam, built to explore the semi-tailless configuration at high transonic speeds. NASA

PART IV

United States of America

In previous sections we have seen how the early development of the turbojet was assisted by knowledge gained in steam turbine and piston engine supercharger work. Also greatly assisting development was the ready availability of heat-resisting alloys. In all these fields the USA was very well provided for and could draw upon considerable knowledge and experience. Regarding piston aero-engines, the USA was particularly well advanced in the field of radial engines, which were further developed, for example, in Germany and the Soviet Union. It was not, therefore, for technological reasons that the USA lagged behind Europe, by some five years, before and during the Second World War. Even when the principles of the turbojet were appreciated, their usefulness was wrongly interpreted or development was held back by lack of official backing. A further, later, impediment was a lack of technical interchange, officially encouraged, between companies that were working on gas turbine projects.

When American engineers did begin to look at the gas turbine for powering aircraft, the potential of the turbojet for high-speed flight was not generally grasped and, in any case, the high-speed, short-range fighter was of less interest than it was in Europe or the Soviet Union. Of greater interest, partly owing to the USA's geography, was long-range flight and therefore American engineers became more interested at first in the gas turbine for use as a turboprop.

By the 1920s many heavy industrial companies in the USA were working on the manufacture of steam turbines. Many ideas were put forward for the progression towards the gas turbine, among which were those of Sanford Moss. He first formulated

a design for a gas turbine before 1900, when he was studying thermodynamics and hydrodynamics at the University of California. In 1901 Moss moved to Cornell University to begin research into gas turbines, but his experiments there were a failure: while the combustion gases operated the turbine, there was insufficient power for compression of air prior to combustion.

In June 1903 Dr Moss (having received his doctorate) returned to General Electric at Schenectady, where he had previously worked as a draughtsman. He continued his gas turbine experiments and, under his direction, various models were built. Similar experiments, in consultation with Moss, were also carried out from 1904 by Prof. E. Thomson and Richard H. Rice at GE's facilities in Lynn, Massachusetts. All of these gas turbines were intended to provide useful shaft power and no thought was given at that time to jet propulsion.

Following on from Moss's theories, GE also developed centrifugal compressors, but

an independent compressed air supply was used for supplying the combustion chambers in their gas turbine experiments. GE's investigations into combustion chambers, turbine wheels and other components were the most thorough in the country up to that time. By 1907, however, work on gas turbines had been shelved due to the lack of suitable heat-resisting alloys, so preventing the use of the high temperatures necessary for high efficiency. As it was, the best fuel consumption anticipated was about four times that of contemporary piston engines. Moss stayed on as a design engineer at GE and the company's centrifugal compressors found considerable application in industry. It was not until late 1937, when GE established its Supercharger Department at Lynn, that its centrifugal compressor work began to have an aeronautical application.

The earliest attempt in the USA to produce a gas turbine to power an aircraft was made by R.E. Lasley. Beginning in

Dr Sanford Moss (right) and R.G. Sanderwick with a GE Type B supercharger for piston engines. GE later fitted a combustion chamber to this type of supercharger in 1943 to create a simple, expendable turbojet for flying bombs.

1925, Lasley had received several patents for gas turbines while working as a steam turbine engineer for Allis-Chalmers. Early in the 1930s he formed the Lasley Turbine Motor Company in Waukegan, Illinois, and by 1934 he had his gas turbine running on the test stand. Lasley's design was very complex and was intended to compete directly with the piston engine and airscrew. However, its best efficiency was only about 12 per cent and Lasley soon had to look outside for development funding. In 1934 he approached the US Navy, but contract conditions could not be agreed.

He next approached the Army, and representatives from Wright Field visited Lasley's workshop in August 1934. After looking over the engine, the Wright Field team sought the opinion of Sanford Moss at GE. The Army memo that then followed

was not favourable to Lasley's engine on the grounds of its inefficiency. To bring the efficiency to a useful level it was thought that an unrealistic turbine temperature of about 1,370°C was needed, and, of course, no metal alloys existed that could run in such a temperature. This marked the end of Lasley's engine, which, with the benefit of official backing and some simplification, may well have led eventually to a viable turbojet or turboprop engine.

Unfortunately Lasley's work failed to point the way. No engine-maker or other body in the USA realized how the turbojet could make a great increase in aircraft speeds possible. Finally, in 1941, a serious American attempt was made to develop a turbojet. As with Heinkel in Germany, this attempt was made by an airframe company, Lockheed, and not by an engine manufacturer.

Strangely, with all the work going on in the USA on turbosuperchargers for piston engines, nobody before 1940 is known to have thought of putting a combustion chamber between the compressor and the turbine, thereby creating a turbojet. Later, when Sanford Moss was asked why this step was missed, he replied: 'Just dumb, just dumb!' In 1943 GE did fit a combustion chamber to a Type B turbosupercharger to create an expendable turbojet for a flying bomb.

By the end of the 1950s American large turbojet and turboprop development was beginning to match that of the British. It had been a long, hard road, travelled by many companies, and those companies were by then reduced to a few, dominated by General Electric and Pratt & Whitney.

CHAPTER TWELVE

Lockheed Aircraft Corporation

Founded in December 1926 by Allan Loughead, the Lockheed Aircraft Corporation had a reputation for innovative aircraft designs by the late 1930s, including its Vega, Air Express and Explorer. In 1940 Lockheed became involved in large-scale manufacture of military aircraft, including Ventura bombers for hard-pressed Britain. In that year the company also embarked on a forward-looking project for a fast jet fighter, known as the L-133. This was to be powered by a turbojet engine designed by Nathan C. Price.

Nathan C. Price

Price began his career in steam turbine work in 1930 at the Doble Steam Motors company, where he designed several light, high-speed, reciprocating steam engines with Velox-type boilers. He also worked on a fuel atomizing burner system for a reciprocating steam engine. Between autumn 1933 and early 1934 Price designed a light steam turbine turboprop to power an aircraft. This engine had a centrifugal compressor, combustion chamber and a turbine that was connected to the compressor and an airscrew. The combustion gases and exhaust steam were expelled through a nozzle designed to give some jet thrust. Price's engine was fitted to a Travel Air biplane that flew in this form on 12 April 1933. It was calculated that this engine was as efficient as a piston engine of the same weight at low altitudes and that its power could be maintained at higher altitudes thanks to the compressor. In 1936 the Doble company stopped work on this project due to lack of interest from engine manufacturers and the Army.

Price began to work on his own on the design of a turbojet from 1938. In January 1939 Lockheed flew the prototype of its radical twin-engined, twin-boom fighter, the XP-38. This was ordered into production

at Burbank by September that year and, as the P-38 Lightning, was to become a famous and successful fighter during the Second World War. It was the Lightning's high diving speed of about 885km/h (550mph) that brought to Lockheed's attention the aerodynamic problems resulting from compressibility, namely a pitching down of the aircraft's nose and also aileron reversal. From this it was apparent that new designs of high-altitude, high-speed aircraft would soon be needed. In the meantime, Lockheed redesigned the P-38 with a pressurized cockpit and new engines. Designated the XP-49, this first flew in November 1942 and was used for high-altitude research. In 1941 Lockheed hired Nathan Price to evaluate the General Electric turbosuperchargers for the XP-49's Continental piston engines. Price also carried out work for Boeing on propulsion systems.

Lockheed L-1000 turbojet (XJ37-1)

By this time Price had his turbojet design largely worked out and he was able to interest Clarence L. 'Kelly' Johnson, Chief Engineer of Lockheed's secret 'Skunk Works', in his engine project. Price's project came at a fortuitous time when Lockheed was already considering high-speed aircraft of the future. Johnson therefore ordered his designers to come up with a jet fighter incorporating the turbojet: these were designated the L-133 fighter and L-1000 engine, respectively. During 1941 the designs of the aircraft and turbojet were both readied for development.

Initially Price tried to design the L-1000 as a turbojet with fuel economy comparable to contemporary piston engines. This effort resulted in a large, heavy, complicated engine that had an axial compressor followed by a reciprocating compressor. By mid-1943 the design had been simplified but

was still complex. It had an axial-flow compressor followed by three centrifugal compressors with intercooling between each centrifugal stage. The combustion system was of the cannular type, whereby twelve separate combustion cans were mounted inside an annulus from which cooling and secondary air was supplied. A five-stage reaction-type turbine was provided and additional fuel could be injected between the turbine stages and in the exhaust nozzle as a form of afterburning. Advanced features included compressor boundary layer control and, between the turbines and the compressors, a variable-speed hydraulic coupling. The purpose of this coupling was to allow the compressor speed to be varied to suit differing air densities with altitude. A static, sea level thrust of 2,315kp (5,100lb) and a weight of 772kg (1,700lb) were expected.

As for the projected L-133 fighter, this was designed as a very sleek aircraft with thin, straight wings having rounded tips. One proposal planned a conventional fin and tailplane empennage, but this was changed to a canard foreplane and a larger vertical fin; at the same time the wing was moved much further aft. Control of the wing's boundary layer was to be provided by suction from the jet efflux duct, a very advanced concept at the time. Other features included a nose air intake, a low-profile cockpit canopy and a tricycle undercarriage. With the adoption of a canard layout, the twin turbojet engines were moved back, with the wing, and given air intakes either side of the fuselage, beneath the wing. The engines exhausted either side of the vertical fin.

On 30 March 1942 Lockheed submitted development proposals for the L-133 airframe and L-1000 engine to the Army at Wright Field. The official reaction was mixed but unsupportive, since the Army considered Lockheed's primary responsibility lay in turning out P-38 fighters and

Three views of the Lockheed L-1000 (XJ-37-1) axial turbojet. In the top left view, Hall L. Hibbard and Nathan C. Price are standing with the engine.

Bottom two photos: Aircraft Engine Historical Society (AEHS), Huntsville, AL

B-17 bombers for the prosecution of the war. Their jet proposal, on the other hand, was seen as a very long-term development and, in addition, a very complicated project fraught with obstacles. By this time the Durand Committee had formulated an American development programme (July 1941) and the Bell company had constructed the airframe of the prototype of America's first turbojet aircraft, the XP-59A, which made its first flight on 1 October 1942.

By November some refining of the L-1000 turbojet had been carried out, resulting in a lower weight of 735kg (1,620lb). The diameter was 0.635m (2ft 1in) and the length 3.73m (12ft 3in). The refinements included using chrome-nickel steel in the combustion chambers. Still there was no support from the Army: Wright Field considered that the engine should be developed separately from the airframe and, in any case, thought that engine development could not be successfully carried out by an airframe company (the same official view held in Germany). For its part, Lockheed was mainly interested in getting into the jet aircraft field, not the engine business, and was beginning to see the problems involved in developing a turbojet.

Nevertheless, following discussions with Wright Field on 19 May 1943, Nathan Price set about radically simplifying the design of the L-1000 turbojet. The single axial and three centrifugal compressors were replaced with two sixteen-stage axial compressors and intercooling was much reduced. Both compressors used casings of constant outside diameter, the rotor blades being mounted on tapered drums. Most of the blades, especially in the first four stages, were of high aspect ratio and none of them had any twist. Circular feet were used for blade attachment, to permit incidence angle adjustments to be made between tests. A unique and advanced feature of the first, low-pressure compressor was that the first four stages were connected to the other twelve stages by a hydraulic torque converter. This permitted them to operate at different speeds to aid starting and acceleration. There were no discs for the compressor blades, these being attached to drums of fabricated shell construction.

It was now possible to use a smaller hydraulic coupling and one turbine less: the compressor was driven by a single-stage, impulse-type turbine, followed by a three-stage mixed reaction and impulse turbine.

The deep-profile turbine rotor blades were of a hollow, sheet metal design and were air- and fuel-cooled, the gas temperature at the first stage being 820°C (less than previously designed for). At the air inlet to the engine, there were twenty-eight directional vanes, at the centre of which was a streamlined boss housing the front bearing. Following this was the low-pressure compressor casing, cast with external circumferential and longitudinal stiffening ribs, and split longitudinally to permit compressor assembly. The high-pressure compressor casing was of similar construction but with longitudinal external ribs only. In between the two compressors were bevel gears and six radial arms to drive the accessories.

The cannular combustion system was extremely short and vortex-stabilized. It was probably designed to burn kerosene and, as always, was the most troublesome component to develop. One source gives the combustion temperature as 1,260°C. Other features of the still mechanically complex L-1000 included the option of burning fuel between the turbine stages, a regeneratively cooled afterburner, a convergent-divergent variable throat and a fixed-area exhaust nozzle.

With the appearance of British and German jet fighters in 1941, the Army became more receptive to Lockheed's wish to develop a jet fighter. The L-133 fighter, however, was not taken up and the L-1000 engine was put on the back burner as a long-range project. Instead, from June 1943, development of Lockheed's XP-80 jet fighter (later the F-80 Shooting Star) was ordered and this was to be powered by the British de Havilland Halford H.1 turbojet.

In July 1943 the Army contracted with Lockheed for the development of the L-1000 turbojet (officially designated the XJ37-1), as a long-term project. Development was to take place in new facilities at Burbank and one engine was to be delivered by 1 August 1945. By the end of the war the prototype L-1000 was about two-thirds complete. Owing to a lack of specialized machine tools, however, Lockheed had been obliged to contract some of the work to the Menasco Manufacturing Company, also in Burbank. By the end of 1945 the complete L-1000 project, including Lockheed's engineering team, had been transferred to Menasco. Unfortunately the project suffered cost and delivery date overruns, due, among other reasons, to a lack of knowledge of the special materials needed, fabrication techniques and a shortage of materials caused by the demands of war. Experimental work and the construction of special test rigs took up more time and money.

L-1000 turboprop (XT35)

At some time in 1946 the L-1000 (or XJ37-1) prototype finally made its first bench run. Subsequent tests apparently showed sufficient promise for the Army to give Menasco a contract for the manufacture of four sets of components. Also proposed was a turboprop version of the L-1000, designated the XT35 Typhoon. For this it was planned to take the drive from the turbine end and drive a pusher airscrew via reduction gearing. Following the axial turbines, it was planned to have a radial turbine with the final hot gas efflux emerging from an annular nozzle surrounding the airscrew gear section. An alternative scheme envisaged the jet efflux passing through a duct in the centre of the pusher airscrews.

In September 1947 Lockheed and Menasco proposed transferring the entire L-1000 programme to one of the major aero-engine manufacturers. Wright Aeronautical took this up, apparently without official funding and in the hope that the XT35 turboprop version of the L-1000 could be used to power the huge global bomber being planned for the Strategic Air Command's nuclear deterrent. A specification for such a bomber had been issued by the USAAF in April 1945 and it seemed then that the range requirements could only be met by an aircraft with turboprop engines. The Model 462 design that Boeing proposed in June 1946 was a straight-winged aircraft to be powered by six 5,500ehp Wright T35 turboprops. However, by 1948, in the light of advances made with turbojets and the fact that Boeing's smaller but swept-wing B-47 Stratojet bomber prototype had flown, it was decided that the global bomber should also have swept wings and turbo jet engines. This, the Boeing Model 464, became the highly successful B-52 Stratofortress bomber. This change of direction was officially accepted and so the hopes for Wright's turboprop were dashed (as were those for Northrop's Turbodyne).

Wright continued to work on the L-1000 turbojet, however, and in July 1953 it delivered three of these engines to the USAF. The Air Force then made these engines and all test data available to gas turbine engine manufacturers without charge. This brought the L-1000 to an end after some $4.5 million, mostly government funds, had been spent on the project.

CHAPTER THIRTEEN

Northrop Aircraft Inc.

The Northrop Aircraft Company was founded in March 1939 by John (Jack) K. Northrop and La Motte T. Cohu, after Northrop left the Douglas Aircraft Corporation of which his company had been a subsidiary. Northrop was an aircraft designer and among his company's wartime products was the P-61 Black Widow night fighter and intruder aircraft. The company's small staff of engineers included Vladimir Pavlecka, one of the Pavlecka brothers from Czechoslovakia, who had joined Northrop because he felt that was the best place to develop an aircraft gas turbine. His inspiration had come from seeing industrial gas turbines at Neuchâtel in Switzerland.

Early in 1939 Pavlecka convinced Jack Northrop of the desirability of developing a turboprop engine to replace the piston aero-engine. Points in favour of a turboprop, Pavlecka suggested, were that it would be simpler, lighter, give less vibration and require fewer accessories. His initial design aims were a specific fuel consumption of 0.55, a compression ratio of 10.5:1 and efficiencies of 85 per cent for each of the axial compressor and turbine. For preliminary design work, Pavlecka was assigned five or six engineers only.

Turbodyne turboprop engine

Northrop's turboprop was named the Turbodyne and, in view of the anticipated great development cost, both the Army and the Navy were approached for a development contract. On 30 June 1941 both services decided to fund the Turbodyne, on a fifty–fifty basis, but this initial sponsorship was limited to the design of a complete engine but the manufacture of only the compressor. Clearly the sponsors saw this as the most difficult problem to be tackled first. After considering both centrifugal and axial compressors, an

eighteen-stage axial compressor was designed and built, but it was then demonstrated that sufficient power to test it could only come from the engine itself.

In the summer of 1942 Frank Whittle visited the USA and toured around the various companies working on gas turbines, his brief being to give assistance to American gas turbine developers. Most of his time was spent at the General Electric works at Lynn, but he also called in on Northrop and studied the Turbodyne drawings and the calculations upon which they were based. These he found very depressing, feeling that the complexities of the Turbodyne were beyond the facilities and capabilities of the company (and probably any other company at that time). It was clear to him that the company was woefully ill-equipped to build such an engine. When pressed by Jack Northrop for an honest opinion, Whittle said he thought the company was wasting its time.

The turboprop was therefore redesigned on Whittle's advice and the US Navy issued a new contract for $1.5 million on 1 July 1943 to cover the cost of building two Turbodynes, one for bench tests and the other for flight tests. The new turboprop, now designated Turbodyne Alpha 1500, was planned to give 2,400ehp at 605km/h (375mph) at 5,500m (18,000ft). Pavlecka and his small team designed it to have an eighteen-stage axial compressor and a three-stage axial turbine. A curiously short, but large volume, annular combustion chamber was designed that gave the engine a large bulge after the compressor section. It was planned to drive a pusher airscrew from a shaft at the turbine end, via gearing.

Late in 1943 Pavlecka resigned from Northrop and was replaced by the British engineer Art Phelan, who had previously headed the engine research division of Chrysler Motors. Soon, despite the redesign, Northrop concluded that this turboprop was beyond its capabilities, in the same

way that Lockheed did with its L-1000. It therefore sought outside assistance and persuaded the Joshua Hendy Iron Works of Sunnyvale, California, to join it on a fifty–fifty basis. Thus, the formation of Northrop-Hendy Inc. brought Hendy's expertise in the design and construction of steam turbines to bear on the project. The Hendy company worked fast and had the two Turbodyne Alpha engines ready for testing early in 1944. Both engines, however, failed on the test bench at about 10,000rpm and, despite the experience and data gained, the Navy left the Army as the sole official sponsor of the project.

XT37 turboprop engine

Early in 1944, before the Turbodyne had been tested, the Army gave Northrop-Hendy a contract to develop a very much more powerful version of the Turbodyne, designated the XT37. It was required to produce 4,000ehp at 11,275m (37,000ft), which meant developing about 10,000ehp at sea level, static. The purpose of this large turboprop was to power a global bomber, later to become the precursor of the B-52 Stratofortress. Development of the XT37 naturally became a lengthy and prodigious task. In 1945 Northrop was able to expand the design team with experts from the General Electric/Whittle programme, including Gene Hunsacker, who had worked on GE's axial-flow compressors, and Bill Crater, who had worked on turbojet combustion systems.

Three prototypes of the XT37 turboprop were complete by late 1947 and testing began. By about May 1948 one of these engines was producing an admirable 8,000shp for a turbine inlet temperature of about 730°C. Another XT37 later achieved 10,000shp and this encouraged the Army to order, in mid-1948, four flight engines. In 1949 the order was given to modify

Northrop's YB-49 Flying Wing bomber as a flying test-bed using two XT37 turboprops with pusher airscrews. The YB-49 was the culmination of Northrop's all-wing aircraft research, which had begun in 1940 with the small N-1M and continued until 1947, when the large, four piston-engined YB-35 lost the competition with the Convair B-36 Peacemaker bomber. Subsequently, two YB-35s were modified as YB-49s to fly on the power of turbojets, one with eight and one with six Allison turbojets. Various test airframes were built but the programme was cancelled by the USAF in October 1949. It was the sole surviving six-jet YB-49 that was to be modified to use two XT37

turboprops and was redesignated the EB-35B. General Motors were to produce the large, contra-rotating, pusher airscrews for this test aircraft.

Late in 1949 the subsidiary Turbodyne Corporation was organized to take over the work from Northrop-Hendy. However, this company was disbanded in 1950 with the closure of the whole programme and all patents and technical data were passed to GE at Schenectady. This came about because the USAF cancelled the EB-35B and after the B-52 was respecified to use turbojets instead of turboprops.

Attempts to interest the Navy in the XT37 engine failed. In any case, the long

development time expended meant that, in the meantime, the turbojet had advanced sufficiently to make it the engine of choice for high-speed, high-altitude bombers. The Northrop Aeronautical Corporation was in the future to create useful jet aircraft, but its work on the aeronautical gas turbine was at an end. There was, however, a small exception to this in 1949 when Northrop engine students developed a small turbojet with a centrifugal compressor and four small combustion chambers. Developing a thrust of 154kp (340lb) for a weight of only 78kg (172lb), this engine was tested in a Ryan Navion aircraft.

Northrop's YB-49 flying-wing bomber prototype powered by eight Allison J35 turbojets. A second prototype, powered by six Allison turbojets, was to be modified as the EB-35B to use two Northrop XT37 turboprops with contra-rotating pusher airscrews. However, the USAF cancelled the EB-35B in October 1949 in favour of the turbojet-powered Boeing B-52. Northrop Aircraft, Inc.

CHAPTER FOURTEEN

National Advisory Committee for Aeronautics (NACA)

As early as 1923 the NACA commissioned the so-called Buckingham Report on Jet Propulsion, which concluded that an engine with a piston-driven compressor, combustion chamber and jet exhaust nozzle, utilized at 400km/h (250mph), would have a specific fuel consumption four times greater than a piston engine with an airscrew. This report was revisited in 1932 but, still, a turbine was not considered to drive the compressor.

NACA ducted fan engines

In spite of the lack of optimism about such engines, Eastman N. Jacobs of the NACA became enthusiastic when he looked at the piston-driven ducted fan project of the Italian Secondo Campini. Campini's ducted fan project, which envisaged burning extra fuel aft of the fan, came to Jacob's attention when he visited the 1936 Volta International Aeronautical Congress. However, it was not until 1939 that Jacobs was able to persuade the NACA to undertake experimental work, and the construction of a Campini-type engine only began the following year. This NACA engine consisted of a 600hp R-1340 Wasp radial engine driving a single-stage fan inside a duct, followed by a combustion section using a vaporizing fuel burner system. Combustion tests began in 1941 but stability could not be achieved and combustion usually occurred outside the duct. A fuel injection burner system was next tried and this gave combustion stable enough to give a measurable thrust.

In January 1942 the NACA ducted fan engine was producing 136kp (300lb) static thrust (which was doubled with combustion on), but the specific fuel consumption was hopelessly high at 6.0. Nevertheless, Dr William Durand, head of the NACA, was sufficiently impressed to recommend that a flight engine be developed. For this, an 825hp R-1535 radial engine was employed to drive the fan and improvements to the burners were incorporated. In July 1942 this engine delivered 410kp (900lb) static thrust cold and 958kp (2,110lb) with combustion on, the specific fuel consumption then being 3.92. Of course, as others around the world found, the use of a piston engine in a jet engine was a dead-end development.

The supersonic compressor and Frederic Flader's turbojet

The aeronautical research of the NACA included work on axial compressors, especially at its Lewis Flight Propulsion Research Laboratory in Cleveland, Ohio, and at its Langley Aeronautical Laboratory at Langley Field, Virginia. Of specific interest was the post-war research carried out on supersonic axial compressors. The advantage of such a compressor was that the pressure ratio per stage was several times that possible with a subsonic axial compressor stage. In order to work, it was necessary for the supersonic flow to occur over the full span of each rotor blade and small deviations were critical. Frederic Flader tested a single-stage supersonic compressor in his small XJ55 turbojet in 1948, but this project ended in failure. During tests at Cleveland, NACA engineers found that the XJ55 compressor worked better at transonic speeds (i.e. speeds close to that of sound). Although supersonic compressors would one day be possible, NACA decided that they were not the path to follow at that time. The NACA's work on more conventional axial compressors became of more use to companies later working in the turbojet field.

General Electric Company

In 1892 the Thomson-Houston Company at Lynn, Massachusetts, was merged with the Edison Electric Company at Schenectady, New York, to create the General Electric Company (GE), which was to become a giant in power generation. Charles G. Curtis joined GE in 1897 and brought with him his patented steam turbine and so the company's development of the turbine began. The first of the company's many industrial steam turbines was installed in Chicago in 1903 to generate electricity.

We have seen earlier how Sanford Moss introduced the idea of the turbine, driven by hot exhaust gases, being used to drive a compressor to supercharge an engine. Moss's work had enabled GE to establish a thriving business producing centrifugal compressors for industry where large quantities of low-pressure air was required, an example being the feeding of blast furnaces in the steel industry. Moss established a Turbine Research department (later known as the Thomson Laboratory) within the Lynn Steam Turbine department, but after the USA entered the First World War in April 1917 this was turned over to the development of submarine detectors, machine guns and even a method of pre-detonating enemy torpedoes.

Sanford Moss and the turbosupercharger

As early as 1906 the idea of supercharging a piston engine using an exhaust-driven turbine and compressor had been put forward by the Swiss engineer Alfred Buechi; by 1916 this was being put to practical use in fighters thanks to the Frenchman Auguste C.E. Rateau. The NACA then proposed that GE would be a good choice of company to develop the turbosupercharger for American aircraft. This came about because the head of the

NACA, William F. Durand, had previously been Moss's professor at Cornell University. He recalled that, as early as 1903, Moss had conducted experiments in which he burned gases in a pressurized chamber to operate a turbine, these probably being the first gas turbine experiments of this nature. At the time Durand was scathing of Moss's experiments, in the room below his: 'whatever Moss was doing, it was not likely to be worth the noise, smoke and smells. In fact it is likely to be worth nothing at all.' Fourteen years later, Moss accepted Durand's proposal to develop the Rateau turbosupercharger at GE.

Moss made an important change in providing for air cooling of the turbine casing. Beginning on 19 June 1918, tests with a 350hp Liberty piston engine fitted with the turbosupercharger were carried out on Pikes Peak, Colorado, which rises to 4,300m (14,000ft). At that altitude, the engine produced only 230hp but this was increased to 356hp with the supercharger working. Following this success, GE received Army orders for its turbosupercharger, only to have these soon cancelled when the war ended in November. Of course, that was not the end of this work but a beginning, although subsequent orders for the successful GE turbosuperchargers were fulfilled in the Street Lighting department since much higher priority was given to the manufacture of industrial equipment elsewhere in the plant.

While Moss continued his research at Lynn, Glenn B. Warren, who had joined GE in 1919 on the company's Test Engineering programme, proposed that industrial gas turbine research should be started at Schenectady. He had previously built two turbine combustion chambers in his garage and had his mind set upon creating a successful gas turbine. In due time, Warren was to rise to become vice president and general manager of the company's Turbine Division.

In September 1931 the Army awarded GE a contract for testing high temperature turbine inlet nozzle and blade combinations. Although this was chiefly concerned with turbosuperchargers, the work was to have a bearing on later turbojet work and it continued throughout the 1930s: GE turbosuperchargers were used in such famous wartime aircraft as the B-17, B-24 and B-29 bombers and the P-38 and P-47 fighters. Studies and practical work continued on the gas turbine for a variety of uses in industry, on the land, sea and in the air. Some Schenectady engineers considered using a gas turbine for driving an aircraft airscrew, with powers of up to 10,000hp, but the idea was shelved due to the low efficiency of turbines and compressors at that time.

First thoughts of an axial-flow compressor, in contrast to the widespread centrifugal type, came when Alan Howard from Schenectady visited the NACA's Cleveland laboratory to view their work on an axial compressor. GE now considered that an axial-flow turboprop looked much more attractive. A four-stage axial compressor was then built, with adjustable blades, but at the first stall all the blades broke off.

GE was then given a contract from the US Navy to build and test a combustion chamber and a single-stage turbine as a preliminary to developing a powerplant for torpedo boats. However, because the air supply available at Schenectady was relatively low at that time, the engineers elected to build scaled-down components for testing, using a specially assembled motor and air compressor. Thus a start had fortuitously been made on components suitable in size for an aircraft gas turbine.

The Durand Committee

During 1941 the US military began taking an interest in the turbojet, having received intelligence reports on some of the German work and being aware of the British research. On 25 February 1941 General Henry 'Hap' Arnold, Deputy Chief of Staff for Air, wrote to Dr Vannevar Bush, chairman of the NACA, requesting him to form a special committee to look into jet propulsion with a view to coordinating American jet engine research and development. It seemed implicit that rocket propulsion should be included along with gas turbine engines. The next month Dr Bush formed a Special Committee on Jet Propulsion within the NACA. The committee was headed by William Durand and included representatives from the Army Air Corps, Navy Bureau of Aeronautics, National Bureau of Standards, MIT, Johns Hopkins University and from the three American turbine manufacturers of Allis-Chalmers, GE and Westinghouse. American aircraft engine manufacturers were excluded on Gen. Arnold's specific orders, his reason being that they should remain heavily engaged in and concentrate on piston-engine manufacture. The USA was not yet at war, although it soon would be, but Britain had been at war with Nazi Germany for two years and urgently needed war matériel.

General Arnold, now promoted to Chief of Staff of the US Army Air Corps, was in a hurry and called for a progress report on jet propulsion from his staff before leaving for England on a fact-finding tour. During May 1941 he observed Whittle's engine, the Gloster E28/39 jet aircraft and other gas turbine developments and was duly impressed. Meanwhile the three US turbine companies submitted gas turbine engine proposals, all of which employed an axial compressor: Allis-Chalmers proposed a ducted fan engine, GE (Schenectady) a turboprop and Westinghouse a turbojet engine. By July the NACA had given all three companies the go-ahead to begin development work. In September it was recommended that the work be sponsored by the military. Accordingly, by early 1942, GE was under contract to the Army Air Corps and Allis-Chalmers and Westinghouse were under contract to the Navy. GE's work was to lead to the world's first turboprop engine, the TG-100 (see below).

Returning to Washington, Gen. Arnold contacted GE with the request that they send a knowledgeable engineer to England to assess the British work. GE's D. Roy Shoults, however, had already been in England from the spring of 1941 on turbosupercharger business and he had gradually become aware of Frank Whittle's turbojet work. Shoults worked with Col A.J. Lyons of the Army Air Corps and Maj. Donald J. Keirn from Wright Field, and together they recommended that Whittle's engine should be built in the USA.

Type I-A, the first American-built turbojet

By the autumn of 1941 arrangements had been made at top level for the transfer of British turbojet technology to the USA with the stipulation that it was only to be used for war purposes. Details were worked out, beginning in July, at meetings between the British Ministry of Aircraft Production and Gen. Arnold's AAF Liaison Committee. Although British work on the E28/39 and the F.9/40 Meteor fighter was looked at, the Americans concentrated on the transfer of Whittle's turbojet to the USA. Arnold chose GE to reproduce Whittle's engine because of its great experience with turbo-machinery and the turbosupercharger, and the fact that it was not involved in any piston engine production.

Early in September 1941 GE received preliminary drawings of Whittle's W.1X engine. This was followed in October by the receipt of a W.1X engine (previously used in taxiing tests of the Gloster E28/39), drawings of the Rover W.2B engine and a team from Power Jets that included test engineer D.N. Walker, fitter G.B. Bozzoni and Flight Sergeant J.A. King of the RAF. By 4 October 1941 all matériel and personnel were installed in Building 45 at GE's Lynn plant and work began under conditions of the greatest secrecy. GE's contract was for fifteen Whittle-type turbojets. At the same time, the nearby Bell Aircraft Corporation of Buffalo, New York, had received a USAAF contract to design and build a jet fighter to be powered by GE's turbojet, the aircraft being designated the XP-59A.

To test the W.1X engine, GE quickly built a reinforced concrete test cell with a heavy steel door and only one single, very small, observation slot. Because of the extreme security placed on the work, this test cell was built inside a building and the engine exhaust was led through a slotted brickwork duct into the base of a chimney some 20m (64ft) high. Air was admitted through a short, circular venturi in the roof. A simple control panel was arranged inside the test cell but was soon transferred outside. Silencing baffles fitted inside the exhaust duct were removed after they became distorted and broke away. All the early testing was carried out in this cell; when further cells were constructed, the jet exhaust was directed over open waste ground.

GE's turbojet received the designation of Type I-A. The brief was to improve on the Rover W.2B engine design where possible but not at the expense of production delivery, the first two engines being due by 2 April 1942. Without affecting its turbosupercharger and other work, GE put together a good team to work on the I-A turbojet project. This was headed by Donald F. 'Truly' Warner, a top engineer from the Supercharger Department, and included Reg Standerwick, M.G. 'Robby' Robinson, John Benson and Sam Puffer, also from the Supercharger Department.

It was no straightforward matter to build an engine from the W.1X drawings, since these were incomplete and, in particular, showed nothing of a speed governor; this is why an actual example of the engine had to be obtained. Starting in November 1941, experience was gained by running and stripping down the W.1X. It was decided to base the GE engine on the Rover W.2B reverse-flow engine but to use certain features of the Power Jets's mechanical design such as that for the bearings. Apart from general Americanization, the I-A engine also incorporated GE practices, a strengthened centrifugal compressor and Hastelloy B for the turbine blades instead of the British Nimonic 80. Hastelloy B, comprising 65 per cent nickel and 29 per cent molybdenum, was a recently developed (1940) heat-resisting alloy made by the Haynes Stellite Company. It could be used at a higher temperature than Nimonic 80.

After only five and a half months' work, the first I-A turbojet was ready for testing. It was taken to the specially built test cell, known by the British as 'Fort Knox' owing to its 0.457m (18in) thick concrete walls. On 18 March 1942 the first run was made, but the compressor stalled well before its full speed. This problem was partially solved by fitting thicker vanes in the diffuser, thereby reducing the effective flow area. (Impressed by Whittle's centrifugal compressor, with its 4.0:1 pressure ratio, GE incorporated the design into its turbo-supercharger and obtained a 40 per cent

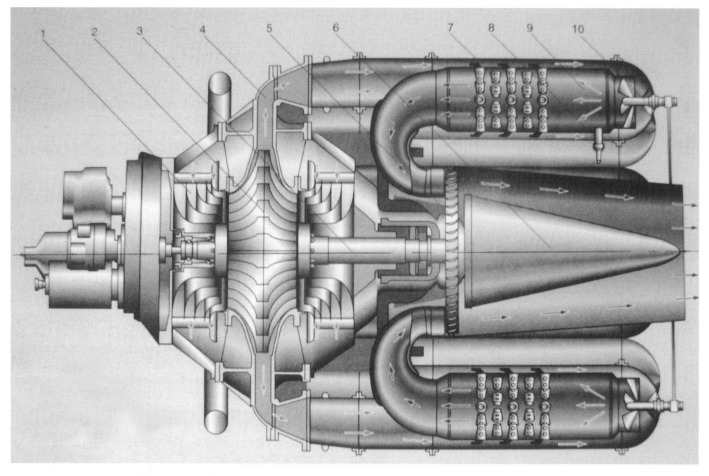

The first turbojet made in the USA, the General Electric Type I-A, based on Frank Whittle's work, first ran on 18 April 1942: (1) impeller blades; (2) double-sided centrifugal compressor; (3) rotor shaft; (4) diffuser; (5) single-stage turbine; (6) fixed-area exhaust nozzle; (7) combustion chambers; (8) igniter; (9) cold air; (10) fuel injector.

increase in its operating altitude.) One month later, on 18 April 1942, a successful run was made, this being the first such for a turbojet produced in the USA.

Donald Warner was the operator for this first successful run and his log read:

Everyone working to finish Type I so that it could go in Fort Knox. We finally took the machine into Fort Knox and hung it from its supports . . . We did a great deal of checking before attempting to start. A great deal of trifling troubles were found and remedied – but after many attempts *Type I RAN*. First run made without shrouding. Speed 7,000rpm for approx 60 seconds and then we shut down. Tail pipe temperature rose to 1,500°F and then started to drop. Mr. Hains was present and had an actual hand in getting it started. J. Benson, A. Price were also on deck. Everyone worked like beavers but all felt well repaid. The check and relief valve was not acting at all right so it was out of operation.

The shroud ring referred to was the sheet metal surrounding the combustion chambers.

Although this run with the I-A engine was considered a success, there were still problems to be solved. The engine ran too hot and surging or stalling occurred. In June 1942 Frank Whittle visited the Lynn works, bringing drawings of his advanced W.2/500 turbojet, and set about redesigning the compressor casing and diffuser section of the I-A engine. Partitions were inserted in the existing compressor casing to give separate passages from the casing to each combustion chamber. With these modifications, the I-A achieved a static thrust of 590kp (1,300lb) without stalling.

Test engines were soon coming steadily out of the workshops ready for testing, but a number of them blew up in the test cell. Examination of the pieces gave no clue to the cause. One day John Benson was passing by a centrifugal compressor that was being

assembled on a balancing stand. As was his habit, he tapped the blades with his nail clippers and the dull sound from almost all of the blades led him to believe that the compressor was cracked. Warner ordered the compressor to be sodium hydroxide cleaned and covered in fluorescent fluid. Ultraviolet light then revealed that fourteen of the sixteen blades were cracked! After the compressor had been redesigned by M.G. Robinson so that it was strengthened with fillets where the blades joined the disc, there was no more trouble from this source. Because there was no shortage of test engines, problems of this kind did not hold up development to any great extent.

America's first jet aircraft, the Bell XP-59A

While GE's development of the I-A turbojet was proceeding, Bell was developing three

A sectioned GE I-A2 centrifugal turbojet, two of which powered the Bell P-59.
Central Arkansas Library System, Aerospace Education Center (AEC), Little Rock, AR

XP-59A fighter prototypes, each of which was to be powered by two I-A engines. Bell was chosen for this task because of its proximity to GE's plants, the fact that it was not overloaded with production work, its innovative engineers and the fact that it had isolated facilities conducive to carrying out secret work. Larry Bell and his chief engineer H.M. Poyer were briefed on the project in Washington on 5 September 1941. Back at the works in Buffalo, Poyer organized a small design team known as the Secret Six.

Within two weeks an aircraft proposal and model had been prepared for Gen. Arnold and approved. Bell then received a fixed-fee contract for three XP-59A aircraft on 30 September 1941, the first to be delivered by June 1942. In the design of this fighter, Bell was given an almost free hand, the main stipulations being that it should use two GE turbojets and carry a full military load. For security reasons the designation of XP-59 was reused from an earlier, cancelled, Bell piston-engined fighter project. Bell's designation for the XP-59 was Model number 27.

Fitting one of the two GE I-A2 turbojets into the Bell XP-59.

Despite lacking data on the turbojet engines, the Bell engineers decided that the fighter would be at its best at high speed and high altitudes of between 7,600m (25,000ft) and 15,250m (50,000ft). The altitude and the consideration of a full military load led to wings of large area. For high altitudes, a pressurized cockpit was necessary and due consideration had to be given to the effects of very low temperatures on the airframe. Unfortunately the secrecy and urgency of the project prevented the use of outside wind tunnels: only the low-speed wind tunnel at Wright Field was used and this enabled the design of the air intakes to include boundary layer bleed slots. However, the area of most uncertainty concerned the engines, for which there was no reliable information regarding even static thrust, and precious little regarding weight, fuel consumption and general dimensions. At first they had to make do with a small, rough sketch that Roy Shoults of GE made when he visited Bell on 13 September 1941. Altogether, Bell's task was greatly handicapped by this excessive secrecy, which also prevented contact with outside aeronautical experts or manufacturers of aircraft equipment.

Responsibility for the airframe structure and engine installation fell to Bob Wolf. The XP-59A was of all-metal, monocoque construction with mid-mounted, tapered wings and an oval-sectioned fuselage. A conventional tail empennage was used, the tailplane being mounted at the base of the vertical fin but well above the line of the jet efflux. All flying surfaces had rounded tips and all control surfaces, including the flaps, were fabric-covered. The two nacelles for the engines were tucked under the wing roots, against the lower fuselage sides, the air inlets protruding slightly ahead of the wing leading edges. The two engine exhaust ducts were well clear of the fuselage, since this tapered upwards to meet the tailfin. The pressurized cockpit was stepped and had a hinged canopy that was heavily framed, resulting in poor vision towards the rear. A retractable, tricycle undercarriage, of extremely wide track, was used. Fuel was carried in the wings in self-sealing tanks and the nose was to be fitted with machine guns and their ammunition. The XP-59A was no beauty and the Bell team were not expecting it to compete even with the next piston-engined fighters then under development. Nevertheless, it was an exciting and milestone project.

For purposes of secrecy, it was decided that flight tests of the XP-59A should take place at the AAF Muroc Bombing and Gunnery Range on Rogers Dry Lake in the Mojave Desert, California. (Muroc was renamed Edwards Air Force Base on 27 January 1950.) The three XP-59A prototypes were completed on schedule but their final assembly was delayed until September 1942 owing to delays in I-A engine deliveries. The first aircraft arrived at Muroc on 19 September and its assembly was begun under somewhat primitive conditions. The first installed engine run-up was made on 26 September.

Following taxiing trials the previous day, the maiden flight was made in the afternoon of 1 October 1942. Bob Stanley was the pilot and the aircraft was known as the Bell Model 27-1 (Ship 1). No serial number was given at that time but the first aircraft later appears to have been assigned the number 42-108786. For this first flight of an American jet aircraft, the XP-59A's tanks were half full and the GE I-A2 engines each gave 568kp (1,250lb) of static thrust. Prior to take-off the cockpit became stuffy from heat and engine fumes, but these disappeared once the aircraft was swung into wind. Take-off was made using an engine speed of 15,000rpm and with flaps up. The aircraft left the ground at about 145km/h (90mph), after a run of about 610m (2,000ft), and a flight of about 30 minutes at a height of 8m (25ft) was made.

Three more flights were made that day, all with undercarriage down, and altitude was limited to 30m (100ft). On the following day two flights were made by Stanley, one at 1,830m (6,000ft) and the other at 3,050m (10,000ft). A flight was then made by Col L.C. Craigie of the Army Air Corps, followed by the final flight of the day by Stanley. He reported that there were no handling problems but that the cockpit was extremely hot. Fuel consumption seemed to be about 150 US gallons per hour and about 52 per cent of the design thrust of 745kp (1,640lb) per engine was available. As repairs and modifications were then needed, no more flights were made until 30 October.

Among the modifications made to the first XP-59A was the provision of an observer's seat in the nose section where the armament was to be. This modification was quite rudimentary and consisted of a seat, instrument panel and a hole in the fuselage with a small plastic windshield. The position was not enclosed but resulted

in the world's first two-seat jet aircraft. E.P. Rhodes, the Bell project engineer, became the first observer when the XP-59A resumed flying on 30 October 1942. Before recorders became available, the main job of the observer was to record the many readings required from the engines.

I-14B and I-16 (J31) centrifugal turbojets

On 12 February 1944 the first XP-59A made its first flight with the slightly more powerful GE I-14B turbojets, rated at a static thrust of 635kp (1,400lb) each. GE had begun the design of the I-14B on 15 May 1942, just after the first flight of the XP-59A, when it was obvious that more thrust was desirable. The new turbojet had a new GE compressor casing and diffuser and, copied from Whittle's W.2/500 engine, an improved turbine. Using fewer, broader and longer blades, the new turbine suffered fewer breakages. Thrust was increased by virtue of an increased air mass flow. For the I-14B, the combustion system was redesigned by A.J. Nerad of GE's Schenectady Research Laboratory. Nerad's combustors had a new liner and used many holes to ensure the fuel mixed thoroughly with the air. This system needed only about a tenth of the fuel pressure of that used in the British system and was thereby more reliable. The I-14B gave its design thrust of 635kp straightaway on its first bench run in February 1943 and, after the first flights, it went into small-scale production.

Just before the first run of the I-14B, GE began design and development of the I-16 (or J31). This design continued with the double-sided, centrifugal, Whittle-type layout of the previous engines and was largely based on Whittle's W.2B design and the GE I-A prototypes. Changes were introduced largely in the interests of simplifying production and to bring the static thrust up to 726kp (1,600lb). The area of the turbine inlet nozzles was increased and the turbine blades were slightly increased in height and width, without altering the inner diameter of the turbine wheel. Without altering its diameter, the compressor was redesigned for an increased air mass flow. Nerad's low-pressure fuel atomization system was again employed and the turbine blades were of Hastelloy B alloy. A completely new control system, however, based on D.F. Warner's patents for steam turbines, was introduced. After minor

A GE I-16 turbojet on outdoor test at Lynn. Judging by the flame length, much work was needed to develop the combustion system.

The GE I-16 (J31) centrifugal turbojet introduced simplifications to facilitate series production.
AEHS, Huntsville

modifications, the engine was redesignated I-16A.

On 24 April 1943 the I-16A made its first test run. For a weight of 365kg (804lb), the I-16A or J31 gave an average static thrust of 647kp (1,425lb) at 16,500rpm, the tail pipe temperature being 635°C. Its specific fuel consumption was 1.23. Some 241 I-16s were manufactured.

The other two XP-59A prototypes had arrived at Muroc by February 1943, but without engines, due to delivery delays. Eventually all three prototypes were being flown with I-A or I-14B engines, the two types being interchangeable. In the meantime, the first of thirteen YP-59As were being built for service evaluation trials. Differences from the XP-59A were minimized but the YP-59A could be distinguished externally by the squarer tips of the flying surfaces, the sliding instead of hinging cockpit canopy and the addition of nose armament. These service evaluation aircraft were also each to be powered by two I-16 turbojets. As for the nose armament, this was to consist of two M4 37mm cannon on each of the first nine aircraft and one 37mm cannon plus three 0.50in machine guns on each of the last four aircraft, which were also to have underwing drop tanks.

The first YP-59A (c/n: 27-4, 42-108771) was delivered to Muroc on 12 June 1943 and others followed. However, the first six of these had to be flown with I-A or I-14B engines due to non-delivery of the I-16 engines. The first flight of the I-16 engine took place on 15 August 1943 using the YP-59A (c/n: 42-108771). During flight tests pilots would often fly the YP-59A until it ran out of fuel, the vast expanse of Rogers Dry Lake providing ample opportunities for making a safe glide landing. The low wing loading made such landings very easy. The large wing area, however, was never going to allow the fighter to exceed the performance of that of the best piston-engined fighters of the day, such as the P-51 Mustang, but this same wing conferred a good high-altitude performance on the YP-59A. An example of this was the unofficial American altitude record of 14,508m (47,600ft) achieved by Bell's test pilot Jack Woolams in the YP-59A (c/n: 27-4) on 15 December 1943. It was GE that solved the problem of engine surge at high altitude before the British solved this problem with the similar W.2B engine. This was thanks to the great resources of GE and the fact that the Bell aircraft made an excellent high-altitude test-bed before British Meteors were making similar flights.

However, all was not well with the I-16, particularly regarding the engine life, which, on average, was a miserable seven and a half hours, or less than that of the first German turbojets in service. Also, unless the pilot used a very delicate touch on the throttle, the uncooled turbine was very easily burned out. The first priority, therefore, was to get the service life increased a great deal, followed by an improvement in the fuel consumption.

The third YP-59A (42-108773) was shipped in crates from the Bell factory to RAF Moreton Valance in England, where it arrived on 26 September 1943. The Gloster company and the RAF jointly assembled the aircraft and it was first flown two days later by 'Doc' Meshako of Bell. It was subsequently tested at Farnborough under the aegis of the RAF and had the serial RT362/G applied, indicating it was to have an armed guard. In exchange, the British sent the first production Meteor I (EE 210) to Muroc in February 1944. The YP-59A was not very well thought of in England (or the USA) and, as a jet fighter, it was not a success. However, as a training exercise and initiation for American industry and the military into jet aircraft, it was a success. In production, the type was limited to twenty P-59As and thirty P-59B Airacomets, which were powered by J31-GE-3 and J31-GE-5 engines respectively. The P-59B Airacomets also had fuel capacity increased by having extra fuel cells fitted in the outer wing panels.

Military evaluation of the type was undertaken by the USAAF's 412th Fighter Group, which was specially formed for the purpose. Their verdict was that the P-59 showed inadequate performance and was an indifferent gun platform. Already military attention was turning to Lockheed's XP-80 jet as the next generation fighter. Jack Woolams continued with company testing through 1944, using the production P-59A. In particular he carried out dive tests, usually resulting in some structural failure of the tailplane, that revealed a tendency to pitch nose up at Mach 0.77. On his fifth dive, the entire tail empennage broke away and Woolams was trapped by a jammed cockpit canopy. Fortunately he was able to twist round in his seat and kick the canopy free, before making a parachute descent from the doomed aircraft. Landing in snow, Woolams was later picked up by one of the earliest helicopters, a Bell Model 30.

An armed Bell P-59A Airacomet (422609), the first American jet fighter, powered by two GE I-16 turbojets. The P-59A (422610) became the first US jet aircraft to land in Alaska, on 9 December 1944. Central Arkansas Library System, AEC

Bell P-59B Airacomet fighter			
Span		13.87m	(45ft 6in)
Length		11.62m	(38ft 1½in)
Wing area		35.84sq m	(385.8sq ft)
Height		3.66m	(12ft 0in)
Empty weight		3,704kg	(8,165lb)
Maximum loaded weight		6,214kg	(13,700lb)
Maximum speed	at 10,670m (35,000ft)	658km/h	(408mph)
Cruising speed		604km/h	(375mph)
Service ceiling		14,080m	(46,200ft)
Range		644km	(400 miles)

I-18 and I-20 centrifugal turbojets

Further development of the I-16 led to the I-18 and I-20. In the I-18, the design of which was begun on 25 May 1943, an increased static thrust of 817kp (1,800lb) was produced by slightly increasing the diameter of the compressor and by modifying the diffuser and exhaust nozzle areas to suit. For this, the weight was increased by only 4.5kg (10lb). The I-18 was first run on 18 January 1944 and first test flown on 1 November 1944. In the I-20, the design of which was begun on 9 June 1943, a static thrust of 908kp (2,000lb) was aimed at, chiefly by increasing the turbine blade height and the air inlet area. The

overall size was the same as the I-16 but weight increased by a modest 44kg (97lb) to 409kg (900lb). First run on 21 April 1944, the I-20 achieved its design thrust at 16,500rpm and gave a specific fuel consumption of 1.20. It was not test flown.

TG-100 (T31) turboprop engine, America's first

While development of Whittle-type centrifugal engines was progressing at the Lynn works, development of an axial-flow turboprop engine was proceeding under similarly secret conditions at Schenectady, New York. After much pondering and discussion, GE decided that it was right to divide the effort and develop these two types of engine separately at the two works. The turbojet was to be a rapid development and the turboprop a longer-term, more advanced project. This turned out to be an excellent decision.

Design work on the turboprop engine, designated the TG-100 (later, T31), was begun at the Steam Turbine Engineering Division at Schenectady on 25 July 1941. This work was under the leadership of Glenn Warren and Alan Howard and benefited from Anglo-American technology exchange. The concept from Britain of separate, multiple combustion chambers in particular helped speed the work along and, as already mentioned, A. Nerad evolved a low-pressure fuel-mixing system for the chambers. In this he was assisted by the talented, young Don Berkey. As a matter of fact, most of GE's turbojet engineers were young because there was no cadre of piston-engine 'old hands' to draw upon. Early development of the TG-100 was continued under the leadership of Dr C.J. Walker, GE's project engineer.

The layout of the TG-100 turboprop consisted of a fourteen-stage axial compressor supplying air to nine reverse-flow combustion chambers, outside the diameter of the compressor casing. This resulted in a large diameter for the single-stage turbine. Forward of the compressor were the reduction gears for the airscrew and the accessories. The original design aim of the TG-100 was to deliver 1,200shp.

Research data from NACA was drawn upon in the design of the axial compressor. It had a compression ratio of between 5 and 6:1 and air was bled from it for thrust balancing and cooling purposes. The compressor casing was of thin, fabricated steel sheet with a horizontal, bolted joint, the rings of stator blades being held in place by clamping rings that also served as spacers. This casing was strong enough to withstand torque loads between the gearbox and the aft mountings on the main frame. The compressor rotor had fourteen aluminium alloy and steel discs shrunk on to a hollow steel shaft, and steel rotor blades were dovetailed into the discs. The nine reverse-flow Nerad-type combustion chambers each had a perforated, stainless-steel liner or flame tube, a duplex-type fuel nozzle and downstream injection.

A large-diameter, single-stage turbine drove both compressor and airscrew and was designed for temperatures of up to 1,030°C. The turbine was of the Curtiss or impulse type and used blades of Vitallium (62 per cent cobalt, 28 per cent chrome, 6 per cent molybdenum and 2 per cent nickel). They were welded to the alloy steel wheel because there was no time to develop dovetail or fir-tree attachments. However, a procedure was developed to replace welded blades when necessary. Reduction gearing for the airscrew shaft consisted of double planetary gearing with an overall reduction ratio of 11.35:1, resulting in an airscrew speed of 1,145rpm. A ring gear, attached to the low-speed planet cage, was used to drive the accessories. A symmetrical, stainless-steel exhaust collector was used on the TG-100B, but a twenty-degree offset exhaust collector was used on the TG-100A. The different arrangements were used according to the aircraft installation. The weight of the TG-100 prototypes peaked at 885kg (1,950lb). Its diameter was 0.89m (2ft 11in) and overall length was 2.92m (9ft 7in). The design of the TG-100 was such that components most likely to need replacement could be changed fairly easily and at a low cost.

The TG-100 was the first turboprop designed and tested in the USA and was also the first to be flown in that country. Although the Army Air Force contracted with Lynn for the centrifugal I-40 (J33) and with Schenectady for the TG-100 (T31) axial turboprop, it made sure that little information flowed between the two plants of the company. By 23 December 1941 the layout of the TG-100 was completed. The first prototype was successfully run on 15 May 1943, albeit without an airscrew. Tests with an airscrew attached were made at Wright Field because there were no facilities for such tests at Schenectady. The first attempt to fly the TG-100 was by fitting it into the starboard nacelle of a Curtiss-Wright C-46, the largest twin-engined transport of the time. Unfortunately the aircraft ran into a tractor during a run down the runway, probably as a result of the exceptionally strong gyroscopic forces produced by the turboprop's airscrew when the tail of the C-46 was raised.

XP-81 and DarkShark turboprop fighters

The first flight of the TG-100 was in the Convair XP-81 mixed-powerplant fighter, the design of which was begun in January 1944. Using a turboprop in the nose and a turbojet in the tail, the aim was to provide the USAAF with a high-performance, long-range fighter for action in the Pacific war. Its first flight was made with an Allison-built J33-GE-5 turbojet in the tail and, because the TG-100 was not ready, a Merlin piston engine in the nose. In this form it

A GE TG-100 (T31) turboprop on an outdoor test rig at Schenectady. On the right is Dr Chapman J. Walker, GE's project engineer, accompanied by Alan Howard.

first flew on 11 February 1945. The first flight of the XP-81 with an XT31-GE-1 turboprop in the nose took place on 21 December 1945, but this engine developed only 1,380shp, about 60 per cent of its rated 2,300shp, plus 275kp (600lb) of residual thrust. Only limited testing of the XP-81 followed and, with the war over, the type was cancelled. Its maximum speed at sea level was 769km/h (478mph).

The US Navy, like the Army, also had thoughts of a long-range, high-performance fighter, but for carrier operation. Already plans were going ahead for the Ryan XFR-1 (later named Fireball) fighter to be powered by a piston engine in the nose and a turbojet in the tail. Sixty-six FR-1 Fireballs were produced and then phased out with the end of the war. One of these aircraft then had its piston engine replaced with an XT31-GE-2 turboprop, the tail engine remaining as a J31-GE-3 turbojet: in this form the fighter was designated XF2R-1 DarkShark. Modifications to the Fireball included lengthening the nose for the turboprop and fitting a fillet to increase the fin area to compensate for the longer nose and larger airscrew.

This aircraft (39661) first flew in November 1946, piloted by Ryan test pilot Al Conover. The XF2R-1, like the FR-1, had a phenomenal rate of climb for its day – in excess of 1,524m/min (5,000ft/min) – and had a maximum speed of about 805km/h (500mph). Air intakes for the J31 turbojet were in the leading edges of the wing's centre section (the outer sections folding) and the exhaust outlets for the

XT31 turboprop were on the fuselage sides below the cockpit. The XT31 drove a specially built 3.28m (11ft) diameter, four-bladed Hamilton Standard, square-tipped, hydraulically controlled airscrew that enabled speed braking to be developed. During a landing approach, the blade pitch was flattened to increase drag, thereby steepening the glide angle and dramatically shortening the landing roll. There was an automatic airscrew adjustment that co-ordinated with the throttle to change blade pitch as power was reduced. Also, when the mainwheels touched the deck, the blade pitch was further reduced to create a reverse thrust and stop the fighter in the minimum distance. On 2 May 1947 Al Conover flew the XF2R-1 to a new world altitude record of 11,936m (39,160ft). Tests at Muroc were impressive enough to plan for the XF2R-2, which would have used the J34 turbojet in the tail, but these and other engine combinations did not go forward. During one ground test, in cold conditions, the XT31 delivered 2,750shp.

GE delivered twelve TG-100A turboprops by 1946, but engineering responsibility was transferred that spring from Schenectady to the Aircraft Gas Turbine Division at Lynn, leaving Schenectady to concentrate on locomotive gas turbines. Thus, the blocking of information between the two plants, desired by the Army, was no longer a problem. At Lynn the GE

A Ryan XF2R-1 DarkShark fighter, powered by an XT31 turboprop in the nose and a J31 turbojet in the tail, air intakes for the J31 being in the leading edges of the wing roots. Philip Jarrett

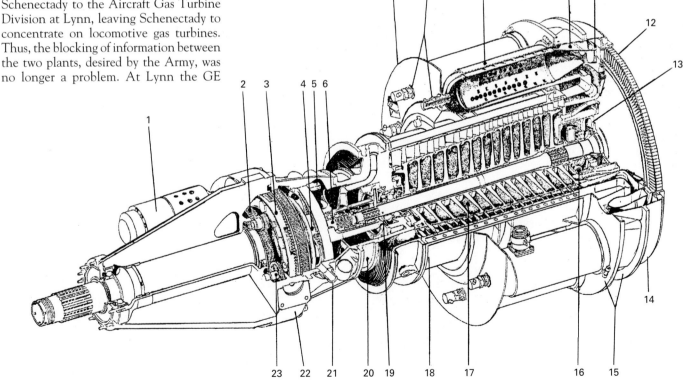

General Electric TG-100B (T31) turboprop: (1) starter; (2) accessory gear drive; (3) low-speed planet gear cage; (4) high-speed planet gear cage; (5) torque arm; (6) high-speed sun gear; (7) fire wall; (8) fuel nozzles; (9) combustion chambers; (10) transition liner; (11) turbine nozzle assembly; (12) single-stage, large-diameter turbine; (13) turbine bearing casing; (14) turbine nozzle casing; (15) main frame assembly; (16) turbine bearing pump; (17) fourteen-stage axial compressor; (18) compressor stator casing; (19) compressor bearing pump; (20) compressor air inlet casing; (21) intermediate casing; (22) forward casing; (23) fuel regulator drive gear.

engineers continued development of the TG-100 and began design of the TG-100B in December 1945. In this the aim was to eliminate poor temperature distribution in the bearings and turbine, the latter having had quite a short life. In the TG-100B, cooling was used for the turbine hub and rim. Other problems that had to be solved in the previous TG-100A were excessive vibration and the design of an airscrew that could change pitch rapidly enough to prevent overspeeding. To eliminate the vibration, after balancing the compressor and turbine rotors individually and as a unit, a metal disc was screwed onto the hub of the turbine wheel and fitted with selected radial studs until perfect balance was arrived at (similar to the way that car wheels are balanced). In the balancing process, one blade was magnetized and passed close by a vibration meter until synchronization was achieved. A new torque and fuel regulator was developed that controlled the pitch of the airscrew directly, as a function of the engine torque output. Hamilton Standard devised an airscrew with a high rate of pitch change.

The TG-100B was first run with an airscrew on 18 November 1947 and it passed a 150-hour Model Qualification Test (MQT) on 16 May 1949. It was funded by both the Navy and the USAAF, but by 20 July 1949 the Navy had taken over all turboprop development. It was the TG-100B that was tested in the XF2R-1 DarkShark. Some sixteen TG-100B (T31) turboprops were built by GE at Lynn before the company dropped turboprop development (until the T58 in 1953). However, the company's experiences with the TG-100 turboprop, especially with the axial compressor, were put to good use in the design of their first axial turbojet, the TG-180 (later J35) described further on.

I-40 (J33), last of GE's centrifugal turbojets

Early in 1943 GE was asked by the USAAF to look into the development of a new turbojet capable of a static thrust of 1,362kp (3,000lb), later revised to 1,816kp (4,000lb). By the standards of the day, this was a large engine and it was more powerful than any then in existence. At Lynn the new engine was designated the I-40 (later, the J33) and its development was begun under the leadership of Dale D. Streid on 9 June 1943. It was also decided to offer the TG-180 in the same performance class and the USAAF ordered both engines into development.

The I-40 turbojet was similar to the series from the I-A to the I-20 in that it used a forged aluminium alloy, double-sided centrifugal compressor and a single turbine, but otherwise it was a new design incorporating GE's experience and new features: straight-through (instead of reverse-flow) combustion chambers, a splined coupling between the turbine and compressor shafts and flooded lubrication for the bearings and shaft coupling. Precision casting of Stellite alloy No. 21 was used for the turbine inlet nozzles and, later, for the turbine blades. Casting techniques were developed as being more conducive to large-scale production. Forged from high-temperature steel, the turbine wheel had cooling airflow vanes milled into each side.

The first drawings for the I-40 were ready by September 1943 and manufacture began as soon as each drawing was issued to the workshops. In January 1944 the first I-40 was ready for testing, but for a couple of days it could not be coaxed to run. Then on 13 January it was finally brought up to a speed of 8,000rpm on an open test stand at Lynn. The turbine required redesigning. After the new one was installed, a run up to 1,816kp (4,000lb) was achieved in February.

Lockheed P-80 Shooting Star jet fighter and its descendants

In the meantime, the USAAF recognized that Bell's P-59 was not suitable for combat and ordered a new fighter, the XP-80, from Lockheed. It will be recalled that officialdom had not been interested in that company's L-133 fighter back in 1939, but now, due to the war, Lockheed was required

General Electric I-40 centrifugal turbojet (J33-GE-5). AEHS, Huntsville

to produce the XP-80 prototype in only 180 days! Kelly Johnson's team at Burbank, California, did better than that and the prototype XP-80 (83020, Lulu-Belle) was ready in 143 days. Because no American turbojet was ready, this prototype was fitted with a British de Havilland Goblin engine giving a thrust of 1,116kp (2,460lb). The Goblin had already done considerable test flying in F.9/40s (Meteors) from March 1943 and, from September, in a Vampire fighter. During the ground running in the XP-80, however, the Goblin was severely damaged when the aircraft's intake ducts collapsed, the engine suction power having been underestimated. A second Goblin was rushed out from England and fitted into the repaired aircraft. In this form the XP-80 made its maiden flight on 8 January 1944, piloted by Milo Burcham.

The all-metal XP-80, designated the P-80 Shooting Star in service, embodied not particularly advanced features, other than the turbojet, in order to achieve success in a short time. Its low-mounted wing was straight but of thin section and the tail unit was conventional. The sleek fuselage had a rounded nose and side air intakes with boundary layer suction. A long jet exhaust duct resulted. Fuel was carried in the wings and armament in the nose. A small bubble canopy enclosed the pressurized cockpit and there was a tricycle undercarriage.

It was not until 10 June 1944 that the first prototype, the XP-80A-LO (83021), was flown with a GE I-40 (J33-GE-5) turbojet, this engine giving 1,737kp (3,825lb) of thrust. This was the fourth I-40 to be produced that year and it resulted in a superior performance to that with the Goblin engine, due to the extra thrust. This was the first all-American jet fighter and during its first thirty-minute flight the XP-80A achieved a speed of more than 805km/h (500mph) and an altitude of 3,050m (10,000ft). Because of this, plans to power the fighter with the Goblin engine were dropped.

Development of the I-40 continued throughout 1944 and early 1945. Problems encountered and solved included exhaust cone buckling, carbon accretion, fuel pump wear, sticking automatic controls and turbine wheel fracturing. By June 1945 the I-40 had passed a fifty-hour Pre-Flight Rating Test (PFRT) and was showing early signs of being a reliable turbojet. It went into production as the J33 of 1,737kp (3,825lb) static thrust, water injection raising this further.

Allison production of GE's turbojets

Unfortunately GE could not produce the J33 in large quantities and was therefore persuaded by the USAAF to licence it for production by the Allison Division of General Motors. GE did produce J33s at Syracuse, New York, for a while but by October 1945 Allison assumed complete responsibility for J33 production.

Before war ended in Europe, two P-80s were in Italy being prepared for combat, primarily to intercept the Luftwaffe's Arado Ar 234 jet reconnaissance aircraft, and two more were in England, but none saw combat. By the late 1940s some twelve squadrons were operating the P-80 (now designated the F-80) throughout the USA and Alaska but the F-80 did not go into combat until 1950 in Korea. Altogether some 1,732 F-80s were built, but plans to

F-80C Shooting Star with an Allison J33-A-35 turbojet			
Span		11.81m	(38ft 9in)
Length		10.49m	(34ft 5in)
Wing area		22.07sq m	(237.6sq ft)
Height		3.43m	(11ft 3in)
Empty weight		3,819kg	(8,420lb)
Maximum take-off weight		7,646kg	(16,856lb)
Maximum speed	at sea level	956km/h	(594mph)
Service ceiling		14,265m	(46,800ft)
Range		1,328km	(825 miles)
Armament	six 0.50in machine guns, two underwing bombs		

An Allison production line for the J33 turbojet. AEHS, Huntsville

An example of the Lockheed F-80 Shooting Star (484998) straight-wing jet fighter, which was just too late to see combat in the Second World War. Powered by the J33 centrifugal turbojet and the USA's first front-line jet fighter, the F-80 served with the USAF, US Navy, US Marine Air Wing and the Air National Guard. It first saw combat in Korea.

build 5,000 were cancelled with the war's end. (For discussion of further GE turbojet development, see Chapter 21.)

Allison produced its first J33 as the J33-A-17 and this passed a 100-hour test in May 1946. Further development produced the J33-A-23, which had a static thrust of 2,088kp (4,600lb) and, with water injection, 2,450kp (5,400lb). It could operate up to an altitude of 14,478m (47,500ft). Then, after considerable effort, Allison developed an afterburner that enabled the J33-A-33 to achieve a thrust of 2,724kp (6,000lb). Continuous development brought the thrust up to 2,680kp (5,900lb) dry, or 3,495kp (7,700lb) with afterburner in the J33-A-29. In due course the J33-A-35 could operate for 1,400 hours without overhaul. Because of this success, Allison went on to produce 15,525 J33 engines for the USAF by the time production ended in 1959, thereby making it one of the most mass-produced turbojets in the world.

Further utilization of the prolific J33 turbojet

The utilization of this large number of J33s will now be briefly outlined. Although the F-80 was successfully introduced as America's first front-line jet fighter, its record was eclipsed by its two-seat trainer version, the T-33. Known initially as the TF-80C, the prototype was created by lengthening an F-80 fuselage to accommodate a second seat, both seats being under a long canopy. The prototype (48-356) first flew on 22 March 1948, piloted by Tony Le Vier. It was powered by an Allison J33-A-35 and had 870ltr (230 US gal) wingtip tanks. The T-33 (or T-Bird as it was nicknamed) saw service in many countries. Lockheed built 5,691, Canadair 656 and Kawasaki 210, making 6,557 altogether. There were many versions of the F-80 and T-33. In Canada, the type was designated CL-30 Silver Star and was powered by a Canadian-built R-R Nene turbojet.

Fears arose in the years after the war of a Soviet over-the-pole bomber attack on the USA, resulting in a requirement for patrolling interceptors. From the F-80, Lockheed developed the F-94 and created the prototype YF-94 by modifying the T-33 prototype (48-356). This was a stopgap interceptor, pending the arrival of a clean-sheet design. It was required to carry radar, a rear-seat observer and air-to-air rocket armament. Le Vier flew the prototype on 16 April 1949. The production F-94A Starfire was fitted with a J33-A-33 with afterburner to give a thrust of 2,722kp (6,000lb), but the afterburner added little to the performance over the F-80 and simply used fuel at a prodigious rate. The definitive Starfire, the F-94C, used the P&W J48-P-5 (licence-built R-R Tay). The C model was, in fact, a complete redesign.

The J33 was also used to power experimental aircraft. Because Bell's P-59 Airacomet, along with all other early jets, had poor endurance due to high fuel consumption, the company contracted to build

A Lockheed T-33 'T-Bird', the two-seat jet trainer derived from the F-80 fighter, was highly successful. Outstanding access to its Allison J33 turbojet was obtained by removal of the complete tail section, which was attached by three bolts. Note one of the engine mountings (in a clamp with a wing nut) on the forward fuselage interface. Philip Jarrett

A Lockheed F-94 Starfire two-seat patrol interceptor, powered by a J33 turbojet with afterburner. Central Arkansas Library System, AEC

the XP-83 for the USAAF. This was along similar lines to the P-59 but with a much larger fuselage to accommodate more fuel. Power was provided by two J33-GE-5 turbojets, each of 1,814kp (4,000lb) static thrust. The first flight of the XP-81 prototype (484990) was on 25 February 1945. Although its range of 2,784km (1,730 miles), with drop tanks, was more than seven times that of the P-59, its general performance was not satisfactory and so

the project was cancelled. Clearly an improvement in turbojet efficiency, rather than more fuel, was required. The Convair XP-81, with a J33 in the tail, has already been mentioned. Convair's XF-92A was a delta-wing research aircraft built under a USAF research contract; Germany's Dr Alexander Lippisch, the champion and pioneer of the delta, was a consultant on the project. It had sharply pointed delta wings and fin, and a nose intake for its J33-

A-23 engine of 2,085kp (4,600lb) thrust. Its purpose was to provide data for the design of the F-102A Delta Dagger interceptor. The first flight of the sole XF-92A (46-682) was on 18 September 1948. This aircraft was later re-engined with an Allison J33-A-29 turbojet and in this form it achieved a speed of 1,014km/h (630mph). In 1952 the XF-92A was handed over to the NACA for research.

Although certain versions of Grumman's excellent F9F Panther carrier-borne fighters were powered with Allison engines, these were all later re-engined with P&W J48 engines. The prototype XF9F-3 Panther (122476) made its first flight on 16 August 1948 with a J33-A-8 engine. Allison then proposed the J33-A-16 turbojet, which gave a take-off thrust of 3,153kp (6,950lb) with water injection, and this was tested in a Grumman F9F-4. However, it was the only one so powered due to many engine problems. It was not until the appearance of the swept-wing Panther, known as the F9F-7 Cougar, that the J33 was once more fitted to the Grumman fighters. The engine used in the F9F-7 was the J33-A-16 turbojet of 2,880kp (6,350lb) thrust.

F-80s in the Korean War

Following the outbreak of war in Korea on 25 June 1950, F-80 Shooting Stars were soon in combat. F-80Cs, powered by the Allison J33-A-23 (and later the J33-A-35) from the 8th, 49th and 51st Fighter Wings were based in Japan and sent against Soviet-built piston-engined aircraft of the North Korean Air Force. Not everyone thought this a good idea because the F-80Cs were short on endurance and their wide turning circle meant that Soviet Yak and Lavochkin fighters could easily turn inside them. On the third day of the war, F-80s of the 8th FBW's 35th Fighter Squadron out of Itazuke shot down four Ilyushin Il-10 ground attack aircraft near Seoul's Kimpo airfield. More F-80 successes followed, with two Yak-9s, for example, being shot down on 30 June. A typical technique used with F-80s was to orbit at altitude for up to twenty minutes. If enemy aircraft appeared, the F-80s would swoop on them but, if not, they would attack enemy road traffic or other targets of opportunity on their way back to Japan. Following the appearance of swept-wing Soviet MiG-15 jet fighters on 1 November 1950, straight-wing jets such as the F-80 and the British Meteor soon found themselves

The sole Convair XF-92A delta-wing research aircraft, powered by a J33-A-23 turbojet, was based on the aerodynamic work of Germany's Dr Alexander Lippisch. Central Arkansas Library System, AEC

outclassed and were therefore relegated to the ground attack role. On 8 November, however, according to the USAF, 1st Lt R.J. Brown in an F-80C found a MiG-15 below him and promptly shot it down in flames. (Disputed by the Soviets. See page 54). In the ground attack role, the F-80C was found to be a stable gun platform but somewhat fast for this duty. The F-94B night-fighter version of the Starfire saw late service in Korea and was credited with shooting down four MiG-15s at night.

TG-180 (J35) axial turbojet

As already stated, early in 1943 the USAF ordered the development of both the centrifugal I-40 (J33) and the axial TG-180 (J35) from GE. Much experience gained with development of the TG-100 (T31) turboprop, especially with the compressor, was of value in designing the TG-180 turbojet. However, having carried out all the development work, GE was to lose out to Allison on the production contracts for both the J33 and J35 engines.

Work on the TG-180 was begun on 3 May 1943 and by June its static thrust aim was raised from 1,362kp (3,000lb) to 1,816kp (4,000lb). The USAF had such faith in the TG-180 that, at an early stage in its development, it based much of its future high-altitude, long-range bomber projects on it. The layout of the engine comprised an eleven-stage axial-flow compressor with a constant tip diameter, a pressure ratio of 4:1 and an air mass flow of 34kg/sec (75lb/sec). It was driven by a single-stage, shrouded turbine and fed straight-through combustion chambers. Accessories were clustered at the front of the engine, inside a large, round-nosed fairing that was inside the air intake. Engine controls and other features were similar to those for the TG-100 turboprop.

On 21 April 1944 the TG-180-A1 was given its first test. It gave a thrust of 1,643kg/sec (3,620lb/sec) for a weight of 1,044kg (2,300lb) and no serious problems were experienced. However, when two J35 engines were delivered to the Douglas Aircraft company in November 1944 to power its XB-43 bomber prototype, one of the engines failed during ground tests: most of the compressor rotor blades came off. The next ten engines also had problems and so it was not until 17 May 1946 that the prototype of the Douglas XB-43 (44-61508) made its first flight, using two J35-GE-3s of 1,700kp (3,750lb) static thrust each. The XB-43, America's first jet bomber prototype, was ordered by the USAAF and was converted from the XB-42 Mixmaster. It had an almost straight wing, mid-mounted, conventional tail and a tricycle undercarriage. Air intakes were located at the fuselage sides for the two J35s, which were inside the fuselage and exhausted beneath the tail. Two crew were housed beneath side-by-side bubble canopies, while the bomb aimer could view through the glazed nose. The XB-43 had a maximum sea level speed of 829km/h (515mph). Due to the delays caused by engine problems, the type was overtaken by technically better designs and the two prototypes were relegated to the flying test-bed role.

XP-84 Thunderjet fighter

In the meantime, a J35-GE-7 engine was shipped to the Republic company to be installed in its XP-84 fighter, this prototype (45-59475) flying on 28 February 1946. At this time the J35 had still not passed a

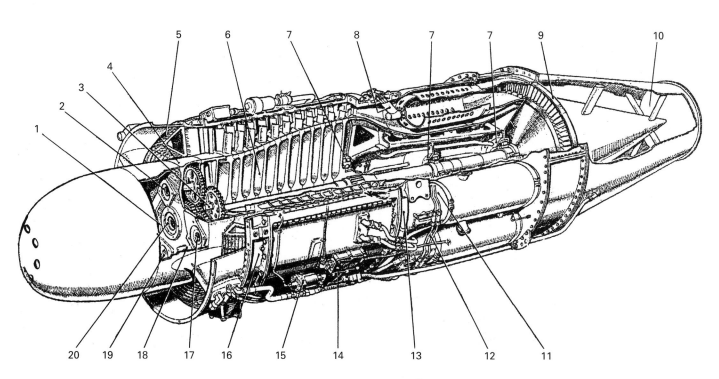

General Electric J35 axial turbojet: (1) starter drive; (2) fuel regulator drive; (3) rpm indicator and generator drive; (4) accessory gear case; (5) inlet air screen; (6) eleven-stage axial compressor; (7) anti-friction bearings (front bearing not shown); (8) fuel nozzle; (9) single-stage turbine; (10) fixed-area exhaust nozzle; (11) mid frame; (12) fuel pipes; (13) cabin pressure manifold; (14) ignition transformer; (15) flow divider; (16) forward frame; (17) fuel pump drive; (18) pressure and scavenge pump drive; (19) hydraulic pump drive; (20) auxiliary drive shaft.

A General Electric TG-180 axial turbojet on the test-bed in 1943. AEHS, Huntsville

Two views of the USA's first jet bomber prototype, the straight-winged Douglas XB-43 (461508). It was delayed due to problems with its two J35 turbojets and so was cancelled by the USAF. Central Arkansas Library System, AEC

General Electric XP-35 axial turbojet. AEHS, Huntsville

150-hour test and its service life was very low. Nevertheless, the XP-84 was destined to be a success. Later named the Thunderjet, the XP-84 was intended to carry on from where the great Republic P-47 Thunderbolt piston-engined fighter had left off. Essentially of simple layout, the all-metal XP-84 had a nose intake for the single J35 engine and a long tailpipe. Its unswept, tapered wing was attached to the fuselage below the centreline and there was a conventional tail empennage. Other features included a framed canopy, tricycle undercarriage and, later, wingtip fuel tanks. Despite a growth in weight during the design phase and then an initially poor turbojet, one of the XP-84 prototypes soon demonstrated the fighter's potential by establishing a new US speed record of 983km/h (611mph) in September 1946.

Responsibility for the J35 engine was handed to the Allison company that September. Some production had been undertaken by the Chevrolet Division of General Motors, but it voluntarily relinquished production to Allison. Soon

after the end of the war, therefore, GE had lost the production contracts for both the J33 and J35 turbojets to Allison (see Chapter 19). These engines needed much development to realize their potential and so the first American aircraft that they powered were also not performing as well as they could. With the improvement of the J33 and J35 in Allison's hands, however, the performance of these early jet fighters, especially the P-84 Thunderjet, greatly improved. Of course, this is not to say that GE did not know what they were about.

F-86 Sabre and other uses for the J35

Before leaving this period of GE's story, mention should be made of the prototypes flown in 1946 and 1947 using J35s made by GE and Chrysler. The North American FJ-1 Fury, powered by a J35-GE-2 engine of 1,733kp (3,820lb) thrust, was ordered on 1 January 1945 for evaluation by the US Navy in the carrier-borne fighter role. This

fighter had a low, straight wing, a nose intake (flanked by six machine guns) and a bubble cockpit canopy. It was possible to see in it elements of the great F-86 Sabre that was to come. The first of three prototype XFJ-1s (39053) made its maiden flight on 27 November 1946; carrier landings were not made until 10 March 1948. The maximum speed of the type was 880km/h (547mph). Only thirty production aircraft followed, powered by Allison J35-A-2 engines, but it was the first jet fighter to go to sea under operational conditions.

Also from the North American company was the USA's first four-engined jet bomber to fly, the B-45 Tornado. Studies for it had begun late in 1944 using existing bomber technology, the only advance being the use of turbojets. Reminiscent of the Soviet Ilyushin Il-28, the B-45 had a shoulder wing with a straight leading edge and slightly swept forward trailing edge. The four engines were housed in pairs in nacelles projecting well forward of the wing leading edge, and the tailplane had considerable dihedral to clear the jet exhausts. The two

P-80 and XP-84 vs Me 262: an official comparison

The following extract is taken from a letter from Army Air Forces Headquarters, Washington, DC, dated 17 October 1946, signed by Brig. Gen. L.P. Whitten and addressed to Wright Field:

1. The results of the Me 262 – P-80A comparitive speed and climb tests as outlined in Air Matériel Command Flight Test Report, Serial No. TSFTE-2008, are viewed with serious concern by this Headquarters. From the performance data submitted in this report, it is shown that the German Me 262 is superior to the P-80A in acceleration and speed, and approximately the same in rate of climb. Moreover, the Me 262's performance compares quite favourably with the XP-84 at all altitudes and is superior to the XP-84 in speed at high altitude. The fact that the design for the Me 262 originated in 1939 and that this aircraft even now can outperform our latest fighters reflects most unfavorably on the ability of American aircraft designers and on the American aircraft industry in general.

2. It is requested that a study be submitted to this office explaining in detail why the Me 262 is superior in performance to our latest fighters. In particular, the following information will be included in this report:
   a) An explanation of the design features in the Me 262 that permit it to outperform the XP-84 at altitude.
   b) An explanation of the Jumo 004 jet engine and a performance comparison among the Jumo 004 and the J33 and J35 engines at various altitudes.

On 4 December 1946, Army Air Forces, Air Matériel Command, Wright Field, replied to the above letter in the following manner:

1. The study requested in the basic letter has been accomplished and is presented herewith.

2. There are two fundamental facts contributing to the superiority of the ME-262 over present AAF fighters which must be considered before undertaking any comparison of these aircraft:
   a) The advancement of the aeronautical sciences in Germany before 1941 was greatly accelerated apparently as a result of the facilities, personnel and funds allotted to advanced research and design by the German government. This alone could account for as much as four or five years' lag in development of the science in this country.
   b) Soon after this country did begin active war-time development in 1941 it was decided, and the decision has been thoroughly justified, to concentrate the efforts of this Command and the industry on improvement and mass production of existing aircraft types to the extreme neglect of advanced research and design. This fact could account for an additional lag of two or three years in aircraft development in this country.

3. It is pointed out that since the cessation of hostilities in Europe in 1945 the efforts of this Command and the industry have been re-directed almost entirely to advanced research and design work which, with the exploitation of German developments, has in two years erased all lag in the development of aeronautical sciences in this country. It is interesting to note that the development of the ME-262 required approximately three years before the first flight, whereas our XP-80 was completely designed and built in 145 days.

4. Comparison of the physical airplanes as reported in AMC Memorandum Report No. TSFTE-2008 involved too few airplanes of each type to be truly representative of the designs. Also the lack of adequate means for measurement of thrust in flight prevents an accurate analysis of the reports for the differences in performance. However, the fact remains that the ME-262 when tested had a better high altitude performance than the No.1 XP-84. The design features of the ME-262 which permit it to out-perform our latest fighters are primarily those features which give it a slightly higher critical Mach number or better propulsive efficiency, namely:
   a) Thinner wing – 11% versus 13% for the XP-84.
   b) Symmetrical laminar flow airfoil with maximum thickness of approximately 40% chord.
   c) Sweepback of wings approximately 15°.
   d) Shorter and more direct ducting for engines.

5. The Jumo 004 jet engine has been evaluated from the standpoint of performance and maintenance, resulting in the following conclusions:
   a) The performance analysis shows slightly more thrust per pound of weight than for our engines. Thrust versus altitude curves at 500 miles per hour for two Jumo 004B units, the J-33, and the J-35 are shown in Figure I attached.
   b) Specific fuel consumption is greater than for the J-33 or J-35 by about 25%.
   c) Frontal area of the two Jumo 004B engines is approximately 37% greater than that of the J-35 giving comparable thrust.
   d) Reliability and time between overhauls for the Jumo 004B are not considered as good as for our engines.
   e) Maintenance required on the Jumo 004B is excessive.

FOR THE COMMANDING GENERAL:
J. S. STOWELL
Brigadier General, U.S.A.
Chief of Administration

General Electric J35 axial turbojets at the Consolidated Vultee Aircraft Corporation, 1949, ready for aircraft installation. AEHS, Huntsville

A Chrysler-built J35-C-3 turbojet on the test stand. Note the clamp, between the trolley wheels, to counter thrust.

The US Navy chose the straight-wing North American FJ-1 Fury carrier-borne jet fighter with its J35-GE-2 engine rather than wait for a swept-wing fighter (F-86). Central Arkansas Library System, AEC

pilots sat beneath a framed canopy, the bombardier sat in a glazed nose and the rear gunner was housed in a tail turret. The prototype XB-45 (45-59479) made its first flight from Muroc on 17 March 1947, piloted by George Krebs. The B-45A went into USAF service in November 1948 and some ninety-six examples were produced. They were powered by J35-GE-3 engines but most of these, and subsequent versions, were re-engined with J47 turbojets.

A striking, one-off bomber prototype was the Convair XB-46 (45-59582) that first flew on 2 April 1947 on the power of four Chrysler-built J35-C-3 engines, each of 1,700kp (3,750lb) thrust. The XB-46 had a long, slim fuselage with a bubble canopy and a glazed, pointed nose. A high aspect-ratio, equi-tapered, straight wing was shoulder mounted halfway along the fuselage. The four turbojets were housed in pairs in nacelles beneath the wings and the tailplane had sufficient dihedral to keep clear of the jet exhausts. A tall fin had a long, curved fillet on top of the fuselage. The maximum speed of the XB-46 was 909km/h (565mph). The USAF, however, decided in favour of Boeing's swept-wing B-47 Stratojet.

Data from German swept-wing research, which had already been applied by Messerschmitt, became available to aircraft designers after the war. Particular notice was taken at the North American company, where the project staff under J. Lee Attwood and Ray Rice were in favour of scrapping their projects with straight wings. The US Navy, however, would not concur, hence the contract for the straight-winged FJ-1 Fury (see above). On the other hand, the Army was in favour of giving North American its head and so the company promptly redesigned, before it was built, the projected XP-86 fighter with 35-degree swept-back wings. This was the origin of the F-86 Sabre, which was to become an all-time great fighter, produced just in time to challenge the Soviet swept-wing MiG-15s in Korea.

The prototype XP-86 (45-59597) made its first flight on 1 October 1947, piloted by George Welch, from Muroc. It was powered by a Chevrolet-built J35-C-3 turbojet and achieved a level speed of 986.5km/h (613mph), faster than predicted. More powerful J35s from Allison and J47s from GE were soon powering the Sabre (see Chapter 21).

The sole prototype of the finely streamlined Convair XB-46 bomber had four Chrysler-built J35-C-3 turbojets in two nacelles. Seen here landing with the ailerons augmenting the landing flaps, the XB-46 was rejected by the USAF in favour of Boeing's B-47 Stratojet. Central Arkansas Library System, AEC

CHAPTER SIXTEEN

Pratt & Whitney Aircraft Company

The Pratt & Whitney Aircraft Company (P&W) of Hartford, Connecticut, was formed on 14 July 1925 and rapidly built a reputation for reliable piston aero-engines with its Wasp and Hornet air-cooled, radial engines. Going flat out to meet wartime demands for its radial engines for the military, the company had little time to consider jet propulsion. Around 1940 one of P&W's engineers, L.S. Hobbs, did make a study of gas turbines with rotary compressors, but he rejected such engines for aeronautical use on the grounds of unacceptable fuel consumption and weight.

Kalitinsky compound engine

At about the same time, Andrew Kalitinsky of MIT proposed to P&W a supposedly more efficient type of gas turbine. Kalitinsky already had experience of gas turbines in Switzerland but the engine he proposed was derived from the so-called Gotaverken system from Sweden, which employed a diesel engine and a turbine. The diesel engine provided enough power to drive a compressor, while its exhaust drove a turbine connected to an airscrew. For boosting power over short periods, extra fuel could be burnt before the turbine and all exhaust gases provided some residual thrust. Both the diesel engine and the compressor were of the opposed-free-piston type, pioneered by Hugo Junkers. Kalitinsky's compound engine promised to give a fuel consumption about three-quarters of that of a good contemporary piston engine and it became of interest in connection with the early proposals for a long-range, strategic

bomber, which were to lead to the B-36, powered by P&W Wasp Major engines.

PT-1 turboprop test engine

P&W therefore decided, in May 1941, to begin preliminary layouts for a turboprop of up to 5,000ehp. This work indicated that the engine would weigh some 50 per cent more than a conventional piston engine but require fewer accessories. It then decided to build a test engine, designated PT-1, at its own expense. The PT-1 consisted of a turbine section, fed by an external hot gas source, and an exhaust nozzle. From the forward end of the turbine, a short shaft led to a reduction gearbox from which was driven a variable-pitch, three-bladed airscrew. This work, which was carried on until near the end of the war, was kept secret, since P&W knew the armed forces wanted the engine manufacturers to concentrate solely upon piston-engine produc-

tion for the prosecution of the war. However, the protracted development of the PT-1 meant it was already left behind by other turboprops. Therefore, after spending some $3.3 million on the project, P&W abandoned work on the PT-1 in June 1945.

PT-2 (T34) turboprop

Nevertheless, the PT-1 did provide much useful data and this was put to good use in the design of the company's next turboprop, the PT-2. Development of the PT-2, officially designated the T34, was ordered by the US Navy on 30 June 1945.

The wholesale cancellation of orders for war matériel that followed the end of war in the Pacific in August 1945 did not bode well for American industry. P&W found its work vanish overnight as orders worth $414 million immediately shrank to $3 million. The future in aeronautics seemed to be with the gas turbine in either turbojet or

Pratt & Whitney's first experimental turboprop, the PT-1. This was not intended for flight and was supplied with externally generated hot gases via the waste gate and inlet duct indicated. The exhaust nozzle is on the right.

turboprop form, not the piston engine. Furthermore, P&W was some five years behind other companies and was up against the giant companies of General Motors (Allison Division), General Electric and Westinghouse. Some prodigious leap forward was required to catch up but the company's only experience of gas turbines had been the PT-1 experiment and in manufacturing, as a sub-contractor, some Westinghouse 19XB (J30) turbojets.

There was much indecision and disagreement as to where the company's future lay and the majority of its engineers favoured having nothing to do with the gas turbine. On occasions, a shouting match developed between those in favour and those opposed to the new forms of powerplant. Eventually a decision was made to enter the gas turbine field wholeheartedly and to build the gas turbine development facilities known as the Willgoos Laboratory. Construction of this facility, named after P&W's Chief Engineer, Andrew Van Dean Willgoos, began in March 1947 at a cost of $15 million – more than the net worth of the company at that time.

At first, P&W wanted to develop its own engines and actually turned down offers in 1945 to build all of GE's designs and a free licence to build the British R-R Nene turbojet. (The next year Phil Taylor of Pan American Airways bought the Nene licence, since it appeared to him that jet airliners were on the horizon.)

As for the PT-2 (T34) turboprop, development of this engine was actually beyond the company when it was ordered by the Navy in 1945, making the success of the Willgoos Laboratory all the more important. The initial design goal was to produce 3,550ehp and, since it was for naval use, extensive use of stainless steel was to be made. The T34 was the first gas turbine engine designed by P&W to reach the flight stage. It had a thirteen-stage axial flow compressor, a cannular combustion chamber and a three-stage turbine. In September 1947 the first test took place, but the engine could not run in a sustained manner. After redesign, especially to the compressor, a test run was made in December 1949 and 5,375shp was produced. The air mass flow was 29.5kg/sec (65lb/sec) and the compression ratio was 6.7:1. On 22 February 1950 the T34 passed a fifty-hour PFRT at 5,700shp and then made its first flight, in the nose of a Boeing B-17 Flying Fortress bomber, on 5 August 1950. Further development brought the T34 up to 7,500eshp, with water injection, and it went into production in 1953. Some 485 T34s were built by P&W and it was used to power the four-engined Douglas C-133 Cargomaster military transport, first flown on 23 April 1956.

J42 turbojet (R-R Nene)

Meanwhile, the US Navy decided in 1947 that it needed the British centrifugal R-R Nene of 2,270kp (5,000lb) thrust to upgrade its Grumman F9F Cougar fighters, which were powered with the J33 of 1,816kp (4,000lb) thrust. P&W was then asked to manufacture the Nene and reluctantly agreed to do so, at the same time getting the Navy to pay all development costs and the purchase of the Nene licence from Pan Am.

Already, in July 1945, the USAAF had test flown a Lockheed P-80 Shooting Star with a Nene engine. In 1947, the Soviets, who were much impressed with British turbojets, began copying the Derwent turbojet and, to a large extent, the Nene; one wonders how much of this work, if any, was known in the USA. P&W then set about translating British Nene drawings, which they began receiving in July 1947, to use American accessories and to make it suitable for mass production. Since the Nene was not being mass produced in Britain, P&W had to design and procure thousands of machine tools and convert much of its factory space for turbojet production. Under the direction of Willard L. Gorton, the first drawings were ready by August 1947, and the Nene was officially designated the J42. The Navy selected the

Pratt & Whitney's PT-2 (T34) turboprop was the company's first gas turbine engine to reach the flight testing stage. It went into production in 1953. Illustrated is the T34-P-3 of 5,700shp.

At the request of the US Navy, the Rolls-Royce Nene was Americanized as the J42 by Pratt & Whitney.

Nene for use in its fighters because of its power, high power-to-weight ratio, its reliability and durability. In addition, the Navy wanted it to stimulate competition between American turbojet manufacturers and this ploy was highly successful, to the extent that the J42 soon became known as the 'needle engine'.

In any event, the Navy had given P&W only some seventeen months in which to produce the first J42s, a difficult task, and the first engines had to roll off the East Hartford production line by November 1948. Not least of the problems was satisfying the requirement that the J42 had to be capable of running on gasoline as well as the British kerosene fuels. The first P&W J42 was running on 6 March 1948 and completed its 150-hour MQT seven months later, at ratings of 2,270kp (5,000lb) static thrust and, with water injection, 2,610kp (5,750lb) static thrust. A J42-P-6 engine was first flown in a production Grumman F9F-2 Panther fighter (122560) on 24 November 1948.

J48 turbojet (R-R Tay)

Meanwhile, back in England, Rolls-Royce continued development of the basic Nene in accordance with an agreement with P&W and also for its own benefit. The initial aim of this continued development was to obtain 30 per cent more thrust without significantly increasing the external dimensions. P&W also played its part in this development and, eventually, continued this on its own. This led to a J42 of 2,838kp (6,250lb) static thrust, which was renamed the Tay in England and the J48 in the USA. The first test flight of the XJ48-P-6 was made in the prototype of the Grumman XF9F-5 Panther (123085) on 21 December 1949, this version becoming the most important of the Panthers. Then, on 19 January 1950, the first aerial afterburning tests were made with a J48-P-3 in the prototype Lockheed YF-94C Starfire (50-955), the afterburning producing a thrust of 3,768kp (8,300lb). This illustrated the USAF's interest in the J48.

Employment of the J42 and J48 engines

Other USAF jets were soon being tested with the J48 engine. On 25 January 1950 the North American YF-93A/YF-86C (48-316) began service tests with a J48-P-3 with afterburner, and a production Lockheed F-94C Starfire (50-956) was flown with a J48-P-5A with afterburner in July 1951. On 20 September 1951 the first prototype (126670) of the swept-wing Panthers, designated XF9F-6 Cougar, was flown, powered by the J48-P-8, which by now was giving a static thrust of 3,178kp (7,000lb). By November 1952 the F9F-6 was in production.

Although the F9F-5 was the best of the straight-wing Panthers (595 were built), it was the J42-powered F9F-2 that saw action in Korea. These were no match for the similarly powered but swept-wing MiG-15s, but Lt Cdr William T. Amen, the commander of VF-111 (aboard the carrier USS *Philippine Sea*), shot down a MiG-15

A Pratt & Whitney J48 centrifugal turbojet, developed jointly by P&W and Rolls-Royce from the J42 to give more thrust and known in England as the Tay. AEHS, Huntsville

Preparing to attach the afterburner to a P&W J48 turbojet, beneath a Boeing B-29 flying test-bed. The exhaust nozzle of the J48 is temporarily taped over to prevent the ingress of debris. AEHS, Huntsville

A US Navy Grumman F9F-5 Panther (125240), powered by a P&W J48 centrifugal turbojet. Earlier F9F-2s were powered with Allison J33 engines and were active in the Korean War; no match for the MiG-15, Panthers were nevertheless potent fighter bombers. Central Arkansas Library System, AEC

on 9 November 1950. The Panthers were normally used in the ground attack role, their armament being four 20mm M3 cannon and underwing rockets or bombs. A total of 740 Panthers of all types were built.

In the F9F-6 Cougar, the features of a 35-degree swept-back wing and the more powerful J48 engine considerably increased the fighter's speed. Cougars were reaching Korea as the war there ended. In January 1954 the first F9F-8 Cougar exceeded Mach 1 (in a shallow dive): this was one of the few occasions when a centrifugal turbojet went supersonic. More than 3,400 F9Fs of all types, including reconnaissance and

trainer types, were built. The successful production of British-derived centrifugal engines (in turn, derived from Whittle's work) by P&W resulted in about 1,150 J42s and 4,100 J48s being delivered to the US Navy and USAF combined. This production work enabled P&W to enter the turbojet field quickly and gain important official contracts, while at the same time continuing independent development work on its axial turboprops.

Late in the 1940s a Congressional Committee, known as the McClellan Committee, subpoenaed people to answer the question of why British engines were always better than American ones. The

consensus was that the situation would be reversed if American companies had the same funding as the British. In view of Britain's parlous post-war economic state, this reasoning is not plausible. Nobody seems to have mentioned the officially encouraged lack of technical interchange between American companies working in the gas turbine field. However, great American engines were still to come, such as P&W's own J57 turbojet (see Chapter 25), and during the mid-1950s GE and other companies began head-hunting in Europe for engineers to expand their development work.

Grumman F9F-2 Panther			
Span	over wingtip fuel tanks	11.58m	(37ft 11¾ in)
Length		11.35m	(37ft 3in)
Wing area		23.22sq m	(250sq ft)
Empty weight		4,533kg	(9,993lb)
Loaded weight		8,842kg	(19,494lb)
Maximum speed	at 6,700m (22,000ft)	877km/h	(545mph)
Initial climb rate		1,567m/min	(5,140ft/min)
Range with drop tanks		2,177km	(1,353 miles)

A line-up of US Navy F9F-6 Cougars, lashed down on the carrier deck. Powered by the P&W J48-P-8 turbojet, the Cougar had 35-degree swept-back wings. Central Arkansas Library System, AEC

Pratt & Whitney J48 turbojet with afterburner. AEHS, Huntsville

CHAPTER SEVENTEEN

Allis-Chalmers

In 1941 the engineering company of Allis-Chalmers was asked by the US Navy to work on a ducted-fan turbojet. It was brought into this field because it had some experience of industrial gas turbines, being licensees of the Swiss company of Brown Boveri. A contract was issued in January 1942 but the resulting work was so slow that the contract was cancelled in June 1943. The company was then ordered to produce the British de Havilland Goblin centrifugal turbojet under licence, the engine being officially designated the J36. Unfortunately the company's work was once again very desultory, and the contract was cancelled after only seven J36s were built.

The J36, rated at 1,225kp (2,700lb) static thrust, was tested in an XP-80 Shooting Star prototype. The engine was also used in three prototypes of a mixed-powerplant, single-seat fighter ordered by the Navy from Curtiss in April 1944. These aircraft were designated XF-15C and each was to have a P&W 2,100hp radial piston engine and airscrew in the nose and a J36 turbojet mounted in the centre fuselage beneath a long fuselage tail section. The XF-15C was an all-metal, low-wing monoplane with retractable tricycle undercarriage and a bubble canopy over the cockpit. The first was flown on 27 February 1945, without the turbojet installed, but crashed that May. The other two prototypes flew with both engines installed but the conventional tail unit was modified to one using an innovative T-tail. Limited test flying was carried out by the Navy during 1946, the maximum speed reached, using both engines, being 755km/h (469mph). This ended Allis-Chalmers's brief foray into turbojets.

CHAPTER EIGHTEEN

Westinghouse Electric Corporation

The Westinghouse Electric Corporation, since 1900 one of the world's largest manufacturers of steam turbines and heavy electrical equipment, built and ran the first American-designed turbojet, the 19A. This was achieved in March 1943, some eleven months after GE ran the first American-built turbojet, its Type I. Westinghouse had never built an aero-engine previously, and its achievement is all the more remarkable for being made only sixteen months after beginning work in this field.

Westinghouse's interest in the turbojet had been stimulated by the Durand Special Committee (see Chapter 15). Early in 1941 Dr L.W. Chubb, the director of the Westinghouse Research Laboratories (WRL), was appointed a member of the NACA Special Committee to look into the possibilities of using the gas turbine for jet propulsion in aircraft. Dr Stewart Way of WRL made calculations of the thrust to be expected from a turbojet and reported his findings to the Committee in August 1941. On 8 December 1941, the day after the Japanese attack on Pearl Harbor precipitated war in the Pacific, Westinghouse asked the US Navy how they could best fit into the Navy's engine development programme. Due to their work on the main propulsion machinery for warships, Westinghouse was already held in high esteem by the Navy. On 7 January 1942, therefore, the Navy requested that Westinghouse design a small turbojet as a take-off booster for carrier-borne aircraft. The thrust required equated to about 500kp (1,100lb) static at sea level.

The axial 19A 'Yankee', the first American-designed turbojet

During the course of the war, the military services had under contract the development of seven turboprops, five turbojets and three pulsejets, plus several ramjet design studies. Westinghouse and GE were to be at the forefront of this development plethora. On 22 October 1942, Westinghouse was given the order to construct two prototypes of a 0.48m (19in) diameter axial turbojet, the diameter leading to the designation of 19A. Later, to accentuate that it was an all-American turbojet, it was named the 'Yankee'. Work began at the company's South Philadelphia plant on the Delaware River and was undertaken by engineers of the Steam Division.

The engineering team was led by the manager of development engineering, Reinout P. Kroon, while combustion research was directed by Dr Stewart Way in the research laboratories. By mid-December 1941 Westinghouse had brought together a team of fourteen engineers and nine skilled experimental mechanics. The first design studies were made by Dr Way. In February 1945 a new division, the Aviation Gas Turbine Division, was formed, headed by Kroon.

Design of the 19A Yankee turbojet was begun on 10 August 1942. It had a six-stage axial compressor, a twenty-four-can cannular combustion chamber and a single-stage turbine. The compressor was designed for a pressure ratio of 3.4:1 and the conical can-type combustors were arranged in groups of three around the annulus. The exhaust nozzle area could be varied by means of a movable tail cone (similar to previous German practice) and the accessories were enclosed within the compressor cone to minimize the frontal

A Westinghouse 19A 'Yankee' axial turbojet, stood on its intake, in the Science Museum, London. This small engine was the first all-American turbojet, hence the name. Note the criss-cross bracing ribs on the compressor casing. Author

area. The 19A was a three-bearing engine and was designed to run on gasoline as per the piston engine or engines of the aircraft to be boosted.

On 19 March 1943 the first run was made with the 19A turbojet, the static thrust developed being 515kp (1,135lb). Lewis Smith, a Bureau of Aeronautics engineer, tells us of an interesting incident that occurred while the 19A was being tested outdoors at night at the South Philadelphia plant: 'Sparks came out of the tailpipe. They shut down and inspected the engine, but could find nothing wrong. After starting again, more sparks came out. They finally found that mosquitoes were being ingested and catching fire in the combustor. They were so large they were still burning out the tailpipe – which gives a good idea of the size of the mosquitoes along the Delaware River!' By July that year a 19A had passed a 100-hour endurance test, but not without problems. These included overheating of the bearings, excessive oil consumption, a turbine failure and difficulty in operating the movable tail cone. On 21 January 1944 the second 19A prototype was flown for the first time, using a Vought FG-1 Corsair as a test-bed. (The Corsair was an outstanding piston-engined naval fighter. One even shot down a MiG-15 jet in Korea, but was itself shot down by another MiG-15 seconds later.) The inverted gull wings and long undercarriage legs of the Corsair made plenty of room for the turbojet to be carried beneath the fuselage.

The US Navy was impressed by the progress made by Westinghouse, unaided by the British, and considered that the 19A

engine was superior in many respects to British engines, but said nothing about engine life. This was the second axial turbojet to run outside of Germany. The 19A gave, at the most, 545kp (1,200lb) of static thrust; six were built altogether. Westinghouse had done well in this initial development, but its work was to slow down due to a lack of engine development facilities, lack of experience of precision aero-engines and, according to the Navy, a lack of effort.

19XB (J30) turbojet

Further development of the 19A engine was undertaken. The 19B (military designation J30) was to have a static thrust of 613kp (1,350lb) and be used as the main propulsion engine for an aircraft, rather than just a booster. Consequently, more accessories had to added. The layout of the compressor and turbine was similar to the 19A, but four extra stages were added to the compressor to give ten in all. The previous cannular combustion system was replaced by an annular one designed by Dr Way. Redesign of the compressor and combustion system accounted for the increased thrust and overall dimensions were not increased. The 19B came out at a weight of 332kg (731lb) and the specific fuel consumption was 1.27. The first flight test of the 19B was made on 28 September 1944, using a twin-engined Martin JM-1 Marauder as a test-bed. Already in January of that year, however, a production contract for 500 19XB turbojets had been awarded

to P&W, although this was cut back to 190 engines with the end of the war. The 19XB (J30) incorporated improvements developed by Westinghouse.

FH-1 Phantom and the first US carrier jet fighter operations

The main use for the J30 engine was to power the Navy's McDonnell XFD-1. In 1942 the US Navy entrusted the comparatively inexperienced McDonnell Aircraft Corporation with designing and building two prototypes of what was to evolve into the Navy's first turbojet-powered, single-seat carrier fighter, the FD-1 (later FH-1) Phantom (long before the F-4 Phantom). The XFD-1 was a low-wing monoplane with straight, folding wings and a conventional tail empennage, though with a tall fin. Its two J30 turbojets were mounted in the wing roots, and the cockpit was positioned forward of the wing. The retractable undercarriage was of the tricycle type and the armament comprised four 0.50in machine guns mounted in the nose. One aim of the design was to keep it simple for both production and maintenance.

Because only one 19XB-2B (J30) was available, the first XFD-1 used this to make a short hop along the runway at St Louis on 2 January 1945. Once the second engine was installed, the aircraft made its first true flight on 26 January 1945. The second XFD-1, piloted by US Navy pilot Lt Cdr J. Davidson, made the first take-off and landing by an all-jet fighter from an

Westinghouse J30 axial turbojet, developed from its 19A and 19B engines.

Coming in for a deck landing, one of the US Navy's first single-seat jet fighters, a McDonnell FH-1 Phantom (first use of that name). It was powered by two Westinghouse J30 turbojets.
Central Arkansas Library System, AEC

American aircraft carrier on 19 July 1946, the carrier being the USS *Franklin D. Roosevelt*.

Problems with the 19XB engine centred largely around its combustion, which was unstable at altitude. Also, temperature distribution around the annulus and at the turbine inlet nozzles was uneven and this led to a reduced life for the combustion chamber and turbine. The combustion problems meant the operating altitude was limited to about 9,150m (30,000ft), whereas the XFD-1 was designed for a ceiling of 12,500m (41,000ft). Range was also reduced by this problem. Maximum speed of the XFD-1 was to be 771km/h (479mph) at sea level, but it is not known if this was achieved. This fighter entered service as the FH-1 Phantom in May 1948 but only sixty were built. VF-17A had the distinction of being the world's first carrier-based jet fighter squadron. The FH-1 was deemed a success and was developed into the McDonnell F2H Banshee with more powerful Westinghouse J34 engines.

Another, more obscure, use for the J30 engine was in the Northrop XP-79A Flying Ram. This bizarre aircraft was designed to dive on enemy bombers and slice their tails off. The aircraft was a small flying wing with two vertical fins, two turbojets and a prone position for the pilot. Its construction was of heavy-gauge magnesium and steel armour plate. The only flight of the sole XP-79B (43-52437) took place from Muroc on 12 September 1945, but the aircraft crashed fatally following a spin.

J32 expendable turbojet

Apart from developing the J30 from the basic 19A engine, Westinghouse had also derived two other engines from it by January 1944. One was a smaller 0.24m (9½in) diameter turbojet for missile use, designated the J32. It was first tested in June 1944 and produced a static thrust of 125kp (275lb). However, it never went into production owing to its high cost and the decision that rockets were adequate for missile use. Some early use was also made of the pulsejet and, later, the ramjet.

24C (J34) axial turbojet

Of far greater importance was the 24C turbojet, which was derived from the 19A as a larger engine to give a thrust of 1,362kp (3,000lb). The US Navy designated it the J34. Although not a great engine, the J34 was destined to be Westinghouse's best to date and the most used by the Navy up to that time. As its designation implies, the 24C turbojet was 24in (0.61m) in diameter. Its rotary system was similar to the 19A but with an eleven-stage compressor and a two-stage turbine. This compressor could deliver an air mass flow of only 22.7kg/sec (50lb/sec) at a pressure ratio of 3.85:1, and so the engine's specific fuel consumption was no better than that obtained with a centrifugal engine. The compressor's performance was later improved slightly. The combustion system was of a double

concentric annular form with twenty-four downstream burners around the inner flame tube and thirty-six around the outer flame tube. Accessories were grouped outside the front of the engine and in the rounded-nose centre-body in the air intake. An oil cooler was formed as part of the air intake casing.

The 24C turbojet was first tested in April 1945 and typically delivered a static thrust of 1,362kp (3,000lb) for a weight of 570kg (1,255lb). It was first test flown in the prototype of the Chance Vought XF6U-1 Pirate (33532) on 2 October 1946 from Muroc. At that time the 24C was designated as the J34-WE-30 and, with an afterburner in operation, could develop a thrust of 1,816kp (4,000lb). The Pirate was Vought's first jet aircraft and three prototypes were ordered by the US Navy in December 1944. It was a straight-wing fighter with wing-root intakes and wingtip fuel tanks. The cockpit was mounted well forward, near the nose, and it had a tricycle undercarriage and four nose-mounted 20mm cannon. Of special interest was the airframe construction using the company's patented Metalite skins. These consisted of alloy skins bonded with a balsawood core, giving great strength with lightness. The production F6U-1 Pirate entered Navy service in August 1949 but only thirty examples were built. Its maximum speed was 908km/h (564mph).

The McDonnell XF2H-1 Banshee naval fighter was a more important project, the prototype of which (99858) first flew on 11 January 1947 using two J34-WE-22 turbojets. As already mentioned, the F2H Banshee followed on from the success of the FH-1 Phantom. Although still of straight-wing configuration, the Banshee was sleeker and more powerful than the Phantom and was powered, in the case of the production F2H-3 version, by two J34-WE-34 engines of 1,475kp (3,250lb) static thrust each. Consequently its maximum speed went up to 933km/h (580mph) at sea level. The Banshee entered service in August 1948 and it performed as an escort fighter during the Korean War. A total of 892, including fighter and reconnaissance versions, were built and it stayed in service until the mid-1960s. In November 1955 some thirty-nine were transferred to the Royal Canadian Navy, thereby becoming that force's first operational jet fighters.

An interesting use of Westinghouse's J34 was in the powering of the Douglas D-558-2 Skyrocket research aircraft. The Skyrocket was developed from the earlier

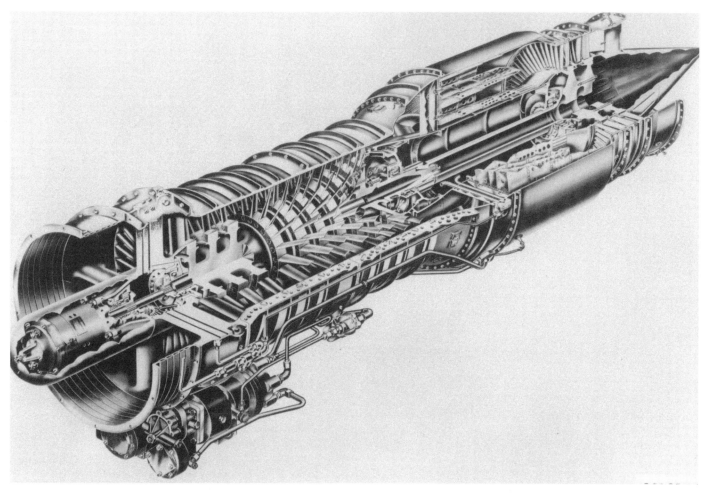

Westinghouse 24C (J34) axial turbojet in section. AEHS, Huntsville

D-558-1 Skystreak (see Chapter 19). A joint NACA/US Navy research programme had the aim of researching higher speeds than the world record of 1,031.04km/h (640.66mph) set by the Skystreak on 20 August 1947. The single 2,268kp (5,000lb) thrust Allison J35 turbojet of the Skystreak was replaced in the Skyrocket by a Westinghouse J34 turbojet plus a 2,722kp (6,000lb) thrust XLR-8 rocket motor. Furthermore, straight flying surfaces were all replaced with swept surfaces, the wings being swept at 35 degrees. It was necessary to enlarge the fuselage to accommodate the mixed powerplant. There was a tricycle undercarriage and air intakes were located in the bottom of the forward fuselage. A particular feature was the emergency jettisonable nose section, from which the pilot could bale out once it had slowed down and descended to an acceptable height. Three examples of the D-558-2 Skyrocket were built, the first (37973) making its maiden flight on 4 February

1948. The Skyrocket programme was highly successful. Due to its high wing loading and low turbojet thrust, however, it became necessary to employ two jettisonable rocket units during take-off, the main rocket motor being reserved for the research flying. This then led to launching being made from a Boeing P2B-1S mother aircraft. Eventually, on 20 November 1953, the Skyrocket became the first piloted aircraft to exceed twice the speed of sound when Mach 2.05 was recorded.

An entirely different experimental aircraft was the XP-87, later named Blackhawk, from the Curtiss company. This was ordered by the USAAF in 1945 as a two-seat, all-weather interceptor. It had straight flying surfaces and was powered by four J34-WE-40 turbojets, paired in wing-mounted nacelles. These nacelles extended considerably fore and aft of the wing, their weight resulting in the wing being mounted mid-way along the fuselage. A bubble canopy enclosed the cockpit, and the

undercarriage was of the tricycle type. Armed with four 20mm cannon, the Blackhawk was a large aircraft, its span being 18.29m (60ft 0in) and its maximum take-off weight 22,634kg (49,900lb). The prototype (45-59600) made its first flight on 5 March 1948. Despite its good performance, including a top speed of 966km/h (600mph), the Army decided to cancel it in favour of Northrop's F-89 Scorpion.

To meet a US Navy requirement for a jet-powered, carrier-based, night-fighter, Douglas produced three prototypes under the designation XF3D-1. The first of these (121457) made its maiden flight on 23 March 1948, powered by two Westinghouse J34-WE-22 engines of 1,360kp (3,000lb) static thrust. The type was a mid-wing monoplane, the wings being of straight, equi-taper planform, with hydraulic folding for carrier stowage. The pilot and radar operator were accommodated side-by-side under a canopy well forward on the fuselage

TOP: This Consolidated B-24 Liberator bomber was used as a flying test-bed for a partially cowled Westinghouse 24C (future J34) axial turbojet suspended from an underwing pylon.

CENTRE: Westinghouse 24C-4B (J34-WE-22) turbojet. AEHS, Huntsville

BOTTOM: McDonnell F2H-2N Banshee night-fighter, powered by two Westinghouse J34 turbojets. The Banshee served with the US Navy in Korea. Central Arkansas Library System, AEC

A Douglas F3D-2N Skynight two-seat night-fighter, powered by two Westinghouse J34-WE-36 turbojets. Only the US Marine Corps used the Skynight, shooting down six aircraft, including four MiG-15s, in Korea. One of these victories was the first by a jet aircraft over another at night. Central Arkansas Library System, AEC

Douglas F3D-2 Skynight		
Span	15.24m	(50ft 0in)
Length	13.97m	(45ft 6in)
Wing area	37.16sq m	(400sq ft)
Empty weight	8,237kg	(18,160lb)
Maximum take-off weight	12,179kg	(26,850lb)
Maximum speed at 6,100m (20,000ft)	909km/h	(565mph)
Service ceiling	11,645m	(38,200ft)
Range	1,930km	(1,200 miles)

nose. Nacelles for the two engines were located beneath the wing roots, the intakes extending well forward beneath the forward fuselage. Armament was four 20mm cannon and there was a tricycle undercarriage, landing hook and provision for underwing drop tanks. The first production models, designated F3D-1 Skynight, used uprated J34-WE-34 engines of 1,474kp (3,250lb) static thrust, but the main production model was the F3D-2, which used J34-WE-36 turbojets of 1,542kp (3,400lb) static thrust. Only the US Marine Corps used the F3D-2 in combat, enjoying considerable success in the Korean War using it as an all-weather fighter. In fact, the Skynight scored the first jet aircraft victory over another at night when one shot down a MiG-15 on 2 November 1952. Skynights, of which 237 were built, accounted for the majority of all US Navy and USMC victories in Korea.

Some continued flying in the electronic countermeasures role as late as 1969 in Vietnam.

A strange, experimental aircraft using the J34 engine about this time was the McDonnell XF-85 Goblin parasite, escort fighter. Since early jet fighters had nothing like the range required to escort bombers, the idea was for the Goblin fighter to be carried within, launched from and recovered by a mother bomber, so providing it with protection when needed. Two prototypes were ordered by the USAAF in March 1947. The Goblin featured a short, fat fuselage, barely large enough to accommodate the pilot and a single J34-WE-7 engine with a nose air intake. The low-set, swept-back wings were foldable and there were six tail surfaces spaced around the rear fuselage. No undercarriage was required, only skids for emergency landing, but there

was a retractable hook to engage in a trapeze on the bomber for recovery. The first XF-85 Goblin (46-523) was launched from a Boeing EB-29 on 23 August 1948, but the two prototypes were soon abandoned when it was found that turbulence around the bomber adversely affected the control of the little fighter. Furthermore, it was realized that this tiny fighter, with a wingspan of only 6.44m (21ft 1½in), would be no match for enemy fighters in prospect.

Another strange-looking but more successful J-34-powered fighter was the Chance Vought XF7U-1, later named the Cutlass. Three prototypes were ordered by the US Navy on 25 June 1946, the first (122472) making its first flight on 29 September 1948. It was powered by two J34-WE-22 turbojets and piloted by Robert Baker. The XF7U-1 had a low-aspect-ratio wing, swept back 38 degrees with two large, swept fins on its trailing edges. There was no horizontal tail surface. Outboard of the fins, the wings were foldable. Large leading edge slats were fitted to the wings, which also had trailing edge elevons. The pressurized cockpit was set well forward in the nose and was equipped with an ejection seat. When on the ground, the aircraft had a pronounced nose-up attitude, due to the long nosewheel leg of the tricycle undercarriage. The two Westinghouse J34-WE-22 engines of 1,362kp (3,000lb) static thrust each were housed side-by-side in the rear fuselage, their air intake ducts being formed between the fuselage sides and the wing roots, with plain inlets. Among the many advanced features of the XF7U-1 were the powered controls with artificial feel and an automatic stabilization system. It was also the first US Navy aircraft capable of being catapulted off a deck with a substantial external stores load (up to 2,270kg or 5,000lb) and became the Navy's first production aircraft to achieve supersonic flight (in a dive).

Unfortunately the Cutlass prototypes and the first few production aircraft (F7U-1s) were plagued with airframe and J34 engine problems. All three prototypes and several early production aircraft crashed. Much development and redesign led to the F7U-3 Cutlass, which was at first powered by Allison J35-A-29 engines, but then by Westinghouse J46-WE-8A engines that each provided a thrust of 2,767kp (6,100lb) with afterburning. Entering US Navy service in 1950, the Cutlass was normally armed with four 20mm cannon and could carry underwing stores; it was the first to use the Sparrow I beam-riding air-to-air missile. A total of 286 production Cutlasses were built, including two used as individual performers in the Blue Angels aerobatic team.

Alongside the US Navy, the USAAF was also ordering more fighters to be powered by the J34 engine, the next being the McDonnell XF-88 (Voodoo) and the Lockheed XF-90 prototypes. With increased production for the military foreseen, Westinghouse was authorized to reopen the US Navy's Industrial Reserve Aircraft Plant in Kansas City, Missouri, and fit it out for turbojet production, initially for the J34. This plant began production in January 1951 and more than 4,500 J34s were built by Westinghouse, P&W and the Ford Motor Company; turbojet parts were also to be made in Columbus, Ohio. Only the XF-88 prototypes of the Voodoo were powered by J34 engines and, owing to their inadequate power, the USAF terminated the programme. The Voodoo was envisaged in 1946 as a long-range escort fighter for the USAAF and the first prototype (46-525) made its maiden flight on 20 October 1948, using two J34-WE-13 engines. Later, with the outbreak of the Korean War, the XF-88 was revived in improved form as the F-101 but with very much more powerful P&W J57 engines (see Chapter 25). Only in a dive could the J34-powered XF-88 exceed Mach 1.0.

On 14 April 1953 an XF-88 made its first flight as the three-engined XF-88B, with an Allison XT38A turboprop driving a small, supersonic airscrew in the nose and the two J34 turbojets with afterburners. The intention was to extend the range of the fighter by flying on the turboprop and then use the turbojets for speed, as required; in this it failed, but part of the exercise was to test the XT38A turboprop.

As for the Lockheed XF-90, as with the XF-88, the J34 engine proved again to be the downfall of a potentially great fighter. The XF-90 was also designed to meet a USAAF requirement for a long-range escort fighter for its bombers. Long range for jet aircraft was proving very hard to obtain in those days, but Lockheed's 'Kelly' Johnson used the very latest knowledge of aerodynamics in the quest for a speedy fighter. The XF-90 had a very sleek fuselage with a long, pointed nose, its rear-hinged bubble cockpit canopy fairing back into a very long strake that led into the swept-back vertical fin. The wings were low-mounted and swept back at 35 degrees, the

Powered by two Westinghouse J34 turbojets, the Chance Vought F7U Cutlass was highly unconventional in configuration. This F7U-3M version was armed with Sparrow I beam-riding air-to-air missiles and was one of the first aircraft in service with guided air-to-air missiles. Central Arkansas Library System, AEC

Chance Vought F7U-3 Cutlass			
Span		12.09m	(39ft 8in)
Length		13.13m	(43ft 1in)
Wing area		46.08sq m	(496sq ft)
Height		5.37m	(14ft 7½in)
Empty weight		8,260kg	(18,210lb)
Maximum take-off weight		14,353kg	(31,642lb)
Maximum speed	at 3,050m (10,000ft)	1,094km/h or Mach 0.92	(680mph)
Service ceiling		12,200m	(40,000ft)
Range		1,062km	(660 miles)

tailplane also being sharply swept back and mounted a third of the way up the fin. Air intakes for the two J34-WE-11 turbojets (with afterburners) flanked the fuselage sides and had boundary layer bleed slots. Fuel cells were fitted between the engines and there were also jettisonable wingtip fuel tanks. Armament was planned as a devastating six 20mm cannon. Apart from power-boosted controls, there was the unusual feature of an adjustable-incidence tailplane that pivoted at its forward end along with the entire upper portion of the vertical fin. The first XF-90 (46-687) made its maiden flight on 3 June 1949 from Muroc, the pilot being Tony Le Vier. The type was badly underpowered and, even

with afterburners (and rocket assistance used in the second prototype), a long take-off run resulted. The XF-90 could exceed Mach 1.0 in a dive, but it was cancelled by May 1950. By then the Banshee, Skynight and Cutlass were in production, all with J34 engines.

One of the most striking experimental aircraft of all time, the Douglas X-3, later named the Stiletto, appeared in 1952. This was designed as a high-speed research aircraft for speeds up to Mach 2.20, one of its research aims being to investigate the effects of kinetic heating on the airframe. It was ordered by the USAF's Air Research and Development Command and was also sponsored by the US Navy, USAF and

NACA. Design work began in 1945 following general arrangement studies under Frank Fleming. Owing to the complexity of the task, however, a mock-up was not built until August 1948 and the order for two prototypes was not given until June 1949. The X-3 had a long, needle nose surmounted by two air intakes that led down to J34-WE-17 turbojets with afterburners. From the top of the fuselage a tail boom led back, over the exhaust pipes, to support the tail empennage. The wing was very small, straight and very thin. There were small, wedge-shaped windows for the pilot just in front of the air intakes, but his view was extremely poor, making an aircraft that was already difficult to handle very tricky to land. Apart from anything else, the pilot had to look through small windows set at an extremely oblique angle.

During the construction of the X-3, many problems had to be overcome in the use of titanium in certain areas. There was further complexity in the task of connecting 590kg (1,300lb) of instrumentation to 850 pin-hole orifices and 150 temperature points distributed over the airframe, plus some 185 strain gauges to record air loads and stresses. The first flight of the only X-3 to fly (49-2892) took place on 15 October 1952, when William Bridgeman inadvertently took off during a high-speed taxi test and flew for one mile at Edwards AFB. Bridgeman made the first official flight on 20 October. Because the J34-WE-17 turbojets gave only 1,544kp (3,400lb) of thrust each (1,907kp/4,200lb with afterburning), the X-3 was badly underpowered. This, coupled with its very high wing loading of 699kg/sq m (143.18lb/sq ft), resulted in an extremely long take-off run, until around 420km/h (260mph) was reached.

Underpowering also resulted in the X-3 not reaching its research objectives. About two-thirds of its fifty-four flights reached just over Mach 1.0 by diving, the highest speed of Mach 1.21 being reached on 28 July 1953. Although its design and research objectives were far from fulfilled, the X-3 pioneered titanium construction. Also, its aerodynamic data, mainly concerning its wing, proved useful in the design of Lockheed's F-104 Starfighter. Furthermore, during a flight in October 1954 the phenomenon of inertia (or roll) coupling was experienced and this led to the solution of a similar problem with North American's F-100 Super Sabre. One of the most surprising things about the X-3 is that, thanks

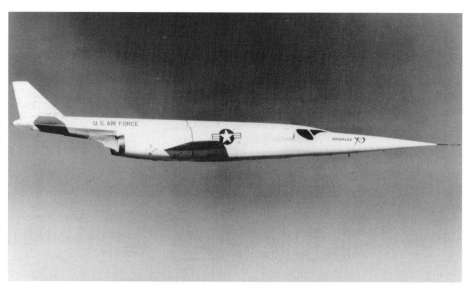

The only Douglas X-3 'Stiletto' (92892) to fly. This striking research aircraft, with its very small, thin wings, was designed to investigate kinetic heating at speeds up to Mach 2.20. However, its two Westinghouse J34-WE-17 turbojets were not powerful enough and the highest speed reached was Mach 1.21. Nevertheless, the X-3 was flown for more than three and a half years, from 1952, and without accident, thanks to the skill of its pilots.

Douglas X-3 Stiletto		
Span	6.91m	(22ft 8¼in)
Length	20.34m	(66ft 9in)
Wing area	15.48sq m	(166.5sq ft)
Height	3.82m	(12ft 6.3in)
Empty weight	7,318kg	(16,120lb)
Loaded weight	10,823kg	(23,840lb)
Maximum level speed	Mach 0.95	
Ceiling	11,580m	(38,000ft)
Endurance	1 hour	

to superb piloting by four pilots, it survived without accident for more than three and a half years.

Despite its problems, more uses were found for the J34 turbojet in the 1950s. Two J34s were added as 'booster jets' to Lockheed's excellent, twin piston engine, anti-submarine aircraft, the P2V Neptune. The turbojets were mounted beneath the wings, outboard of the piston engines, to produce the P2V-5F model (re-designated P-2E in 1962). The first P2V-5F (12863) flew in 1953.

A highly unusual fighter for the US Navy was the Convair XF2Y-1 Sea Dart, powered by two J34-WE-42 engines with afterburners. The Sea Dart featured a delta wing and single fin. Its combined hull and fuselage housed a cockpit, positioned well forward, and two long nacelles for the engines mounted above the fuselage and either side of the fin, keeping the engines as far as possible out of the sea spray. The air intakes began just aft of the small cockpit canopy. The aircraft could rest on its hull on the water but, for take-off and landing, two hydro-skis were extended. The prototype (137634) made its first flight on 9 April 1953. Once again, lack of sufficient power from the J34s (plus serious hydro-ski vibration) resulted in poor performance. More powerful J46 engines were fitted to the prototype and the first production XF2Y-1s but the programme was cancelled in 1956. However, on 3 August 1954 an XF2Y-1 exceeded Mach 1.0 in a shallow dive and thereby became the first supersonic seaplane.

Finally, before J34 production ended in 1962, North American's T2J-1 Buckeye was designed to use a single J34-WE-46 engine. The aircraft was designed to meet a 1956 US Navy requirement for a multi-role jet trainer and the first prototype (144217) flew on 31 January 1958. In production this two-seat trainer was designated T-2A and some 217 were built to equip the US Navy Training Squadrons. A later version, the T-2B, was powered by two P&W J60 turbojets. J34 turbojets were still in service in the 1980s as boosters for P-2E Neptune and C-119 aircraft.

J40 axial turbojet

The fact that the J34 was used in a training aircraft highlights the fact that it was a reliable engine, even though lacking in power. Unfortunately, Westinghouse's subsequent engines and the company's fortunes in the turbojet business were to be attended by failure. This fact was unknown in the early 1950s when the Korean War was in progress and the company's Kansas City plant was gearing up for the development and production of the J40 and J46 axial turbojets. It was expected that, between them, these two engine types would power almost all US Navy fighters and attack aircraft.

The J40 was ordered into development in June 1947 by the US Navy as a 2,724kp (6,000lb) static thrust engine. In time the design thrust grew to 4,540kp (10,000lb) and a number of naval aircraft, such as

The first supersonic seaplane, the prototype of the delta-wing Convair XF2Y-1 Sea Dart fighter (137634). Powered by two Westinghouse J34-WE-42 turbojets with afterburners, the Sea Dart took off and landed on retractable hydro-skis. It could also rest on its hull on the water or, as illustrated here at San Diego, taxi onto a beach or mat towed behind a ship. Note how cleanly the engines burn at high altitude, the environment turbojets are designed for.

the Douglas F4D Skyray, Douglas A3D, McDonnell F3H Demon and Grumman F10F Jaguar, were confidently being designed around it. The J40 was very long for its diameter, its fineness ratio being high even without the afterburner fitted. It was a completely new design with a ten-stage axial compressor, a double concentric annular combustion chamber and a two-stage turbine. For most installations the J40 had a bifurcated air intake with all accessories being conveniently arranged between the ducts, ahead of the engine. However, where the engine was to be installed in a pod (for example in the A3D bomber), a single, circular air inlet was provided, the accessories then being grouped beneath the compressor casing. In either case, the intake was de-iced using hot air bled from the delivery end of the compressor.

The J40's compressor casing was split longitudinally and bolted together, the forward half being in aluminium alloy and the rear, high-pressure half being in steel. All compressor blades and discs were also of steel. The annular combustion chamber was of the so-called step-wall type whereby concentric rings admitted compressed air to cool the perforated flame tubes. Sixteen duplex burners were fitted, fed with fuel from a dual gear pump. Air cooling was used for the turbine inlet nozzles and the two steel turbine discs. These were bolted together around their peripheries and carried solid blades made from Stellite heat-resisting alloy. The engine's length was increased by about fifty per cent when the afterburner was attached, this being by means of a flexible coupling and quick-release connectors. Fuel was injected midway along the afterburners. Sideways-opening eyelids were provided to vary the exhaust nozzle area, the actuating rod for these being about 6.4m (14ft) long, since the electric screw jack had to be mounted beneath the turbine section.

A prototype of the J40, an XJ40, was first run on 28 October 1948 and an early J40 passed a 150-hour MQT in January 1951. However, all was far from well with this turbojet and every type of problem, involving combustion, aerodynamics and mechanics, manifested itself. Westinghouse was

very unlucky to have so much wrong with an engine and the result was considerable unreliability and a failure to reach the design thrust of 3,405kp (7,500lb) or 4,767kp (10,500lb) with afterburner. Even by the summer of 1952 only 2,724kp (6,000lb) static thrust was being obtained, without afterburner. A downrated version was tried but the problems were not resolved. In January 1953 the Navy announced millions of extra dollars to increase the pace of development and get the engine right, but by March 1953 it had changed its mind and began seeking alternative engines from P&W and Allison for its aircraft. The J40 contract was cancelled in September 1953, only 107 engines having been delivered. A twin-spool version of the J40, designated the J50, remained on the drawing board.

In an effort to increase its technical expertise, Westinghouse signed a technical collaboration agreement with Rolls-Royce on 15 June 1953. Rolls-Royce was hoping also for a licence agreement to sell its successful Avon turbojet into the USA, but this proved to be illusory as far as Westinghouse was concerned. Instead Westinghouse decided to press on with its own designs, despite the devastating failure of the J40.

J46 axial turbojet

The company's J46 axial turbojet fared no better than the J40, despite the use of Rolls-Royce technology. The J46 was a direct, but enlarged, descendant of the J34 and it was to have powered several US Navy fighters, including the swept-wing F3D-3 Skynight (which was cancelled), the Chance Vought F7U-3 Cutlass and the Convair F2Y Sea Dart. Endless problems and delays with the J46 resulted in only the twin-engined Cutlass being left to use the engine. It was not until May 1953 that the J46 made its first flight in a Cutlass, but most of the test flying of this aircraft had to be carried out with Allison J35 engines due to a lack of or, at best, only a trickle of flight-cleared J46 engines. At the beginning of 1954 numerous Cutlass aircraft were parked outside the factory awaiting J46 engines and

thousands of Chance Vought employees were laid off. In October 1955 a Congressional investigation, following the crash of several J40-powered Demon fighters, found that Westinghouse had become complacent after its early successes. That December, the Navy cancelled Cutlass production after only four squadrons had been equipped with this potentially excellent fighter. Subsequent Demons were powered by Allison J71 engines.

Westinghouse leaves the turbojet business

By now Westinghouse personnel must have been having many a sleepless night, worrying about the sorry state of the turbojet side of the business. Final throws of the dice were made with their XJ54 and XJ81 turbojets. The axial XJ54, built with Westinghouse funds, was a R-R Avon engine scaled down to give a thrust of 2,815kp (6,200lb) for a weight of 680kg (1,500lb). It was a good engine, far better than the J46, but paradoxically it found no customers. As for the XJ81-WE-3, this was actually the USAF designation given to the Rolls-Royce Soar turbojet; it had a thrust of 790kp (1,740lb) for a weight of 138kg (304lb). Only twenty-four examples were supplied (built by Rolls-Royce) and were used to power the Northrop XQ-4 drone in tests during 1958.

In 1962 Westinghouse decided to leave the turbojet business, a sad ending considering its pioneering work in the early days and the high esteem in which it was held by the US Navy owing to its steam turbine and other experience. Among the reasons for the company's later failure with the turbojet were the insufficient funds and resources expended on research and development and an inability to modify its long-standing steam turbine practices to the ways of the aeronautical gas turbine. This led to a lack of competitiveness against P&W and GE. Even the J34, a good engine, had not been designed for upgrading to meet the ever-increasing military needs for more thrust. Finally, the US Navy decided to rely primarily on P&W, while the USAF chose mostly GE.

CHAPTER NINETEEN

Allison

The Allison company's experience with engines goes back to 1909, when it was involved in the founding of the famous Indianapolis race track and the subsequent development of cars and engines. The company entered into aero-engine development and construction in 1926, leading up to the building of the USA's only production, liquid-cooled piston engine of the Second World War, the V-1710. The most famous use of this engine, in supercharged form, was to power the twin-engined Lockheed P-38 Lightning fighter. In April 1945, with the end of the war in Europe in sight, the USAAF terminated volume production of the V-1710 and this left thousands of the company's personnel without work.

Development and production of GE's J33 and J35 turbojets

However, the future was not entirely bleak. Already, in June 1944, something of the future of aero-engines was glimpsed when Allison's general manager, Ed Newill, visited Wright Field. There he was asked to quote in one week a price for building (not developing) a turbojet. The only information available was a photograph, rough dimensions and weight. A price was quoted, based on the cost per pound of contemporary piston engines, and Allison won the contract to build what turned out to be the GE J33 turbojet. Also that June, GE's I-40 (J33-GE-5), developed from British technology, was flown in the prototype of Lockheed's P-80 fighter.

At the time, nobody at Allison knew anything beyond the theory of jet propulsion, but a team of about twenty technicians was organized to work out tooling and manufacturing procedures. This process was helped by visits to GE's Lynn works. A start was made by building GE's I-16 and then the I-40 (J33) centrifugal engines. At

this stage Allison was involved purely in production and no changes to GE's designs were allowed without first clearing them with GE at Lynn (who, in turn, cleared them with GE at Schenectady).

The J33, however, still had much development potential and so Allison became gradually involved in development, with subsequent benefit on the aircraft so powered. Allison's Director of Engineering at this time was Ron Hazen and some of his chief engineers were T.S. McCrae, J.B. Wheatley, Fred Luker, Charlie McDowall, A.W. Green, W.C. Oestrike, J.C. Fetters and R.P. Atkinson. The first Allison-produced J33 was delivered on 3 February 1945 and seven months later, in September 1945, responsibility for GE's J33 engine was transferred to Allison, a division of General Motors. Meanwhile service tests were being carried out with the P-80 powered by a GE-produced J33 engine.

The first prototype of Lockheed's P-80 Shooting Star fighter was built in only 143 days, the first flight being on 8 January 1944, piloted by Milo Burcham. Only sixteen examples were ready by VE Day, with two in Italy awaiting combat, but none saw action. Allison's J33-A-11 of 1,814kp (4,000lb) thrust, its J33-A-19 of 2,359kp (5,200lb) thrust and its J33-A-25 of 2,449kp (5,400lb) thrust powered the Shooting Star production models P-80A, P-80B and F-80C respectively. By the late 1940s about

twelve squadrons were operating the F-80 throughout the USA and Alaska. Despite the fact that it was a straight-wing fighter, it proved to be a very successful design from 'Kelly' Johnson's team. It captured a number of speed and distance records: a one-off machine, the highly modified P-80R, set a new world speed record of 1,003.88km/h (623.8mph) on 19 June 1947.

With the outbreak of the Korean War, Shooting Stars were soon in combat and had no trouble dealing with the piston-engined aircraft that the North Korean Air Force at first committed to combat. However, with China's physical entry into the war, Soviet swept-wing MiG-15s quickly outclassed the Shooting Stars, which were then switched to ground attack missions. Altogether some 1,830 Shooting Stars were built.

On 23 November 1948 the first production Grumman F9F-3 Panther fighter (123016) made its first flight with the Allison J33-A-8 engine of 2,088kp (4,600lb) thrust. This was followed by the first flight of the production Lockheed F-94A Starfire (48-356) on 1 July 1949, powered by the Allison J33-A-33 that was then giving 2,360kp (5,200lb) of static thrust, or 2,724kp (6,000lb) in afterburner mode. By July 1950 the J33-A-16 was giving a static thrust of 2,655kp (5,850lb) and was flown in the XF9F-4 Panther prototype (123084).

Lockheed F-80C Shooting Star		
Span	12.7m	(39ft 11in)
Length	10.52m	(34ft 6in)
Maximum take-off weight	7,646kg	(16,856lb)
Maximum level speed	933km/h	(580mph)
Cruising speed	707km/h	(439mph)
Range	2,221km	(1,380 miles)

Allison's early development effort was mainly concerned with afterburners for the existing engines but they also made detail changes. Initially, afterburner technology from the Solar Company was used. Allison also worked on water injection, increasing the thrust of the J33-A-27, for example, from 2,883kp (6,350lb) to 3,178kp (7,000lb). Altogether, Allison produced 15,525 J33 engines for the USAF by 1959, making it one of the most prolific production turbojets. As related earlier, the J33 was a centrifugal engine derived from Whittle's W.2B design; Britsh production, Soviet copies and worldwide licence production of this basic layout make it the most produced and most successful engine type of all time.

As for the J35 axial engine, the first item needing improvement was the lubrication system. The original air/oil mist spray system had led to bearing failures and so was replaced by Allison with a full scavenging oil system. This was first used on the J35-A-17B version, greatly improving engine

life and reliability. The J35 came to be in demand by both the USAF and US Navy and was used to power fighters, bombers and experimental aircraft.

In April 1947 the Republic YP-84A Thunderjet fighter (45-59482) began service tests using the J35-A-15 of 1,702kp (3,750lb) static thrust. At this time Chrysler was brought into J35 production and four J35-C-3 engines were used to power the Convair XB-46 bomber prototype. Another experimental bomber, the six-engined Martin XB-48 prototype (45-59585), first

flew on 22 June 1947 powered by J35-A-5s. Eight of these engines were used to power the Northrop flying-wing bomber, the YB-49 (42-210367), for its first service tests on 21 October 1947.

None of these bombers went into production but it was a different story for Boeing's B-47 Stratojet bomber. The XB-47 prototype (46-065) first flew on 17 December 1947, powered by six J35-A-7s of 1,816kp (4,000lb) static thrust each. This successful bomber went into production but with more powerful GE J47

BELOW: The Northrop YB-49 flying-wing bomber needed eight Allison J35-A-5 turbojets. However, this aircraft, like other experimental bombers such as the XB-46 and XB-48, could not compete with the B-47. The use of multiple turbojets was necessary until large engines were developed.

ABOVE: The Martin XB-48 experimental bomber, seen landing, was powered by six Allison J35-A-5 turbojets. Depressed ailerons are being used to supplement the small flaps. The J33 and J35 engines were taken over from General Electric and, after improvement, became much in demand. Central Arkansas Library System, AEC

The huge Convair B-36 Peacemaker strategic bomber used four underwing J35 turbojets as boosters but these were later changed to J47s. Central Arkansas Library System, AEC

Douglas D-558-1 Skystreak			
Span		7.62m	(25ft 0in)
Length		10.88m	(35ft 8½in)
Wing area		14.0sq m	(150.70sq ft)
Height		3.70m	(12ft 1¾in)
Maximum take-off weight		4,584kg	(10,105lb)
Maximum speed	at sea level	1,048km/h or Mach 0.855	(651mph)
Ceiling		12,000m	(39,360ft)

engines. Four J35s were used as boosters in a giant Convair B-36 bomber test-bed (92057) first flown on 28 March 1949, but again this aircraft later used J47s as boosters.

As for experimental aircraft, the first of these to use the J35 engine was the Douglas D-558-1 Skystreak. First conceived in 1945, the Skystreak was sponsored by the US Navy and the NACA as a high-speed research aircraft for speeds up to Mach 0.85. The all-metal design was kept as simple and as clean as possible, a straight, low-mounted wing being used. The slender, circular-section fuselage was just large enough to accommodate an Allison J35-A-11 turbojet of 1,816kp (4,000lb) thrust (some sources say 5,000lb st), there being a simple nose air intake. Its tiny cockpit had a canopy with a V-shaped windshield. A large vertical fin was fitted, carrying the tailplane at about halfway up the fin. The undercarriage was a retractable, tricycle type. Because of the high design speeds, it was decided to devise the nose section as jettisonable in an emergency, the pilot baling out from it once it had slowed down sufficiently. To gather data, the airframe had 400 pressure measuring points and there were also strain gauges fitted to the wings and tail empennage.

Three D-558-1 Skystreaks were built, the first (37970) flying on 15 April 1947

from Muroc, piloted by Gene May. Immediately after take-off, the aircraft suffered a partial power loss but May was able to land safely straight ahead on the lake bed. A similar engine failure occurred on 21 April. However, this aircraft later established a new world speed record of 1,031.04km/h (640.66mph) on 20 August 1947. The second prototype (37971) was destroyed on 3 May 1948 when its J35 compressor disintegrated soon after take-off. Many successful research flights were completed, largely by the third prototype (37972), until the programme was completed in June 1953. (For discussion of the swept-wing version of the Skystreak, the D-558-2 Skyrocket, see Chapter 18.)

Another research aircraft made its maiden flight sometime later, on 20 June

1951, powered by the J35-A-7A turbojet of 2,270kp (5,000lb) static thrust. This was the Bell X-5 (50-1838), which had its roots in the wartime Messerschmitt Me P.1101. The P.1101 was intended to investigate variations in the wing sweep, the wing being adjustable on the ground, and the almost complete prototype was captured at the end of the war. The X-5 was designed by Robert J. Woods and two prototypes were constructed. Each featured a short fuselage with a boom leading back to support the tail empennage, the single J35 being housed in the lower fuselage with a nose air intake. The mid-mounted wings could have their sweep angle varied in flight from 20 degrees to 60 degrees, there being three positions. The first sweep variation was made on 27 July 1951, the pilot being

Skip Ziegler. Unfortunately the second prototype crashed on 13 October 1953, killing the pilot Raymond Popson. The maximum level speed of the X-5 was about 1,046km/h (650mph).

The J35 was called upon to power many fighters. In June 1947 the first production F-84B Thunderjet (45-59497) made its maiden flight, powered by a J35-A-15. The XP-86 prototype (45-59597), later to become the famous Sabre, powered by a Chrysler-built J35-C-3 engine, first flew on 1 October 1947. First flights during 1948 include those of the production FJ-1 Fury (130342) in March (J35-A-4) and the prototype XF-89 (46-678) Scorpion in August (two J35-A-9s). Allison's first J35 with an afterburner, the J35-A-21, was used to power the twin-engined Northrop YF-89A Scorpion (49-679) on its first flight on 15 November 1949. The A-21 version of the J35 gave a static thrust of 2,315kp (5,100lb) or 3,087kp (6,800lb) in afterburner mode. Finally, the prototype of the Douglas XF4D-1 Skyray naval fighter (124586) first flew on 23 January 1951, using the J35-A-17 engine.

These examples suffice to show the strength of demand for the J35. Although some aircraft, such as the Fury and Sabre fighters and the B-47 bomber, went on to use GE's more powerful J47, the J35 went into production for the Scorpion, Cutlass and Thunderjet fighters. Altogether, Allison produced a remarkable 14,454 J35 turbojets. This great production activity was not just because of the need to re-equip the USAF and the US Navy with jet aircraft, but also owed much to the demand and urgency created by the Korean War, during which Allison engines powered 69 per cent of all the conflict's jet fighter missions. The success of the J33 and J35 engines allowed Allison to go from the precarious situation brought about by the sudden end of piston aero-engine pro-

duction to becoming the USA's first volume builder of turbojet engines.

Although the decision to launch the Korean War was made by North Korea's Kim Il-sung, he was encouraged and then massively supported by China's Mao Zedong. Mao's aim was to persuade the Soviet Union to help build up China's military forces and also to pass on to China the technology to build atomic bombs. Mao did not care how many Chinese troops were killed, since manpower was something he did not lack. After a year of war, Kim Il-sung had had enough but the conflict was perpetuated by Mao. This war was also a chance for the Communist countries to test the resolve of the West in a conflict and also to test their latest weapons, such as the MiG-15 fighter. However, it also gave a great spur to the West to speed up development and production of its latest weapons, including jet aircraft.

Allison powers the first US missiles in service

It is of historical importance that Allison J33 turbojets powered the first guided missiles in service with the US Navy and the USAF. The Regulus 1 (SSM-N-8) missile, for which the prime contractor was Chance Vought, first flew in 1951 and was designed as a submarine-launched surface-to-surface flying bomb. The US Navy had already experimented with submarine-launched (on the surface) American copies of the German V1 flying bomb, but these pulsejet-powered missiles were not specifically designed for the job. Regulus 1 had a cigar-shaped fuselage and mid-set swept-back wings and a vertical fin. The outer wing panels folded for stowage and there was radio command guidance. It was powered by an Allison J33-A-14 of 2,088kp (4,600lb) static thrust and was boosted at

From August 1951, North America was defended by Northrop F-89 Scorpions in Air Defense Command (ADC) and Alaska Air Command. Unlike a number of aircraft that had their J35 engines supplanted by more powerful J47s, the Scorpion remained J35-powered; TOP: F-89C-15 Scorpion, the first production model, armed with cannon; BOTTOM: F-89D in Alaska and armed with 104 Mighty Mouse rockets housed in the front half of each wingtip fuel tank. Both versions were powered by two Allison J35-A-33 engines. Central Arkansas Library System, AEC

A Regulus, with wings folded, submarine-launched (on the surface) surface-to-surface missile, powered by an Allison J33-A-14 turbojet. The Regulus was the first guided missile to enter service with both the US Navy and the USAF. Central Arkansas Library System, AEC

take-off from the deck by two 14,980kp (33,000lb) thrust solid-propellant rockets that were jettisoned at burn-out. A two-megaton nuclear warhead was carried.

Regulus 1 missiles entered US Navy service in 1955 and were carried by both diesel- and nuclear-powered submarines, the purpose-built USS *Grayback* being an example of the former. Regulus submarines patrolled in Soviet waters, including the Bering Sea, and took part in the Cuban Missile Crisis. At any one time, there were always four submarines on patrol and it was not until 1964 that Polaris submarines began replacing those equipped with Regulus. A total of 514 Regulus missiles were built, including training and target drone versions that were fitted with a retractable undercarriage for recovery and re-use.

The first guided missile to enter USAF service was the Matador (TM-61C) surface-to-surface missile, the prime contractor for which was the Martin Marietta Corporation. The Matador had a bullet-shaped fuselage with high-set swept-back wings and a T-tail. It was powered by a J33-A-37 engine of 2,088kp (4,600lb) static thrust, the air intake for which was underneath the midpoint of the fuselage. For take-off, one 22,700kp (50,000lb) thrust solid-propellant rocket was attached under the rear fuselage and was jettisoned at burn-out. A radio navigation guidance system was used and a nuclear or high-explosive warhead could be fitted.

The Matador entered USAF squadron service in 1959 and more than 1,000 were

built. Its range was over 805km (500 miles) and speed 1,095km/h (680mph), but it was susceptible to electronic jamming and so the improved Mace (TM-76) was developed. This was of similar configuration but powered by the J33-A-41 turbojet of 2,360kp (5,200lb) static thrust and featured the Goodyear ATRAN self-contained guidance system, which could not be jammed. Because of its greater weight, Mace had a more powerful take-off rocket of 45,400kp (100,000lb) thrust. With its wings

folded, Mace was transported with all its support equipment on a tractor train of vehicles. First deployed with the USAF's 38th Tactical Missile Wing in Europe, Mace went on to equip Japanese and French air force units.

T38 turboprop

Because of its interest in long-range patrol aircraft, the US Navy also had an interest

Regulus 1 (SSM-N-8) missile			
Span		6.40m	(21ft 0in)
Length		10.05m	(33ft 0in)
Fuselage diameter		1.37m	(4ft 6in)
Loaded weight		6,593kg	(14,522lb)
Speed	Mach 0.79	966km/h	(600mph)
Range		925km (575 miles)	

Mace (TM-76) surca-to-surface missile			
Span		6.98m	(22ft 11in)
Length		13.41m	(44ft 0in)
Fuselage diameter		1.37m	(4ft 6in)
Loaded weight		8,172kg	(18,000lb)
Speed	Mach 0.85	1,045km/h	(650mph)
Range	(TM-76A)	1,045km	(650 miles)
	(TM-76B)	1,930km	(1,200 miles)

in the turboprop engine. Accordingly in December 1945 it issued a design and development contract to Allison for a 4,100shp turboprop. Allison had already begun design studies, late in 1944, and originally planned to build a turboprop in the 4,000shp class. It then decided that two smaller engines, which could operate independently or together, would offer greater operational flexibility. (Armstrong Siddeley in England applied the same reasoning to its Double Mamba turboprop.) Allison's basic engine, to be developed first and then later coupled, was designated the T38 (Model 501). It featured a nineteen-stage axial compressor of 6.2:1 compression ratio, eight combustion chambers and a four-stage turbine. A noteworthy feature was the mounting of the airscrew reduction gearbox remote from the engine: it was driven by a shaft with a flexible coupling from the front of the engine, this feature giving the opportunity of mounting the turboprop without a break in the aircraft's main wing spar. Although Allison's engineers had learned much from the production and some development of J33 and J35 turbojets, their first original work on gas turbines began with the T38 turboprop. In terms of turnover, this work resulted in Allison falling behind GE and P&W, but the Navy's funding at least spared it the burden of finding research funding. One of the difficulties Allison (as a division of General Motors) had to overcome was the need to train automotive engineers to understand the aeronautical market.

The engineering team working on the T38, headed by Ronald M. Hazen, included Jack C. Fetters (chief turbine engineer), John Wheatley (project engineer), O.P. Pracher (aerodynamicist) and engineers Art Gaubatz and Bob Hicks. As usual, problems that had to be overcome concerned gearbox vibration (coupling with engine vibrations) and combustion. The XT38 was first run in 1947 and gave about 2,000shp. Its first test flight was made on 19 April 1949, fitted to the nose of the company's Boeing B-17G Flying Fortress test-bed, from Weir Cook Municipal Airport in Indianapolis. By then the XT38 was developing 2,250shp. During 1950 it was tested in an Allison-owned twin-engined Convair CV-240 (then dubbed the Turbo-Liner) and the power of each T38 was 2,750eshp. This CV-240 replaced the B-17G as a flying test-bed. Remarkably compact, the T38 was, with its gearbox, smaller than a J35 turbojet and measured approximately 0.51m (1ft 8in) in diameter by 2.13m (7ft) in length. Its weight was 556kg (1,225lb).

The T38 never saw an application on its own because the Convair T-29E transport, a military derivative of the Convair 240 that it was intended to power, was cancelled by the USAF. The T38 design was later used as the starting point for the famous T56 turboprop. The T39 was a design for a large turboprop of 9,000ehp that remained as a project. The experience gained by Allison in its original gas turbine designs, however, was most valuable and work began on the coupled T38, the T40 (Model 500). The Navy contract for the T40 was signed on 28 June 1946 but Gaubatz and Pracher had already designed much of this turboprop earlier that year.

T40 (coupled) turboprop

The T40 comprised two T38A-1 gas turbine engines mounted side-by-side and driving a contra-rotating airscrew through a common, remote, reduction gearbox. The two engines were connected so that each drove both airscrews but could be operated independently. By now the T38 had a seventeen-stage compressor, but still retained eight combustion chambers and a four-stage turbine. The compression ratio was 6.3:1 and the air intake was heated by air tapped from the compressor to prevent icing. All four turbine stages drove the compressor and, through it, the drive shaft to the main gearbox. Thus, two drive shafts led into the rear of the gearbox and a coaxial shaft led from the front of the gearbox to drive the contra-rotating airscrews. The two drive shafts from the two T38s each embodied a clutch so that each engine could be operated independently. The reduction gearing was of the compound type, with an overall reduction ratio of 15.75:1, and incorporated an airscrew brake to prevent windmilling after shut-down.

A master control unit, combining throttle and airscrew controls, was mounted with other accessories above the compressor casings and a pneumatic-type starter was mounted on the gearbox. The three-bladed, reversing, square-tipped airscrews were made by Aeroproducts and were 4.27m (14ft) in diameter. The T40 was a complicated engine and it presented the Allison team with plenty of problems during its development. Probably the biggest headaches were caused by vibration: the reader will recall that this was the same story

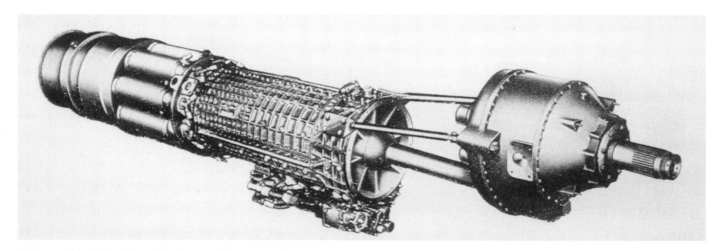

The layout of the Allison T38 axial turboprop with its remote reduction gearbox for the airscrew.

A Boeing B-17G Flying Fortress bomber 'Anudderone' converted as a flying test-bed with an Allison T38 turboprop in the nose.

An Allison T40 turboprop (coupled T38A-1s), with contra-rotating airscrews, in a test cell at Indianapolis. The cones in the exhaust nozzles appear buckled by the hot exhaust gases.

in other countries developing turboprops. Concentrating on the T40's gearbox, the engineers ascertained the meshing frequencies of the teeth of every gear and then redesigned them to avoid troublesome frequencies. The result was a very smooth-running gearbox.

The XT40 ran for the first time on 4 June 1948. The Allison engineers realized that it was essential to have a good and rapid system of de-coupling a failed engine since, if this was not done, the drag from the failed engine would soon cause the other engine to fail. What seemed like a good opportunity to test the de-coupling system occurred during bench tests across San Diego Bay when an internal oil leak in one of the engines produced a long flame across the water. However, the engine refused to actually stop running. Next, a fire hose was directed into one engine, but this simply shrank the casings and all the blades were stripped off. Finally, debris was thrown into one engine until its compressor collapsed and the de-coupler was found to work in an emergency. By about November 1949 the XT40 had completed around 1,500 hours of test-stand running and was declared ready for flight tests.

Convair flying boats

The first test flights of the T40 were not in the company's flying test-bed but in the prototype of the large Convair XP5Y flying boat. Originally this aircraft was to be powered by four Westinghouse T30 turbo-props, but this engine had fallen behind schedule, owing to industrial disputes. In May 1946 Convair was awarded a US Navy contract for two prototypes of its proposed long-range, multi-role, flying boat, to be powered by four turboprops. (It is thought that the design of the XP5Y gained considerable benefit from wartime German work on large flying boats by the Blohm und Voss company, especially the Bv 222 Wiking, which was of a similar specification.) In Convair's design the large hull was particularly slim, beamwise, and had a high-mounted wing that carried the engines and floats. The vertical fin was very tall and angular and carried the tailplane at its base. For its main anti-submarine (ASW) role, the aircraft carried a heavy load of electronic equipment, bombs, mines, rockets and torpedoes.

The prototype XP5Y-1 made its first flight, from San Diego, on 18 April 1950.

It was powered by four T40-A-4s, each of 5,250shp and weighing 1,312kg (2,890lb). In August this aircraft set a turboprop endurance record of 8 hours 6 minutes. Also in August, however, the Navy changed its role from ASW to that of passenger and cargo carrying. This involved considerable reworking, including the deletion of all armament, the provision of a side cargo hatch and the installation of pressurization and air conditioning. Thus revised, the aircraft was designated the R3Y-1 Tradewind. In April 1952 Allison delivered its first production turboprop of the developed T40-A-10 rated at 5,332shp (one source states 5,850shp).

The R3Y-1 Tradewind first flew on 25 February 1954. The first of five Tradewinds built (128488) made a record flight on 24 February 1955 from San Diego to the Navy Test Centre at Patuxent River, Maryland, in 6 hours at an average speed of 649km/h (403mph). Other records followed and the US Navy transport squadron VR-2 received the first of its mixed fleet of R3Y-1 and R3Y-2 flying boats on 31 March 1956. Six examples of the R3Y-2 were built, these featuring an upward-opening nose section to allow men and matériel to be landed directly onto a beach. First flown on 22 December 1954, the R3Y-2 made history in September 1956 when a tanker version simultaneously refuelled in flight four Grumman F9F-8 Cougar fighters from VF-111.

All was not well with the T40 turboprop, however. On 10 May 1957 VR-2's Tradewind *Coral Sea* went out of control after the in-flight separation of an airscrew and the aircraft was written off. A complete

gearbox separated from an engine on VR-2's Tradewind *Ocean Trade* on 24 January 1958, causing the aircraft to hit a sea wall. Although no crew were lost in these accidents, all Tradewinds were effectively grounded by the Navy. In addition to engine problems, the Tradewinds were found to be unstable in flight and generally expensive to build and run.

Allison turboprops powered their share of experimental aircraft. One of the prototypes (46-525) of the McDonnell XF-88 was modified as the XF-88B with an XT38 turboprop in the nose. The XF-88 was a twin-jet, heavy, long-range 'penetration' fighter, intended to escort bombers over long distances (it was later revived as the basis for the F-101A Voodoo fighter). The XF-88 had swept-back wings, wing root air intakes and a high-set tail empennage well above the two jet exhausts. The purpose of fitting the XT38 engine was to create a test-bed for supersonic airscrews. The XF-88B first flew on 14 April 1953. Its turboprop was offset to port in the nose and the nosewheel was moved to starboard in order to accommodate these items. It was possible to test 27 combinations of airscrew, their diameters ranging from 1.22m to 3.05m (4–10ft).

In July 1955 another fighter prototype, the XF-106 (later redesignated XF-84H) was first flown. This had been completely rebuilt from a Republic RF-84F reconnaissance machine in order to test supersonic airscrews and was powered by an Allison T40 turboprop of 5,850shp. In order to clear the airscrew wash, the XF-84H had a high-mounted T-tail.

The long-range, multi-purpose Convair R3Y Tradewind flying boat was powered by four Allison T40-A-10 turboprops giving a total power of about 22,000shp plus residual thrust. Central Arkansas Library System, AEC

VTOL flight with the T40

Early in 1950, the US Navy launched a design competition to produce a sea-going VTOL fighter for operation from small decks. Five companies submitted ideas but the final contracts were awarded to Lockheed and Convair to produce competing prototypes. It was specified that the fighter would be a tail sitter and be powered by the Allison 7,100shp YT40-A-6 turboprop driving Curtiss-Wright 4.88m (16ft) diameter contra-rotating airscrews with electric pitch control. This arrangement provided some 2,270kg (5,000lb) of thrust at lift-off. (Some inspiration for this project may have come from the German Focke-Wulf 'Triebflügel' project.)

Lockheed's VTOL aircraft was designated the XFV-1 Salmon. It had tapered wings (with wingtip fuel tanks) and a cruciform tail, there being ample control due to the great slipstream over the control surfaces. Strangely, no vertical flights were ever attempted with the XFV-1 and all of its twenty-seven flights were made in the conventional manner, using a long, temporary, fixed undercarriage.

Convair's VTOL aircraft was designated the XFY-1 Pogo. It had a delta wing, with wingtip fuel tanks, and a large vertical fin above and below the fuselage, thus making a cruciform arrangement with the wing. Its spinner for the airscrews was more elongated than that on the XFV-1. Testing began in 1954, using a tethered flight rig inside an airship hangar at Moffett Field, California. Following extensive tethered flights, the XFY-1 was first flown outdoors in August 1954 and its first full VTOL flight was made in November 1954. However, even though a swivelling seat was provided, the manoeuvre of landing backwards while looking over his shoulder was extremely difficult for the pilot and a testimony to his great skill. In addition, problems were experienced with the T40 and its airscrews. Therefore, although this VTOL programme was short-lived, the XFY-1 Pogo had demonstrated the first transition from horizontal to a vertical, tail-sitting landing of a non-helicopter aircraft.

T56 turboprop (and civilian 501-D13)

In 1949 the US Navy sponsored development of a new turboprop engine, the coupled T54, which was to have about 28 per cent more power than the T40. Therefore, with the expertise gained from its earlier turboprop work, Allison began design of the T54. Soon after, in 1951, it also began work on the T56 turboprop. This was derived from the T38 and was funded by the USAF to power a new transport aircraft (the C-130 Hercules). The Chief Project Engineer was Jack Fetters. The design team included Joe Barney (compressor), Don Zimmerman (turbine) and Victor Petersen (reduction gearing). Very soon, work on the T56 overtook that on the more complicated coupled T54, which was then dropped. The T56 was an expanded, improved derivative of the T38 and used a cannular combustion system instead of separate combustion chambers. Its axial compressor used only fourteen stages and its speed was only 13,820rpm instead of the 14,300rpm of the T38. Nevertheless, it gave an air mass flow of 14.52kg/sec (32lb/sec) at a pressure ratio of 9.25:1.

The first T56 was ready for testing in just under two years from the start of design work, and the first T56-A-1 passed a 50-hour PFRT in September 1953. The T56 gave 3,460shp plus 330kp (726lb) of residual thrust, or a combined total of 3,750ehp. Allison was anxious to produce a really reliable turboprop, especially after some of the earlier misfortunes with the T40, and wanted to offer such an engine to both military and civilian operators. Therefore, beginning in December 1954, it pursued more extensive testing than on any other engine up to that time.

The programme included thirteen 150-hour test runs. The first test flight of a T56 was made on 26 March 1954, using the B-17G test-bed. By November 1954 the T56-A-9 was in production as the Series I and Allison, after all its earlier tribulations, had at last got a world-class turboprop that was a winner. Developed in parallel with the T56, a commercial derivative known as the 501-D13 was also ready for certification testing in 1954. The new Allison turboprops were noteworthy for their small size, when considering their power.

Lockheed C-130 Hercules STOL transport

The first production T56 engines were ready in time for the four-engined Lockheed C-130 Hercules transport and it was in this aircraft that they were first flown. The first of two YC-130 prototypes (53-3396) made its first flight from Lockheed's Burbank, Los Angeles, plant on 23 August 1954, its pilots being Stan Beltz and Ray Wimmer. Designed as a short take-off and landing (STOL) tactical transport, the C-130 was destined to become one of the world's most important aircraft for both military and civilian use.

The C-130 utilized large, integrally machined panels, especially for the cargo hold floor and the wing main skins, these giving great strength with lightness. Titanium and new high-strength aluminium alloys were used and considerable use was made of bonded metals. Its cavernous fuselage was kept clear by using a shoulder-mounted wing and by mounting the retractable, tandem, twin main wheels in side fairings outside of the fuselage lines. The fuselage swept upwards to the tail at the rear, allowing the large rear doors to be opened hydraulically in flight, if required. The rear fuselage had a ramp that could be lowered to the ground for easy loading. This ramp led into a cargo hold measuring 3.05m by 2.74m (10ft × 8.9ft) with a length of 12.62m (41ft 5in). Excellent accommodation, including a galley and rest bunks, was provided for the crew and the view from the cockpit was first class. A total of 19,876ltr (4,372gal) of fuel was carried between the main spars of the wings and was later supplemented by two pylon-mounted tanks below the wings. The four, slim engine nacelles extended considerably forward from the wing leading edges and each nacelle contained a long drive-shaft leading from its T56 to a strut-mounted gearbox. Originally, Curtiss Turboelectric three-bladed airscrews were used, but these were soon changed to Aeroproducts four-bladed, square-tipped airscrews or Hamilton Standard four-bladed, reversible-pitch airscrews. The tail empennage, especially the vertical surface, was of generous area.

Large Fowler flaps, low-pressure tyres and reverse thrust from the airscrews aided the Hercules to make short landings on unprepared strips, the Fowler flaps occupying most of the wing's trailing edge. The power available from the T56 engines was such that a Hercules could be pulled up into a full stall and then have its height maintained by immediately opening up the engines to full power.

The C-130 went into production at the vast plant at Marietta, Georgia, and the first C-130A (53-3129) took off from there on 7 April 1955. Apart from going into service with all US air arms, the Hercules (or 'Herky

The Lockheed XFV-1 'Salmon' experimental VTOL aircraft with an Allison 7,100shp YT40-A-6 turboprop engine driving contra-rotating airscrews. All of its take-offs were made horizontally on a temporary undercarriage, before the programme was cancelled.

Convair's competitor to Lockheed's XFV-1 was its XFY-1 'Pogo', also powered with an Allison T40 turboprop. Shown are its snugly fitting 'hangar' and the pilot about to start up. The XFY-1 carried out VTOL flights, requiring great skill from the pilot, especially when landing 'backwards'. The aim of the programme was to provide the US Navy with a VTOL fighter for operation from small decks.

Many of Allison's successful T56 turboprop engines were used to power the ubiquitous Lockheed C-130 Hercules transport. Illustrated is a C-130A. Central Arkansas Library System, AEC

Lockheed C-130A Hercules			
Span		40.41m	(132ft 7in)
Length		29.79m	(97ft 9in)
Wing area		162.11sq m	(1,745sq ft)
Height		11.66m	(38ft 3in)
Empty weight	approx.	30,000kg	(66,150lb)
Loaded weight		52,600kg	(115,983lb)
Maximum speed		612km/h	(380mph)
Range, with maximum fuel		8,200km	(5,090 miles)

Bird' as it was dubbed) was exported all over the world. The variants produced included cargo and personnel transports, ground attack and air-to-air refuelling types. A civilian cargo version was known as the L-100. One of the last military versions of the Hercules was the C-130H, which was powered by the 4,508ehp T56 known as the Dash-15. Pilots serving in Vietnam began using the so-called Kasong dive when an airfield was under enemy fire. In this, the Hercules was dived steeply from a considerable height and then flared at the last moment to land. The rear doors of the Hercules, opened in flight, made air drops easy, as well as such operations as dropping Special Forces personnel from great heights. Its quiet approach, short landing and cargo doors also made it an excellent choice for rescue missions, such as that made by Israeli forces at Entebbe. Development of this most versatile aircraft continued and production approached 2,000 examples worldwide. Apart from its wartime utilization, many people requiring life-saving aid in disaster zones have reason to be grateful for the Hercules and its reliable T56 turboprops.

Besides powering the civilian L-100 Hercules, the 501 turboprop was used to re-engine the Lockheed Electra airliner (as the L-188A and C Electra) and later powered the Convair 580 transport. After two L-188A Electras crashed, NASA at Langley identified the cause in May 1960 as the phenomenon known as propeller whirl flutter (PWF). The engine mountings, probably weakened in hard landings, were found to flex enough to allow PWF to occur at a frequency that matched the natural frequency of the wings. The result was a fracture of the wing structure that was otherwise perfectly adequate to deal with all forces it was expected to meet. Subsequently, the engine mountings were reinforced and the Electra went on to be extremely successful and long-lived in the form of the P-3 Orion ASW aircraft for the US Navy. T56 turboprops powered these and also Grumman E-2 Hawkeye early-warning aircraft for the Navy.

Almost 15,000 T56 and 501 turboprops had been built by the end of 1990. Uprating of the engine was achieved by designing it to run hotter instead of faster, because an

increase in rpm would have reduced gearbox reliability. By 1987 the T56-427 was giving 5,250shp and a lower specific fuel consumption (about 0.52), its weight being 829kg (1,825lb).

J35-A-23 (J71) turbojet

In April 1949, while Allison were still working on the XT38 turboprop and the afterburning J35-A-21 turbojet, the company began design of an all-new turbojet. In order to utilize development funding for the J35 and to avoid the process of seeking funding for a new engine, Allison designated the turbojet the J35-A-23. Later, it was re-designated the J71.

In the design of the J71, Allison entered into a phase of its turbojet work that was almost entirely its own original work. The design team was headed by Project Engineer Dimitrius Gordon and Director of Engineering Ronald Hazen. Their brief was to produce a turbojet within the basic 0.94m (37in) diameter of the J35 but with at least double the previous thrust. With this achieved, the new engine could not only be fitted into existing aircraft but also allow the design of new supersonic fighters. To obtain the much greater air mass flow required of at least 70kg/sec (154lb/sec), a sixteen-stage axial compressor was designed, its pressure ratio being 8.25:1. Similarly, the turbine stages of the earlier J35 were increased from one to three in order to extract the necessary shaft power for the compressor. The previous cannular combustion system was replaced with one similar to an annular system. However, a total of ten individual liners were mounted around the circumference of the annulus. The liners had perforations to admit the compressed air to the flame tube at the interior, the resultant hot gases then passing through the inlet nozzles to the turbine. Besides anti-icing of the air intake section by hot air tapped from the compressor, there was an unusual system of air intake screening to prevent the ingress of foreign objects while on the ground and during climb out. Once at altitude, these screens folded forward and down against the circumference of the air intake.

An early type of electronic computer was mounted under the engine accessory section of the engine. This controlled the engine fuel supply and exhaust nozzle area in accordance with air density, exhaust gas temperature and engine speed. The computer provided

Developed from the Lockheed L-188 Electra airliner, the P3V Orion became a very successful ASW/maritime patrol aircraft for the US Navy. Powered by four T56 turboprop engines, the Orion was produced in many specialized forms and sold worldwide. Illustrated is 'NOAA 42', a WP-3D flying laboratory (re-equipped P-3C), one of two used for atmospheric research, weather modification experiments and other projects by the National Oceanic and Atmospheric Administration (NOAA).

automatic control of engine conditions to accommodate changes in aircraft altitude and speed as determined by the pilot's throttle setting. Variation of the exhaust nozzle area was accomplished by use of a hydraulically operated nozzle bullet.

The first J71 was built in eleven months from the beginning of design work, and testing began at the end of 1950. Its designed continuous static thrust was 3,673kp (8,090lb) for a dry weight of 1,857kg (4,090lb). Its maximum static thrust (5 minutes) was 4,630kp (10,200lb). Production of the engine was shared between Allison at Indianapolis (one third) and the Chevrolet division of General Motors at Tonawanda, New York (two-thirds); in both cases many parts were made by subcontractors. Unfortunately, the J71 was never able to penetrate the high-performance combat aircraft market dominated by the more advanced GE J79 and P&W J57 turbojets, both of which were more powerful and, crucially, had considerably better fuel economy than the J71.

The J71 was used to power the initial versions of Northrop's S-62 Snark intercontinental missile. The first aircraft designed to use the engine was the Douglas RB-66A Destroyer: the prototype (53-2828) first flew on 28 June 1954 and used two J71-A-9 engines of 4,404kp (9,700lb) thrust each. The RB-66 was a highly modified,

USAF reconnaissance version of the Navy's A-3 Skywarrior. It was also produced as the EB-66 electronic countermeasures (ECM) aircraft. Their main use in combat was as electronics jamming platforms during the Vietnam War. The type was only built in small numbers.

The prototype of the US Navy's McDonnell XF3H-1 Demon fighter, designed to combat the Soviet MiG-15, first flew on 7 August 1951. It was intended to put 150 of these aircraft into production using the Westinghouse J40 turbojet. However, the failure of this engine caused some two years of delay. After a number of accidents, caused by the aircraft being underpowered with the J40, it was decided to fit Allison's J71 engine into F3H-2 production aircraft. By 1959 some 519 Demons had been built and equipped eleven naval squadrons. Although the Demon had plenty of power, it was not very successful and was withdrawn from first-line service in September 1964. Using the J71-A-2E turbojet, which gave 6,350kp (14,000lb) of thrust with afterburning, the F3H-2 could achieve Mach 0.95 at 9,150m (30,000ft).

A completely different aircraft that was powered by the J71 was the Martin XP6M-1 Seamaster four-engined flying boat. The prototype (133821) first flew on 14 July 1955 using afterburning J71-A-4 turbojets. This aircraft was designed to meet a US

Navy requirement for a high-performance, multi-role flying boat. It had a shoulder-mounted, sharply swept wing with considerable anhedral so that wingtip floats could be permanently mounted. The four J71 engines were mounted in paired nacelles above the wing's centre section. A very tall, swept fin had at its top a swept horizontal stabilizer with considerable dihedral. An extremely ambitious design, the Seamaster was the fastest flying boat ever built and one was actually dived faster than sound. Two prototypes and six pre-production YP6M-1 flying boats were powered with the J71 engine but production P6M-2 aircraft were to be powered by P&W J75 engines. After two pre-production machines had fatal accidents, only three P6M-2s were eventually built and the order was cancelled in August 1959.

With the phasing out of the above aircraft in the late 1950s, Allison failed to find new work for the J71 and so just 1,707 were manufactured. Up to this point Allison had not been too successful in the turbojet field, but its work on turboprops, leading to the highly successful T56, kept it in the marketplace alongside General Electric and Pratt & Whitney. Two Allison turbojet projects, the J56 and J89, were in the 11,350kp (25,000lb) thrust Mach 2.5 class but were never built.

The prototype Martin XP6M-1 Seamaster (133821) high-performance, multi-role flying boat being rolled out at Baltimore (4 January 1955). Powered by four Allison J71-A-4 turbojets with afterburners, the Seamaster was one of the fastest flying boats ever built, one being dived faster than sound. Rubber pressure pads, removed before flight, are cemented onto the wings for simulated loads tests.

CHAPTER TWENTY

Wright Aeronautical Corporation

This company can trace its lineage back to the famous Wright brothers. From small engine beginnings, the Wright Aeronautical Corporation was formed in 1919 by F.B. Rentschler. The company later became famous for the production of reliable, air-cooled radial engines, exemplified by its J-5 Whirlwind engine which carried Charles Lindbergh across the Atlantic on his famous flight in May 1927. A merger with the Curtiss aircraft company that year formed the Curtiss-Wright Corporation and these companies worked together from 1931 in Wright's plant at Paterson, New Jersey. Production of piston engines was boosted by wartime demand. After the war the company saw a use for gas turbines in boosting, and making more efficient, its piston engines.

In the mid-1930s the Wright company was dissatisfied with the performance of the GE superchargers used on its Cyclone radial engines. Consequently, it carried out its own research on superchargers and produced its own type before the outbreak of war. Wright turbosuperchargers turned out to be as efficient as those on the Rolls-Royce Merlin XX engine and came to be manufactured by GE also.

The Wright company's interest in turbojets began in 1941 when it tried to obtain a licence from Britain to build the Whittle turbojet. However, these negotiations were overshadowed by the US Army, which obtained the rights to manufacture the turbojet and then turned it over to GE. In 1947 Wright took up development of the Lockheed L-1000 engine, in both its turbojet and turboprop forms, from Menasco (see Chapter 12). The USAF cancelled the turboprop work, leaving Wright to continue work on the L-1000 turbojet until 1952.

R3350 Turbo-Cyclone compound engine

The company's next foray into gas turbines concerned its R-3350 two-row, eighteen-cylinder radial Turbo-Cyclone, which was sponsored by the US Navy. The idea behind this engine was to use the exhaust energy, normally wasted, by ducting it into three turbines that, via shafts and gearing, added their power to the rear of the engine's crankshaft. The turbines were spaced around the rear section of the engine at 120-degree intervals and each was fed by the hot exhaust gases from six cylinders. These turbines had chrome-nickel steel alloy blades welded to Iconel X discs. Their connection to the crankshaft was via quill shafts and fluid couplings and each turbine produced about 180hp, which was added to the engine's output. By this means, the engine's maximum output for take-off was 3,250hp at 2,900rpm. The R-3350 Turbo-Cyclone passed its 150-hour MQT in January 1950. Beginning with Lockheed R7V Super Constellations, the engine was widely used in both military and civilian aircraft. A masterpiece of engineering, the Turbo-Cyclone represented a last throw of the dice for piston aero-engines, albeit compounded with gas turbines, in the face of the turbojet.

J65 (Sapphire) turbojet

In the meantime, despite resistance to turbojets from many of Wright's piston engine engineers, the company's president, Roy T. Hurley, had bought manufacturing licences from Britain for the Armstrong Siddeley Sapphire and the Bristol Olympus turbojets, both excellent engines with great potential; in their Americanized forms the Sapphire would be the J65 and the Olympus the J67. The company's Chief Engineer at this time was Wilton G. Lundquist and its Director of Engineering was Jack Charshafian.

Americanization of the Sapphire took about three years, far longer than expected, and involved, for example, replacing the central, machined forging of the engine with welded fabrications. The J65 was destined to power the Republic F-84F Thunderstreak fighter but the prototype flew with an Allison J35 on 3 June 1950; performance was disappointing and the second prototype flew with an imported Sapphire engine. Finally, a YF-84F Thunderstreak (11344) flew on 14 February 1951 using a YJ65-W-1 engine of 3,269kp (7,200lb) thrust. Eventually all 2,713 of the Thunderstreaks built had the J65 engine, most using the J65-W-3 of 3,275kp (7,220lb) thrust. The more powerful J65-W-7 of 3,538kp (7,800lb) thrust was used in the RF-84F Thunderflash reconnaissance version of the fighter, which featured wing-root air intakes instead of a nose intake; 715 RF-84Fs were built.

The US Navy also employed the J65, beginning with the unsuccessful North American FJ-2 Fury. The prototype of this fighter (131931) first flew on 3 July 1953, using a J65-W-2 of 3,269kp (7,200lb) thrust. A similar engine was also used to power the prototype of Lockheed's extraordinary XF-104 Starfighter (37786), which first flew on 4 March 1954 (see Chapter 21).

Douglas A4D Skyhawk

The McDonnell Douglas A-4 Skyhawk carrier-borne attack aircraft, powered by the J65 engine, turned out to be one of the US Navy's most successful post-war aircraft. The Skyhawk had a small, low-set delta wing (small enough not to require folding for carrier stowage) and also a delta-shaped tailplane at the base of its vertical fin. Air intakes flanked the fuselage just aft of the cockpit. The design of this aircraft was begun under the very experienced designer Edward H. Heinemann, with no official funding. Thus, when the US Navy began looking for a jet aircraft to replace its very successful Douglas Skyraider, McDonnell Douglas was already in a position to offer something. The ingenious Heinmann had produced a design that was less than half

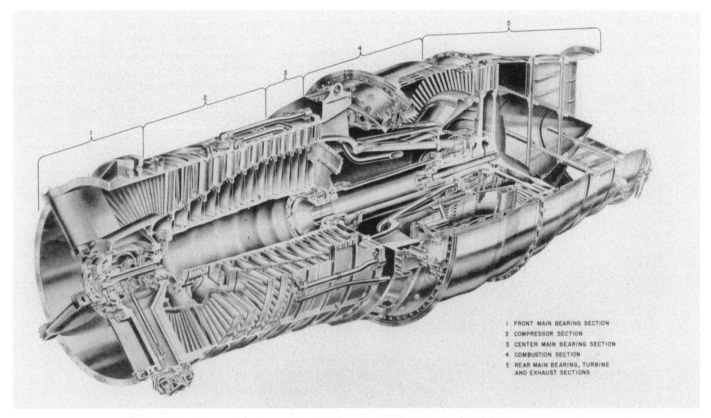

1 FRONT MAIN BEARING SECTION
2 COMPRESSOR SECTION
3 CENTER MAIN BEARING SECTION
4 COMBUSTION SECTION
5 REAR MAIN BEARING, TURBINE
  AND EXHAUST SECTIONS

Cutaway of the Wright YJ-65-W-1 axial turbojet, Americanized version of the Armstrong Siddeley Sapphire engine. AEHS, Huntsville

the weight that the Navy's specification considered feasible. This was done by extreme attention to detail and, in selecting the J65 or Sapphire engine, Heinemann considered he was using the best engine available at the time. The only shortcoming of this excellent aircraft was its short range. The Korean War brought an order for the Skyhawk but the prototype (137812) did not make its first flight until 22 June 1954. The first production A4D-1 Skyhawk (147813) flew on 14 August 1954, powered by the J65-W-2 engine. First deliveries to the US Navy began on 26 October 1956 and to the US Marine Corps in January 1957. Both services employed the type in Vietnam and it remained in service for many years (and even longer with foreign air forces). Despite its small size the Skyhawk could carry external stores of up to 4,085kg (9,000lb), in addition to its two 20mm cannon. Some 1,346 were built with J65 engines before a switch was made to either J52 or TF30 engines, when another 1,614 were built. The Skyhawk actually stayed in production until 1980. The A-4F became well known as the mount for the US Navy's Blue Angels aerobatic team, which used a four-ship formation.

A Republic F-84B Thunderjet fighter, one of the best of the straight-wing jets but still no match for swept-wing fighters such as the MiG-15. The Thunderjet was especially successful in the ground attack role in Korea and most were powered with the Wright J65 turbojet. Later, swept-wing developments of the Thunderjet were produced (Thunderstreak and Thunderflash). Central Arkansas Library System, AEC

This Republic F-84 Thunderjet (5216) was used in zero-length launching experiments using a jettisonable, solid-fuel rocket.

McDonnell Douglas A-4F Skyhawk		
Span	8.38m	(27ft 6in)
Length	12.29m	(40ft 4in)
Wing area	24.16sq m	(260sq ft)
Height	4.57m	(15ft 0in)
Empty weight	4,581kg	(10,100lb)
Maximum take-off weight (on land)	12,437kg	(27,420lb)
Maximum speed, without external stores	1,054km/h	(655mph)
Radius of action	612km	(380 miles)

Grumman F11F Tiger, the US Navy's first supersonic aircraft

The US Navy's first operational, just supersonic aircraft was the Grumman F11F Tiger, powered by the J65 engine. Its prototype, designated YF9F-9 (138604), first flew on 30 July 1954 powered by a J65-W-7 of 3,540kp (7,800lb) thrust, without afterburner. The Tiger's fuselage was area-ruled to reduce drag and the swept-back wings had leading-edge slats. The tricycle undercarriage was fuselage mounted and the air intakes flanked the fuselage just aft of the cockpit. Armament consisted of four 20mm cannon and four underwing Sidewinder air-to-air missiles. Deliveries to the US Navy began on 15 November 1954 and some 199 were built. However, the Tiger had a relatively short operational life and was superseded by the Vought F-8 Crusader. Relegated to the training role, the Tiger was perhaps best known as the mount of the US Navy's Blue Angels aerobatic team and so it was certainly agile enough.

Martin B-57 Canberra

The USAF found itself in desperate need of a new tactical bomber when the Korean War broke out. To speed the introduction of a jet-powered tactical bomber, a contest was held at Andrews AFB from what was available and the winner was the twin-engined English Electric Canberra. The Martin company was chosen to produce the Canberra under licence as the B-57, but Americanization of the entire airframe had to be undertaken and it was not until 20 July 1953 that the prototype flew. It was not long before the British semi-spherical bubble canopy was found unsuitable for the ground attack role and so a new nose section with a long canopy enclosing the crew in tandem was produced, as the B-57B. Many successful versions of the B-57 were manufactured, the RB-57D, for example, even competing with Lockheed's U-2 spy plane for altitude and range. SAC used the B-57 to overfly the Soviet Union and Taiwanese pilots flew the RB-57D over China, during the latter of which it was discovered that the country was developing an atom bomb. (Yin Chin Wang's RB-57D became the first aircraft shot down by a SAM missile, a few months before Gary Power's U-2 was shot down over the Soviet Union.) A special Canberra, flying from Germany and fitted with a Robin camera, took the first photographs (from 19,800m or 65,000ft) of the Soviet's Kapuskin Yar rocket base. Some 315 B-57s were produced with J65 engines, after which various other engines were used, depending on duty.

T49 turboprop

While the J65 was being produced, Wright began developing a 10,000shp turboprop version, designated the T49. Extra turbine stages were fitted to drive a large reduction gearbox for a four-bladed airscrew. The airscrew was of the Curtiss turbo-electric type, 4.57m (15ft) in diameter with paddle-type blades 610mm (24in) wide and with a ducted spinner. The T49's first test was in December 1952 and it eventually developed 8,000shp. Flight tests began on 26 August 1955 when two T49s replaced the inner paired turbojets on a two Boeing B-47Bs (51-2046 and 2103), these being redesignated B-47Ds. Although 9,710ehp was by then being developed, the engine was never qualified and no buyer was found.

J67 (Olympus) turbojet and the end for Wright

Following the eventual success in producing the J65 turbojet, Wright should have also had a winner in licence-producing the excellent Olympus turbojet as the J67 for the USAF. Wright made a long and thorough job of Americanizing and redesigning this engine and included a civilian version known as the JT38 Zephyr. In fact, it took too long, because P&W's J57 and JT3 turbojets claimed the whole market before them. This, unfortunately, was the end of Wright in the aero-engine field.

A Grumman F11F Tiger fighter of the US Navy's Blue Angels aerobatic team. Its engine was the Wright J65-W-7 turbojet. AEHS, Huntsville

Grumman F11F-1 Tiger			
Span		9.64m	(31ft 7½in)
Length		14.31m	(46ft 11¼in)
Wing area		23.23sq m	(250sq ft)
Height		4.03m	(13ft 2¾in)
Empty weight		6,091kg	(13,428lb)
Maximum take-off weight		10,052kg	(22,160lb)
Maximum speed	at sea level	1,224km/h or Mach 1.0	(760mph)
Service ceiling		12,770m	(41,900ft)
Range		2,044km	(1,270 miles)

Martin RB-57E Canberra with two J65-W-5 engines			
Span		19.51m	(64ft 0in)
Length		19.96m	(65ft 6in)
Wing area		89.19sq m	(960sq ft)
Empty weight		12,247kg	(27,000lb)
Maximum take-off weight		24,948kg	(55,000lb)
Maximum speed	at 6,096m (20,000ft)	968km/h or Mach 0.85	(601mph)
Service ceiling		16,154m	(53,000ft)
Range		3,700km/h	(2,300 miles)

CHAPTER TWENTY-ONE

Continuation of the General Electric Story

Soon after the end of the war General Electric had, by military command, lost its two most important engines to a competitor, following the loss to Allison of its J33 centrifugal turbojet in 1945 and then the J35 axial turbojet in 1946. This had been officially promulgated so that Allison could bring its great production capacity to bear on the turbojet. Undaunted, GE then set about building up a new Aircraft Gas Turbine Division with development and production concentrated at its Lynn plant. (Meanwhile, GE's Turbine Division at Schenectady concentrated on developing the gas turbine as a power source for locomotives, ships and industrial power generation.) Harold D. Kelsey was charged with overseeing the development of the new division at Lynn. Kelsey worked out an engine development plan that included turbojets of 2,724kp (6,000lb) thrust, turboprops of 3,000shp and test facilities that included a 30,000hp drive for testing compressors. Strangely, he received little support from the GE hierarchy and was kept chronically short of funds and facilities. In particular, a compressor drive of only 12,000hp was authorized but the head of test engineering, Eugene Stoeckly, persuaded the US Navy to donate a powerful steam turbine from a cancelled warship for compressor testing. Thus, the stage was adequately set for a great future in turbojets, no thanks to the GE executives.

TG-190 (J47) turbojet

Following Kelsey's plan, it was decided to develop an axial turbojet within the confines of the J35 but with at least 2,270kp (5,000lb) of thrust. This engine was designated the TG-190, later the J47, and the first design studies were submitted to the USAAF in May 1946. Very soon afterwards, development began under engineer Neil Burgess. The TG-190 was based on the J35 but had

a new, twelve-stage compressor giving an air mass flow of 41kg/sec (90lb/sec) at a pressure ratio of 5:1, its speed being 7,950rpm. The compressor casing consisted of two aluminium alloy castings, bolted together horizontally, and supporting one row of steel inlet guide vanes, twelve rows of steel stator blades and one row of steel straightening vanes. Twelve aluminium alloy discs were shrunk onto a hollow steel shaft to form the compressor rotor, each disc carrying a row of steel blades. The rotor shaft was supported by a roller bearing at each end and was connected to the turbine shaft by a splined coupling.

There were eight interconnected, tubular stainless-steel combustion chambers, developed for higher pressures and airflow. Each had a perforated flame tube and a duplex fuel burner with downstream injection. There was provision for water/alcohol injection halfway along each combustion chamber wall. The turbine was a single-stage type, preceded by sixty-four hollow, air-cooled steel nozzle guide vanes. There were ninety-six alloy rotor blades inserted into the rotor disc, the shaft of which was supported by a roller bearing at each end. A fabricated, stainless-steel casing surrounded the turbine and led to an exhaust nozzle with a short, fixed centre cone. A new, dry sump lubrication system was used. Almost all auxiliaries were housed in the centre of the air intake, streamlined with a large, rounded-nose fairing. The vacuum tube electronic control system devised for the J47 was not rugged enough and was the cause of many an engine stopping. Consequently, a hydromechanical system had to be used for production engines.

Development of the TG-190 was funded by the USAAF as the J47 and large-scale production was envisaged. The first example was test-run on 21 June 1947. Subsequent development did not run smoothly and there was also a need to reduce the weight, which was more than the earlier J35. To this end,

a change was made from aluminium alloy to magnesium alloy for the engine's centre casting and some of the compressor discs. Unfortunately, this was unsuccessful and so aluminium alloy was reverted to. Another problem, turbine blade failures attributed to vibration frequency coupling, was solved by redesigning the blade root fillets.

In September 1947 the first J47s were delivered to the USAAF (redesignated the USAF that month), and the first test flight was made on 20 April 1948 using a B-29 bomber as a flying test-bed. On 18 May a J47-GE-1 made its first flight in a fighter, a P-86A (47-605), which was to be designated the F-86 Sabre in 1949. That engine gave a static thrust of 2,200kp (4,850lb).

In summer 1948, J47 turbojets went into production at Lynn but larger production facilities were sought and new facilities were set up in October at Lockland, Ohio, where Wright Aero had previously built and tested piston aero-engines. The first J47s left Lockland in February 1949 and all J47 work was transferred there by November that year.

The first flight of the second prototype of the Boeing XB-47 Stratojet (46-066), powered by six J47-GE-3 engines, took place on 21 July 1948. Four of these engines were also used to power the first production North American B-45A Tornado bomber (47-001) in November 1948. The USAF obviously had faith in the eventual success of GE's J47 engine, specifying it for some of its key new aircraft, especially the F-86 fighter and B-47 bomber – both destined for fame.

North American F-86 Sabre fighter

Although the prototype F-86 Sabre had flown on a Chrysler-built J35 engine, it was the J47 engine that subsequently powered it and took it to greatness. The P-86 began

Building up a General Electric J47 turbojet. In the foreground, a compressor half casing, complete with stator blades, waits to be bolted on. AEHS, Huntsville

A cutaway display J47-GE-25 turbojet on an exhibition stand. Note the pipes leading to water injection rings halfway along each combustion chamber. AEHS, Huntsville

General Electric J47 turbojet, with and without an afterburner. AEHS, Huntsville

The straight-wing North American B-45 Tornado bomber was powered by four GE J47 turbojets. It went into service with the USAF and was well liked by its crews. Illustrated is an RB-45C reconnaissance version. Central Arkansas Library System, AEC

life as a straight-wing jet fighter for the USAF and US Navy but, after study of German wartime swept-wing research, it was redesigned to have sharply swept-back wings. The delay caused by this redesign meant that North American temporarily lost the lead to its competitors such as Republic (who were sticking with straight wings), but resulted in one of the greatest jet fighters of the 1950s. The USAF accepted this delay for the promised advantage of a swept wing but the Navy did not and purchased the straight-wing and unsuccessful FJ-1 Fury fighter.

The P-86 was designed under the leadership of J. Lee Atwood, Ed Schmued and Ray Rice. It utilized a low-mounted wing swept back at 35 degrees, with full-span leading-edge automatic slats, hydraulically boosted ailerons and slotted flaps.

Later, beginning with the F-86F advanced models, the wing was redesigned with 'hard' leading edges without the automatic slats. Great strength was given to the wings by the use of skins machined from the solid and double skins sandwiching corrugated metal between the two main spars. Fuel was carried in the wings and the centre section. The tail empennage was fully swept and there were hydraulically operated airbrakes on both sides of the rear fuselage. Later, on the F-86E, the tailplane was made of the all-moving type. The cockpit was pressurized, its bubble canopy affording a superb view, and was equipped with an ejector seat. Three 0.50in calibre machine guns were mounted on each side of the nose air intake and the tricycle undercarriage retracted inwards. A small, distinctive lip above the intake housed

a radar antenna and there was a radar gunsight. Extra fuel could be carried in underwing drop tanks. About the only mistake made in the design of the Sabre was in arming it with machine guns instead of cannon, as combat experience later showed.

The first of many P-86As entered USAF service in May 1948. No control problems were experienced in diving the fighter vertically, faster than sound. On 15 September 1948 a regular F-86A took the world speed record at 1,080km/h (671mph), its engine being a 2,359kp (5,200lb) thrust J47. In March 1949, after much difficulty in developing its afterburner, the J47-GE-7 passed the 150-hour MQT, although by the end of 1949 J47s were still averaging only seventeen hours between overhauls. Clearly, with the threat of war in Korea,

The famous North American F-86 Sabre swept-wing fighter, powered by the GE J47 turbojet, was the only fighter available at the start of the Korean War that could match the equally famous Soviet MiG-15. This Sabre has its air brakes partially opened. Central Arkansas Library System, AEC

bombers, mainly B-29s from Kadena in Japan, which were rapidly destroying North Korea's industry and strategic infrastructure. In addition, UN jets carried out a great many ground attack missions, notably the destruction of two dams by F-84 Thunderjets in May 1953. By the end of the Korean War, exaggerated claims were being made for UN air forces over the Communist air forces, although it now appears that the kill ratio of 2:1 in favour of the UN forces is about right. Most aerial victories were scored by the extraordinary F-86 Sabre. When UN pilots were matched against Soviet pilots, scores were about even. However, when UN pilots were matched against undertrained Chinese or North Korean pilots, the score was heavily in favour of the UN.

Something unique happened with jet aircraft during the Korean War when one F-86 pushed another. Following a dog fight between F-86s and MiG-15s over the latter's Antung airbase, Capt. R. Risner, one of the USAF's greatest pilots, found that his wingman was shot up and losing too much fuel to make it back to base. Risner then ordered his wingman to shut down and proceeded to push his aircraft with the upper lip of his intake against the lower edge of the other aircraft's tailpipe. Having thereby pushed his wingman within range of Cho-do island, from where he could be rescued, this valiant effort ended in tragedy when the baled-out wingman was drowned when the wind caught his parachute.

One unwelcome feature of the F-86, especially on primitive airfields, was that its

much development work was still needed on the engine. Already icing problems had been solved (by diverting some hot compressor air to hollow, inlet guide vanes) and some progress was made in weeding out cracked compressor rotors prior to assembly. On 13 December 1950 an advance detachment of the 4th Fighter Interceptor Wing (FIW) flew some F-86A Sabres to Kimpo in Korea to combat the North's swept-wing MiG-15 fighters. Although Kimpo was at first totally unsuitable for the sophisticated F-86s, the numbers based there soon grew. The first of many victories by an F-86 over the Soviet-built MiG-15s came on 17 December 1950. Something of the combat between these two legendary fighters is related in the Soviet section above.

Most combat between the F-86 and the MiG-15 took place over North Korea, along the Yalu river in what was nicknamed 'MiG Alley'. The F-86, however, was also used in the ground attack role, usually flying out of Taegu in the South. In combat the F-86 experienced many mechanical problems, as might have been expected with a new aircraft rushed into service. Examples varied quite a bit, so that there were good and not-so-good Sabres, the good ones being known by the pilots as Honchos. Against the MiG-15, the F-86 was at a disadvantage regarding operational ceiling, rate of climb, thrust-to-weight ratio and armament. However, the F-86 could accelerate in a dive more quickly, had a better gunsight and better trained pilots. On the other hand, the

cannon of the MiG-15 could more readily destroy an F-86, since it usually took a great number of machine gun bullets to destroy the very tough MiG-15.

Early in January 1951 invading Chinese troops pushed the Sabres and other United Nations' forces out of Kimpo. In the turmoil an airman was sucked into the intake of an F-86 and killed. Subsequent operations were conducted largely from Suwon, which meant consuming more fuel in order to fly north to meet the MiGs. While this was the main job of the F-86s, the MiGs were principally concerned with shooting down

Close-up showing the air intake and clean lines of the F-86 Sabre (8242) fighter. The six gun ports have been faired over in this preserved example at Duxford. Author

J47 engine needed a big electrical cart to start it, the cart plugging in at the port side of the fuselage, near the wing trailing edge. On the other hand, the T-33 jet trainer started on its own battery. It therefore came to pass that, at the Hahn airbase in Western Germany, the practice began during the later 1950s of starting an F-86 by running a T-33 in front of it. A T-33 would be placed about 5m in front of the F-86 and its engine run up to about 80 per cent. This windmilled the F-86's J47 up to about 6 per cent, which was enough to get the turbojet started.

The Sabre was exported and built under licence, seeing service in twenty countries. In Australia the F-86E was modified and built with a 3,402kp (7,500lb) thrust Rolls-Royce Avon 26 turbojet instead of the J47, while in Canada the Sabre was built with the Orenda engine. The most powerful Sabre was the F-86H fighter-bomber, which was powered by GE's J73-GE-3 of 4,046kp (8,920lb) thrust. The F-86H, built for Tactical Air Command, was the only aircraft powered by the J73 engine (successor to the J47). It was considerably more potent than the earlier Sabres and was armed with four 20mm cannon, although only 477 were built. 'Chuck' Yeager, however, managed to dive an F-86F (with J47 engine) faster than an F-86H that had 50 per cent more power. He achieved this by getting his crew chief to crank in the cooling scoops on the tailpipe, thereby causing the exhaust gas temperature to rise (dangerously) and, along with it, the thrust. Much loved by all who flew it, some 8,890 Sabres were built worldwide, including all versions.

Boeing B-47 Stratojet bomber

Before the Korean War broke out, various bomber prototypes were tested with GE engines. The huge Convair B-36 bomber, with six P&W piston engines driving pusher airscrews, had already been tested with an additional four turbojets (Allison J35s) to boost take-off and over-target dash. On 11 July 1949 the first production B-36D (49-2647) made its first flight with four J47-GE-19 turbojets as boosters and received the appellation of 'six turning, four burning'. The USAAF's first jet bomber, the well-liked North American B-45 Tornado, was re-engined with J47 engines. The Martin XB-51 was designed as a medium bomber for the USAAF and the prototype (46-685) first flew on 28 October 1949. This was a swept-wing bomber with the unusual engine installation of two J47-GE-9s beneath the forward fuselage plus one in the fuselage. Despite its good performance, only two XB-51 prototypes were built.

Already, in 1947, a far more advanced bomber, the XB-47, had been produced by Boeing in its Seattle plant. The first two prototypes of this bomber had flown with Allison J35 engines, but on 7 October 1949 the re-engined first prototype (46-065) first flew with six J47-GE-3 engines. Whereas Convair's B-46 and Martin's B-48 were similar in concept to the B-45 Tornado and remained only as prototypes, the B-47 was delayed while Boeing engineers assimilated German wartime swept-wing research data. Swept wings gave the B-47 more than an edge over the competition, in the same way that they did for the F-86 Sabre fighter. The B-47 had all flying surfaces swept, particularly the high aspect-ratio, laminar-flow, thin wings, which were swept back at 37 degrees. Three turbojets were suspended beneath each wing, two in paired nacelles and one further out in a single nacelle. The location of the engines helped resist loading on the wings, which were so thin that they had no room for fuel or landing gear. Consequently all fuel was carried in the fuselage and the main wheels, arranged in tandem fashion, retracted into the fuselage. Outrigger wheels deployed from the paired engine nacelles. In order to allow room for a large bomb bay (early nuclear weapons were large and heavy), the fuel was distributed along the fuselage and had to be managed in a manner that kept the bomber in balance. The crew of three were housed in a pressurized cockpit having a bubble canopy and some glazed nose panels.

The very clean lines and high wing loading of the B-47 resulted in a very long landing run and this could only be shortened by use of a large braking parachute. A second, smaller drogue chute was also developed for use as an in-flight air brake. The purpose of this was to allow landing approaches to be made at relatively high engine power, since acceleration in the event of an overshoot was very poor with early turbojets. In case an overshoot became necessary, the drogue chute was jettisoned and high engine power was already available. In a normal landing the drogue chute was simply left attached. Again, because of poor acceleration characteristics, a built-in jet-assisted take-off (JATO) system was developed, the rockets exhausting from nine nozzles on each side of the fuselage, aft of the wings.

With the flight of the prototypes, it was soon found that the B-47's performance was even better than predicted. This was mainly due to the drag being 25 per cent less than estimated, with consequent benefit on speed and range. A batch of ten B-47A production aircraft was built for the training of factory and USAF personnel and then production began in earnest with the B-47B. By now the bomber was known as the Stratojet. In service with the Strategic Air Command (SAC), the B-47 did not have the range for intercontinental missions, which became the province of its big sister, the B-52. To power the B-47B, GE developed the J47-GE-23 and 25 turbojets, which developed 2,633kp (5,800lb) of thrust. These engines featured a thin disc turbine wheel, a high-airflow compressor and provision for water injection. They

North American F-86A Sabre			
Span		11.31m	(37ft 1½in)
Length		11.44m	(37ft 6½in)
Wing area		26.76sq m	(288sq ft)
Height		4.47m	(14ft 8¾in)
Empty weight		4,582kg	(10,093lb)
Loaded weight		7,208kg	(15,876lb)
Maximum speed	at low level	1,090km/h	(677mph)
	at 10,670m (35,000ft)	958km/h or Mach 0.90	(595mph)
Initial climb rate		2,277m/min	(7,470ft/min)
Service ceiling		14,630m	(48,000ft)
Range, with drop tanks		2,045km	(1,270 miles)

The Martin XB-51 jet bomber of 1949 performed well, with two J47 engines beneath the forward fuselage and one in the rear fuselage. However, only two prototypes were built, the first (6685) being shown at its roll-out. Central Arkansas Library System, AEC

Outclassing all other American, straight-wing, jet bombers was the revolutionary, swept-wing Boeing B-47 Stratojet, seen here landing. It used six GE J47 turbojets. Central Arkansas Library System, AEC

Inspecting No. 2 engine, a GE J47, of a Boeing B-47 Stratojet bomber at Wright-Patterson AFB, Dayton, Ohio, January 1951. Central Arkansas Library System, AEC

This fine study of a B-47A Stratojet illustrates its clean lines to good effect. The fastest bomber of its day, it could reach 965km/h (600mph) on the power of its six GE J47 engines. Visible on the rear fuselage side are the nozzles of some of its eighteen built-in rockets for heavy take-offs. This particular Stratojet (49-1900) was the first of a production batch of ten used for training purposes. Boeing Airplane Company

also had conical shutters that could be closed over the engine air intake in the event of a breakdown, thereby minimizing asymmetric drag. This feature indicates that engine failures were not uncommon.

While the Lockheed and Douglas companies were brought in to boost B-47B production (altogether 2,060 B-47s were built), Packard Motors and the Studebaker Corporation were brought in to increase production of the J47 engine as the J47-PM-25 and J47-ST-25 respectively. The J47-GE-25 developed a thrust of 3,269kp (7,200lb) with water injection, which was standard on that model. The final model was the J47-GE-33, which had the electronic control system and gave a thrust of 3,473kp (7,650lb). At the peak of production, in 1954, J47s were being produced at an unprecedented rate of 975 per month. The bulk of the engines went to power B-47 bombers and F-86 fighters, made more urgent by the Korean War. Production of the J47 ended in 1956, by which time 36,500 had been made.

XJ53 and J73 turbojets

During the long and difficult development of the J47 turbojet, GE had acquired a considerable bank of knowledge and expertise and, by 1951, was able to begin looking at more advanced projects. The first of these had its roots in late 1947 when the USAF asked GE to study a turbojet of unprecedented power for a Mach 1.8 bomber. Designated the XJ53, the engine had a thirteen-stage axial compressor with variable-incidence inlet guide vanes, a compression ratio of 7.7:1 and an air mass flow of 120kg/sec (264lb/sec). It made use of titanium and had a two-stage turbine and cannular combustion chambers. The XJ53 first ran in March 1951 and passed a fifty-hour PFRT two years later at 8,150kp (17,950lb) static thrust. A J53-GE-3 version, of similar size and weight, gave a thrust of 9,534kp (21,000lb) and was intended for missile propulsion. However, achieving this thrust was one thing but keeping the weight within reasonable limits was another: at 2,950kg (6,500lb), the J53 was far too heavy and failed to find any application.

The next stage was to scale the J53 down to J47 size to produce the J47-GE-21, later redesignated the J73. This turbojet featured a twelve-stage axial compressor with variable inlet guide vanes, a compression ratio of 7:1 and an air mass flow of 64.47kg/sec (142lb/sec). A two-stage turbine was used and a fixed-area exhaust nozzle. The J73 gave a maximum thrust of 3,550kp (7,820lb) for a dry weight of 1,657kg (3,650lb). Only the F-86H Sabre fighter used this engine, of which only 870 were built.

To help with its engine development, GE began head hunting in Europe for capable

Boeing B-47E-II with J47-GE-25 engines			
Span		35.36m	(116ft)
Length		32.92m	(108ft)
Wing area		132.8sq m	(1,428sq ft)
Height		8.53m	(28ft)
Empty weight		36,663kg	(80,756lb)
Loaded weight		93,842kg	(206,700lb)
Maximum speed	at 4,968m (16,300ft)	975km/h or Mach 0.83	(606mph)
Cruising speed	at 11,735m (38,500ft)	897km/h	(557mph)
Climb rate		740m/min	(2,430ft/min)
with water injection		1,420m/min	(4,660ft/min)
Service ceiling		12,344m	(40,500ft)
Ferry range		6,496km	(4,035miles)

engineers. During the early 1950s, for example, Gunther Diedrich (formerly head of Germany's Argus pulsejet work) was interviewing engineers in London who answered advertisements placed by GE. Examples of successful recruitment were engineers from BMW, including Bruno Bruckmann and Peter Kappus. Others had earlier gone to the USA under Operation Paperclip.

Variable stators

In the summer of 1951, under Gerhard Neumann (previously of BMW), the question was addressed of how to design a compressor that could deal with very high flight speeds and also low speeds without stalling, the latter condition usually occurring due to excess airflow through the compressor at low flight speeds. Neumann, who had joined GE in 1948 and was to become head of the Jet Engine Department in 1955, chose to investigate variable incidence stator blades as a solution. He tells us:

We laid out on paper a new type of jet engine, about which I had talked with La Pierre (and Roy Shoults), with a modified

type of compressor that had variable stators … Our aerodynamicists were convinced that engine performance and fuel consumption could be improved dramatically if the angle of the vanes somehow could be varied 10 to 30 degrees around their bases during engine operation. To accomplish this, I proposed a system that would let the stators change angles during flight without affecting their reliability. Thus, the name 'variable stators' was created.

A standard fourteen-stage compressor was then modified as an eleven-stage compressor with the first five stages of stator blades being variable. Tests were completed on this compressor (V.511) by January 1952 and pronounced a success, since the compressor was found to be stable and stall-free under all conditions. GE then filed a patent for the variable stator compressor, with Neumann's name as the inventor. While these tests were being made, the design of a demonstration engine, designated VSXE (variable stator experimental engine) or GOL-1590, was begun. Further variable stator tests were made with a fourteen-stage compressor and the GOL-1590 engine made its first run on 16 December 1953.

J79 turbojet, first US Mach 2.0 engine

Meanwhile, the USAF issued GE with a study contract for an engine able to cruise at Mach 0.9 and attain a combat speed of Mach 2.0, while at the same time having good fuel consumption and low weight. To meet these demanding requirements, GE formed a project team under Perry T. Egbert and design work began on 1 January 1953 of what was to become the J79-1 turbojet. (Owing to illness, Egbert was later replaced by Neil Burgess, formerly project manager on the J47.) Considerable argument had ensued between the engineers over the three ways to design the compressor of a Mach 2.0 turbojet: dump or bleed excess air overboard; use a twin-spool rotor; or use variable stators. The twin-spool would lead to complexity and considerable weight, while bleeding air was thought unattractive for a large engine. General Manager C.W. La Pierre made the final choice of variable stators and there was welcome support for this choice after the test compressor gave first-class results. This decision was at variance with most engineers elsewhere, such as those at P&W and Rolls-Royce, who

General Electric J79 axial turbojet. On the right, inlet end, can be seen the rings and bellcranks used to alter the incidence of the compressor stator blades. On the left can be seen the relatively short afterburner and two of the actuators for the variable-area exhaust nozzle. The J79 engine made Mach 2.0 fighters and bombers practical. Central Arkansas Library System, AEC

favoured the twin-spool approach and, nevertheless, achieved excellent results.

In April 1954 the USAF issued a contract to develop the GOL-1590 as the J79 turbojet. The world's first production Mach 2.0 engine made its debut on 8 June 1954 with the first run of the J79-GE-1 variable-stator turbojet. To comfortably cope with Mach 2.0, the engine had a maximum capability of Mach 2.4. The first (subsonic) test flight of the J79 was made on 20 May 1955, the engine being mounted in a retractable pod beneath a B-45 Tornado bomber.

The J79 had a seventeen-stage axial compressor with variable inlet guide vanes and six stages of variable stator blades. Its maximum pressure ratio was 13.5:1 and the air mass flow was 77.18kg/sec (170lb/sec). The incidence of the stators in each stage was altered by means of a short arm on the outer end of each stator blade engaging in a slot in a ring surrounding the casing. The rings for all the stages were moved circumferentially by means of bellcranks, all linked together and powered by a servo. The engine had a ten flame tube cannular combustion chamber, giving a turbine temperature of about 930°C. Following the three-stage turbine was a high-augmentation-ratio afterburner and a variable-area convergent-divergent exhaust nozzle. Most of the accessories were clustered below the compressor casing. The J79, with afterburner, actually came out as lighter than the basic J47, a remarkable achievement, but it initially had a number of faults, chiefly the failure to meet the specific fuel consumption guarantee. At the end of its development the J79-GE-17 was giving a normal continuous thrust of 5,040kp (11,100lb), or 8,090kp (17,820lb) with afterburner on, its afterburning thrust augmentation ratio being the highest developed up to that time. At its normal continuous thrust, the specific fuel consumption was 0.810 (rising to 1.965 in afterburner mode). The J79-GE-17 weighed 1,740kg (3,835lb) dry, had a length of 5.30m (17ft 4½in) and a diameter of 0.99m (3ft 3in).

Development of the J79 had been greatly facilitated by the large test chamber built in Building 29G at Lynn, under Gerhard Neumann's supervision. Power for the chamber was derived from a 35,000hp ex-Navy steam turbine and altitudes from sea level to 18,285m (60,000ft) and speeds from zero to supersonic could be simulated.

Lockheed F-104 Starfighter

With the promise of a Mach 2.0 engine came the possibility of Mach 2.0 fighters and even bombers: here manufacturers were thinking ahead of the military. Results of the first jet aircraft combat in Korea were of great interest and in 1952 the USAF commissioned designers to go to Korea and solicit the views of pilots and generals. Their brief was to find out how American aircraft could better meet the challenge from Soviet aircraft. The MiG-15 had clearly shown that greater speed and altitude performance was needed.

At the Lockheed factory, under Clarence 'Kelly' Johnson's direction, studies of many fighter layouts, some large, had been under way since the company's F-80 was initiated. Following his trip to Korea, Johnson decided in November 1952 to go for a small fighter concentrating almost entirely on the parameters of high speed, fast climb rate and high ceiling. The resulting design showed a fighter with virtually everything packed into the fuselage and a tiny, unswept wing having an extraordinary thickness ratio of only 3.36 per cent! Lockheed was successful in selling this design to the USAF and received an order for two prototypes, designated XF-104, in March 1953. During

the development of the airframe, which bristled with novelty, thin flying surfaces were mounted on five-inch air-to-ground rockets (sent back from Korea) and fired skyward from Edwards AFB. Sometimes the wings (or tailplanes) were torn away by flutter, but the recording equipment was parachuted down at the end of the burn. In the design of the thin wings, direct benefit was gained from the research carried out by Douglas on its X-3 Stiletto (see Chapter 18).

By the time the XF-104 prototypes were nearing completion, no J79 engine was ready. The only suitable engine available for test flights was the Wright J65-W-3 (licence-built British Sapphire) of 3,270kp (7,200lb) thrust. This thrust was lower than the aircraft was designed for, but sufficient to get started, and so the engine was fitted into the airframe. On 4 March 1954 the XF-104 prototype (37786) made its maiden flight, piloted by Tony Le Vier, from Edwards AFB. Later the 4,767kp (10,500lb) thrust J65-W-6 was fitted but the aircraft was barely supersonic and plain, sharp-lipped side inlets were used, without conical shock bodies. These early flights met with numerous problems but provided initial data on the airframe. Already, in January 1954, the USAF had ordered 15 YF-104As, now named the Starfighter, and this was followed in 1955 by an order for 155 F-104As. All these fighters were to be powered by J79 engines. From 5 May 1954 Lockheed engineers began meeting with GE engineers to coordinate the development of airframe and engine. Extensively redesigned, the F-104A was externally most recognizable by the addition of half-cone shock diffusers in the air intakes.

Lockheed XF-104 prototype. With its powerful GE J79 engine and tiny, thin wings, this interceptor was tailored for high speeds (up to Mach 2.0), a fast climb rate and a high ceiling. However, if the engine failed, the aircraft flew like a brick and a successful landing was unlikely. While the USAF eventually rejected it, many F-104 Starfighters were made and exported. Central Arkansas Library System, AEC

Once Lockheed received a J79-GE-3A engine, the prototype YF-104A (55-2595) was able to make its maiden flight on 17 February 1956. In afterburner mode, this engine could provide a thrust of 6,720kp (14,800lb). Although GE was said to have resolved problems with the J79 engine, after the J79-GE-3 passed a fifty-hour PFRT on 1 December 1955, engine problems were responsible for various accidents and groundings of the YF-104. During the development programme, aircraft were lost after the eyelids of the afterburner opened, reducing the thrust below that needed to keep the aircraft in the air: with its tiny wings, the YF-104 flew like a brick if its thrust was cut. Airframe problems, such as jettisoned wingtip tanks striking the tail, were also met and resolved. On 27 April 1956 the F-104 exceeded Mach 2.0 for the first time and was soon flying at altitudes of up to 18,300m (60,000ft). Finally, on 26 January 1958, the first deliveries of the F-104A commenced to the 83rd Fighter Interceptor Squadron (FIS) at Hamilton AFB.

The essence of the F-104A was its very small, sharp wing, tailored for flight at Mach 2.0. Indeed, the leading edge of its wing was so sharp that felt and wood guards were fitted on the ground to prevent personnel having nasty accidents. This wing, with a 26-degree taper on leading and trailing edges, was a mere 6.68m (21ft 11in) in span (a third of which was taken up by the fuselage width) and its maximum depth at the root was only 107mm (4.2in), tapering down to a mere 50mm (1.96in) at the tip. The wings had 10 degrees of anhedral and had conventional spars covered with a single, machined-from-solid skin top and bottom. Attachment to the fuselage was via five forged alloy rings forming part of the fuselage structure. Wing controls consisted of full-span, leading edge flaps for landing and take-off, ailerons and, inboard of the ailerons, blown flaps for landing, take-off and manoeuvring. The idea of the blown flap was that air, bled from the engine, was blown through small nozzles and directed over the upper surfaces of the trailing edge flaps to smooth out the airflow and hold it to the surface of the wing and the flap. By this means, greater lift was generated and acceptable take-off and landing speeds were achieved. Since the wing was so thin, almost nothing could be fitted inside it. Therefore, hydraulic jacks to operate the leading and trailing edge flaps were housed in the wing root fillets; to operate the ailerons, servo valves were inside the wings to operate ten miniature hydraulic jacks per aileron, since there was no room for a full-size jack. Of course, the problem with getting such a 'hot ship' onto the ground using blown flaps was that these were not available in the event of an engine flame-out. An all-moving tailplane was fitted to the top of the fin.

The long, slim fuselage had a pointed nose and a cockpit positioned well forward. Originally a downwards-firing ejector seat was fitted, due to fears about an ejected pilot clearing the tall tail empennage. Fuselage side air intakes were positioned before the wings and these intakes had half-cone centre bodies to provide, in conjunction with the sharp lips of the intakes, appropriate shock waves to slow the supersonic airflow and aid pressure recovery. This technique followed on from wartime research in Germany by Dr Klaus Oswatitsch. To readily adapt to high and low speed conditions, a large amount of secondary airflow was ducted around the engine and discharged around the exhaust nozzle, one aim of this being to cool the ducting of the large afterburner. The exhaust nozzle was fully variable by means of hydraulically driven petals. For start-up and taxiing, there were hinged doors on the side of each intake, aft of the centre bodies, to admit low-speed air.

The tricycle undercarriage retracted into the fuselage and there was an emergency ram-air turbine (in case of engine failure), fuselage side air brakes, an emergency runway arrester hook and a revolving barrel M61 20mm cannon firing at the rate of 6,000 rounds per minute. Little electronic equipment could be fitted into the fuselage beyond what was strictly necessary and so all-weather capability was not possible. Furthermore, the reliability of the J79 was poor. A flame-out faced the pilot with either a landing at 442km/h (275mph), since there was no compressor bleed air available for the blown flaps, or downwards ejecting, which was not possible at low level. With the introduction of the F-104G and other models for other countries, the upwards-firing British Martin Baker ejection seat was fitted.

It was soon found that the F-104A, striking and as fast as it was, was of limited use to the USAF and dangerous. Most were grounded by April 1958 after more than seventy had been lost, and it was virtually withdrawn from service by 1959, with fewer than 200 supplied. Most were designated surplus and sold to foreign air forces, but this was not before USAF pilots had chalked up many records with it, including the world speed record of 2,259.83km/h (1,404.19mph).

Following this disappointing failure with the USAF, Lockheed set about adapting the F-104A to take all types of underwing armament and electronics. The weight and engine power grew but, surprisingly, not the wing. Ground attack was now included in its missions. The USAF remained not particularly interested and so the Starfighter finished up largely as an export and licence-built machine, in various forms, particularly for the air forces of West Germany, Japan, Canada and Italy. In the ground-attack role the F-104 was successful, but the F-104G of the West German Luftwaffe suffered a high rate of attrition, owing, it was said, to a lack of experience in its crews. The fine-looking Starfighter was also very unforgiving of mistakes. Including all variants worldwide, some 2,600 F-104s were built, a considerable number for an aircraft that was dangerous, of limited use and with a very short range. The major variant was the F-104G ground-attack version.

Lockheed F-104G Starfighter with J79-GE-11A turbojet		
Span without wingtip tanks	6.68m	(21ft 11in)
Length	16.69m	(54ft 9in)
Wing area	18.22sq m	(196.1sq ft)
Height	4.15m	(13ft 6in)
Empty weight	6,390kg	(14,082lb)
Maximum loaded weight	13,054kg	(28,779lb)
Maximum level speed at 12,200m (40,000ft)	2,092km/h or Mach 1.969	(1,300mph)
Service ceiling	16,750m	(55,000ft)
Radius of action	507km	(315 miles)

Convair B-58 Hustler bomber

In its day, the performance of the F-104 was hard to believe. Even more so, however, was that of the B-58 Mach 2.0 bomber, also powered by the J79 engine. The technical challenges posed in the building of a Mach 2.0 bomber were enormous and unprecedented. In 1949 the USAF was already looking far ahead for its future bombers and its Air Research and Development Command sought the views of the aircraft industry regarding a supersonic bomber. A competition was organized and the Convair company at Fort Worth was considered to offer the best ideas, based on the company's experience with its F-102 Delta Dagger interceptors. Originally two or even three GE J53 turbojets were envisaged to power the bomber. After a great deal of study, research and many proposals, the bomber that eventually emerged was a delta-winged aircraft powered by four J79 turbojets and, curiously, carrying its weapons in a large, jettisonable pod beneath the fuselage and other external racks. Finally Convair received a USAF contract in August 1952 for two XB-58 prototypes, the weapons systems and all support and maintenance equipment.

The B-58 had a 60-degree delta wing with a cambered leading edge and only 3.46 per cent thickness ratio at the root. The wing was almost filled with fuel tanks, apart from space to accommodate the retracted undercarriage, and had a set of three large elevons on each trailing edge. Further fuel was carried in the fuselage and the weapons pod, and there was an in-flight refuelling receptacle in front of the cockpit windshield. The fuselage was 'waisted', or shaped according to area rule with the wing, carried a single fin and rudder, and a single radar-controlled M-61 Vulcan cannon in its tail cone for rear defence. Air conditioning and ejection seats (in capsules) were provided for the crew of three. The four J79 engines were each in separate nacelles suspended from pylons raked forward of the wing leading edges. Each nacelle intake had a circular, sharp lip and a movable, conical centre body. As in the F-104 fighter, the engines had variable bypass, cooling air flows and variable exhaust nozzles. The fuselage was packed with complex electronics for navigation, bombing and systems management.

Convair B-58A Hustler with J79-GE-5B engines		
Span	17.32m	(56ft 10in)
Length	29.49m	(96ft 9in)
Wing area	143.35sq m	(1,543sq ft)
Height	9.58m	(31ft 5in)
Empty weight, without pod	25,202kg	(55,560lb)
Maximum take-off weight	73,937kg	(163,000lb)
Maximum speed at high altitude	2,128km/h or Mach 2.0	(1,322mph)
Take-off speed (loaded)	400km/h	(248mph)
Initial climb rate	5,180m/min	(17,000ft/min)
Range without refuelling	8,248km	(5,125 miles)

Lockheed B-58 Hustler Mach 2.0 bomber. Four GE J79 turbojets were suspended beneath the delta wing and the unusual weapons pod beneath the fuselage also carried some of the fuel. The prototype began flying in 1956 but the complex development was so lengthy that the Hustler did not enter service with Strategic Air Command until 1960. Central Arkansas Library System, AEC

On 11 November 1956 the prototype XB-58 (55660), without the under-fuselage pod, made its first flight piloted by B.A. Erickson. This machine was powered by four J79-GE-1 engines of 4,360kp (9,600lb) thrust each. By now the XB-58 had been named the Hustler. Aerodynamically it seemed promising, but there were plenty of engine, airframe and other problems requiring attention. Indeed, the potential for problems with such a complex machine was great. Altogether thirty aircraft were ordered for development, including the two prototypes and 28 YB-58s, but numerous accidents occurred.

Problems affecting the J79 engines included troublesome control of the afterburners that gave asymmetric thrust, leading to yawing of the bomber at supersonic speeds. The engines were also subject to vibration, which caused fatigue cracks in the ducting and both forward and aft sections of the fuselage within the short time of about fifty hours of flight. Instability in the YB-58s was caused by fuel moving around too much as the aircraft accelerated or slowed down. Problems also occurred with the tyres, brakes and electronic systems.

Naturally all these problems took time to solve. It was not until 1 August 1960 that the B-58A Hustler became operational with SAC's 43rd Bomb Wing at Carswell AFB. The bomber's usual warload was five nuclear bombs carried in a pod almost two-thirds the length of the fuselage. The Hustler's mission could be carried out with one refuelling. SAC's B-58As achieved numerous records that eclipsed the performance of many contemporary fighters: these included a speed of 2,095km/h (1,302.7mph) in May 1961 and a flight up to 26,018m (85,361ft) with a 5,000kg (11,023lb) bomb load. As well as development aircraft, just over 170 B-58s were built to equip SAC wings. They were finally withdrawn from service in the late 1960s, due to very high operating costs. The CV-58-9, a projected civil version powered by four J58 engines and designed to carry twenty-six passengers, was not built.

Other J79 projects

While the B-58 was being developed, GE endeavoured to speed up development of the J79 engine by simultaneously working on three different models. These were the J79-GE-2 destined for the North American

A5 Vigilante and the F-4 Phantom fighters, the J79-GE-5 for the B-58 Hustler and the J79-GE-7 for the F-104 Starfighter. Thus, both the USAF and the US Navy were anxious to get the J79.

The prototype YF4H-1 Phantom (142259) first flew on 27 May 1958, powered by two J79-GE-3A engines of 4,360kp (9,600lb) thrust, or 6,720kp (14,800lb) in afterburner mode. This aircraft was designed as a multi-role fighter/strike aircraft for the US Navy and, after much modification, eventually proved to be a highly capable aircraft that subsequently also served with the USAF and the US Marine Corps. Used worldwide, more than 5,000 had been built by the time production ended in 1979, well beyond the timeline of this book. Also largely beyond this book's timeline was the Vigilante Mach 2.0 tactical strike aircraft for the US Navy. The prototype A-5A first flew on 31 August 1958, piloted by Dick Wenzell and powered by two J79-GE-2 engines of 4,360kp (9,600lb) thrust, or 7,330kp (16,150lb) with the afterburner. The A-5A was extremely advanced and featured blown flaps, variable configuration air intakes, computer systems and storage between the engines for fuel, and a nuclear weapon that was ejected rearwards. In place of ailerons and a rudder this aircraft had, respectively, differentially moving tailplanes and an all-moving vertical fin. The Vigilante was operational with the US Navy until 1979, by when some 205 of all types had been built.

For a long time the TBO and serviceability of the J79 was very poor, due, it was said, to underfunding by the USAF slowing down development. As we have seen, underdeveloped engines were often put into aircraft with dire results. Even by 1959, for example, the J79-GE-8 had only just passed its 150-hour MQT. However, funding was later increased and the J79 was turned into a good turbojet. Aircraft powered by it have set forty-six world records. In October 1953 GE was reorganized to develop and build its big engines only at the giant plant renamed Evendale, outside Cincinnati, Ohio. A total of 17,309 J79s were manufactured for military use, all from GE's Evendale plant. At the same time, a small engine division was set up at the Lynn plant under Jack Parker as general manager and Ed Woll as engineering manager; its products were to be small turbojets and, for helicopters, turboshaft engines.

Civilian CJ-805 turbojet

A simplified, civil version of the J79, the CJ-805, was produced in 1956. The CJ-805-3B turbojet had a take-off thrust of 5,290kp (11,650lb) at 7,684rpm. It had no water injection and was fitted with sound suppressors and thrust reversers. Test flying of a CJ-805-3 of 5,080kp (11,200lb) thrust began in October 1958 by replacing the two engines of a Douglas RB-66A Destroyer (22828) of the USAF. Four CJ-508s powered the Convair CV-880 jet airliner that first flew on 27 January 1959 from the San Diego plant. It was intended to be a slightly smaller but faster rival to the similarly configured Douglas DC-8 and Boeing 707 airliners. The CV-880 began airline service in May 1960 with TWA and was the first aircraft to fly with sound suppressors. Production ended in 1962 after small numbers had been built. At this time, the variable stator system had still not been perfected, since, at least in the case of CJ-805s used on the CV-880 airliners, the variable stators would sometimes stick in the low-incidence position after engine start-up. In such a case, the ground crew would free the stators.

Civilian CJ-805-23 turbofan

A turbofan version of the CJ-805, designated the CJ-805-23, was then built by adding a ducted fan with its own turbines to the rear of a CJ-805. Each fan blade was connected to its own turbine blade mounted in an inner annulus in the exhaust flow, there being no mechanical drive from the engine. The design was led by Peter Kappus, who had been with BMW during the war. (The reader may recall, however, that exactly this layout was proposed by Frank Whittle in his W.2/700 projected turbojet with aft fan, but such work, including his L.R.1 turbofan engine, was cancelled by the British government in 1944. Also in Britain, the work of Metropolitan-Vickers on turbofan engines with aft fans was cancelled in 1946.) The static thrust of the CJ-805-23B was 7,310kp (16,100lb) and the specific fuel consumption was dramatically lower than the turbojet. This turbofan had a thrust reverser but no water injection or sound suppressor. In fact, the engine was very quiet due to the low-velocity, cold air stream from the fan surrounding the high-velocity, hot turbojet exhaust. Four CJ-805-23B engines powered the Convair

CV-990 Coronado jet airliner (derived from the 880), which first flew on 4 January 1961. This airliner went into limited service but the economy and range promised by the turbofan engines could not be realized since, disappointingly, the drag of the airframe turned out to be higher than estimated. Therefore, only thirty-seven CV-990 airliners were sold and the CJ-805-23 turbofan found no other markets. However, GE went on to develop successful turbofan engines that did find worldwide military and civilian markets.

J85 turbojet

As already mentioned, a small engine division was set up at Lynn in October 1953. Late in 1954 GE's Lynn plant proposed to the USAF the development of small turbojets for various uses. It happened that the Air Force needed a small turbojet to power the projected McDonnell GAM-72 Quail, which was to be carried by the B-52 bomber and released purely as a decoy. GE then received a contract in November 1954 to develop what was to become the J85 turbojet. Simplicity and a high thrust-to-weight ratio were the keynotes of this engine.

The specification called for a turbojet of 1,135kp (2,500lb) thrust, a compressor pressure ratio of 7:1 and a thrust-to-weight ratio of an unprecedented 10:1. This engine was designated the X104 by the USAF. GE designed it with a six-stage axial compressor, an annular combustion chamber, a two-stage uncooled turbine and a simple, two bearing arrangement. One bearing was behind the first four compressor stages and the other bearing was in front of the turbines, this leaving the turbines and part of the compressor overhung. However, this engine was not built.

In December 1954 GE's Project Manager at Lynn, Joe Buechel, led the design of another engine that was to become the J85. (It was in competition with Fairchild's J83, which was later cancelled.) The J85 had a short, six-stage axial compressor, a combustion chamber of the annular type and a two-stage turbine. It had a long afterburner and a variable, petal-type, convergent exhaust nozzle. The rotor shaft had two central, anti-friction bearings, leaving the compressor and the turbine overhung. However, a hollow in the compressor allowed the forward bearing to be positioned partly inside the length of the compressor.

The experimental Ryan XV-5A lift fan VTOL aircraft (24506) at San Diego. It used two General Electric J85-GE-5B turbojets as gas generators to drive the lift fans in the wings and nose. The flaps over the wing fans, shown closed, hinged upwards from each wing fence. Louvres over the nose fan are also shown closed. The J85s exhausted below the tail for forward flight. The first flight was made on 25 May 1964 and the first transitional flights were made in December 1964. Ryan

Northrop T-38 Talon with two J85-GE-5As		
Span	7.70m	(25ft 3in)
Length	14.14m	(46ft 4½in)
Wing area	15.79sq m	(170sq ft)
Height	3.91m	(12ft 10½in)
Empty weight	3,250kg	(7,164lb)
Maximum take-off weight	5,485kg	(12,093lb)
Maximum speed at 10,975m (36,000ft)	1,381km/h or Mach 1.3	(858mph)
Service ceiling	16,335m	(53,600ft)
Range	1,759km	(1,093 miles)

The first J85 was put on the test bench within a year of design commencing, but would not run owing to inadequate airflow and pressure at the design speed. GE found that part of the compressor problem was due to the blades being manufactured in the same way as large engine blades (i.e. by forging and cropping) and the accuracy was not good enough for smaller blades. The compressor was redesigned as a seven-stage and then an eight-stage axial. Mechanical changes included a new front frame at the inlet that included variable inlet guide vanes, an anti-icing system and an extra front bearing for the rotor, giving the engine three bearings. The variable-area exhaust nozzle was redesigned as the convergent-divergent type. The engine being developed for the GAM-72 decoy missile did not have an afterburner and was designated the YJ85-GE-3. Development of the afterburner came about to suit an application in Northrop's T-38A Talon supersonic trainer that arose in 1956. The afterburning version was designated XJ85-GE-5. It seemed that 1956 was to be an excellent year for the J85 programme, since not only the T-38 Talon but also North American's T-39 Sabreliner were set to utilize it.

When the YJ85-GE-1 with a seven-stage compressor was run in January 1956, it gave a static thrust of only 776kp (1,710lb) and it was, in any case, not self-sustaining. It also exhibited vibration and surging problems. The surging eventually damaged the engine and it was abandoned. In January 1959 the redesigned J85-GE-5 with eight-stage compressor, three bearings and afterburner first went on test, but many problems remained to be solved. Deadlines for aircraft installation could only be met by using interim engines. Thus the prototype North American T-39 Sabreliner (NA-246 UTX) made its first flight on 16 September 1958 with two J85-GE-3 engines, this representing the first manned flight of J85 engines. The prototype of the Northrop YT-38 Talon (N-156F) made its first flight on 30 July 1959 using two YJ85-GE-1 engines. The first flight of the afterburning XJ85-GE-5 was completed in September 1959 by mounting one in a retractable pod lowered from a Convair F-102 fighter's missile bay. Finally, in December 1960, J85-GE-5 engines began to come off the production line and the engine went on to be a great success for the company. It found many applications, including the T-38 Talon (the first supersonic trainer) and the F-5 Freedom Fighter.

Many versions of the engine were developed and some 12,000 in all were manufactured. The afterburning J85-GE-21, for example, gave a thrust of 1,590kp (3,500lb) dry or 2,270kp (5,000lb) with reheat. It had a nine-stage compressor giving an air mass flow of 24.06kg/sec (53lb/sec) at a pressure ratio of 8.3:1. Its dry weight was 310kg (684lb), diameter 0.51m (1ft 8.2in) and length 2.94m (9ft 7.7in). With reheat, its thrust-to-weight ratio was high at 7.3:1. This made it a suitable engine for VTOL aircraft experiments in the Ryan XV-5. (The J85's best thrust-to-weight ratio was exceeded by the Rolls-Royce RB 108 lift engine at almost 8:1, without afterburning, first run in July 1955.)

Civilian CJ610 turbojet

Civil versions of the J85 were developed, chiefly to power the first small business or executive jets. These engines were the CJ610 turbojet and the CF700 small turbofan. The CF700 continued the theme of utilizing a bypass aft fan unit. The story of these engines belongs to the early 1960s and beyond, but it is of special interest to mention that CJ610-9 engines were used to power new-build Messerschmitt Me 262s in the USA, the first of which flew in 2005.

T58 turboshaft engine

Apart from these small turbojets, the Lynn plant was also involved with developing and producing turboshaft engines for helicopters. The first turboshaft design study was made in 1953 and, after estimating the requirements of military helicopters expected by 1958, work began in February 1954 on the XT58 project. This project was managed by Harold T. Hokanson under design engineering manager Bill Lawson. The goals for the XT58 were to eclipse the Lycoming T53, have a power of 1,050shp and a weight of 114kg (250lb) without gearbox.

By March 1954 the XT58 design was firmed up. The prototype was to have an eight-stage axial compressor with a pressure ratio of 8.3:1. Very thin rotor discs were secured together by explosive rivets. For the first time in a GE engine, the combustion chamber was of the annular type. This was made possible because the small size allowed entire combustion chamber tests to be made, using the airflow capacity available at the plant. J.A. Benson was responsible for combustion chamber design. A separate, or free, power turbine was positioned behind the compressor's turbine with an output shaft to the rear to connect to the gearbox. The exhaust duct was bifurcated either side of the output shaft.

By June 1954 the US Navy approved development of the XT58 turboshaft engine and the prototype went on the test bench on 11 March 1955. Unfortunately the engine would not run in a self-sustaining manner. By removing the power turbine, it did run on 5 April 1955 but its performance was down. Faults and problems were many and included power turbine blade failure due to vibration. By developing dampers that changed the turbine blade natural frequency, this latter problem was solved. Poor aerodynamics and fatigue caused by vibration also afflicted the compressor. These and other problems arose from the lack of component testing and that was blamed on budget and time constraints. It was decided that only detailed testing and redesign would achieve satisfactory results.

Because of the difficulty at the time of instrumenting a small compressor, an elongated version was built that was more easily instrumented. From this it was found that the required performance could be obtained from the original compressor design. It was, therefore, redesigned as a ten-stage compressor with some new aerofoil profiles and variable inlet guide vanes. The riveted rotor was replaced with a one-piece, smooth rotor (for the last eight stages) and this gave exceptional mechanical stability and excellent control over blade tip clearances. Circumferential dovetails were used to fasten the blades to the rotor.

Testing of the redesigned XT58 began in January 1956 and, thanks largely to the new compressor, the military rating of 1,050shp was surpassed on 2 February. Indeed, so successful was the new compressor that this so-called smooth spool compressor became a standard feature in both small and large future GE engines. In April 1956 tests began with two XT58s driving a Sikorsky S-58 helicopter rotor and transmission system on a test stand at Schenectady. On 4 August 1956 the XT58 turboshaft engine passed its fifty-hour PFRT and, on 30 January 1957, two T58 engines powered a modified S-58 helicopter for the engine's first hovering flight.

Subsequent development of the T58 engine encountered a few problems. Some rear blades of the compressor failed due to fatigue caused by torsional vibration of the blades. This was solved by strengthening the dovetails and by altering the blade vibration characteristics. Hot spots and premature structure collapse was caused in the combustion chamber by uneven temperature distribution. Here a solution was to fit an annular flow splitter ring between the compressor diffuser and the combustion chamber's inner liner, thereby giving a positive distribution of airflow over the inner and outer liners of the combustion chamber. The difficult job of developing a reliable control system for the turboshaft in a helicopter was tackled jointly by GE and Hamilton-Standard, and such a system, with the T58-GE-2, passed a 150-hour MQT in September 1957.

The prototype of the Sikorsky HSS-2 anti-submarine helicopter, powered by two T58-GE-6 turboshaft engines of 1,050shp each, made its first flight on 11 March 1959. Known as the Sea King, this helicopter went into US Navy service in 1961. An internal system of fresh water spray and corrosion inhibitor was developed to combat the effects of salt water in naval service. A variant designated the HH-3E was powered by two T58-GE-5 turbo-shafts of 1,400shp each and went into service with the USAF. The T58 went on to power various other military helicopters and also, in its CT-58 form, civilian helicopters.

The T58 was GE's first small gas turbine engine and a combined military and civilian total of more than 6,000 had been built by the time production ended in March 1984. To this must be added an unknown but large number built under licence. Among the licensees was de Havilland, this company calling it the Gnome. The Gnome included modifications to use a Lucas fuel system and computer controls and first ran on 5 June 1959. The most noteworthy achievement made with the T58 was the successful production of a small-scale, reliable axial compressor. A typical example of the engine is the 1,500shp T58-GE-10 with a ten-stage compressor driven by a single-stage turbine, and a two-stage free, power turbine. Its compressor has a pressure ratio of 8.4:1 and an air mass flow of 6.35kg/sec (14lb/sec). Speed is 27,200rpm and specific fuel consumption 0.61. The T58-GE-10 measures 1.49m (4ft 10½in) long by 0.51m (1ft 8¼in) high and weighs 156kg (345lb) dry.

T64 turboshaft and turboprop engines

In the autumn of 1953, GE work began on a second, more powerful turboshaft engine of 2,500shp. This work started by developing a new compressor and only then, at the end of 1956, was the US Navy's interest sought. Because of convincing data obtained from the compressor tests, GE was awarded a contract to develop a complete engine in April 1957, after competing against Lycoming. Designated the T64, this engine was to be developed in both turbo-shaft and turboprop forms. Because, at the time, such engines were still competing against the piston engine, a guaranteed specific fuel consumption of 0.506 was called for, even at the expense of weight. Therefore, at an early stage, GE decided to go for a pressure ratio of at least 12:1. Also, because the engine was to be used for turboshaft and turboprop applications, it was considered more convenient to bring the drive shaft from the power turbines through the engine and out at the front.

The T64 had a fourteen-stage axial compressor with a pressure ratio of 12.6:1 and an air mass flow of 11.2kg/sec (24.5lb/sec). The incidence of its inlet guide vanes and the first four stages of stator blades was variable in order to avoid surging and allow for easy starting. The compressor had three forward discs, connected by couplings, followed by two smooth, integral spools having eight and three stages respectively. An annular combustion chamber, based on the T58 design, was used. To drive the compressor, a two-stage turbine was provided, this having air-cooled blades for the first stage. A separate, free, two-stage power turbine was fitted, this having air-cooled first-stage stator blades. A drive shaft led through the engine from the power turbines to the gearbox for the rotors or airscrew. A fixed-area exhaust nozzle was used and all auxiliaries were clustered beneath the compressor casing. Because the engine was small but used high pressures, particular attention had to be paid to seals and blade tip clearances. Features used to achieve this included abradable labyrinth seals (pioneered in Britain) and turbine blade shrouds. Attention to detail included cast turbine blades with hollow tips to minimize centrifugal stresses at the blade roots.

Of special interest was the work GE conducted into the manufacture of small,

accurate titanium blades for the compressor of the T64. Research was carried out at the Lynn plant, where the best method of manufacture was found to be to precision forge the tiny blades oversize and then chemically mill them to final size. By this means, as the forging dies wore, adjustments could be made in the chemical milling process to give the final size. Later, as the T64 grew, the compressor blades were made in stainless steel. In any case, the internal system of fresh water spray and corrosion inhibitor (developed for the T58) was used to counteract the deleterious effects of salt water in naval service.

In August 1958 the first run was made with the gas generator section of the engine (minus the power turbine section). The first complete engine, the XT64-GE-4, made its first run in January 1959 but achieved only 1,850 shp, barely 70 per cent of what was designed for. The cause of this shortfall was traced to various small leaks that reduced the overall efficiency. The cure was found to be to use sealant where possible to bond together flanges and joints and to fit extra bolts to other flange joints. Also, clearances for labyrinth seals and blade tips were further reduced. The engineers were rewarded for their efforts in April 1959 when an engine run produced 2,850shp, considerably more than the power guaranteed.

Very extensive testing of the T64 followed, this being demanded by the Navy to ensure service reliability. As part of the test programme, GE built two large test cells that could accommodate the airscrew of the turboprop version. It was this version that threw up the main problem. Due to fractures appearing in the airscrew reduction gear housing, it was necessary to redesign the whole gearbox, with the result that the gearbox casing became heavier.

The first flight of the T64 was made with the turboprop version on 22 September 1961, using a Canadian-supplied de Havilland DHC-4 Caribou. The T64 went on to power various aircraft and large helicopters. In the CH-53E Sea Stallion helicopter, three T64-GE-416s were used for power. It was also licensed to de Havilland, but not used by that company. Eventually the engine was developed up to 4,750shp in the T64-GE-419 version. It was a technological and commercial success for GE and more than 3,215 were built by 1999. GE went on to be one of the world's great producers of gas turbine engines of all types.

CHAPTER TWENTY-TWO

AVCO Lycoming

We have seen above that GE competed with Lycoming in the field of turboshaft engines. Lycoming Manufacturing was founded in Williamsport, Pennsylvania, in 1908. It manufactured many automobile engines and made its first aero-engine in 1929. Many thousands of reliable radial engines were produced, ranging in size up to 285hp. In due course a great number of larger aero-engines of the piston type were made. By 1947 the company was known as AVCO Lycoming, following the merger with the Aviation Corporation in 1932.

It was not until the early 1950s that AVCO Lycoming began thinking about gas turbines. The company had been approached by Dr Anselm Franz, formerly of the Junkers company and father of the famous wartime Junkers 109-004 turbojet. After the war Franz arrived in the USA under the terms of Operation Paperclip and initially worked at Wright-Patterson AFB as a consultant. He then sold the idea to Lycoming that it would be worthwhile to develop small gas turbine engines and he was hired to do just this. Since Lycoming had no experience of gas turbines, Franz was given a free hand to create his own team and this he did with a mixture of Americans and wartime colleagues. Most important of the latter was Heinz Moellmann, who later became Lycoming's chief engineer. Also noteworthy was Dr Heinrich Adenstadt (formerly of Junkers), who was initially used as a materials consultant at Wright-Patterson, while Franz covered the aerodynamics side. The full-time team under Franz was actually quite small, only about ten members strong.

T53 turboshaft and turboprop engines

In summer 1952 Lycoming was awarded a gas turbine development contract by the Army, which desired more power for its growing number of helicopters. A turboshaft engine of 600shp was called for. Considerable feedback was being received from the early use of helicopters in the Korean War. Soon after the signing of the contract, the new team moved from Williamsport to the vast plant at Stratford, Connecticut. During 1953 Dr Adenstadt, Dr Siegfried Decher and Dr Friedrich Bielitz, all former colleagues of Franz from Junkers, joined the team. From then on, personnel at Stratford kept increasing. Under Franz, the team set to work on the company's first gas turbine engine, designated the T53. He envisaged an engine with rugged qualities, capable of being maintained by semi-skilled personnel under front-line conditions. Furthermore, he foresaw a multitude of uses for the T53, but mainly that of a turboshaft for helicopters.

The T53's compressor system consisted of a five-stage axial unit followed by a centrifugal stage. This gave an air mass flow of 5.45kg/sec (12lb/sec) at a pressure ratio of 6.0:1. From the centrifugal stage, the air was led into a reverse-flow annular combustion chamber with eleven fuel vaporizing tubes. Reversing back to the aft direction, the hot gases fed into two axial turbines, one to drive the compressors and the second, free turbine to drive the gearbox via a short, inner coaxial shaft that led through the engine to the front. The gearbox was at the centre of the annular air intake. The turbine, stator blades and vanes were all uncooled. Controls for the engine were hydromechanical, there was a fixed-area exhaust nozzle and all accessories were conveniently grouped around the smaller diameter of the axial compressor section.

The first run of the XT53 was made during April 1955, but in the meantime the Army had decided that a more powerful engine of 860shp was required. This first test threw up typical vibration problems, affecting the compressor and turbine blades

and the power turbine drive shaft. The vibration frequency of this shaft was most readily altered by enlarging its diameter along its length between the bearing points. Naturally, this also entailed enlarging the hollow shaft between the compressor and its turbine. Other remedies involved appropriately modulating the frequencies of the gear teeth with that of the turbine. Problems with combustion also had to be solved, but soon the T53 was proving to be an excellent design and its 150-hour MQT was passed in June 1958. The first flight of the T53 as a turboshaft was on 27 September 1956, when it powered a Kaman Model K600-1 helicopter with inter-meshing rotors. Soon afterwards, on 22 October 1956, the first flight of the Bell XH-40 helicopter prototype with an XT53 took place. The T53 went on to great success, powering many helicopters, in particular the legendary Bell UH-1 Huey. The turboprop version of the T53 powered the Grumman OV-1 Mohawk surveillance aircraft, the first turboprop aircraft developed for the US Army. Continuous development of the T53 turboshaft engine brought it up to 1,100shp for a specific fuel consumption of 0.682 and a weight of 228kg (502lb). This, the T53-L-11D, had a length of 1.21m (3ft 11.6in) and a diameter of 0.60m (1ft 11.7in). By 1999 about 18,000 T53 turboshaft engines had been constructed, including licensed production.

T55 turboshaft and turboprop engines

Following the success of the T53, the Lycoming team began studying, in 1953, a turboshaft engine in the 1,500shp class. After receiving a development contract from the USAF in April 1954, this engine was designated the T55. This turboshaft engine had a seven-stage axial compressor followed by a centrifugal stage. The inlet

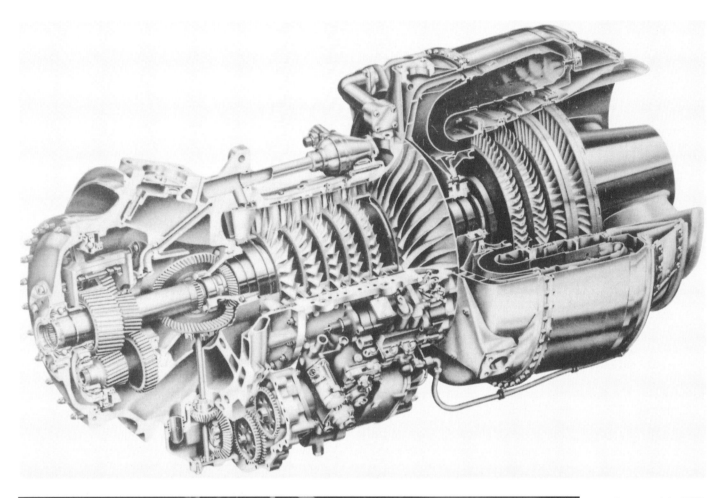

TOP: Cutaway of the AVCO Lycoming T53-L-13 turboshaft engine; BOTTOM: AVCO Lycoming T53-L-11A turboshaft engine. Very solid construction is apparent, this engine being designed for front-line maintenance by semi-skilled personnel. Author

guide vanes and seven stages of stator blades were of the variable incidence type. The combustion chamber was an annular, reverse-flow type, similar in configuration to the T53. A two-stage turbine drove the compressor and another free power turbine, also of the two-stage type, provided power through an inner, coaxial shaft that led forwards. The T55 was a simple, rugged engine of generally the same layout as the T53.

In December 1955 the gas generator section of the T55 was run and then, in June 1956, came the first run of a complete engine. Both turboprop and turboshaft versions were developed, the work being aided considerably by feedback from the T53 programme. Most famously, the T55 turboshaft was used, beginning in the 1960s, to power the twin-engined, twin-rotor Boeing CH-47 Chinook helicopter. The T55 later became the core of America's first high-bypass turbofan engine, the PLF1A-2, which had a thrust of 1,960kp (4,320lb) and a bypass ratio of 6.1:1. Engines of this type powered the British Aerospace BAe 146 regional jet transport. As Textron Lycoming, the company went on to be a world player in gas turbines for helicopters, aircraft, tanks and other applications, all thanks to the founding work of Dr Anselm Franz.

An AVCO Lycoming T53 turboshaft engine powers this Bell XH-40 helicopter prototype (S4461) that was developed into the legendary Bell UH-1 Huey assault helicopter. Central Arkansas Library System, AEC

The Vertol Model 76 or VZ-2 tiltwing aircraft (56-6943) making a transition from hovering to horizontal flight in July 1958. It was powered by an AVCO Lycoming YT53-L-1 560shp turboshaft engine mounted above the fuselage and just behind the wing, a cross-shaft transmitting the power to the two airscrews.

Another successful military helicopter was the Boeing CH-47 Chinook, a CH-47C being illustrated. Power was provided by two AVCO Lycoming T55 turboshaft engines mounted at the base of the rear rotor pylon. Central Arkansas Library System, AEC

CHAPTER TWENTY-THREE

Boeing

Having dealt with small gas turbine and turboshaft engines in the previous chapter, it is appropriate here to outline the famous Boeing aircraft company's brief development of such engines. In June 1943 the study of jet propulsion was begun at Boeing and a laboratory was established at its Seattle plant. Beginning with axial and centrifugal compressors, various gas turbine engine components were constructed and tested in the laboratory until finally, in 1947, a complete turbojet was built. This turbojet, designated the Model 500, gave a thrust of 68kp (150lb) for a weight of 39kg (85lb). It had a centrifugal compressor, two can-type combustion chambers and a single-stage turbine. Gradual modification of the compressor and turbine enabled the Model 500 to give an increased thrust of 88kp (195lb) for a weight of 54kg (120lb) and a specific fuel consumption of 1.3. Easily lifted by one man, this small turbojet was aimed at missile and small aircraft applications and possibly also to start larger engines, but no orders materialized.

Model 502 turboprop and turboshaft engine

The Model 500 was then developed as the basis of the Model 502 turboprop by the addition of an opposed, single-stage, free power turbine and gearbox. This engine, like the 500, was first run in 1947 and produced 120shp for a weight of 64kg (140lb) and a specific fuel consumption of 1.8. Under the designation T50 (Model 550), the US Navy then began backing the engine as a potential power source for naval

vessels. By 1949 the 502 had been developed to give 160shp and the specific fuel consumption had been reduced to 1.5. At that stage, six 502s were delivered to the US Navy for testing and feedback from these tests enabled Boeing to carry out considerable beneficial redesign: this largely involved improvement of the aerodynamics and fuel control system, the addition of a third bearing and structural strengthening. In 1950 Boeing received a contract for Model 502-6 turboshaft engines from the Navy, for use as power generators aboard minesweepers.

The world's first gas turbine-powered helicopters

On 10 December 1951 a Model 502-2E turboshaft engine was used to power a Kaman K-225 two-seat, intermeshing rotor helicopter (125477) to make the world's first gas turbine-powered helicopter flight. This was followed by the world's first twin gas turbine-powered helicopter flight when, in March 1954, the Kaman HTK-1 first flew, powered by two Model 502-2 engines. The great leap forward in helicopter development, by providing plenty of power, was thus begun using Boeing engines.

The turboprop version of the Model 502 was first flown in November 1952 when one such engine was used to power a Cessna XL-19B Bird Dog, making it the world's first turboprop-powered light aircraft. Using a Model 502-8 turboprop of 210shp, this aircraft set a world light aircraft altitude record of 11,297m (37,063ft) on 16 July 1953. Further use of the 502

turboprop included the powering of Army aerial targets. By 1959, following much development, the Model 502-10C turboshaft version of the engine was producing 240shp for a weight of 145kg (320lb) and specific fuel consumption of 1.02. Some 1,500 of all types of Model 502 had been produced by the time production ended in 1965.

Model 520 turboshaft engine

Boeing's Model 520 turboshaft featured a quite different layout to the previous engines. Begun early in 1954, as a joint venture between Boeing and the US Navy, the 520 had a double-sided centrifugal compressor, two reverse-flow combustion chambers and a radial turbine. This was followed by a single, axial, free power turbine. Both turboshaft and turboprop versions of the 520 were developed with powers of up to 550shp and specific fuel consumption as low as 0.65. Unfortunately no orders came from the Navy and no production ensued.

Despite Boeing's pioneering work with small gas turbine engines, the running of a large gas turbine facility and wages bill, coupled with insufficient sales volume, rendered the business unprofitable. In addition, when Boeing began putting all its resources into development of its giant 747 airliner, the gas turbine business became a burden and so the decision was made to sell it to the overhaul and repair company of Steward-Davis Inc.

CHAPTER TWENTY-FOUR

Fairchild

The Fairchild Engine and Airplane Corporation had worked on piston aero-engines from 1928 until just after the Second World War. Then, soon after Boeing began its gas turbine studies, the Fairchild engine division started on the design and development of the 9,850shp XT46 turboprop for the US Navy. This large engine had multiple power sections driving into a single gearbox, but work on it was stopped after the initial development phase.

J44, the first expendable US turbojet

Studies began in 1946 for a small, in-expensive turbojet for use in the guided missiles that the company was developing.

In June 1947 the US Navy awarded a contract to develop such an engine to power an air-to-underwater torpedo-carrying missile. This engine, designated the J44, was America's first expendable turbojet and was required to have a life of only ten hours. In order to meet the requirements of simplicity and ease of manufacture, thereby keeping the cost low, the design engineers worked closely with the manufacturing engineers from the inception of the project. The J44's compressor was a mixed-flow, axial/centrifugal type with curved inducer vanes, and it was made from a one-piece magnesium alloy casting that required no machining of the blades. Similarly, the diffuser section, with three rows of guide vanes, following the compressor was a single casting requiring no machining. An annular

combustion chamber was made from sheet metal and used commercially available oil burners. This was followed by an inlet nozzle ring that was a single casting complete with blades. The single-stage turbine had its blades welded on to a forged steel disc. A simple, stock stainless steel tube, with a welded flange at each end, formed the rotor connecting the turbine to the compressor. There was a bearing before the compressor and aft of the turbine and a fixed-area exhaust nozzle was used. The main structural support for the engine was its outer shell, this being generally smooth and requiring no nacelle.

In August 1948 the XJ44 made its first run. In due course, the engine gave a thrust of about 455kp (1,000lb) for a weight of 127kg (280lb) and a diameter of only 0.56m

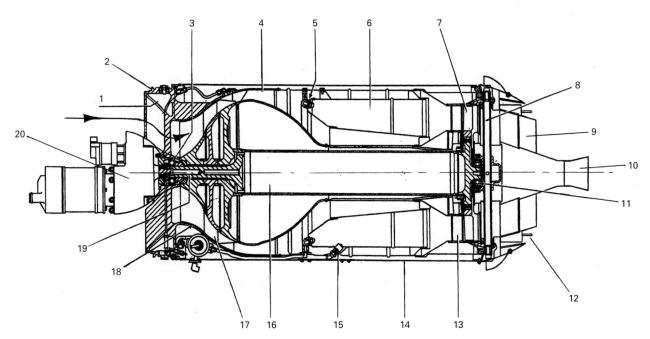

Fairchild J44 R-12 expendable, monocoque turbojet: (1) oil reservoir, for oil mist lubrication system; (2) mounting ring; (3) front ball bearing; (4) annular diffuser system; (5) fuel manifold; (6) annular combustion chamber; (7) single-stage turbine; (8) rear supporting strut; (9) fixed-area exhaust nozzle; (10) cooling air ejector nozzle; (11) rear ball bearing; (12) studs for tail cone attachment; (13) turbine inlet nozzles; (14) engine monocoque supporting shell; (15) sparking plug; (16) machined tubular rotor shaft; (17) mixed-flow axial/centrifugal compressor; (18) compressor housing; (19) compressor shaft; (20) bolt-on accessory section.

(1ft 10in). The first flight of the J44 was made in 1950 when it powered Fairchild's Petrel missile. This missile released its wings and engine just prior to its torpedo entering the water, in a manner pioneered by Germany's Henschel company during the war. At this time tests also began of the J44 powering the Ryan Firebee high-speed target drone, a project sponsored by all three services. In 1950 Fairchild's engine work was moved from the original Farmingdale works to the Deer Park works, both locations being on Long Island, New York.

As service trials proceeded, so problems with the J44 were thrown up, most of them attributable to over-simplified production. Variations in the casting of the compressor diffuser and turbine inlet nozzle sections led to mismatching between the compressor and the turbine and also led to compressor surging. It therefore became necessary to machine the diffuser vanes and turbine nozzles. Serious vibration and balancing problems occurred due to the use of a stock tube for the rotor, owing to a variation of tube wall thickness. Here, the solution was

to use a heavier tube and machine it down both inside and out. The oil system for the bearings had to be changed from a pressurized one to an oil mist one to suit the variation in operational altitudes. Development of the J44 was completed by October 1954.

From 1954 the J44 was developed to have a longer life as the J44-R-3. The aim of this was to produce a turbojet suitable as a booster for Fairchild cargo aircraft. Generally this process consisted of the use of better, heat-resisting metals, more machining, improved bearings and strengthening. The improved engine was mounted above the Fairchild C-82 cargo aircraft and, later, to each wingtip of the Fairchild C-123B cargo aircraft. Another use of the J44 was where two swivelling engines were mounted in the experimental Bell Model 65 VTOL aircraft. The main use of the J44, however, was to power the Firebee drone, although, with a specific fuel consumption of 1.55, it could not compete with Continental's J69 (a licensed version of Turboméca's Marbore) and it was taken out of production by 1959.

XJ83 turbojet

Fairchild's last foray into turbojets was the XJ83 engine. This was developed (in competition with GE's J85) to power bomber decoy missiles and was sponsored by the USAF. The XJ83 had a seven-stage axial compressor, an annular combustion chamber and a two-stage turbine. It was first run early in 1957 and eventually produced a thrust of 1,112kp (2,450lb) for a weight of 165kg (363lb) and a specific fuel consumption of 0.94. Its first flight was in a Fairchild XSM-73 Goose surface-launched decoy missile in June 1957. Unfortunately, XJ83 development was cancelled in favour of GE's J85 in November 1958. Hopes of using the engine to power a trainer were also dashed and so Fairchild's turbojet operation was closed down in 1959.

The Bell experimental ATV or Air Test Vehicle (N1105V) used two Fairchild J44 turbojets, each rated at 454kp (1,000lb) thrust, for vertical and horizontal flight. These engines were mounted at the aircraft's centre of gravity and could be rotated between vertical and horizontal positions. A Turbomeca Palouste gas turbine (mounted above and behind the cockpit) provided compressed air for reaction stabilizing jets. Flight tests were made from November 1954 to spring 1955, but no transitions from the hover to forward flight were made. Bell Aircraft Corporation

CHAPTER TWENTY-FIVE

Continuation of the Pratt & Whitney Story

P&W started on turbojet work by producing Rolls-Royce Nene and Tay centrifugal engines as the J42 and J48, respectively (see Chapter 16). Work on these engines, and also some early work on turboprops, such as the T34, was carried out somewhat reluctantly by P&W. This inauspicious start was later expunged by the fact that the company built some of the world's great engines in the shape of two-spool and turbofan turbojets.

By 1950 the opinion at P&W was that they were lagging behind other companies making turbojets and that the only way to make good was to jump considerably ahead of what the competition was doing. To do this it was recognized that much higher pressure ratios were needed, perhaps double the current 6:1, and that an engine was needed that could better cope with conditions above and below the optimum. Already, in the spring of 1946, P&W's R.G. Smith and W.H. Sens had studied the possibilities of a two-spool turbojet, a type with separate low- and high-pressure compressors, each driven by its own turbine. Such an engine was thought to have considerable flexibility, allowing it to give optimum performance while its speed and power altered. (In October 1945 Frank Owner, of the Bristol company in England, had also been thinking of a two-spool turbojet, with a pressure ratio of about 9:1; about five years later the first Olympus engine was running as the world's first two-spool turbojet. Two spools had also been demonstrated in Rolls-Royce's Clyde turbo-prop, although with a pressure ratio of only 6:1. The Clyde produced 4,000ehp and a specific fuel consumption of 0.71, but was shelved in 1949 because there was no aircraft in prospect for it.)

JT3 (J57), the USA's first two-spool turbojet

P&W's engineering manager, Leonard S. 'Luke' Hobbs, then set about obtaining military sponsorship for a new, two-spool turbojet, planned to be more powerful and

Pratt & Whitney's two-spool J57 axial turbojet took a long time to develop but was eventually a good engine. It is shown with the air intake on the right. Standing with it are (from left) Wright A. Parkins (engineering manager of P&W), Leonard S. Hobbs (vice president for engineering of United Aircraft Corporation) and William P. Gwinn (general manager of P&W). AEHS, Huntsville

efficient than GE's successful J47. However, the US Navy had already awarded GE a contract to develop a J47 successor (the J40, cancelled in 1953) and so Hobbs went to the USAF. In order to avoid what appeared to be a duplication of the Navy's programme, P&W was directed to begin its engine development as a turboprop and Boeing's B-52 was designed to use such engines accordingly. It is said that this was a subterfuge to avoid awkward funding issues since it was planned to change the sponsored turboprop later to a turbojet, and then the USAF would have a turbojet that competed with the Navy.

Therefore, late in 1947, P&W began work on the two-spool PT-4 turboprop (or XT45) as a 10,000shp engine with a thirteen-stage axial compressor having a total pressure ratio of 8:1. In 1948 the USAF changed its requirement to that of a 4,540kp (10,000lb) thrust, two-spool turbojet and P&W's PT-4 design was relatively easily converted to such a turbojet, designated the JT3. Design work on the JT3 began in March 1948 under the direction of Chief Engineer Andrew Willgoos for mechanical work and his assistant Perry Pratt for aerodynamic work. At about this time the company discovered that its JT3 was in competition with Westinghouse's J40 turbojet as the powerplant for Boeing's XB-52 bomber.

In September 1948 the USAF terminated the XT45 (PT-4) turboprop and decided to concentrate on the high pressure ratio turbojet for its future long-range bombers. Accordingly, a specification for the J57-P-1 was issued and P&W's workshops began building two prototypes, the JT3-8 and the JT3-10. At an early stage during this construction, tests indicated that JT3 performance would be poor, the chief reasons for this being poor turbine design and very small high-pressure compressor blades. In addition, the engine weight was coming out as excessive. Nevertheless, it was decided to complete the two prototype engines and the JT3-8 first ran on 27 June 1949 while the JT3-10A first ran in February 1950. Their predicted poor performance was confirmed by these first runs. The JT3-8, for example, gave only 2,950kp (6,505lb) of thrust. Both the prototypes suffered from excessive seal leakages.

In the meantime, from February 1949, the teams under Willgoos and Pratt began a complete redesign of the engine so that it went from a parallel, barrel shape to a waisted shape. The new JT3 (JT3-10B) turbojet had compressor rotor discs of a constant diameter but had the casing tapering down towards the high-pressure end, as the blades became shorter. The new compressor had a higher efficiency, assisted by better sealing, and overall some 272kg (600lb) of weight was saved. In addition, a more compact engine resulted because its accessories could largely nestle in the waisted section of the casing. Construction of the JT3-10B began in October 1949; on

1 December the USAF ordered eighteen YJ57-P-3 prototype turbojets, specifying the static thrust as 3,950kp (8,700lb). On 21 January 1950 the new engine made its first run and the JT3-10B was redesignated JT3A by P&W and J57 by the military. Another three years of development then lay ahead to resolve problems with the engine, mainly concerning the bearings, the seals, compressor blade vibration and hydrogen embrittlement of titanium parts. Despite its two spools, the J57 was never completely stall-free but was rugged enough to withstand the rigours of hundreds of stalls without requiring maintenance. Fortunately for P&W, the USAF decided to keep faith with the development and did not cancel it. In the long run, this was good for all concerned.

The J57 completed its fifty-hour PFRT on 9 March 1951, by when it was giving a thrust of 4,085kp (9,000lb) and a specific fuel consumption of 0.80. Its first flight was then made that month, the engine being suspended beneath a B-50 bomber. During November 1951 a J57-P-3 production engine completed a 150-hour MQT.

Many derivatives of the J57 were produced during the production of 21,000 examples, but the original engines were laid out as follows. The low-pressure compressor had nine stages driven by a two-stage turbine, the shaft between the two being inside the high-pressure shaft. The following, high-pressure compressor had seven stages and was driven by a hollow

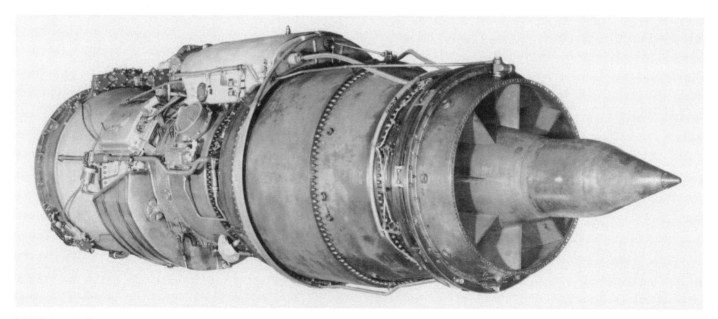

A P&W J57 turbojet, with exhaust end on the right (exhaust duct removed). AEHS, Huntsville

Final inspection of new P&W J57 two-spool turbojets. Thousands of such engines were despatched to power B-52 bombers and the new Century fighters. AEHS, Huntsville

and also the particularly famous B-52 bomber. Also, in its JT3D turbofan form, it was destined to power the famous Boeing 707 airliners.

The mighty Boeing B-52 Stratofortress bomber

On 15 April 1952 eight J57-P-3 turbojets, each of 3,950kp (8,700lb) static thrust, powered the huge YB-52 (9231) on its maiden flight (before the XB-52). This flight, which lasted three hours, took place from Larsons AFB and the pilot was Boeing's test pilot Tex Johnson. The B-52, designed by a team under Ed Wells, was required to replace the B-36s of Strategic Air Command (SAC) as the strategic nuclear bomber deterrent. Having very clean lines, the B-52 carried on the design philosophy of the smaller six-engined B-47 Stratojet but had its eight engines in four paired nacelles suspended from pylons beneath the 35-degree swept-back wings. The first two prototypes each had a low-profile, framed canopy for two pilots in tandem, but subsequent aircraft had stepped windscreen panels at the front of the fuselage. Various unusual features that are not apparent from its clean lines should be mentioned. Owing to its great loaded weight of 184 tonnes, the aircraft was not rotated for take-off but simply lifted from the runway, at the correct speed, by virtue of its wing being set at an incidence of 8 degrees with the fuselage horizontal. The gigantic, all-moving tailplane was then used to trim the aircraft for cruise attitude once airborne. The equally large vertical fin could be power-folded at its hinged base in order for the bomber to enter normal hangers. Roll control was by means of spoiler panels on the upper wing surfaces and there were very large trailing edge Fowler flaps. An unprecedented total of 38,865 US gallons of fuel was carried in the upper fuselage (largely above the bomb bay), wings and in underwing tanks. The main undercarriage consisted of four twin-wheel bogies that could be slewed to allow the bomber to make cross-wind landings without attempting to yaw the aircraft straight just before touchdown. There were

shaft by a single-stage turbine immediately in front of the low-pressure turbines. This two-spool compressor had a pressure ratio of 12.9:1 and an air mass flow of 84.4kg/sec (186lb/sec) that was delivered to the diffuser section at a temperature of about 460°C.

The J57 had an excellent combustion system that achieved a combustion efficiency of virtually 100 per cent at sea level. An annular combustion zone housed eight combustion cans, each having six fuel injectors that injected a fine fuel spray downstream. Each can consisted of rings of Iconel nickel-chrome steel alloy with slots for cooling air. Part of the airflow entered each can through large holes and another

part entered through a central intake. Upstream baffles ensured good fuel/air mixing. In essence, each can was a smaller annular combustion chamber housed inside a large annulus. Temperature in the turbines was about 680°C but only in later models was air cooling used for the first stage. Typical speeds were of the order of 10,000rpm for the high-pressure rotor and 6,700rpm for the low-pressure rotor. The size of a typical J57 included a length of 6.78m (22ft 3in) with afterburner, a maximum height of 1.19m (3ft 11in) and a dry weight of 2,197kg (4,840lb). The J57 was used to power a number of famous fighters for both the USAF and US Navy,

A prototype (9230) of the huge Boeing XB-52 Stratofortress with eight P&W J57-P-3 turbojets. Development led to the very successful B-52, the strategic nuclear bomb deterrent of SAC. Entering into service in 1955, some are still flying today. Philip Jarrett

also retractable outrigger wheels near the wingtips. Curiously, compressed air turbines were used throughout the aircraft to generate electricity and hydraulic power and also to operate the air conditioning, the air being tapped from each engine and directed through stainless steel ducting. Parts of this ducting glowed with the heat. Aft of the tail empennage, the fuselage housed a tail gunner (later, remotely controlled guns instead) and a large braking parachute.

The USAF was so impressed with the design of the B-52 that it ordered 500 aircraft even before the first flight took place. To cope with this enormous production task, a programme was organized to sub-contract many companies nationwide, Boeing at Wichita eventually being the programme leader. During development, and also in service, many problems occurred. The main problem with the J57 engines concerned the early type of vacuum tube electronic control system, which proved unreliable and was eventually replaced with a hydro-mechanical system. Using the electronic control system, Guy Townsend, the USAF test pilot, tells us: 'I never had an eight-engine take-off, always seven. You didn't know which seven, but they kindly failed one at a time!' The first B-52A service test aircraft was flown on 5 August 1954. The B-52B was cleared for SAC service on 29 June 1955, the first bomber being stationed at Castle AFB, California. Among the problems with the B-52 in service were exploding compressed

Boeing B-52D-25-BW with eight 5,489kp (12,100lb) thrust J57-P-29WA turbojets		
Span	56.39m	(185ft 0in)
Length	47.727m	(156ft 7in)
Wing area	371.6sq m	(4,000sq ft)
Empty weight	85,730kg	(189,000lb)
Maximum loaded weight	204,120kg	(450,000lb)
Cruising speed	893km/h or Mach 0.84	(555mph)
Service ceiling	13,716m	(45,000ft)
Range	11,861km	(7,370 miles)

air turbines, which, since these and their ducting ran extremely hot, caused fire and other damage. Other failures included undercarriage bogies jammed at the wrong angle and fatigue breakages of hot-air ducting and the Fowler flaps.

Despite all these vicissitudes, more than 800 B-52s were built and the type went on to stay in service decades beyond its intended time. Early in its life, in January 1957, its impressive range was demonstrated when three B-52s, using in-flight refuelling, flew non-stop around the world and covered 39,146km (24,325 miles) in 45 hours 19 minutes at an average speed of 837km/h (520mph). Perhaps the most regrettable operations with the B-52 were the so-called Arclight raids on North Vietnam, when the bombers flew very high, out of earshot, and the first sign of their presence was when the enormous bomb loads were actually exploding on the ground.

North American F-100 Super Sabre fighter

Further fame awaited the J57 turbojet when it powered the world's first supersonic aircraft in production, the North American F-100 Super Sabre. This was the first type of what became known as the Century fighters. Other fighters were planned around the J57 and, for this new generation of supersonic aircraft, P&W developed an afterburner that could bring thrust up to 5,610kp (12,350lb), and later much more than this. In time for the F-100, the J57-P-7 was developed to produce a thrust of 4,400kp (9,700lb) or 6,720kp (14,800lb) in afterburner mode. To cope with an increased air mass flow, this engine had a steel compressor and also a variable-area exhaust nozzle.

Extensive use was made of titanium in the structure of the F-100. It had a thin wing swept back at 45 degrees and a plain, oval, sharp-lipped air intake at its nose. The wing was low set and the all-moving tailplane slightly lower set. To avoid the risk of the then-feared aileron reversal (caused by wing twist), the ailerons were set inboard along the trailing edge. This left no room for landing flaps and so the only aid at low speeds was the full-span leading edge slats. Later, ailerons were fitted in the normal position and flaps were fitted (F-100D).

On 1 November 1951, North American received a USAF contract for two YF-100 prototypes and 110 production aircraft. During 1952 refinement of the design took place to the extent that it was redesignated as the YF-100A. The prototype YF-100A (25754) was flown by George Welch from Edwards AFB to make its first flight on 25 May 1953. Using the afterburner, Welch took the aircraft beyond Mach 1.0 on this first flight. The first production F-100A made its first flight on 29 October 1953, by which time the fighter had been named the Super Sabre.

In November 1953 the F-100A, armed with four 20mm cannon under the nose, entered service with the 479th Fighter Day Wing. Within a year, however, the type was grounded following a number of mid-air break-ups. The cause was traced to inertial roll coupling that caused a hard swerve to starboard during the pull-out from a dive at high speed. The solution of this serious problem was aided by data obtained from the X-3 flights (see Chapter 18). Redesign of the airframe included a taller fin and increased wingspan. The original engine was also soon replaced with the more powerful J57-P-39, in which the afterburning thrust went up to 7,265kp (16,000lb).

The F-100C was the first fighter-bomber version and, on 20 August 1955, Col H.A. Hanes of the USAF flew one of these to a new world speed record of 1,323.03km/h (822.09mph), or Mach 1.245, at high altitude. (On 10 March 1956 this record was broken by the Fairey F.D.2 at 1,822km/h [1,132mph] or Mach 1.73.) The definitive version, the F-100D, was equipped to carry a considerable amount of ordnance, on six underwing pylons, for the ground attack role, while still remaining capable as a fighter. Its engine was the J57-P-21A of 7,695kp (16,950lb) thrust in afterburner mode. Considerable exports of the Super Sabre were made to foreign air forces, including those of Turkey, France, Denmark and Taiwan, and a total of 2,651 of all types were built.

Powered by a P&W J57 turbojet, the North American F-100 Super Sabre, first of the 'Century fighters', was the first supersonic aircraft in series production. Illustrated is a two-seat F-100C rebuilt as the prototype F-100F, with J57-P-21 engine. Central Arkansas Library System, AEC

North American F-100D Super Sabre		
Span	11.82m	(38ft 9½in)
Length	14.36m	(47ft 1¼in)
Wing area	35.77sq m	(385sq ft)
Height	4.945m	(16ft 2½in)
Empty weight	9,526kg	(21,000lb)
Maximum take-off weight	15,800kg	(34,832lb)
Maximum speed at altitude	1,390km/h or Mach 1.3	(864mph)
Initial climb rate	5,045m/min	(16,550ft/min)
Service ceiling	14,020m	(46,000ft)
Range with drop tanks	2,494km	(1,550 miles)

The J57 went on to power other famous Century fighters for the USAF, notably the Convair F-102 Delta Dagger and the McDonnell F-101 Voodoo. The prototype YF-102A made its first flight on 24 October 1953 using a J57-P-11 engine with afterburner. However, despite using the 5,605kp (12,350lb) thrust of this engine in full afterburner mode, this delta fighter refused to go supersonic until the newly discovered area rule was applied to its fuselage and the aircraft was completely redesigned. The resulting F-102A, first flown on 11 January 1954, then easily reached Mach 1.25. Thus was born a very successful all-weather interceptor, of which almost 900 were built and which gave excellent service for almost twenty years.

As for the F-101, this was originally envisaged as an escort fighter for SAC bombers but finished up in the USA defence role. The prototype F-101A (34218) made its first flight on 29 September 1954, from Edwards AFB, and Mach 1.0 was exceeded in a shallow dive. This aircraft had swept wings, a high-mounted tailplane and was powered by two J57-P-13 engines, each giving a thrust of 4,540kp (10,000lb) or 6,755kp (14,880lb) with afterburner on. At that time this engine was still prone to compressor stall. More seriously, however, the F-101 was subject to longitudinal instability and would sometimes pitch up, with fatal results. The pitch-up problem was only finally eradicated after many years. The type's best role was as the RF-101 reconnaissance machine. Service was with the USAF and Canada's RCAF.

The McDonnell F-101 Voodoo was built as an escort fighter for bombers but was then modified as a nuclear bomber for Tactical Air Command (TAC). Illustrated is an F-101A powered by two P&W J57 afterburning turbojets. Central Arkansas Library System, AEC

Vought F-8 Crusader

The J57 turbojet also powered US Navy aircraft, notably the Chance Vought F8U Crusader and Douglas F4D Skyray fighters and the Douglas A3D Skywarrior bomber. P&W had never expected to supply the Navy, but this opportunity arose following the failure of the rival Westinghouse J40 engine.

The prototype of the Chance Vought XF8U-1 Crusader, or XF-8A (138899), made its maiden flight on 25 March 1955, powered by a J57-P-4 with afterburner. During the Korean War, Chance Vought beat considerable competition to win a contract to develop a carrier-based supersonic fighter. Their fighter had a shoulder-mounted swept wing, large tail empennages on a short moment arm and a chin-type air intake below the cockpit that was positioned right at the nose. The aircraft was the first designed from the outset to use area

rule on the fuselage. The tailplane was of the all-moving type, but the most unusual feature of the XF8 was its two-position, variable incidence wing. By increasing the wing incidence, the landing approach could be flown with the nose down, thereby giving the pilot the best possible view of the carrier deck.

After going supersonic on its first flight, development of the F8U went ahead at great speed and with few problems. The F8U-1 production fighter had a maximum speed of Mach 1.53 and joined VF-32 combat unit aboard the USS *Saratoga* in late 1957. Landings were also made aboard small carriers such as the USS *Hancock*. On 17 December 1956 the first of the F8U-1P unarmed reconnaissance versions made an in-flight refuelled flight from Los Angeles to New York at an average speed of Mach 1.1 in 3 hours 23 minutes. The pilot was Maj. John H. Glenn, who was later the first American astronaut to orbit the Earth, and

this was the first transcontinental supersonic flight. Throughout its successful life, the Crusader was produced in various versions, re-engineered and re-engined, always with the J57 turbojet. More than 1,200 were made of all versions, excluding rebuilt and re-engineered existing aircraft during the 1960s. The most powerful engine used was the J57-P-420 fitted to re-engined F-8Js to operate from small carriers of the French Aéronavale. This engine had a thrust of 8,165kp (18,000lb) in afterburner mode.

The second major application of the J57 by the US Navy was to power its twin-engined Douglas A3D Skywarrior strategic bomber. This was the Navy's heaviest carrier-borne aircraft and was to be a faster nuclear bomber than those being built for SAC. In this application, Westinghouse's J40 powered the prototype but then lost out to P&W's J57. A similar story prevailed with the Navy's Douglas F4D Skyray all-wing fighters, which were re-engined with

The Vought F8U-1 Crusader took the US Navy into the supersonic age. Prototypes were first flown in March 1955 and the type entered service only two years later. Illustrated is an F8U-1 of VF-32 from the carrier USS *Saratoga.* Central Arkansas Library System, AEC

Vought F-8E Crusader			
Span		10.72m	(35ft 2in)
Length		16.61m	(54ft 6in)
Wing area		32.52sq m	(350sq ft)
Height		4.80m	(15ft 9in)
Empty weight		9,038kg	(19,925lb)
Maximum loaded weight		15,422kg	(34,000lb)
Maximum speed	at 12,200m (40,000ft)	1,800km/h or Mach 1.7	(1,120mph)
Service ceiling		18,000m	(59,000ft)
Radius of action		1,000km	(620 miles)

J57s replacing the troublesome J40s. The Skywarrior also appeared as the B-66 in USAF service.

Boeing 707 and Douglas DC-8: the first American jet airliners

Successful as the J57 was in its military form, even more success was to come in civilian service with turbofan versions of the engine and such engines were also fed back to the military. America's first jet airliner, the Boeing 707, was derived aerodynamically from the B-47 bomber, with a 35-degree swept-back wing and four underwing podded engines, and was made possible by the P&W JT3C-1 turbojet, the civilianized version of the J57. The prototype 707 (N70700) made its maiden flight on 15 July 1954. Its similarly configured competitor, the Douglas DC-8 airliner, first flew on 30 May 1958 and was powered by four JT3C-6 turbojets.

The Boeing 707 came into being following the original idea of a jet-powered tanker to refuel in flight SAC's new jet bombers. However, the USAF vacillated over whether to sponsor the tanker development and the US government would not fund the development of a jet airliner, despite the initial success of Britain's de Havilland Comet. Boeing thought it could develop the jet airliner on $18 million, but the eventual cost was something like $185 million (more than the company was worth), and this was raised by loans from forty-two banks. Fortunately, in October

Pratt & Whitney's JT4 (J75) two-spool, axial turbojet with afterburner was used to power the Republic F-105D and F Thunderchief fighter bombers. In afterburner mode its maximum thrust was 11,110kp (24,500lb). Illustrated is a J75-P-5 with its two-position convergent exhaust nozzle on the left. Central Arkansas Library System, AEC

1954, Boeing received a USAF order for tanker versions of the aircraft, designated KC-135. This helped to carry development of the airliner, but Boeing still had to battle against the Douglas DC-8 for airline orders.

An interesting proof of the toughness of the 707 came on 7 August 1955 when Tex Johnson eschewed a mere flypast of the valuable 707-80 prototype at a hydroplane racing event on Lake Washington, near Boeing's Seattle plant. Instead, in front of thousands of spectators, including Boeing's president Bill Allen, Tex barrel-rolled the 707 just 120m (400ft) above the lake. He then flew back the other way and repeated the manoeuvre, a perfect 1g barrel roll. This event did much to impress the airline executives, but Tex was asked to desist from repeating it in the future!

The JT3C engines provided neither the 707 nor the DC-8, like the Comet, with a transatlantic range. For this a turbofan or bypass engine of much lower specific fuel consumption was needed. By 1958 the JT3C turbojet had been developed to give a TBO of 8,000 hours (much higher TBOs were to come) and had been considerably lightened, but its specific fuel consumption was still too high for the new jet airliners.

JT3D (TF33) turbofan engine

The turbofan version of the J57, the JT3D, was actually developed under a military contract with the designation of TF33 since it was foreseen to be beneficially applicable to the B-52 bomber. The design plan to produce the turbofan from the J57 turbojet was to substitute two fan stages in place of the first three compressor stages and add a fourth turbine stage to produce the power needed to drive the low compressor stage and the new fan. The fan was 1.35m (4ft 5in) in diameter and had an air mass flow of 204kg/sec (450lb/sec). Strengthening of the low-pressure shaft was necessary to transmit the power to the fan, since this was to produce about 50 per cent of the thrust. A new, short discharge duct was designed for the fan, at the front of the engine, in the interests of minimizing duct losses. Elements employed from previous development and research included the advanced compressor blades used in the J91 nuclear turbojet programme, which assisted in the design of the fan, and the very long and thin turbine blades used in the T57 turboprop programme.

Other previous research that brought about important advances came from vacuum-melting technology, which made great weight reductions possible (compressor and fan components were some 40 per cent lighter) and the elimination of fatigue failures in fan discs. P&W's 'Waspalloy' vacuum-cast turbine blades were claimed to be superior to all other wrought alloys in the region of 815°C to 870°C. (Vacuum-melting techniques were also developed by GE and the F.J. Stokes Machine Company.)

The design of the JT3D turbofan resulted in an engine that provided 50 per cent more thrust than the J57 but had a 13 per cent better specific fuel consumption and considerably less noise. Almost two and a half times the air mass flow of the J57 was required and yet the new engine could use about 90 per cent of the J57's parts. It was even stated by P&W that conversion of a J57 into a JT3D could be carried out in the overhaul shop and would not need factory reworking. Conversion kits were designed for this marvellous prospect.

Once the first JT3D ran, on 13 June 1958, USAF funding for the TF33 military version began. The JT3D passed a fifty-hour PFRT on 7 November 1959 and its first test flight was made on 21 July 1959. The first deliveries of TF33s to the USAF were made in May 1960. The promise that J57 turbojets could be readily converted into JT3Ds in the maintenance facilities was fulfilled by the production of a kit of parts that included a new compressor, fan and fan duct. By this means, each engine could be converted to give a third more thrust for 20 per cent less fuel consumption and less noise.

Boeing's prototype 707-80 was used for very extensive testing for a number of years, not least for P&W's engines. For more than two years it flew with a JT3C-6 in one inner pod, an improved JT4A in the other inner pod and the original JT3C-1s in the outer pods. Later it was flown with four JT3D-1 turbofans. The 707 entered airline service with Pan Am as the 707-120, which used the JT3C-6 turbojet rated at 6,124kp (13,500lb) thrust with water injection, thrust reversers and a large noise suppressor having twenty separate tubes. Despite the suppressor, take-offs were very noisy affairs and the water injection resulted in trails of black smoke. The JT4 was sponsored by the military as the J75 turbojet, later used to power the Republic F-105 Thunderchief fighter bomber (nicknamed the Thud). The JT4 was a scaled-up JT3 turbojet to give a maximum thrust of 6,490kp (14,300lb) or, with an afterburner, 11,120kp (24,500lb).

Not until 1962 did the 707-320B go into service with JT3D-3 turbofans, these giving a static thrust of 8,170kp (18,000lb) each.

No. 3 engine on a Boeing 707-120 airliner, a P&W JT3C-6. The engine has a six-nozzle sound suppressor. Such sound suppressors were only partially successful, pending the introduction of much quieter turbofan engines.

Boeing 707-120B with JT3D-1 turbofans and thrust reversers			
Span		39.88m	(130ft 10in)
Length		44.04m	(144ft 6in)
Wing area		226.27sq m	(2,433sq ft)
Height		12.80m	(42ft 0in)
Empty weight		54,813kg	(120,734lb)
Maximum take-off weight		117,132kg	(258,000lb)
Normal operating speed	Mach 0.90 above	7,680m	(25,200ft)
Range		6,000km	(3,725 miles)

The 707-420 had earlier been introduced in 1959 with Rolls-Royce Conway engines, but these were never specified in the same quantity as the P&W engines, despite the fact that the Conway was more fuel efficient and lighter. In any event, the 707 became a phenomenal success, way beyond the timeline of this history. The DC-8 was also flown with similar engines to the 707 but did not enjoy quite the same success. In the end, some 556 DC-8s were sold, compared with 930 707s. P&W's JT3D-3 turbofan ushered in a new era of economical and fast jet airliners and transports, and the company at last had an engine that was competitive with British engines. The TF33 turbofan also went on to enjoy great success in powering USAF B-52 bombers, KC-135 tankers and C-135 passenger transports.

The TF33 had a maximum thrust of 7,720kp (17,000lb) and a specific fuel consumption of 0.52. Its length was 3.46m (11ft 4½in), diameter 1.35m (4ft 5¼in) and a dry weight of 1,773kg (3,905lb). Among its other great engines, P&W went on to develop the military TF30, the world's first afterburning turbofan engine.

T57, the most powerful US turboprop

Besides the turbofan development of the J57 turbojet, there was the derived PT5 turboprop, the development of which was sponsored by the USAF as the T57. At 15,000shp, this was the most powerful turboprop outside the Soviet Union. An extra low-pressure turbine was added to the J57 to give three stages driving the low-pressure compressor and a reduction gearbox. The gearbox was mounted at the centre of the annular air intake and drove a Ham Stan airscrew consisting of four hollow, square-tipped blades, each of 0.76m (2ft 6in) chord. The annular intake was surrounded by an annular fuel/oil heat exchanger and an oil tank. The XT57 prototype was tested in 1956 and passed a fifty-hour PFRT. It was flight tested in the nose of a C-124C Globemaster II. However, although the engine was expected to have a development potential of 20,000shp, it was cancelled in 1957 owing to the cancellation of its specified aircraft, the Douglas C-132 military airlifter.

The turbofan version of the J57, the Pratt & Whitney JT3D. This development produced more thrust, better specific fuel consumption and far less noise. Pratt & Whitney even produced kits so that JT3C turbojets could be converted into JT3D turbofans. Philip Jarrett

A Boeing 707-123 airliner with P&W JT3D-1 turbofan engines. Central Arkansas Library System, AEC

CHAPTER TWENTY-SIX

The Nuclear Turbojet Engine

In the early years after the war, the USAF was concerned with obtaining the range necessary from its planned jet bombers to provide a credible strategic nuclear deterrent force. Conventional turbojets and turboprops were not efficient enough at first to give aircraft great range without refuelling. The idea then arose of investigating the viability of a nuclear-powered bomber that would have unlimited range. Gen. Curtis E. Le May, head of SAC, set up the Nuclear Energy Programme for Aircraft (NEPA) to study the subject. The matter seemed all the more urgent after the Soviet Union had developed its own atomic bomb by September 1949 and with the outbreak of the Korean War in the following year. President Harry S. Truman then created the Atomic Energy Commission (AEC) to control nuclear research and bombs, since he did not want to leave such matters in the hands of the 'hawks'.

Nuclear bomber projects

In 1951, therefore, the USAF and the AEC combined to issue a five-year research contract to GE and P&W to study nuclear materials and shielding systems. Data from this programme was then to be used to help the government decide if a nuclear-powered aircraft was practical. There were many things to consider, not least being the weight of shielding required, the distance the nuclear reactor needed to be from the aircraft crew and safety issues in the event of a crash.

The programme began with radiation shielding experiments: it was actually thought acceptable for a bomber crew to receive some radiation providing they were over child-rearing age and this led to the appellation of 'NEPA Man'. A Convair B-36 bomber was modified to carry a small nuclear reactor in the rear bomb bay, part

of the protection from radiation being by means of water jackets. Since lead shielding was too heavy, other lightweight shielding was used, some around the reactor and some around the crew. This modified B-36 was redesignated the XB-36H, and then NB-36, and was named by its pilots 'The Crusader'. The first flight of the NB-36 was made on 17 September 1955. In case the NB-36 crashed, every one of its flights was accompanied by another aircraft carrying Marines (known as the Glow in the Dark Brigade) who would parachute in and seal off the site. Attempts were made to decrease the reactor size but progress was slow.

The US Navy also began its own nuclear aircraft project and favoured a large, modified flying boat. At first the Martin Seamaster was considered, but then thoughts turned to the British Saunders Roe Princess flying boat. This was to accommodate the nuclear reactor in the upper deck, take-off being made on turbine fuel. The Navy, however, abandoned these ideas in favour of the Nautilus nuclear submarine in which shielding was not a problem. By now the USAF and US Navy were deadly rivals in the business of a nuclear deterrent.

Meanwhile, work went ahead on the propulsion systems for a nuclear bomber and GE set up its Aircraft Nuclear Propulsion department (ANPD). Roy Shoults originally headed the project and David Shaw later became the general manager of ANPD. A similar programme was pursued at P&W and both companies expended major effort on the work.

While the NB-36 tests and engine work was under way, Gen. Le May had plans drawn up for a nuclear bomber and in 1954 the USAF identified a weapons system requirement for a nuclear-powered bomber, designated WS-125A. The following year GE was teamed up with Convair and P&W was teamed up with Lockheed to develop, in competition, their engine/airframe ideas.

Whether by official policy or by company decision, GE pursued the development of a direct-cycle engine and P&W pursued an indirect-cycle engine. In the direct-cycle type some of the engine's airflow passes directly through a nuclear reactor instead of a normal combustion chamber. In the indirect-cycle type the engine's airflow is heated by passing it through a nuclear-powered heat exchanger.

GE's X211 nuclear turbojet

The ultra-secret programme at GE's Evendale plant was divided between the nuclear power source at ANPD and the engine at the Jet Engine department. The engine programme was managed by Bruno Bruckmann, with Gerhard Neumann making many of the design decisions. At first, tests were made with a modified J47 turbojet running on nuclear heat; after much study the projected X211 engine was decided upon.

The X211 would have been the world's largest turbojet, had it been completed, and was some 12.50m (41ft) long. It consisted of two colossal, parallel, afterburning turbojets (XJ87s) with a nuclear reactor in between them. These engines had variable stator compressors, each designed to give an air mass flow of 136kg/sec (300lb/sec) and an unprecedented pressure ratio exceeding 20:1. Half of this airflow was to pass through the reactor for heating while the other half bypassed the reactor through large pipes to the turbine section. Several reactors were tested, with core temperatures of up to 1,100°C, and it was estimated that the combined thrust of the X211 would be in the order of 15,700kp (34,620lb). The effects of rendering the engines radioactive and of pouring radioactive gases into the atmosphere scarcely bear thinking about. Apart from environmental concerns, one wonders how radioactive engines would be serviced. In any event, only the XJ87 turbojet element of the X211 was tested.

P&W's nuclear turbojets

While this work was proceeding at GE, P&W was working on its indirect-cycle nuclear turbojet, this being certainly more environmentally friendly. At 20.6m (67ft 7in) long, this engine was to be even larger than GE's X211 and was to use a pressurized-water reactor and a 4.0m (13ft 1½in) diameter ducted fan. However, by 1953 this project was replaced by one using a reactor heating molten salt, which was circulated to a heat exchanger to heat the compressed air for six J91 turbojets. The J91 was to be a single-shaft turbojet with a variable inlet and a giant convergent/divergent exhaust nozzle, its maximum diameter being 1.83m (6ft), but it was never built.

Two experimental engines, variants of the J91 and known as the X287 and X291,

were built in spring 1957. They each had a nine-stage compressor giving a pressure ratio of 7:1, an annular combustion chamber and a two-stage turbine, and achieved a thrust of 11,000kp (24,255lb) or 15,750kp (34,730lb) in afterburner mode. The X287 (or JT9A-20) was especially successful and it contributed to the design of the JT3 turbojet. Later still, P&W studied a scheme using four modified J58 turbojets, of higher than normal pressure ratio, their heat being provided by two or four reactors. This multiple J58 engine was to be tested in a large projected Convair aircraft known as the NX-2.

About this time it was mistakenly thought that the Soviets were testing a nuclear bomber and so President Eisenhower increased the US nuclear bomber budget. In fact, it was not until 1961 that the Soviet Union tested a Tupolev Tu-95 Bear bomber fitted with two conventional turboprop engines and two crude, direct-cycle nuclear engines. Gurenov piloted this aircraft on some forty flights between 1961 and 1969.

It is said that the crew were not shielded from radiation and that some died as a result.

By late 1956 turbojets were becoming more efficient and the government decided to cancel the projected WS-125A strategic aircraft, since it was premature to develop an airframe when a possible nuclear power system was so far away. There was no consensus between industry and official bodies regarding the desirability or otherwise of nuclear-powered aircraft. Therefore, although the aircraft programme was cancelled, GE and P&W continued with their engine investigations, without any specific applications in mind. GE's Direct Cycle engine was working well but without enough power. The NB-36 made its last flight on 28 March 1957 and was then scrapped. All work on nuclear engines for aircraft was terminated in March 1961 when official funding stopped. By now the future was seen to be in Intercontinental Ballistic Missiles (ICBMs), not strategic bombers, the future for the pilots of which was seen to be as 'Silo Sitters'.

As early as 1956 Pratt & Whitney began the design of its JT11 turbojet, military designation J58. It was the first turbojet designed for Mach 3.0 and had a take-off thrust of 13,600kp (30,000lb) in afterburner mode, for a weight of 3,175kg (7,000lb). The J58 powered the four-engined Lockheed A-12 and SR-71 Blackbird aircraft. J58s were also to be used in one of P&W's nuclear propulsion projects. Philip Jarrett

PART V

Other Turbojet-Producing Nations

CHAPTER TWENTY-SEVEN

Japan

Japan, although technologically advanced enough to develop gas turbine-powered aircraft in parallel with Europe during the Second World War, did not begin to do so until it was too late to help it militarily. This was due to an initial lack of interest by the military. Japan had been fighting in Manchuria since 1931, but did not enter the global conflict until December 1941, when it attacked the American fleet at Pearl Harbor. Thus began the Pacific War or, as the Japanese call it, the Greater Asian War. All went well for Japan for six months and then the Allies, chiefly led by the USA with its huge industrial capacity, began the long fight back. In mid-1944 the Marianas Islands came under Allied control and provided a base for B-29 bombers to begin the decimation of Japan. Soon the Japanese military saw the need for jet aircraft. Despite the very unfavourable war conditions by then, Japanese engineers did make some remarkable progress, albeit too late to affect the war's outcome. However, this story has its roots very much earlier.

As early as 1919, a Lt Kohichi Hanajima of the Imperial Japanese Navy (IJN) became interested in turbines and other rotating machinery and was stimulated by developments in Europe. During a visit to France in 1926 he purchased ten Rateau turbosuperchargers (designed for Hispano Suiza piston engines) and brought them back to Japan. One of these was given to the Tokyo Imperial University (TIU) for study, but the general interest in Japan was slight. One of the turbosuperchargers was fitted to the Army Air HQ Model 3 experimental fighter, on which work began in June 1926 and was completed a year later. This aircraft had a 300hp Hispano-Suiza engine and was tested in 1928, but the improved performance expected from the turbosupercharger was not realized. By 1936 Hanajima was a Rear Admiral and had been made the head of the Engine Division of the Kaigun Kokusho (Naval Air Arsenal), shortened to Kugisho, at Yokosuka. This establishment was to Japan what Farnborough, Wright Field and Rechlin were to Great Britain, the USA and Germany respectively.

An interest in ramjets then arose in Japan, apparently triggered by references to ramjets made by various participants at the November 1935 Volta Congress in Rome. In May 1938 the French engineer René Leduc received a letter from the Japanese Ambassador in Paris asking him to contact Mitsubishi, since that company was interested in building, under licence, the ramjet and the aircraft that Leduc was working on. Needless to say, Leduc did not follow this up and his work on the ramjet aircraft was soon shelved until after the war.

Around 1937 a number of foreign publications concerned with jet propulsion became available in Japan. These included patent applications from Whittle and Campini, plus articles by Goddard. Such publications stimulated the interest of Hanajima, and also that of the TIU and the Mitsubishi Aircraft Company, in jet propulsion. Prof. Nakanishi and his assistant Prof. Hatta at TIU carried out theoretical calculations and experiments on the thermodynamic cycles involved in propulsive ducts with internal combustion. A series of pressure ratios, air mass flows, temperatures and so forth were assumed for these studies, in which ramjets were given most attention. The experiments centred on air passage shapes and the internal flow through ducts. For this study project a Prof. Kawada was the aerodynamic consultant. In 1937 a young student named Hibi, who had worked under Prof. Nakanishi, began work at Mitsubishi on ramjets. Up to 1939 many small ramjet models were tested, and by 1943 the Imperial Japanese Army (IJA) had taken an interest in applying ramjets to kamikaze suicide aircraft. That year, the Army made flight tests of a larger ramjet but none of this work had any useful outcome. Nevertheless, Hibi continued with his research until the end of the war.

During 1940 Capt. Tokuyasu Tanegashima of the IJN visited France and Switzerland and thereby became interested in gas turbines, bringing back to Japan one of Brown Boveri's turbosuperchargers from Switzerland. He also visited the USA and bought a sample of the Moss-designed turbosupercharger from General Electric. Armed with his new knowledge of gas turbines, Tanegashima replaced Hanajima as head of the Engine Division of Kugisho at Yokosuka. Despite a continued lack of official interest, Tanegashima was permitted to pursue supercharger and gas turbine study with limited funds. In this work, he consulted with Hanajima and, through his enthusiasm, stimulated the interest of individuals in the IJN and industry, who made additional funds available. Study of European and American turbosuperchargers led to the development of similar equipment by Mitsubishi. However, teething troubles with turbosuperchargers led to a continuation with gear-driven superchargers (the Mitsubishi J2M4 Raiden interceptor, for example, had to have its turbosupercharger changed to a gear-driven one in the J2M5 model).

Initially Tanegashima's gas turbine work went down a dead end by investigating the Junkers-type free piston compressor (fine when used in Junkers piston aero-engines) as the gas generator for a turbine. In this he was influenced by an advertisement from the Pescara company in *La Nature* magazine and also by the thoughts of the respected Prof. Aurel Stodola of the University of Zürich. It was claimed that the free piston compressor would have efficiencies that would make the gas turbine a practical proposition.

In 1941 the Mitsui Seiki company was commissioned to design and construct a free piston gas generator. At the same time, Lt Cmdr Osamu Nagano, aided by Masanori

Dr Osamu Nagano in 1977. During the Second World War he was the Technical Manager of turbojet development at Kugisho and was a pioneer of early Japanese turbojets.

Miyata, designed and built at Kugisho a small 100mm (4in) diameter turbine to be driven by the gas generator. The whole unit was then tested and gave about 0.1hp at 12,000rpm. As a demonstration, it drove a magneto to power a small electric lamp. Tanegashima was not very impressed with this machine and he decided that industry was not then capable of building a good free piston engine.

By this time, a Thrust Division had been established within the Engine Division of Kugisho. In 1941 another dead-end was investigated in the shape of the Tsu-11 compound jet engine. (This may have been a dead-end in so far as turbojet development was concerned, but at least Japanese thoughts were being concentrated on jet propulsion.) In 1938 Genzo Shoji had been sent to Italy as the Japanese representative on technical matters and quickly showed interest in the Campini motorjet propulsion system. Full design details of the Campini engine were flown to Japan in July 1942 on an SM-75, this being the only direct flight between Italy and Japan. Like the Italian Campini jet unit and others developed elsewhere, the Tsu-11 consisted of a piston engine (in this case a 130hp air-cooled Hatsukaze 11, four-cylinder, in-line type) driving a geared-up ducted fan as a compressor, following which extra fuel was burned in an exhaust duct. Vanes straightened out the airflow from the compressor before the extra fuel was injected.

The Tsu-11 is said to have had a static thrust of 200kp (441lb) at 3,000rpm (the fan itself rotating at 9,000rpm), for a weight of about 200kg (441lb). The overall diameter of the Tsu-11 was 0.640m (2ft 1in) and its length was 2.20m (7ft 2½in). Consideration was given to this engine as a booster for conventional aircraft, the powerplant for a fighter and to power a suicide bomb (see below). However, when the Navy tested one in 1944 beneath the fuselage of the third prototype of their Yokosuka P1Y1 Ginga (Milky Way) twin-engine bomber, its top speed of 547km/h (340mph) was increased by only 20km/h (12mph). A much larger Tsu-type powerplant was to have a 1,280hp Kinsei 50 (Golden Star) radial engine driving the compressor and was expected to deliver some 900kp (1,985lb) of thrust. However, its size would have been of the order of 4.5m (14ft 9in) long by 1.25m (4ft 1in) diameter. Uninspired by this type of engine, Tanegashima came to the conclusion that it was better to investigate a gas turbine with an axial compressor and a separate combustion chamber. From this came the idea of developing a turboprop engine.

In designing the turboprop, the services were retained of Japan's leading specialist in axial compressor theory, Prof. Numachi of the University of Sendai, who had actually volunteered his services at Navy Headquarters and then been referred to Tanegashima at Yokosuka. Also active in this field was Y. Shimoyana, who carried out experiments with aerofoil cascades at the Faculty of Engineering at Kyushu Imperial University at Fukuoka. Minami, one of Prof. Numachi's students, then designed a sixteen-stage quarter-scale axial compressor that was built to demonstrate the feasibility of the axial compressor. In 1942 tests with this compressor demonstrated a compression ratio of 3:1 and an adiabatic efficiency of 78 per cent. This was a worthy achievement for a first axial compressor and gained Tanegashima further support for his turboprop project.

The turboprop was designated the GTPR (Gas Turbine Propeller Rocket), indicating that considerable residual thrust was expected, and the Ishikawajima-Shibaura Turbine Company and the Ebara Blower Company were commissioned by the Navy to undertake its construction. Only component tests were undertaken and official interest in the GTPR was slight. The Army also sponsored a minor variation of the GTPR, but this work was not completed. Later, there existed projects for turboprops at Mitsubishi, one being for a 5,000shp engine.

By 1943, news that jet aircraft were being actively developed in Germany aroused much interest in Japan and so turbojet projects were begun. The Chief of Kugisho, Vice Admiral Misao Wada, directed turbojet development to begin at Yokosuka. Later that year Lt Cmdr Kato, assistant to Tanegashima, was working on the design of a turbojet designated TR (Turbine Rocket). This featured a centrifugal compressor, adapted from a turbosupercharger and expected to give a pressure ratio of 4:1, and a single-stage turbine. A centrifugal compressor, instead of an axial one, was chosen, against the advice of Tanegashima, because his assistants believed it would prove to be more efficient than the axial type. The TR turbojet was developed into the TR-10, which was built by the Ebara company. A bench test of the TR-10 was made in 1943 but the compressor gave a pressure ratio of only 3.5:1 and overall efficiency of the engine was only about 50 per cent. Various modifications were then made but none were successful. Finally, a redesign incorporated a four-stage axial compressor and new inlet duct in front of the centrifugal compressor, with a view to easing the load on it. This turbojet was designated the TR-12. When completed, at 350kg (772lb), it was found to be heavier than the thrust it produced. It was then refined to lighten it and was designated the TR-12B.

The TR-12B was never developed into a satisfactory engine despite forty examples being built and work with them continuing until the end of 1944. The TR-12B produced a static thrust of 320kp (706lb) at 15,000rpm, for a weight of 315kg (695lb). Its diameter was 0.86m (2ft 10in) and length 1.80m (5ft 11in). The turbine was 0.476m (1ft 6¾in) in diameter and operated in a temperature of 700°C. Fuel consumption was 510kg (1,125lb) per hour. It was planned to flight test the TR-12B beneath a Mitsubishi G4M2 Betty bomber in November 1944, but it is not known if this was actually done. In any event, all

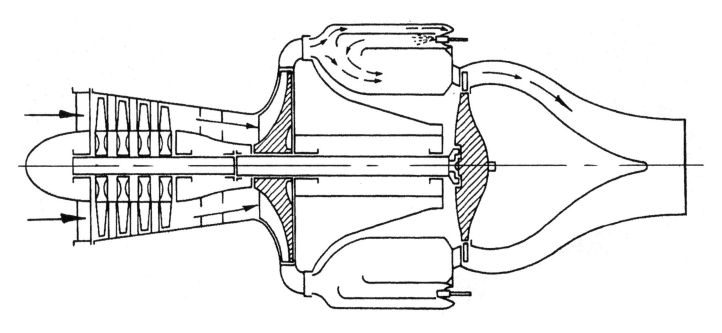

The layout of the TR-12B turbojet with a four-stage axial compressor, a centrifugal compressor and reversed-flow combustion chamber.

work on the TR-series of engines was abandoned early in 1945 when the first information of developments in Germany was received. At some point, 'TR' designations were changed to 'Ne' (Nensho for combustion rocket) designations.

German–Japanese collaboration

On 27 September 1940 the Axis powers of Germany, Japan and Italy signed the Tripartite Pact to promote cooperation for their mutual benefit in economic, political and military matters throughout Europe and Asia. Of greatest interest to Japan were Germany's advances in aviation, but optics, radar and other technical innovations were also of interest. By 1940 Japan had begun negotiations with the Junkers aircraft and engine companies and negotiations were later opened up with other companies such as Messerschmitt and Heinkel. Prior to Germany's invasion of the Soviet Union, matériel was transported between Germany and Japan by the Trans-Siberian railway. After that, it went by sea and, finally, by submarine. Ships and submarines of all Axis powers were used. The exchange of matériel from Japan to Germany largely comprised rubber, zinc, tungsten, molybdenum, quinine, tin and oil and, from Germany to Japan, details of technical advances in aeronautics, torpedoes, optical and radar

equipment, special steels, aluminium, lead, platinum, mercury, industrial diamonds, ball bearings and chemicals.

In January 1943 the German-Japanese Economic Agreement was signed to ratify the exchanges between the two countries, although such exchanges had been going on for some time. By 1944 the imbalance of naval power in the Allies' favour meant that the only means of transporting matériel was by submarine and soon even that method was fraught with danger, such was the Allies' control of the seas. The exchange of information on secret weapons really meant Germany helping Japan and required further consideration by the former. During March and April 1944 negotiations began between Japanese representatives in Berlin and the German OKL concerning the release of details for the production under licence in Japan of the Messerschmitt Me 163B-1a rocket-powered interceptor, the Me 262A-1a jet fighter, the Walter rocket motor and the Junkers 109-004 and BMW 109-003 turbojets. This would require the assistance of technicians from Messerschmitt and Junkers in Japan and also the training of Japanese technicians in Germany.

The main Japanese representatives in Berlin coordinating the acquisition of German matériel on jet aircraft were Maj. Gen. Otani, working for both Japanese Army and Navy air forces, Admiral Koshima (Naval Attaché at the Japanese

Embassy) and Lt Gen. Komatsu (Japanese Army Air Force Attaché). Apparently, Komatsu cared little about technical matters and was happy to leave these for Otani to deal with. German industry showed considerable reluctance to release details of their hard-won technology, but all resistance was overruled by Hitler and all agreements had been finalized by July 1944. The Japanese agreed to pay Germany considerable sums for the details and production rights of weapons of war and industrial processes. These sums amounted to RM20 million for each item and it is interesting to note that, even in the last weeks of the war in Europe, Japanese representatives in Berlin were anxious to settle their country's debts.

Meanwhile, in May 1944, Technical Commander Eiichi Iwaya (an airframe specialist) and Capt. Yosikawa left Germany on the Japanese Fleet submarine I-29 with matériel on board that included turbojet and jet aircraft drawings. En route, the I-29 put in at Singapore and here Iwaya elected to speed up his journey and report by flying the rest of the way to Japan. While the submarine was later sunk with all its valuable cargo, west of Manila, Iwaya arrived in Japan on 17 July 1944 with a few photocopies, including a cross-section of the BMW 109-003 turbojet and some general material concerning the Me 262 fighter and Me 163 interceptor. Further sets of drawings and matériel were then to be sent to Japan on different German U-boats. An example of a crated Me 163 and an Me 262, together with examples of turbojets and various components and equipment, were also to go by U-boat. Besides I-29, the Japanese submarines I-8, I-30, I-34 and I-52 were also sent to French ports but only the first three reached Brest and Lorient to collect matériel. No Japanese ships went to European ports, and only German and Italian freighters attempted the run to Japan.

Early in 1944, members of the Japanese Army and Navy air forces attended a demonstration of the Me 262 at a Messerschmitt factory. They also witnessed operation of 109-004 turbojets at the Junkers plant at Dessau. In August 1944 the Japanese began an intensive study of the 109-004 turbojet by visiting all of the dispersed Junkers assembly plants; they were especially interested in the light metal works, since it appears that they were deficient in this field. During one of his visits to the Dessau plant, a Maj. Taruntani said to Ulfried Gold (in charge of Japanese transactions since 1939) that Japan was very interested in producing the 109-004 turbojet, but that they were also in great need of construction calculations to assist in the development of a turbojet already under way in Japan. Following this, helpful calculations and data were encoded and radioed to Japan (this being well before the advent of the fax machine). In the last few months of the war in Europe, some design

and performance details of the Ar 234B, Ba 349, He 162A, Fi 103, Ju 287 and Me 263 jet and rocket aircraft were also radioed to Japan; this was known to the Allies from 'Ultra' code-breaking intercepts.

Junkers was also requested to provide a construction engineer, an assembly engineer and a foreman to help with the turbojet project at the assembly stage. Only a foreman, Herr Trappiel, could be spared by Junkers, but Dipl.-Ing. R. Schomerus from Messerschmitt, who had already been to Japan, volunteered to step in and assist on the manufacturing side as possible. Meanwhile, full sets of 109-004 drawings were being prepared, along with hardware, and these were delivered to an OKL courier on 6 November 1944 for transport to the port of Kiel. Similar material was prepared by BMW regarding its 109-003 turbojet. All this material, together with a crated Me 262, Me 163 and other aircraft was put on board the U-boats U-234 and U-864.

An idea of the matériel on board these U-Boats may be gained from the manifest for U-234: on board were some 300 tonnes of cargo and sufficient fuel and supplies for up to a nine-month trip. Its cargo included 8 tonnes of documents and technical drawings and about 210 tonnes of war matériel, including the Messerschmitt aircraft, production jigs and tools, turbojet and rocket engines and half a tonne of uranium oxide. U-864 left Kiel for Bergen in December 1944 but was damaged in an air raid on Bergen; after repairs, it departed

from Bergen on 9 February 1945, intending to reach Japan via Penang, but was sunk on the same day by the Royal Navy. U-234 left Kiel on 25 March 1945 but had to put into Kristiansand for repairs after being hit by U-1301 under water. Once repaired, U-234 was under way again when the Allies' order for all U-Boats to surrender was given on 10 May 1945. U-234 surrendered on 15 May and was taken to Portsmouth Harbor, New Hampshire, USA. Thus, with the war over for Germany, the only useful turbojet technical material to reach Japan was the Junkers data encoded and radioed and the brief documents, mainly concerning the 109-003 turbojet, delivered by Iwaya.

When details, brief as they were, of the BMW 109-003 reached Japan in July 1944, the Army and Navy held a joint conference (a rare event) at which it was decided that a Japanese version of this turbojet held more promise in the short term than Japanese work still in its early stages. Therefore, all domestic projects were frozen and the available details of the 109-003 and the Junkers 109-004 were issued to various companies. Details of the Heinkel-Hirth 109-011 turbojet may also have been made available. This resulted in four turbojet projects:

- Ne 130, by the Ishikawajima-Shibaura Turbine Company: designed for a static thrust of 900kp (1,985lb) at 9,000rpm for a weight of 900kg (1,985lb). It was similarly configured to the BMW

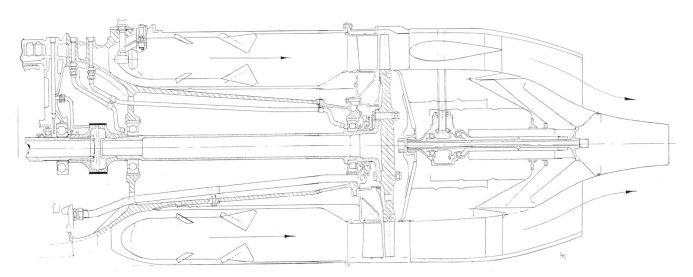

Ne 130 axial turbojet. The badly damaged state of the microfilm that was found made possible a reconstruction of only the 'hot end' of this engine, which had a seven-stage axial compressor. However, this is enough to show how closely this engine was based on the BMW 109-003A turbojet, the main differences being in details and the use of Japanese components such as bearings and the flexible coupling between shafts. It was also larger and heavier than the BMW engine. Author

109-003 and had a diameter of 0.850m (2ft 9½in) and a length of 3.85m (12ft 7½in). A fuel consumption of 1,600 litres per hour was estimated.

- Ne 230, jointly by the Nakajima Engine Company and the Hitachi Turbine Company: designed for a static thrust of 885kp (1,951lb) at 8,100rpm for a weight of 870kg (1,918lb). It was apparently based closely on the BMW 109-003A and had a diameter of 0.762m (2ft 6in), a height of 0.914m (3ft) and a length of 3.430m (11ft 3in).
- Ne 330, by the Mitsubishi Engine Company: designed for a thrust of 1,300kp (2,866lb) at 7,600rpm for a weight of 1,200kg (2,646lb). It may well have been based on the Heinkel-Hirth 109-011 turbojet and had a diameter of 0.880m (2ft 10½in), a height of 1.18m (3ft 10½in) and a length of 4.0m (13ft 1½in). A fuel consumption of 2,530 litres per hour was estimated.
- Ne 20, a Navy project headed by Osamu Nagano at Kugisho in Yokosuka.

The Ne 20 was to become Japan's most successful turbojet and the other three projects were not fully developed in the time available.

Nevertheless, a look at Nakajima's work on the Ne 230 should be of interest. For this project, Nakajima had rooms totalling 420sq m (4,520sq ft) and the total of personnel in its Experimental Division at the end of the war numbered 217, of which 53 were engineers. Chief of this division was Shigeto Ueda. His engineers gained their first experience of turbojets by cooperating with Hitachi in the construction of the Navy's Ne 10 engine. An Ne 10 was then borrowed from the Navy and run on the test bench at the Tanahashi plant to familiarize them with the turbojet. Much difficulty was found in starting the Ne 10 and it was confined to only a few runs owing to the critical lack of fuel, which, at this stage of the war, meant that Japan's aircraft rarely flew and condemned the huge battleship *Yamato* to a one-way, suicide mission. In any case, the Ne 10 was found to have a very high fuel consumption. In developing the Ne 230, based on BMW's engine, problems encountered included premature wear of the hydraulic fuel pumps (both gear and reciprocating types), starting difficulties and compressor problems. Also, a control system still had to be developed. In fact the Ne 230 had so many problems

in need of solution and so few engineers available to solve them that it is doubtful whether a successful turbojet could ever have been developed. Incredibly, the engineers and their assistants, even those of long experience, were expected to join up for military service at a predetermined date, regardless of their value to the work. Naturally, for many, this had a bad effect on their enthusiasm for the work. In general, engineers were young and, technically, 'jacks of all trades', and the shortage of skilled personnel was acute. Parts for the Ne 230 were produced at Nakajima's Mitake and Ogikubo plants and finally assembled at Hitachi's Takahagi plant and at Kugisho, Yokosuka. The Ne 230 was run several times at the Hitachi plant but was never fully developed.

Of the Ne 130, Ne 230 and Ne 330 engines, the last of these was expected to be the best and was scheduled to power the Yokosuka R2Y2 Keiun (Beautiful Cloud) two-seat attack aircraft, a derivative of the R2Y1 reconnaissance aircraft. The fuselage-mounted piston engine of the R2Y1 was to be replaced by two underwing Ne 330 turbojets. A projected use of the Ne 130 (or the Ne 230) was to replace the piston engine and pusher airscrew in the Kyushu J7W1 Shinden (Magnificent Lightning) canard fighter. With turbojet power, this fighter was designated the J7W2 and, in fact, it was designed from the outset to eventually use a turbojet engine. The first flight of the J7W1 was not made until 3 August 1945, from Fukuoka Airport, and only one other prototype was built, but not flown, by the war's end.

Of much greater import was the Ne 20 axial turbojet developed under project engineer Cmdr Osamu Nagano, assisted by Tanegashima, at Kugisho. He made the initial layout in the autumn of 1944 and, under great pressure, detail design and construction was begun in January 1945. The layout was guided by the GA cross-section drawing of the BMW 109-003A-0 (plus, perhaps, some photos). Of particular value in saving much development time was the guidance given by the BMW drawing of the combustion chamber. This clearly indicated an annular chamber with hollow fingers to introduce secondary air into the hot combustion zone. Because the Ne 20 was only about 75 per cent the size of the 003, however, only twelve (instead of sixteen) burners were used, although of the same size. Although the BMW drawing confirmed that Japan had largely been

developing its own engines along the right lines, the best features of the 003 engine, as far as they could be ascertained, were retained. However, many material substitutions had to be made. Nickel, in particular, which all heat-resisting alloys used, was not available and so the turbine blades were a steel alloy using manganese, chromium and vanadium. The Special Steels Section of Kugisho at Yokosuka, with the help of several universities, developed and tested some fifty-two special steels, nine of which were selected for use in gas turbine and rocket engines.

The Ne 20 had an eight-stage axial compressor, an annular combustion chamber and a single-stage turbine. The compressor had a pressure ratio of 3.4:1 and delivered an air mass flow of 14kg/sec (30.87lb/sec) at a speed of 11,000rpm. The turbine inlet temperature was between 700 and 750°C, the gases passing to the turbine through only twelve inlet nozzles (BMW used thirty-six). Cooling air was directed to the rear face of the turbine wheel, to which the solid rotor blades were welded. Rotor bearings comprised two ball races in front of the compressor, a single ball race behind the compressor and a roller race in front of the turbine wheel, which was thereby overhung. The oil lubrication system for the bearings included a pressure and scavenge pump outside the engine and a second scavenge pump inside this engine that was driven by spur gears from the rotor shaft behind the compressor rear bearing.

An electric motor, mounted in front of the compressor, used 4:1 gearing to spool the engine up to 2,250rpm but starting usually occurred at around 1,500rpm. Petrol was used to start, but during acceleration the fuel was switched to pine root distillate containing about 25 per cent petrol. This may have been one answer to the acute fuel shortage and crude pine root oil was used to test the Maru-Ka 10 pulsejet engine (based on the German Argus 109-014 V1 flying bomb pulsejet) at Yokosuka. Unlike earlier designs, starting of the Ne 20 was not difficult and was usually achieved in 10 to 15 seconds. Careful use of the throttle, however, was necessary to avoid stalling. Accessories, such as twin fuel pumps, oil pumps and a magneto were clustered around the compressor casing and driven by radial shafts and bevel gears. Shaped oil tanks were fitted top and bottom of the intake casing.

The main structural member of the Ne 20 was the compressor casing, cast in alloy and with strengthening ribs. At its forward

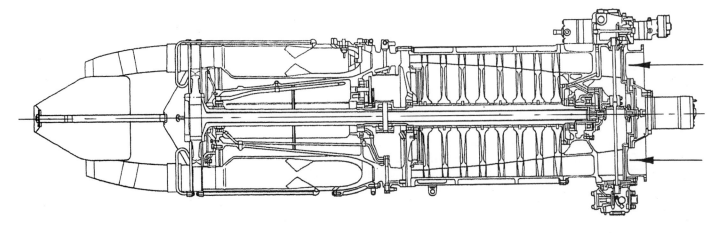

The Ne 20 axial turbojet was partly based on BMW's 109-003 engine, but was smaller. Development work on all other turbojets in Japan was shelved in order to concentrate on the Ne 20. Robert C. Mikesh

end was bolted the flange of a cast ring containing four streamlined struts and a central housing for the accessory gears and drives and the front compressor bearings. The air intake duct was bolted to a forward flange on this cast ring. At the rear of the compressor casing was a cast ring supporting the rear bearing for the compressor and having slots for the exit of air from the compressor. The cast ring and the rear of the compressor casing had the main support points (for attachment to the aircraft's wing) and the cast ring had a conical section that led rearwards to support the turbine bearing and the combustion chamber. The structure aft of the cast ring was largely of sheet metal construction, the exhaust nozzle being of the fixed-area type, pending information on a variable-area type. The Ne 20 weighed about 470kg (1,036lb), had a length of 2.70m (8ft 10¼in) and a diameter of 0.62m (2ft 0½in).

Working day and night, and with help from Nakajima, Mitsubishi and the Ishikawajima Shibaura Turbine Company, Kugisho had the first example of the Ne 20 ready by March 1945. About four hundred machine tools were used in this heroic effort, with the casting and machining of large components being performed by the industrial concerns mentioned. On the surface, the Naval Air Station at Yokosuka did not look very impressive, particularly once enemy aircraft began bombing and strafing it, but that was because much of the organization was out of sight: in the solid limestone of the Yokosuka hills was built a whole underground experimental aircraft factory comprising workshops, hangars, storage and living quarters.

The first Ne 20 was run on 26 March 1945, using a test cell in a cave. A static thrust of about 475kp (1,047lb) was achieved at 11,000rpm and tests were encouraging enough to warrant abandoning all other Ne projects in order to concentrate on the Ne 20. Of course, much development was still needed and problems to be solved. Due to increased attention from enemy aircraft and the deteriorating conditions at Yokosuka, Tanegashima considered it wise to move the turbojet group to a dispersed location. By then, the Kugisho workshops were in a bad way, with dirt and disorganization everywhere. Everyone was working in a mess, using hand tools and benches to make small pieces and with no apparent organized effort.

Dispersal of the turbojet group was made to warehouses and a tobacco factory at Hadano at the southern edge of the Tanzawa mountains, about three hours by road from Yokosuka. Engine test stands were erected under bamboo camouflage in a nearby farm. Conditions at Hadano, in a wide valley, were very pleasant for the two hundred workmen and about ten officers, with plenty of food and other comforts. It also seems to have been free from air attacks and was much more conducive to concentration on the engine work.

By now, the turbojet group could not depend on much help from industrial companies such as Hitachi and Mitsubishi, due to transport and other difficulties engendered by the war situation. Modifications and the manufacture of small parts were all that could be done. An example of this was the modification of the compressor to achieve a higher compression

ratio. The talented Nagano increased the camber of the stator blades by bending their trailing edges using a hammer and anvil. This modification was tested on the second Ne 20 and proved successful; all succeeding engines were fitted with similar stator blades.

Another problem was that the front bearings, taking the thrust from the compressor, were overheating and burning out quite quickly. Nagano again worked on this problem and eventually solved it by fitting sprung rings between the two ball races, thereby ensuring that they shared the load equally. Also, to equalize the loads between the turbine and the compressor, a balancing piston was fitted at the centre of the shaft.

Fatigue cracks appearing in turbine blades after only one or two hours running were tackled by making the blades thicker at the expense of turbine efficiency, which fell to about 70 per cent. By this means, up to five hours running could be obtained without trouble. If this applied to the whole engine, it was as good as the life of early German turbojets. No doubt due to the lack of drawings, the engineers seem to have been unaware of the important detail of the bulb root fitting of turbine rotor blades used by BMW, and used welded attachment instead. Specific fuel consumption of the Ne 20 was high at about 1.5.

By the end of the Pacific War in August 1945, the group at Hadano had managed to assemble nine Ne 20s and the Yokosuka Naval Yard had built twelve. From February 1945, Kugisho at Yokosuka was re-designated as the Dai-Ichi Kaigun Koku Guijitsho (1st Naval Technical Arsenal).

Of the twenty-one Ne 20s built, those from Yokosuka were considered to be of poor quality owing to the lack of experience in building engines there and the chaotic conditions. Had the war continued, the next production runs were to have been at the rate of 100 engines per month from the combined output of various Naval Air Arsenals, a figure that was to be later increased by contributions from Mitsubishi and Hitachi.

In view of the lack of scientists and engineers available for the development and the shortage of special metals, the Japanese managed to produce a surprisingly useful turbojet in only eight months from the start of detailed design work. This was largely thanks to the leadership of Osamu Nagano and owed only a little to German technology.

After the war the US Navy delivered an Ne 20 turbojet to Chrysler for repair and test. The electric starter motor at the front of the compressor had received a blow and it was necessary to have its armature rewound. Also, a replacement set of bevel gears and a support bracket were installed. The engine was reassembled and on the test stand early in October 1946. Several runs were made at speeds up to 9,000rpm and totalling some 78 minutes. A small photopanel was made up and used to record data on the engine's starting characteristics. Unfortunately, on the last run the compressor was badly damaged by the ingestion of a small wood screw, which seems to have come loose from the inlet fairing supporting the oil cooler. The turbine wheel was only slightly damaged.

Chrysler then received another Ne 20, apparently an earlier model, from the US Navy in a dismantled condition. Using the compressor rotor and stator from this engine, the first engine was rebuilt and on the test stand by November 1946. Altogether, 11 hours and 46 minutes running was made on this Ne 20 and it gave a static thrust of 475kp (1,047lb) at 11,000rpm and a high specific fuel consumption of 1.55. The engine was then dismantled for individual component testing and a complete report made to the Navy. Chrysler found this programme of great educational value and showed that the Ne 20 would probably have had a useful

life for the Japanese. Its wartime utilization will now be discussed.

Japan's first jet aircraft, the Nakajima Kikka

After Technical Cmdr Eichi Iwaya returned to Japan with brief details of German jet aircraft in July 1944, the Naval Headquarters held a meeting with the country's largest aircraft manufacturer, Nakajima, and also the much smaller Kawanishi company. The Navy required a single-seat, twin-jet attack aircraft, based on the Messerschmitt Me 262 fighter, and specified a modest maximum speed of 695km/h (430mph) and a range of 200km (125 miles) with a 500kg (1,103lb) bomb load, or 280km (175 miles) with a 250kg (551lb) bomb load. Take-off was to be within 350m (1,148ft) with the assistance of two 450kp (992lb) thrust rockets. The wings were to be foldable to allow hangarage in caves and tunnels and also for ease of production by semi-skilled labour.

Soon after this meeting, Nakajima's chief designer, Kenichi Matsumura, and engineer Kazuo Ohno produced the general layout of a twin-engined jet aircraft that resembled a smaller Messerschmitt Me 262, although only sparse details of the latter were available since the main drawings had been lost in the submarine transporting them. By

mid-September the project had been accepted by the Navy planners residing at Nakajima's Koizumi factory and detail designing went ahead. In this the designers were helped by what Iwaya, as an airframe specialist, could remember of his inspections of the Me 262. At that time, the design was based on the use of two TR-12 turbojets and, due to a lack of engine details, underwing mounting of the engines was advantageous for last-minute changes. A punishing work schedule ensued, with Nakajima staff working day and night shifts on detail drawings. These were expected to be ready by October, followed by production aircraft by December 1944. Initially the aircraft was to be a Special Attack or kamikaze aircraft carrying a bomb to the Allied fleets closing in on Japan. Early in December, however, the Navy revised the unrealistic schedules and the aircraft mission was changed to that of a close air support bomber. Thus, the aircraft was dissimilar in purpose to that of the Me 262 fighter. A revision of the official specification included a maximum speed of 620km/h (386mph) with a 500kg bomb, a range at full power and at sea level of 300km (186 miles) and a landing speed of 93km/h (58mph). As before, rockets were to be used to assist a loaded take-off. By now, the aircraft had been named the Kikka (Wild Orange Blossom), but had no type designation.

Preparing Kikka, Japan's first jet aircraft, for flight. Mesh safety guards over the Ne 20 turbojet intakes were removed before flight.

A wooden mock-up of Kikka was inspected by Navy officials, including Admiral Wada from Kugisho, on 28 January 1945 and the proposed engines were changed to Ne 20s. Within two weeks a revised mock-up was ready and approved on 10 February, whereupon the Navy immediately placed a production order. Every effort was made to achieve simplicity in construction and many important materials were constantly being substituted: in particular, steel sheet was used where possible instead of aluminium alloy sheet. The Japanese had earlier made strenuous efforts to obtain licences for plywood processes from Germany. By June 1945 Kugisho had ordered that work on Nakajima's G8N Renzan (Mountain Range) four-engine bomber (in the same factory) should stop and materials for it be diverted to the Kikka. Initially, a line of about twenty-five Kikkas was laid down at the Koizumi plant, but B-29 bomber raids had caused serious damage to the plant and so, from February 1945, much work was dispersed to safer locations. The engineering staff went to Sano City, east of Tokyo, most of the airframe construction was undertaken at Kugisho, Yokosuka, and even small parts manufacture was moved from the Koizumi factory to various dispersed locations throughout central Honshu. Therefore, the Kikka prototype, which was also the first production machine, was put together in a farm. For the period from July to September 1945, production of ninety-four Kikkas was planned. As far as possible, parts from other aircraft had been adapted and designed into Kikka, examples being some of the undercarriage, cockpit and fittings adapted from the Zero fighter. The strenuous efforts made to simplify Kikka resulted in an estimated production time of 7,500 man-hours each; an even lower time had been striven for, but this was only half that required, for example, to produce a Zero fighter.

On 20 May 1945 the first structural tests were begun and the airframe of the first prototype was completed by 25 June. It was then dismantled and trucked to the Koizumi plant, where it was completed with two Ne 20 turbojets two days later. On 30 June the engines were started for the first time but, because the runway at the plant was considered too short for safety, the Kikka was again dismantled and then trucked to Kisarazu Air Base bordering Tokyo Bay. There, during an engine test on 14 July, a nut was sucked into one engine, destroying

Lt Cmdr Susumu Takaoka of the Imperial Japanese Navy prepares to fly Japan's first jet aircraft, the Kikka fighter, powered by two Ne 20 turbojets, probably on its second flight. Officers and other personnel watch with great interest.

its compressor. After a new engine was fitted, taxiing tests were begun on 27 July with the pilot Lt Wada. All was now ready for Japan's first jet aircraft flight.

The Kikka had a fuselage of rounded, triangular section, of metal monocoque construction with twenty-four formers. Light stringers were covered in a light alloy skin except for a portion in front of the cockpit that was covered in a steel skin. The fuselage was built in three sections, bolted together, the centre section being built integral with the wing centre section. The wing centre section had twin spars, spanning 5.0m (16ft 6in), and, outboard of the two engines, carried light alloy outer panels that hinged inwards for storage. A laminar flow section was used for the wing and there were nine main support ribs between the spars. A sweepback of twelve degrees was used on the leading edge and

there were wingtip leading slots to delay a tendency to wingtip stall. The tailplane was mounted at top fuselage level to clear the jet efflux and all control surfaces were fabric covered. Three-position, plain flaps were provided inboard of the engines.

The cockpit canopy had a sliding section for access, and there was a 50m shatter-proof windscreen. The pilot was also protected by 12mm armour plating in front and behind and had a standard parachute. A total of 725ltr (160gal) of fuel was carried in two fuselage tanks, fore and aft of the cockpit, and there was an automatic CO_2 fire control system. An inwards-retracting, hydraulically actuated, tricycle under-carriage was provided; at the prototype stage there was no armament.

Following the first taxiing tests, high-speed taxiing tests were carried out by Lt Cmdr Susumu Takaoka, who found that,

Two Ne 20 turbojets ready for fitting to the Kikka fighter in the background. The close-up of the Ne 20 shows the front of the axial compressor, the bolts for attaching the electric starter motor and, at the bottom, two fuel pumps.

The war-torn Koizumi plant of Nakajima in November 1945. A partially completed Kikka fighter is illustrated and, in the close-up, one of its Ne 20 turbojets. The saddle tanks are for oil. In the background are partly-built Nakajima G8N Renzan bombers, the materials for which were diverted to Kikka construction.

at a speed of 130km/h (80mph), the brakes were barely adequate. Despite this, in the afternoon of the next day, 7 August 1945, the Kikka was prepared for its first flight, with a partial fuel load sufficient for about sixteen minutes of flight, to minimize weight. The weather was very favourable, with a light crosswind on Kisarazu's main runway, which pointed out to Tokyo Bay. After slowly opening the throttles to 11,000rpm and releasing the brakes, Takaoka flew the Kikka off the runway in 25 seconds after a run of 725m (2,378ft).

The smoothness and quietness of this, Japan's first turbojet aircraft flight, was something that Takaoka was not prepared for. He found it disquieting since, as a test pilot, he was used to the sound and vibration of an engine being part of his overall monitoring as a flight progressed. Because it was decided not to retract the under-carriage on this first flight, he had to limit the speed to 170km/h (106mph) and was constantly and cautiously easing the throttles back accordingly. After a turn over Tokyo Bay, Takaoka began his final approach a long way from the runway threshold in order to make it a shallow one.

Nakajima Kikka			
Span		10.0m	(32ft 10in)
Wings folded		5.26m	(17ft 3in)
Length		9.25m	(30ft 4in)
Wing area		13.20sq m	(142sq ft)
Height		3.05m	(10ft 0in)
Empty weight		2,300kg	(5,070lb)
Normal loaded weight		3,550kg	(7,828lb)
Maximum loaded weight		4,312kg	(9,508lb)
Estimated maximum speed	at 6,000m (19,700ft)	680km/h	(423mph)
Estimated initial climb rate		500m/min	(1,640ft/min)
Estimated service ceiling		10,700m	(35,100ft)
Estimated range		555km	(345 miles)

With the engines at 7,000rpm and with 40 degrees of flap, he touched down and cleared the runway in about 1,200m (3,935ft). This historic flight had lasted eleven minutes and the aircraft had performed well enough to require no adjustments at that stage. Furthermore, and more significantly, examination of the engines showed no

An Ne 20 turbojet removed from a Kikka fighter. The mesh intake safety guard lies on the floor.

noteworthy problems either. Altogether, the production of this first Japanese turbojet aircraft was a great achievement, brought about in barely more than a year. However, with the explosion of the atomic bomb over Hiroshima the previous day, the end of the Pacific War was nigh.

Nevertheless, the elation of those involved with Kikka was great and an official demonstration before Navy and Army officers was planned for 10 August. This official flight had to be delayed until the next day, due to enemy aircraft activity in the area. The Kikka carried more fuel than on the first flight and, fitted beneath the wing roots, there were now two rockets to assist the take-off. Takaoko fired these rockets after about four seconds of the roll from releasing the brakes. Unfortunately, the Kikka then reared up, scraping its tail skid on the runway. At first the speed was too low for elevator effectiveness, but after nine seconds the rockets burned out and the aircraft's nosewheel forcibly struck the runway. Takaoko elected to abort the take-off and cut the engines. He braked as hard as possible and executed a partial ground loop to stop the aircraft. It passed the end of the runway and over a drainage ditch, which sheared off the undercarriage, and finally came to rest on the sandy shore of the bay. It seems that this accident was not due to any fault with the aircraft or the pilot but was due to the misalignment of the rockets. Takaoka, although humiliated and guilt-ridden by this disaster, had done an excellent job in a difficult situation. However, this was the end for Kikka. A second atom bomb had been dropped on 9 August, this time at Nagasaki, and Japan surrendered on 14 August 1945. The Allied fleets entered Tokyo Bay, over which Kikka had been flown, and the formal instrument of surrender was signed on board the battleship USS *Missouri*.

An Ne 20 turbojet partly dismantled for examination and with a damaged starter motor on the left. At the top centre of the engine, and across it, are the main mounting points for attachment under a wing. This is probably the Ne 20 repaired and tested by Chrysler in the USA after the war; it gave surprisingly good results.

An Ne 20 turbojet in Smithsonian NASM, USA, now on display. Two oval supports for the front of the nacelle can be seen on the left.

Other Japanese jet aircraft projects

While the Japanese Navy was negotiating with Junkers for the rights to build its 109-004 turbojet under licence, the Japanese Army Air Force negotiated with the Messerschmitt company for production rights to the Me 163 interceptor, its Walter rocket motor, the Me 262 fighter and the BMW 109-003 turbojet. Because of this dividing line and the fact that the two forces rarely cooperated, there were often difficulties in the negotiations. The Messerschmitt company wanted to go further than signing construction licences and was keen to help advance Japanese aeronautics by injecting advanced ideas into Japanese fighter development. No doubt Messerschmitt had been urged to follow this path by Hitler and signed a contract with the Japanese to place some of its best experts at their disposal: Dipl.-Ing. Rolf von Chlingensperg (planning), Dipl.-Ing. Riclef Schomerus (leading aerodynamicist) and Dr.-Ing. August Bringewald (assembly expert). It was also planned initially to make many aircraft and engine components for the Japanese, such as the Riedel starter for turbojets, and to supply the heat-resisting alloys Tinidur and Chromadur.

Schomerus, Bringewald, Ruf, Chlingensperg and some Japanese specialists, together with much matériel, sailed for Japan in December 1944 in U-864, but this U-boat was sunk (see above). Preliminary drawings and illustrations of the Me 163, its Walter rocket and the Me 262, however, had reached Japan in autumn 1944. Both designs had to be considerably adapted to Japanese production methods and to use substitutes for special materials that were not available, such as thin, malleable steel sheet. German efforts to get details and examples of their advanced aircraft and other equipment to Japan were, by this time, quite determined. In mid-February 1945, a further nine U-boats left for Japan, full of matériel. These were the U-518, U-530, U-546, U-548, U-879, U-880, U-995, U-1001 and U-1230. By April all had sailed clear of Allied patrols and were in the South Atlantic, but at least six of these were sunk. The fate of U-234 and U-874 has already been noted. Much of the Allied success in sinking Axis submarines, and much else, could be attributed to the breaking of codes and interception of radio messages.

Late in October 1944 the Germans were advised that only the Japanese Army Air Force was interested in building a version of the Me 262, but some Messerschmitt engineers were of the opinion that building this aircraft was currently beyond the capability of Japanese industry. Detail design drawings for the Ki-201 Karyu (Fire Dragon), the Japanese Army Air Force version of the Me 262, were begun on 12 January 1945 and were due for completion in June 1945. This work was led by Iwao Shibuya and resulted in an aircraft similar to the Me 262, but larger. The first prototype was planned to be ready by December 1945 and was to be built at Nakajima's Mitaka plant. Power was to be provided by two Ne 130s or Ne 230s but, probably, two Ne 20s would have been used, provided the Navy agreed. Intended as a fighter and attack aircraft, the Karyu was to be armed with two 20mm and two 30mm cannon in the nose and be capable of carrying an external bomb load of up to 800kg (1,764lb). It was also to have airborne radar and be directed to interception by ground radar. It was intended to begin production of the Karyu at Nakajima's Kurosawajiri Research Works at Kitakami, with eighteen examples ready by March 1946, but the drawings were only half complete by the war's end and no Karyu was ever built.

The information on German developments brought to Japan in July 1944 included general details and a booklet concerning the Me 163B rocket-powered interceptor. This aircraft was of great interest to both the Army and the Navy as possibly an ideal way of intercepting the B-29 bombers pounding Japan. Such Me 163 details as were known were given to Mitsubishi to help produce its version.

Although superficially very similar to the Me 163, many compromises had to be made due to shortages of materials and the avoidance or simplification of components difficult to make in Japan. Design work began in July 1944. The rocket interceptor was designated the Ki-200 by the Army and J8M1 by the Navy, the name of Shusui (Sword Stroke) being applied. Armament was to be two 30mm cannon in the wing roots. The Japanese must have had good information on the Walter HWK 109-509 rocket that powered the Me 163. Japanese experts had certainly studied this unit and its C-Stoff/T-Stoff liquid propellant system in Germany; in any event, they produced the rocket motor designated KR 10 (or Toku Ro 2) for the Shusui. The KR 10 had a thrust of 1,500kp (3,308lb) and a weight of 170kg (375lb); the Shusui carried sufficient fuel for four minutes of power. By June 1945 two examples of the Shusui were ready for testing, one by the Army and one by the Navy, and a glider version with water ballast, designated the MXY8, was also made.

The Navy lost no time in ground testing their J8M1 and this was followed by the interceptor's first flight, at Yokosuka, on 7 July 1945, the pilot being Lt Cmdr Inuzuka. After a typically steep climb to 400m (1,312ft), however, the rocket cut out and the ensuing stall and crash was fatal to the pilot. Only about seven Shusui were built by the end of the war.

A number of versions of the Oka (Cherry Blossom) Special Attack or suicide bomb were designed, the original concept being that of IJN Ensign Shoichi Ota. The original Oka Model 11 was designed in 1944 by IJN technician Lt Cmdr Tadano Miki as a rocket-propelled aircraft with small wings, twin fins and rudders and a bubble cockpit

Nakajima Ki-201 Karyu			
Span		13.71m	(45ft 0in)
Length		11.50m	(37ft 9in)
Wing area		25.01sq m	(269sq ft)
Height		4.06m	(13ft 4in)
Empty weight		4,500kg	(9,920lb)
Maximum loaded weight		7,000kg	(15,432lb)
Maximum speed	at 10,000m (32,800ft)	853km/h	(530mph)
Initial climb rate		915m/min	(3,000ft/min)
Landing speed		160km/h	(99mph)
Range at altitude and throttled back		980km	(609 miles)

canopy. It was carried to its launch area by a G4M2 bomber and then released to power dive at its target, guided by the kamikaze (Divine Wind) pilot. Power for the Oka was provided by three solid-fuel rockets, each giving 800kp (1,764lb) of thrust for nine seconds. With a wingspan of only 5.0m (16ft 4¾in) and a length of 6.066m (19ft 10¾in), the Oka Model 11 carried 515kg (1,136lb) of high explosive to the enemy ships that were its target. In an attempt to improve performance, the Oka Model 22 was produced, powered by the Tsu-11 compound jet engine (see above). Air intakes for this version were on the fuselage sides, just behind the cockpit. The wingspan was reduced to 4.12m (13ft 6in), while the length was increased to 6.88m (22ft 6¼in). This Oka was a failure and its estimated top speed was only about 425km/h (264mph). The first one flight tested went into a stall and spin after being released from its bomber. The Model 22 was then projected as the Model 33 powered by an Ne 20

turbojet, but appears to have not been built. The Oka Model 43 was designed as a lightweight fighter, powered by the Ne 20 turbojet and armed with two cannon. It was to be catapult launched from the ground and return for a landing on its skid. By May 1945 the stress analysis on the Model 43 had been completed and the first prototype was almost finished by the war's end. The only data known for it are a span of 9.0m (29ft 6¼in), a length of 8.15m (26ft 9in) and a loaded weight of 2,340kg (5,160lb). The last known derivative was the projected Oka Model 53 fighter, designed for air-launching. It was to be powered by an Ne 20 turbojet and armed with two 20mm cannon.

Japan, which was almost totally destroyed in the war, was gradually rebuilt with the aid of the American Marshall Plan. Soon Japanese military forces began to emerge but only for the purpose of self defence, including the Japanese Air Self Defence Force (JASDF). As the country's industries were rebuilt, the assembly of foreign aircraft

was begun, notably the North American F-86F Sabre by Mitsubishi. In July 1953, with Allied post-war restrictions lifted, leading Japanese aircraft manufacturers collaborated to form the Japan Jet Engine Company (JJE) under the auspices of the government. One of the member companies was Fuji Heavy Industries Ltd, which produced two turbojets, the design being headed, it is believed, by Nagano. The first of these, the Jo-1, was on the test bench in 1954. This engine was a single-shaft, axial turbojet with an eight-stage compressor giving a pressure ratio of 4.5:1 and an air mass flow of 18.96kg/sec (41.8lb/sec). There were eight combustion chambers and a single-stage turbine. The Jo-1 gave a static thrust of 1,000kp (2,205lb) at 12,000rpm and had a dry weight of 450kg (992lb) and a specific fuel consumption of 1.01. Its dimensions included a diameter of 0.68m (2ft 2¾in) and a length of 2.80m (9ft 2¼in).

Other turbojets (studies only) included the Jo-3-1 and the Ji-1. The Jo-3-1 was to

The Japanese Air Self Defence Force (JASDF) was formed after the war and training began with American aid. Here, an Allison J33 turbojet, used in a Lockheed T-33 trainer, is being studied. Such lectures were usually given in English with an interpreter standing by.

have an eight-stage axial compressor, an annular combustion chamber and a single-stage turbine; it was designed for a static thrust of 1,200kp (2,646lb) at 13,600rpm and to have a specific fuel consumption of 1.08. The Ji-1 was also an axial engine and was to have a twelve-stage compressor, eight cannular combustion chambers and a two-stage turbine; it was designed for a static thrust of 3,000kp (6,615lb) at 8,000rpm. This work kept most of the wartime Japanese turbojet teams involved and included Osamu Nagano.

In April 1954 the Fuji Automotive Company obtained a licence to build small turbojets from the US Continental company, these engines being derived from French Turboméca designs. Fuji then set about designing Japan's first post-war jet aircraft, the Fuji T1F2 *ab initio* jet trainer. This was to replace the North American piston-engined T-6 in JASDF service. The T1F2 (later designated T-1A) closely resembled the F-86 Sabre and had low, swept wings, swept tail empennage and a nose intake. A rear-hinging canopy enclosed the cockpit, which had two seats in tandem. At the same time, the Ishikawajima-Harima Heavy Industries Co. Ltd (IHI) began developing turbojets. IHI began by building the General Electric J47 turbojet under licence for the F-86. Kawasaki also built engines under licence and began to gain experience by over-hauling Allison J33 centrifugal engines for the US Far East Logistic Force.

The maiden flight of the Fuji T-1 was on 19 January 1958, this aircraft being a T-1A powered by a Rolls-Royce Orpheus 805 of 1,815kp (4,000lb) static thrust. The pilot was none other than Susumu Takaoka, who had piloted the Kikka on its historic first flight (by this time he was a General in the JASDF). The T-1B version was powered by an IHI J3-IHI-3 turbojet of 1,200kp (2,645lb) static thrust. Some T-1Bs were later converted to T-1C standards and were then powered by the IHI J3-IHI-7 turbojet of 1,400kp (3,085lb) static thrust. Only forty-six T-1As and 20 T-1Bs were built and these served alongside Lockheed T-33s in JASDF service. IHI went on to become the largest manufacturer of turbojets in Japan. Later examples of its work are the small F3-IHI-30 turbofan of 1,670kp (3,680lb) static thrust and the licence-built General Electric J79 turbojet. The former was used in the twin-engined Kawasaki T-4 trainer and the latter in the F-104J Starfighter, licence-built by Mitsubishi.

Dr Osamu Nagano (wearing glasses) beside a Fuji Jo-1 axial turbojet of 1954. This was Japan's first post-war turbojet.

A cutaway example of the Ishikawajima-Harima J3-IHI-7 turbojet, first run in July 1956. It was a straightforward axial engine with an eight-stage compressor, an annular combustion chamber with thirty nozzles and a single-stage turbine. It was used as a booster for the turboprop-powered Lockheed-Kawasaki P-2J Neptune maritime patrol aircraft, one turbojet being mounted under each wing.

Fuji T-1A jet trainer		
Span	10.50m	(34ft 5in)
Length	12.12m	(39ft 9in)
Height	4.09m	(13ft 5in)
Maximum take-off weight	5,000kg	(11,025lb)
Maximum speed	925km/h	(574mph)
Cruising speed	620km/h	(385mph)
Initial climb rate	1,981m/min	(6,498ft/min)
Range	1,280km	(795 miles)

CHAPTER TWENTY-EIGHT

France

Before relating the French story, a brief explanation of the aircraft industry organization in France will be useful. Six state-controlled groups of aircraft manufacturers were formed in 1936, leaving others as independent companies. Each group had the initials SNCA... (Société Nationale de Construction Aéronautiques ...) followed by initials according to its approximate location in the country:

SNCAC   ... du Centre at Fouchamboult, Bourges and Billancourt

SNCAM   ... du Midi at Toulouse

SNCAN   ... du Nord at Meaulte, Sartrouville, Caudebec-en-Caux, Les Mureaux and Havre

SNCAO   ... de l'Ouest at Nantes, Saint-Nazaire and Issy-les-Moulinaux

SNCASE   ... de Sud-Est at Clichy, Argenteuil, Berre, Vitrolles, Cannes and Marseille

SNCASO   ... de Sud-Ouest at Courbevoie, Châteauroux, Bordeaux, Rochefort and Suresnes

At the end of 1940 the SNCASO and SNCASE took over the activities of the SNCAO and SNCAM, respectively, the latter two going into liquidation. From July 1941 the occupying German authorities and the Vichy government laid down what aircraft and engines, largely for German use, should be built by the French industry. During this period such work as could be carried out on turbojets, turboprops and jet aircraft was performed secretly from the Germans. Following the Liberation of France, from August 1944, the government embarked on the complete nationalization of the aircraft and engine industries, in accordance with a plan worked out before the Liberation. For economic reasons,

merging of groups continued to take place, for example, SNCASO and SNCASE merged on 1 March 1957 to form Sud-Aviation (later Aérospatiale).

Early ideas and projects

France is one of those nations never at a loss for new ideas and innovations and so, as one would expect, the country had plenty of early schemes for jet engines and turbines of all kinds, well before the state of technology made them practical propositions. In this matter, they paralleled Germany and Great Britain and, but for the German occupation of most of the country from 1940, France would doubtless have been at the forefront of turbojet development. Once the yoke of German domination had been lifted in 1944, France then had a long job catching up with Britain, helped by the British and the employment of many German physicists and engineers.

A brief review of some of the country's early ideas concerning jet propulsion and gas turbine machines may be of interest. As early as December 1863, Jean de Louvrié applied for a patent (60,712) for an apparatus that he called an Aéronave and which embodied a gas turbine. Then, in 1887, Alphonse Beau de Rochas published a paper on the use of a rocket using compressed air or steam. The country's earliest functioning gas turbine is attributed to C. Lemale, whose machine worked for several hours in 1904. In 1908 René Lorin applied for a patent (390,256) for a motor-jet in which air compression was powered by a piston engine, and then fuel added and burned to create a propulsive jet. Georges Marconnet patented a pulsejet in 1909 (412,478) and, in the same year, Victor de Karavodine and Alfred Barbezat succeeded in operating a de Laval turbine from an explosion chamber. Attracted by its simplicity, the pulsejet in various forms

received the attention of a number of inventors, including Hayot (1913), Henri Melot (made tests in 1914) and Oscar Morize (1917).

The elements of the classic axial turbojet engine are seen in Maxime Guillaume's patent 534,801 of 1921. Experimental gas turbines were built and demonstrated by Antoine Odier in 1924 and Jean Mely in 1926: the former was of 400hp and the latter 500hp. From 1930 René Leduc began studying ramjets, following (probably unknowingly) the earlier ideas of René Lorin, and in 1933 proposed a thermo-propulsive duct fed by a gas turbine; Leduc began ramjet tests in 1936.

Thus, ideas for jet propulsion and gas turbines were never in short supply. In 1937 Sensaud de Lavaud began experimenting with a turbojet engine, France's first. A renowned scientist, researcher and technician, de Lavaud's inventions and researches were prolific. He developed his small turbojet with the help of the engineers André Brunet and Édouard Primet. It comprised a twelve-vaned centrifugal compressor followed by a row of sixty stator blades. The combustion chamber was of the annular type and had fingers to aid mixing and temperature regulation. After passing through a single-stage turbine, the exhaust gases ejected into the centre of a long, diverging exhaust duct. This duct also acted as a thrust augmenter by drawing in atmospheric air through an annular intake, at the centre of which was the exhaust nozzle of the engine. The solid rotor shaft was carried on a bearing behind the compressor and another in front of the turbine, the compressor and turbine wheels having bosses that threaded onto the ends of the shaft. The turbine blades were 35mm (1.37in) long and made from a drawn profile with a slight twist at the leading edge. Measuring 1.127m (3ft 8¼in) in length and with a diameter of 0.265m (10½in), de Lavaud's turbojet was tested and gave a thrust of 100kp (221lb), its weight being only 50kg (110lb) with accessories. Unfortunately, due to poor attachment of the turbine rotor blades, a breakdown occurred in about ten minutes. Nevertheless, this was a creditable and historic effort and it proved the turbojet concept.

In May 1941 SNCASO began studies to build another turbojet based on de Lavaud's engine. Components were built but the project was stalled after the German occupiers showed an interest. De Lavaud and Brunet later buried these components in their garden near Paris. Once France was liberated, Primet recovered the turbojet and presented this historically important engine to the Musée de l'Air.

On 1 July 1940 the government of Marshal Henri-Philippe Pétain moved to the town of Vichy, in the south-east corner of the country, and proceeded to set itself up as the Government of Unoccupied (or Vichy) France. Despite the main part of France being occupied, engineers continued to work clandestinely on projects whenever possible, perhaps looking forward to a time when their country was once again free. One such engineer was René Anxionnaz of the Société Rateau company, who had applied for a patent for a bypass turbojet engine in 1939; the patent (864,397) was granted on 17 January 1941. Anxionnax's bypass engines were envisaged in various forms, but the principle remained the same. (Frank Whittle's patent for a bypass engine was granted in 1936.) From 1940 both the

Sensaud de Lavaud's experimental turbojet, partially cut away. Note the annular intake of the thrust augmenter. Musée de l'Air

Société Rateau and SOCEMA companies were engaged in secret turbojet research during the Occupation (see below).

In November 1942 the Germans broke the armistice with Vichy France and moved into the regime's territory under Operation Lila in an attempt to capture the bulk of the French fleet; this was forestalled when Admiral Laborde ordered the sinking of thirty-nine warships and submarines. From June 1944 France was gradually liberated by the Allies until, by December, Allied forces began reaching the River Rhine, the last natural barrier to Germany. The German counter-attack that month in the

Ardennes was a short-lived setback, but by May 1945 Germany had been crushed between Soviet forces in the East and Allied forces in the West. With the collapse of the German Reich, chaos ensued in the ruins. The fortunes of Germany's scientists and engineers were extremely varied: some went into hiding and some eventually served the victorious countries, either voluntarily or forcibly. The fate of those in Soviet hands has already been noted in that section. In order to build up its own turbojet industry and make up for the lost years of war, France needed experienced technicians and German personnel presented a golden

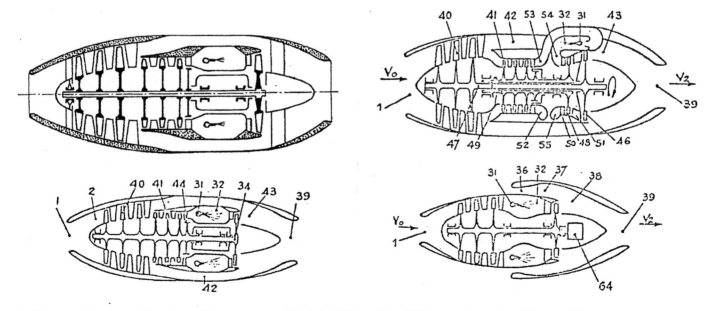

René Anxionnax's bypass turbojet schemes. The patent was applied for in 1939 through Société Rateau and granted on 17 January 1941. French patent 864,397

opportunity: the turbojet teams at the BMW company were a particular target for the French.

SNECMA

Dr Hermann Oestrich and 200 senior technicians at BMW had been developing the 109-003A axial turbojet during the war, as related in the German section. The bombing of Berlin eventually forced the dispersal of the company and, in February 1945, Oestrich's team moved to a salt mine some 400m (1,310ft) below ground at Stassfurt, near Magdeburg, in Saxony. A number of provisional test benches were installed on the surface, in the open air. The work of this group ended the day before Stassfurt surrendered to US Army forces on 12 April 1945. Already, however, Oestrich had hidden his technical records in the town's cemetery.

On 13 April 1945 a ten-man American technical team, consisting mainly of Pratt & Whitney engineers, arrived in Stassfurt to interrogate Oestrich and others. These Americans took a tough line and ordered BMW to restart production despite the fact that Berlin had still not surrendered. A demonstration run of a BMW 109-003 turbojet was made for the Americans, who were very impressed with its performance. Around 11 May Oestrich and one of his designers, Hans Munzberg, were flown to Munich for more intensive interrogation. While they were there, the Americans cleared out the Stassfurt facility and most of its personnel were evacuated, only hours before Soviet forces arrived, to BMW's partially destroyed Milbertshofen plant near Munich. Oestrich joined them there and, under the direction of Lt-Col Robertson, they prepared reports on turbojet development for the Americans. For this work the BMW engineers were paid.

With this work completed, Oestrich and his colleagues waited for work. In July 1945 Sir Roy Fedden, on behalf of the British authorities, asked for the BMW engineers to work out a project for a two- or four-engined turboprop transport aircraft. The take-off weights were calculated as 8.5 tonnes for a twin-engined aircraft and 13.5 tonnes for a four-engined aircraft. Oestrich worked out a turboprop (PTL) with a ten-stage axial compressor, an annular combustion chamber and a four-stage axial turbine, much along the lines of the projected BMW 109-028 turboprop. This

engine was to have a take-off power of 1,600shp at 11,800rpm, a specific fuel consumption of 350gm/hp and was to drive a 3.0m (9ft 10in) diameter three-bladed airscrew via 6.5:1 reduction gearing. Its total weight was to be 640kg (1,411lb), diameter 0.55m (1ft 9½in) and length 2.735m (8ft 11½in).

As the French Army advanced into Germany at the beginning of 1945, they recovered German turbojets in operable condition and these were examined by French technicians. During that summer, a Capt Mirles headed the search in the French Zone of occupation and considerable data and material pertaining to turbojet development was acquired. This was sent to France and gave its technicians a good insight into the German work. Oestrich was then approached in secret by DGER agents and, with his colleague Dr Donath (who had been responsible for the pre-production of the BMW 109-003A-0 turbojet), was flown to Paris for talks with the Ministère de l'Air. There they began initial negotiations to take about one hundred of his best engineers, with their families, to work for the French.

Upon his return to Munich, Oestrich was taken to Britain, where he remained from 25 August to 5 September in the company of twenty-four other important German specialists including Helmut Schelp of the RLM (German Air Ministry) and Wernher von Braun, the rocket specialist. Lengthy interrogations were undertaken in a school in Wimbledon in south-west London. Returning once again to Munich, Oestrich was offered a six-month contract by the Americans for himself and about twelve colleagues, but without their families. They were not happy with this offer, since it excluded their families and was quite restrictive. Furthermore, the Germans were threatened with permanent unemployment if they refused the offer. In any case, they were more inclined to work for the French, whom they trusted after associating with them during the war.

Atar 101 axial turbojet

By September 1945 Oestrich and several of his key associates were working in a small office in the old Dornier plant at Rickenbach, near Lindau, on Lake Constance in the French Zone of occupation. This group was named the Atelier Technique Aéronautique Rickenbach (ATAR) and worked on the design of a new turbojet

based closely on the BMW 109-003A. Soon, the group at Rickenbach were joined by almost 200 specialists, many of whom were former colleagues of Dr Oestrich, but there were also former technicians from the companies of Junkers, Daimler-Benz, Heinkel-Hirth, VDM, Arado and Dornier. By October the design of the new engine, designated the Atar 101, was largely complete and, that December, the Ministère de l'Air awarded the group a development contract for it, with the proviso that all manufacturing was carried out in France. Until June 1946 the ATAR group was headed by Engineer Gen. Paul Mazer and Chief Engineer Delbégue, with Dr Oestrich as director of projects and design.

In January 1946 the French concluded an excellent contract with the Germans in the ATAR group. It was for a five-year term, with their earnings protected against inflation and provisions made for the specialists' families. There were to be few restrictions on travel and there was the opportunity of French citizenship within two years. This contract was signed on 25 April 1946 and, that month, the first drawings for the Atar 101 V turbojet prototype were sent to SNECMA for manufacture to commence. This company, newly reorganized, was the only one in France with the means to take on the turbojet project; it possessed five plants and had a long experience in manufacturing piston aero-engines.

Cooperation between the project office at Decize and SNECMA actually proved to be poor and the 300km distance between the two concerns, without today's electronic means of communication, promoted inefficiency. The last of the Atar 101 V drawings were sent to SNECMA in July and, in the same month, some 120 of the German specialists moved to Decize, on the River Loire in the Nièvre département, to continue work on the Atar engine. This group, soon 500 strong and destined to double, was then named Aéroplanes G. Voisin, Groupe 'O'. They lived in the old police barracks at Decize and were only gradually allowed to mix with their French neighbours in case of hostility, but such animosity as there was from the local populace soon dissipated.

From May 1946 the components of the Atar 101 V were manufactured in SNECMA's Usines Kellerman and Genne Villiers plants. The testing of components such as the combustion chamber, compressor and turbine commenced in 1947. Testing of the hydro-mechanical governor, based on that of the Junkers 109-004, also began at that time. In March 1948 these components were assembled at the company's new Milun Villaroche complex and the first run of the Atar 101 V1 was made on 26 March 1948. The entire Atar 101 V1 was made from ordinary commercial steels, since nothing else was then available in France. The engine had a seven-stage axial compressor giving a pressure ratio of 4.2:1 at 8,050rpm. Its combustion chamber was of the annular type, with twenty burners, and the single-stage turbine had fifty-three wrapped-sheet, air-cooled rotor blades. The exhaust nozzle had a large central bullet, moved by an hydraulic piston acting on the centre line.

On 5 April 1948 the Atar 101 V, which by this time had accumulated only one and a half hours of running, attained a thrust of 1,680kp (3,700lb) at 7,500rpm. In April 1949 the Atar 101 V4 prototype completed a fifty-hour endurance test, and by October that year the V1 prototype had accumulated some 350 hours of endurance runs at thrusts of between 1,800kp (3,970lb) and 2,200kp (4,850lb). In January 1950, running of Atar

engines on the bench amounted to 1,000 hours and, that April, a thrust of 2,700kp (5,955lb) was reached. At the end of 1951 an Atar 101 prototype achieved an endurance run of 150 hours.

TA 1000 and TB 1000 turboprops

While work on the turbojet was proceeding, a turboprop project was being pursued under the leadership of SNECMA's chief engineer, the very competent Michel Garnier. This was actually the company's first gas turbine project and was begun in February 1946. Designated the TA 1000, this turboprop was intended to develop 3,750eshp and was to power a transport aircraft projected by SNCASE. The TA 1000 had a centrifugal compressor followed by a ten-stage axial compressor, twelve reverse-flow combustion chambers and a two-stage turbine. Finally, there was a single-stage turbine for driving the two contra-rotating airscrews via 6.67:1 reduction gearing. The TA 1000 was designed to give 5,800shp plus 240kp (529lb) of residual thrust at 8,400rpm. The compressor was to produce an air mass flow of 25kg/sec (55.12lb/sec) at a pressure ratio of 7.0:1, the total engine weight being

3,900kg (8,600lb). The construction of three prototypes was begun but, curiously, this turboprop was abandoned in 1949 when SNCASE dropped its aircraft project. There was also a bypass turbojet version of this engine projected and planned to give a thrust of 3,280kp (7,230lb). Evaluation of SNECMA's turbojet projects came down in favour of the Atar 101, and so the TA 1000 was terminated.

Continuing with the turboprop theme, a much smaller turboprop, the TB 1000, was begun in 1947. This was to be in the 1,500eshp class with a nine-stage axial compressor, six can combustors and a two-stage turbine. The compressor was designed for a pressure ratio of 4.5:1 and an air mass flow of 9kg/sec (19.85lb/sec) at 14,000rpm. Eight prototypes were ordered, the first running in the summer of 1950 at around 1,000shp. At the end of 1951 a typical TB 1000 was giving 1,240shp plus 250kp (551lb) of residual thrust at 14,000rpm, for a total weight of 480kg (1,058lb). After these initial tests, however, there did not seem to be any way of improving the performance without considerably increasing the engine's weight and bulk.

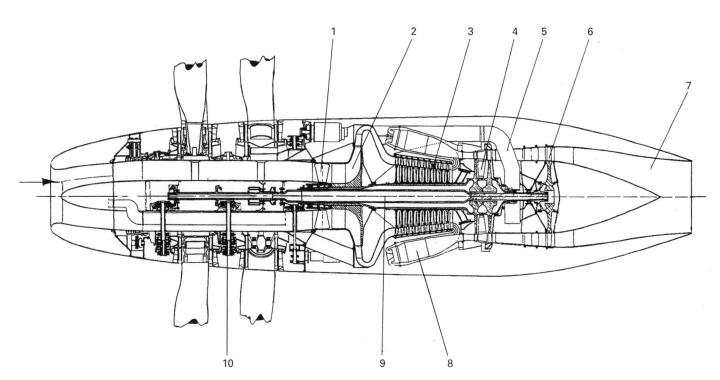

SNECMA TA 1000 coaxial turboprop: (1) inducer fan; **(2)** centrifugal compressor; **(3)** ten-stage axial compressor; **(4)** two-stage turbine; **(5)** cooling air duct for turbine bearings; **(6)** single-stage turbine, driving airscrew gears; **(7)** fixed-area exhaust nozzle; **(8)** twelve reverse-flow, interconnect combustion chambers; **(9)** coaxial hollow rotor and shaft; **(10)** reduction gears for contra-rotating airscrews.

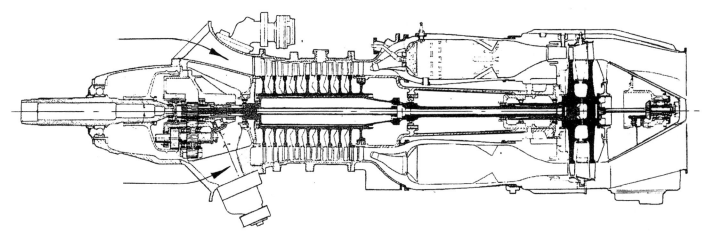

SNECMA TB 1000 B turboprop.

Therefore, a new version, the TB 1000 A, was bench run in January 1952 and was more encouraging. With air mass flow increased to 11kg/sec (24.25lb/sec) and pressure ratio to 5.0:1, this version produced some 1,750shp plus residual thrust of about 350kp (772lb) at 15,400rpm for a weight of 450kg (992lb) and plans were in hand to test the prototype on a Nord 2501 freighter. Unfortunately, after more than 1,000 hours of bench testing, the project was terminated in 1952 due to government cutbacks. Both TB 1000 and TB 1000 A variants were around 0.70m (2ft 3½in) in diameter and 2.750m (9ft 0¼in) in length. There was also a projected TB 1000 B turboprop, which some considered could have rivalled the R-R Dart. It was to have

a nine-stage axial compressor, six can combustors and a two-stage turbine. The drive to contra-rotating airscrews was to be via three-stage gearing having a total reduction ratio of 8.62:1. Various transport aircraft were planned by Breguet and SNCASO using four TB 1000 turboprops, but all projects were terminated.

SNCASO S.O. 6000 Triton, France's first jet aircraft

Concurrent with SNECMA's turboprop and turbojet developments, French aircraft designers and builders were flying their first experimental jet aircraft on the power of captured German turbojets and also Rolls-Royce turbojets made in Britain and under

licence by Hispano-Suiza in France. The country's first indigenous jet aircraft was the SNCASO S.O. 6000 Triton, the design of which was begun secretly in 1943. The all-metal Triton was designed by Lucien Servanty as a two-seat (side-by-side) jet trainer. It was intended to power the aircraft with a Rateau SRA-1 bypass turbojet, but, since this interesting engine was not completed, use had to be made of a captured Junkers 109-004B-2 turbojet found in a production centre in Vichy France at the end of the war.

The Triton was a mid-wing monoplane with thin-sectioned, equi-tapered wings of only 9.20m (30ft 2in) span. The fuselage was quite rotund, with a stepped windscreen for the cockpit. A tricycle undercarriage

SNECMA TB 1000 turboprop. Musée de l'Air

France's first jet aircraft, the SNCASO S.O. 6000 Triton, near completion and being weighed and checked for balance. Its powerplant was a captured German Junkers 109-004B-2 turbojet, since a French engine was not ready, and the air intake was under the nose. Musée de l'Air

retracted into the fuselage and there was a conventional tail empennage, the tailplane being low set. Construction of the first prototype, S.O. 6000-01, was begun in 1945 in the Suresnes factory. It had a nose air intake, the duct passing through the cockpit, between the seats. This inelegant arrangement was replaced in subsequent prototypes by two air intakes ('elephants' ears') on the fuselage sides just before and above the level of the wings. To prepare the pilot Daniel Rastel for the first flight, he first flew a recovered Messerschmitt Me 262A fighter, beginning on 13 September 1946 at Brétigny. After a number of flights in the Me 262, Rastel then flew the Triton (possibly the 03 prototype, F-WFKY) for the first time on 11 November 1946, accompanied by test engineer Armand Raimbeau. Due to the low installed power of the Junkers engine (of only 750kp or 1,655lb duration thrust), a speed of only 300km/h (185mph) was attained on this first, ten-minute, flight. Three more S.O. 6000s were built, all to have been powered by a R-R Derwent 5, but were each eventually powered by a single R-R Nene, licence-built by Hispano-Suiza, of 2,268kp (5,000lb) thrust. Rastel was later injured in a crash. Other pilots who flew the Triton also gained their initial jet experience in an Me 262A, the first of six transferred to France at the war's end together with a two-seat Me 262B. One of the highest speeds attained by a Triton was 911km/h (565mph) on 7 May 1949 with the 04 prototype (F-WFDH). Interestingly, two ejection seats from

Heinkel He-162A-1 Salamanders were sent to SNCASO for installation in the S.O. 6000-03 and -05 Tritons. A French modified version of this seat was later installed in the S.O. 6020-01 and -02 Espadons.

Of much sleeker appearance, and also powered by a single Junkers 109-004B-2 turbojet, was the small Arsenal VG.70 research aircraft designed under the leadership of Jean Galtier. The VG.70 had a 40-degree swept, shoulder-mounted wing and swept tail surfaces. The slim, streamlined fuselage had a bubble canopy over the cockpit and a semicircular ventral

air intake for the engine inside the fuselage. A tricycle undercarriage retracted its nosewheel into the fuselage and its mainwheels into the wings. The first flight of the sole VG.70, the second French jet aircraft to take to the air, was made at Melun-Villaroche by Arsenal chief test pilot Modeste Vonner on 23 June 1948 and was followed by a research flight programme. The maximum speed reached was about 900km/h (559mph) at 7,000m (23,000ft). A proposal to replace the Junkers 109-004B turbojet with a R-R Derwent did not proceed since it would have required a completely redesigned, wider fuselage to accommodate the centrifugal engine.

Experimental jet aircraft, using British engines

France's first multi-jet aircraft to fly was the extremely curious Aérocentre N.C.1071 experimental carrier-borne bomber. This large aircraft had a mid-mounted, straight wing of 20m (65ft 7½in) span, designed to fold in a complicated manner for storage. The fuselage was a short, rotund affair with stepped cockpit glazing and also some glazing at the nose and tail. It was powered by two H-S built R-R Nene 101 engines, each of 2,050kp (4,520lb) thrust. Each engine and retracted main undercarriage leg was housed in a nacelle (almost as long as the fuselage) mounted beneath each wing. At the end of each nacelle, on a short moment arm, was mounted a tall fin and rudder, the two fins being connected at

The SNCASO S.O. 6000-04 prototype of the Triton (F-WFDH), powered by a Rolls-Royce Nene turbojet, at Bricy-Mars in 1948. It was the fastest Triton and attained a speed of 911km/h (565mph). Note that the air intakes are now on the fuselage sides and dubbed 'elephants' ears'. Musée de l'Air

their tops by a tailplane and elevator. There was no connection between the tail empennage and the fuselage, which barely extended beyond the tailplane. The NC.1071 prototype (F-WFOA) made its first flight on 12 October 1948 at Toussus-le-Noble, piloted by Fernand Lasnes, accompanied by Marcel Blanchard, and in the course of some eighty flights showed that it was capable of attaining 800km/h (497mph). Although several variants were proposed, such as the N.C. 1072 all-weather fighter and the N.C. 1073 ground-attack bomber, not surprisingly its development was truncated.

Another Aérocentre aircraft, also powered by an H-S built Nene 102 of 2,268kp (5,000lb) thrust, was of much more orthodox appearance and was designated the N.C.1080. It was designed to meet an Aéronavale requirement for a fast, carrier-borne fighter-bomber and was flown for the first time on 29 July 1949. The N.C.1080 had a low-mounted wing and all flying surfaces were swept back, the tailplane being mounted about halfway up the vertical fin. The cockpit was positioned close to the nose and there was a tricycle undercarriage. First flown at Melun by Marcel Lasne, the sole N.C.1080 (F-WFKZ) crashed on 7 April 1950, not far into the test programme, and the project was terminated in favour of building the de Havilland Sea Venom under licence.

Dassault MD. 450 Ouragan, France's first jet fighter

The country's first jet fighter prototype was the Dassault MD. 450 Ouragan (Hurricane), albeit powered by an H-S Nene 102 pending the availability of an Atar engine. Relatively simple to ensure success, the Ouragan was designed by a first-class team led by the redoubtable Marcel Dassault, who had designed the MB 151 and MB 152, France's best wartime piston-engined fighters (in those days Dassault was known as Marcel Bloch). Dassault's brief was to produce a fighter to outperform the British Vampires that the Armée de l'Air was cutting its teeth on. The Ouragan featured a sharp-lipped, circular nose air intake and a low-mounted, barely swept wing. The tail empennage was also slightly swept, the tailplane being mounted halfway up the vertical fin. Control surfaces had hydraulic boosting and the cockpit, with its bubble canopy, was pressurized and equipped with a Martin Baker ejection seat. Armament was to be four 20mm cannon plus underwing rockets or bombs; the short tricycle undercarriage was hydraulically retractable.

Construction of the prototype Ouragan began in April 1948 and this made its first flight on 28 February 1949. Two more prototypes were flying by June 1950, these being powered by H-S built Nene engines. Very few problems were encountered in

the development of this fighter, which went into production at Bordeaux Merignac at the end of 1949 and into service early in 1952. Some 350 Ouragans were built for the Armée de l'Air, but numbers of them were also exported, notably to India and Israel. Both these countries used the fighter-bomber in their various wars. In service, the Ouragan proved to be an agile and stable weapons platform and was easy to maintain. Its further development led to the first Mystère fighters.

Throughout 1948 and 1949 the French were obliged to continue using British turbojets for their first jet aircraft, mostly using the R-R Nene and Tay engines, both later licence-built by Hispano-Suiza. SNCASO was particularly active with experimental aircraft and continued to work with its S.O. 6000 Triton. The company then took part in the first French post-war military aircraft programme with the S.O. 6020 Espadon (Swordfish). This was an experimental, single-seat interceptor with mid-mounted, swept-back wings, and powered by a single H-S Nene 2 of 2,268kp (5,000lb) thrust. The unarmed prototype S.O. 6020-01 first flew on 12 November 1948, piloted by Daniel Rastel. The second,

The prototype of France's first jet fighter, the Dassault MD. 450-01 Ouragan (Hurricane).
Philip Jarrett

MD. 450 Ouragan		
Span, with wingtip fuel tanks	13.16m	(43ft 2in)
Length	10.74m	(35ft 2¾in)
Wing area	23.80sq m	(256sq ft)
Empty weight	4,140kg	(9,127lb)
Maximum loaded weight	6,800kg	(14,994lb)
Maximum speed at sea level	940km/h	(584mph)
Initial climb rate	2,280m/min	(7,478ft/min)
Service ceiling	15,000m	(49,200ft)
Range	1,000km	(620 miles)

modified 02 prototype was armed with six cannon and first flew on 30 December 1949. In 1952 the 01 prototype was modified to be additionally powered by two Turboméca Marboré turbojets (see below) mounted on the wingtips. Later still, the 01 prototype had, in addition to the main engine and wingtip engines, a rocket engine installed in the rear fuselage beneath the main engine exhaust nozzle; in this form it was redesignated the S.O. 6026. The third of the original prototypes, the S.O. 6020-03, was completed with a liquid-fuelled rocket and propellant tanks in a jettisonable nacelle beneath its fuselage and, in this form, was redesignated as the S.O. 6025 (F-WFRG). This experimental work led to the S.O. 9000 Trident mixed-powerplant research aircraft (see below).

Immediately after the end of the war France began seeking a force of aircraft carriers, with fighters and bombers to go with them. To begin with, it made do with refitted British carriers and also British and American aircraft. The country's ambitious programme of building its own carrier aircraft had to be abandoned at the stage of prototypes, due to its weak economy and the burden of fighting a new war in Indo-China. Nene-powered prototype fighters included the Aérocentre NC. 1080 (F-WFKZ), first flown on 29 July 1949, the Arsenal VG. 90 (F-WFOE), first flown on 27 September 1949, and the SNCAN Nord 2200 (G), first flown on 16 December 1949. Again, while waiting for the opportunity to build its own jet aircraft, France utilized British aircraft such as the SNCASE S.E.535 Mistral (licence-built Vampire) and the Gloster Meteor.

SNCASE was also building its share of experimental aircraft, such as the S.E. 2410 Grognard. This was a single-seat attack aircraft with swept wings and tail surfaces and was powered by two H-S Nene 101 turbojets, each of 2,200kp (4,850lb) thrust. These engines were mounted one above the other inside the fuselage and were fed from wing-root air intakes. The S.E. 2410-01 first flew on 30 April 1950 and was followed by the S.E. 2415 Grognard II (F-WFRX), which first flew on 14 February 1951 and had an extended forward fuselage to house radar equipment. It was projected to have a second seat in its production form.

Meanwhile SNCAN produced its N.1601, a single-seat, twin-engined experimental aircraft produced to investigate the swept wing and high-lift devices. It had a mid-mounted wing of 12.46m (40ft 10½in) span, swept back 33 degrees on the leading edges and incorporating leading-edge slats, spoilers, ailerons and flaps. The tail surfaces were also swept and there was a tricycle undercarriage and a cockpit with a stepped canopy and ejection seat. Two R-R Derwent 5 turbojets, each of 1,588kp (3,500lb) thrust, were housed in nacelles below the wing roots, projecting forward of the wing leading edges, thus being close to the fuselage sides. First flown on 24 January 1950, the N.1601 achieved a speed of 1,000km/h (621mph) and became a valuable research vehicle.

While all this experimental flying was being done, SNECMA was working hard and methodically to develop the Atar engine up to flying status. The improved Atar 101 A series of engines was ready for test flying by 1949. In the A series, a more rigid rotor was introduced and the accessories were disposed in a better manner. New intake guide vanes were also fitted to give better first stage loading of the compressor, and a minor modification of the exit guide vanes helped to reduce compressor losses.

Thus, on 10 November 1950, the first flight of a French turbojet engine was made, using a twin-engined Martin B-26G Marauder (F-WBXM) as a test-bed; the Atar 101 A of 2,200kp (4,850lb) thrust was carried, with a lengthened jet pipe, inside the Marauder's fuselage. Soon this test-bed was joined by a four-engined S.E.161 Languedoc (F-BATA), which first flew in November 1951 with an Atar 101 A mounted above it on a pylon. Another similarly equipped Languedoc ('P') joined the test programme in December 1951. Other flying test-beds included a SNCASO S.O.30 Bretagne (F-WAYD), a SNCASE S.E.2060 Armagnac and a Meteor F.4 (RA491).

Unfortunately, by this time the fiscal affairs of SNECMA were in a chaotic state caused by gross over-manning (16,950 personnel in 1947) and vast overheads; the only income came from sales of some licence-built Bristol Hercules piston aero-engines. The workforce was therefore drastically pruned to 6,600 and Oestrich's group was formally absorbed into the company in June 1950; the Atar engine became SNECMA property. In such a crisis, being a nationalized company was of great benefit. Up to 1948 SNECMA had an Administrator, André Maroselli, but in the 1950s Henri Desbruères was appointed as its President.

R.104 Vulcain turbojets

In June 1951 work began on the design of the R.104 Vulcain, which was essentially the enlargement of an early Atar turbojet. First run on 21 May 1952, in November that year the R.104 A Vulcain completed its acceptance tests at a static thrust of 4,500kp (9,920lb) and, following ground runs at 5,000kp (11,023lb) thrust, flying tests were begun with the engine in a nacelle beneath the Armagnac flying test-bed in 1954. The planned series-production R.104 Vulcain was expected to have a design static thrust of 5,500kp (12,128lb) at 6,700rpm, a pressure ratio of 6.0:1 and a weight of 1,525kg (3,363lb); its diameter was 1.160m (3ft 9¾in) and length was 3.235m (10ft 7¼in). Twelve prototypes of the Vulcain were ordered and six were completed in 1952/3 but later the project was terminated with the cancellation of the Mystère IV D, which was planned to use it.

In December 1953 another development saw the scaling down of the Vulcain to suit it as the powerplant in twin-engined, light fighters. This brought the small Vulcain

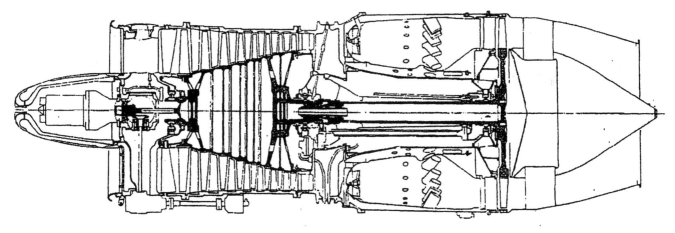

The 5,500kp thrust **SNECMA Vulcain R.104** turbojet (designed for twin-engined, lightweight fighters) with an eight-stage axial compressor and single-stage turbine.

down to an air mass flow of 24kg/sec (52.92lb/sec) at 12,900rpm, from the previous 90kg/sec (198.45lb/sec) at 6,700rpm. The small Vulcain ran in December 1954 but was then terminated before planned afterburner trials could begin. By then the larger R.104 Vulcain was developing a thrust of 6,000kp (13,230lb) with an air mass flow of 110kg/sec (242.5lb/sec), before it too was abandoned in January 1955.

R.105 Vesta small turbojet

Also in 1953, SNECMA worked on a small turbojet to compete with the H-S R.800 and Turboméca Gabizo in roughly the 1,000kp (2,250lb) thrust class. The new turbojet was designated the R.105 Vesta and was based on the company's experience thus far with the Atar and Vulcain, and used certain components that were scaled reductions of these engines. The Vesta had an eight-stage axial compressor, an annular combustion chamber with ten combustors, a single-stage axial turbine and a fixed exhaust nozzle. Four Vesta prototypes were built and the first was run on the bench in October 1954, producing a thrust of 1,250kp (2,756lb). Vibration in the compressor proved difficult to master and so a new compressor was designed, based on that for the Atar 101 E-3, giving an air mass flow of 24kg/sec (52.92lb/sec) at a pressure ratio of 4.7:1. With this, the Vesta completed a twenty-hour certification run in October 1955 at a thrust of 1,300kp (2,866lb) at 12,900rpm. The engine weighed 290kg (639lb) and had a specific fuel consumption of 1.10, without reheat. Some of the uses envisaged for the Vesta

engine were to power the Payen PA-59 and the Morane-Saulnier MS 800 projected aircraft. In 1955, however, the Vesta lost the competition to the Turboméca Gabizo turbojet and so was abandoned.

Early Atar 101 turbojet development

Although the Atar 101 turbojet was not an advanced engine (some would say it was outmoded), its intensive development in incremental stages led to an excellent engine with eventually far more power than its original basis, the 1945 BMW 109-003A. To lead its development more effectively, Oestrich spent more and more time at SNECMA plants rather than at the Decize offices. During development of the Atar 101, the usual problems, such as blade fracturing, needed solving. Compressor blades fractured at the first and seventh stages. The cause of fractures at the first stage was vibrations instigated by aerodynamic forces and the remedy was to reduce the air inlet slightly with a diaphragm and other minor modifications. At the seventh stage, the fractures were caused by resonance from the ten supporting arms at the entry to the combustion chamber, the offending arms being quite unsuspected at first since they were far away from and upstream of the compressor. The trouble was increased by the exit vanes between the compressor's seventh stage and the supporting arms. A cure was found by slightly thickening the blades and by thickening the turbine inlet guide vanes to raise the resonance level above the maximum operating speed.

Cracks also appeared in the turbine rotor blades after a very short time; the cure

proved hard to find, but a special welding method and an improved chrome/nickel Sirius HT alloy cured the problem. The turbine stator blades were made of PER 2 alloy (similar to the British Nimonic 75) and all blades and inlet guide vanes were air cooled. These developments, carried out on the prototype engines, produced a turbine that could run for 500 hours without failing. All improvements were incorporated into the Atar 101 B engine. By the beginning of 1950, however, soon after the 500-hour endurance run was achieved, a nickel-chrome alloy became available that permitted a change to solid turbine rotor blades. Thus, costly air cooling of these blades was dispensed with and blades with an efficient twist could be made (difficult with the previous hollow blades), which gave a better turbine performance and an improved specific fuel consumption.

An increase in the compression ratio was obtained by increasing the number of stator blades in the compressor. An improved combustion chamber was also introduced with the 101 B by replacing the multiple nozzles for secondary air with a mixing system with a step on the inner wall and a number of longitudinal slots in both walls. In production, slots and holes were punched out after the annular walls had been welded up. In February 1951 an official 150-hour duration test on the Atar 101 B at Melun-Villaroche produced a thrust of 2,400kp (5,290lb) at 8,050rpm, for a dry weight of 850kg (1,875lb) without starter motor, its specific fuel consumption being 1.1. The Atar 101 B had a diameter of 0.906m (2ft 11in) and a length of 2.84m (9ft 4in).

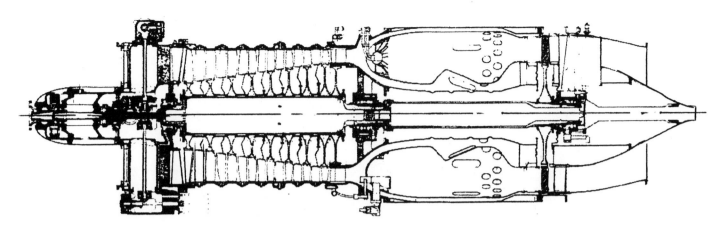

SNECMA Vesta R.105 axial turbojet.

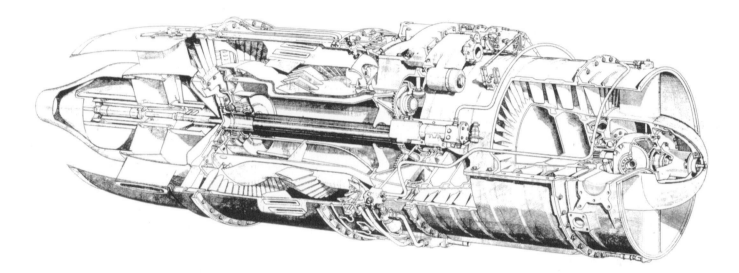

SNECMA Atar 101 B axial turbojet. Musée de l'Air

SNECMA Atar 101 B axial turbojet. Musée de l'Air

A SNECMA Atar 101 B axial turbojet at an exhibition in 1950. Note the Atar 5000 remote, shaft-driven gearbox for the auxiliaries. Musée de l'Air

The first flight test of the Atar 101 B (c/n: 1012) was made in an MD. 450-11/12 Ouragan fighter on 5 December 1951, when the engine gave a maximum thrust of 2,600kp (5,732lb) at 8,050rpm. From 27 March 1952 test flights, using two 101 B engines, were made in a Gloster Meteor F.4 (RA491).

S.O. 4050 Vautour multi-role jets

The first aircraft specifically designed to use the Atar 101 engine was the SNCASO S.O. 4050 Vautour, a twin-jet aircraft aimed at carrying out various roles. The 01 prototype ('U') made its first flight on 16 October 1952, powered by two Atar 101

Bs. SNCASO began the development of this aircraft in 1949, starting with an air-launched, half-scale, unpowered model, the S.O. M1, and then a second model, the S.O. M2, powered by a R-R Derwent engine. (The S.O. M1, first flown on 26 September 1949, was actually preceded in flight by the S.O. M2, first flown on 13 April 1949.) Data

The prototype S.O. 4050-03 Vautour two-seat jet bomber of December 1954, about to land. This aircraft was powered by two Armstrong Siddeley Sapphire turbojets, but production versions were powered by SNECMA Atar 101 E engines. Philip Jarrett

from these tests helped in the design and construction of the S.O.4000 prototype, which had mid-mounted, swept-back wings, a conventional all-swept tail empennage and accommodation for a crew of two in tandem, and was powered by two H-S built Nene 102 engines mounted in the rear fuselage. The S.O.4000 (F-WBBI) first flew on 15 March 1951. From this prototype, the smaller S.O.4050 Vautour was developed for various roles in Armée de l'Air service. It differed considerably from the S.O.4000 prototypes and had all wings and tail surfaces swept back and the two engines mounted in nacelles beneath the wings. Small outrigger wheels retracted into the engine nacelles, the main undercarriage comprising two twin-wheel units in tandem. On each side of the rear fuselage there were large air brakes.

Three Vautour prototypes were ordered and these flew as the S.O.4050-01 two-seat all-weather fighter, the S.O.4050-02 single-seat ground attack aircraft on 16 December 1953 and the S.O.4050-03 two-seat bomber on 5 December 1954. The 02 was powered by Atar 101 D engines and the 03 by Armstrong Siddeley Sapphire engines. After service evaluation, all three types were ordered into production, using the Atar 101 E as their common powerplant. Of the 140 Vautours built, only 40 were Vautour II-B two-seat bombers, but they represented France's first jet bomber. Eighteen Vautours were also supplied to the Israeli air force.

M.D. 452 Mystère fighter and Atar 101 development

Following the great success of Dassault's Ouragan fighter, a prototype was fitted with 30-degree swept-back wings and made its maiden flight on 23 February 1951, the pilot being Constantin Rozanoff. Powered by an H-S Nene 104B of 2,300kp (5,070lb) thrust, this fighter was designated the MD.452 and received the name of Mystère I. From the start, this aircraft was virtually trouble-free and it was the prototype of the country's most famous fighters. In April 1951 a batch of seventeen prototypes was ordered. The first six were each powered by an H-S built R-R Tay 250A turbojet of 2,850kp (6,280lb) thrust, the first (05) making its maiden flight on 5 April 1952 as the Mystère IIA. The other eleven Mystère prototypes were powered by various versions of the Atar 101 engine: the first, designated Mystère IIC, made its maiden

flight on 21 February 1954 with an Atar 101 D of 2,800kp (6,170lb) thrust. In Britain there had been high hopes of supplying the turbojets for France's new jet aircraft, but the French were determined to develop their own powerplants and this was finally coming to pass.

Development of the Atar 101 engine from the B model took the following course. The Atar 101 C had improvements to the compressor and combustion chamber and had its speed raised from 8,050 to 8,400rpm to give a thrust of 2,800kp (6,170lb). A Rotax starter was fitted in the central intake casing. In the Atar 101 D, the speed was reduced to 8,300rpm but a larger turbine was fitted. Its diameter was increased from 802 to 840mm (31½in to 33in) and this increased the engine's diameter from 0.886m to 0.920m (2ft 10¾in to 3ft 0¼in). As nickel-chrome-cobalt alloys became available, the temperature in the turbine was allowed to rise by 100°C or more and this increased the thrust to 3,000kp (6,615lb) at 8,500rpm. Also, the movable bullet to alter the exhaust nozzle area was replaced by movable upper and lower eyelid flaps or clamshells in the 101 D. In the 101 D-3 model a special ignition chamber was fitted to facilitate restarting at altitudes below 6,000m (19,700ft).

The 101 D-3 model was soon replaced by the 101 E, which had a new compressor. Tested in 1954, the new compressor had an additional, or zero, stage added at the front to give a pressure ratio of 4.8:1 at 8,400rpm. To give more protection from the ingestion of debris, the first row of the rotor blades was changed from aluminium alloy to steel. The gradual improvement of the compressor in the D model led to a 16 per cent increase in airflow and a 20 per cent increase in pressure ratio over the original prototype. A new compressor in the E model increased the pressure ratio by another 15 per cent. Also in the E model, the combustion chamber diameter was increased to match the new, larger turbine and the hydraulically operated clamshell flaps were improved. The Atar 101 E-4, for example, gave a thrust of 3,700kp (8,160lb) for a weight of 880kg (1,940lb).

In 1952 an afterburner with large eyelid flaps was tested and this was fitted to the D model in 1954 to produce the 101 F, which had, in afterburner mode, a thrust of 3,800kp (8,380lb) at 8,300rpm. Similarly, the E model was fitted with the afterburner to produce the Atar 101 G, the thrust of which went up to 4,700kp (10,365lb) at

8,400rpm in the 101 G-4 version. The first Atar afterburning flight tests were made using the Languedoc test-bed in July 1953 and, beginning in August 1954, in the Mystère II. To accommodate the afterburner, it was necessary to enlarge and extend the rear fuselage. SNECMA also tested a thrust reverser in which compressor bleed air was used to blow the jet exhaust into surrounding deflector rings, but this did not go into production.

Although the Mystère IIC was only a modest advance on the Ouragan's performance, production of the latter was stopped at the 350 mark and switched to the Mystère IIC. One prototype of the Mystère III was built, this being a night-fighter with air inlets on the fuselage sides to feed a centrifugal H-S Tay 250 turbojet, a new nose being designed to house radar equipment. The Mystère IV, although superficially like the Mystère II, was really a new fighter, the prototype making its first flight on 28 September 1952. This aircraft had a completely redesigned, stronger air-frame with a thinner wing swept back a further 8 degrees (to 38 degrees), fully powered flight controls and an all-flying tailplane. Unfortunately for SNECMA, the Atar 101 was not chosen to power the new Mystère IVA that went into production. Instead, the H-S built Tay 250A of 2,850kp (6,285lb) static thrust at 11,000rpm was chosen. Later, the Verdon 350 development was used. The Armée de l'Air ordered 240 Mystère IVAs (225 being funded by the USA as a contribution to European NATO forces), with further orders of 110 for India and 60 for Israel. All three countries used the Mystère in battle, the French using it during the Suez Crisis of November 1956.

The Mystère IVA was a well-liked, thoroughly useful fighter and it had a long life. Before the US funds were released for these purchases, pilots from the USAF visited France to test the available pre-production Mystère IIB, which was fitted with an Atar 101D. Capt. Davies was detailed to fly this aircraft and, on 28 October 1952, he was surprised to find that the aircraft exceeded Mach 1.0 in a dive, a performance unknown to the French until then. This was at a time when, in Europe, only the British had exceeded Mach 1.0 in dives.

Following the Mystère IVA there was a plethora of derivatives, mostly unbuilt, but again SNECMA did not receive a contract to power them. The Mystère IVB, first flown on 16 December 1953, had a new chin-type

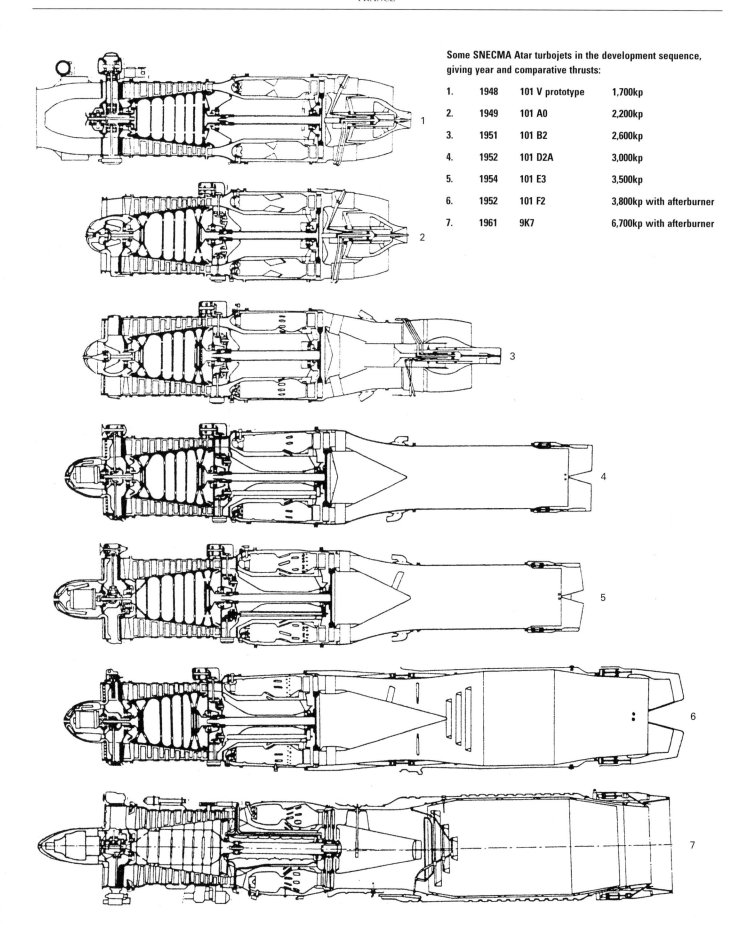

Some SNECMA Atar turbojets in the development sequence, giving year and comparative thrusts:

1.	1948	101 V prototype	1,700kp
2.	1949	101 A0	2,200kp
3.	1951	101 B2	2,600kp
4.	1952	101 D2A	3,000kp
5.	1954	101 E3	3,500kp
6.	1952	101 F2	3,800kp with afterburner
7.	1961	9K7	6,700kp with afterburner

A SNECMA Atar 101 F at the Paris Air Show, 1951. This version has an afterburner and eyelid flaps to vary the exhaust nozzle area. A shaft-driven, remote accessory gearbox is also shown.

air intake with a duct curving below the cockpit instead of the previous bifurcated arrangement. This was done so that the nose above the intake could house gunsight radar and followed similar lines to North American's F-86H Sabre. Nine of these aircraft were built for developmental purposes and they were each powered by a R-R Avon RA.7R engine of 4,310kp (9,500lb) thrust in afterburning mode. On 24 February 1954 the Mystère IVB-01 exceeded Mach 1.0 in level flight, using the afterburner, and became the first European aircraft to achieve this. The reliance upon engines such as the British Avon occurred because the afterburning Atar 101G was not ready and raised the hopes at Rolls-Royce that the supply of its Avons would continue. Not until November 1956 was the Atar 101G-3 of 4,400kp (9,700lb) thrust tested in flight in a Mystère IVB and also the first Mirage 001 Balzac.

Throughout the 1950s the French aircraft industry carried out much experimentation with jets, their aircraft usually being powered by Atar 101 turbojets. From SNCAN came the Gerfaut and Griffon aircraft. The Gerfaut had its origins with the SFECMAS (previously Arsenal) company, which was later merged into SNCAN. As the N.1402A Gerfaut 1A research aircraft, it had very thin delta wings with

a leading sweepback of 58 degrees, a swept vertical fin and a high-mounted delta tailplane. It had a tricycle undercarriage and was powered by an Atar 101 C of 2,800kp (6,175lb) thrust. The prototype ('H') made its first flight on 15 January 1954 and, on 3 August that year, it became the first European aircraft to exceed Mach 1.0 in level flight without any power augmentation. This was another milestone for

SNECMA's engine. The N.1402B Gerfaut 1B had larger wings, was powered by an Atar 101 D-1 turbojet and first flew on 17 April 1956. The last of the series was the N.1405 Gerfaut II ('E') of similar layout but with structural refinements and powered by an Atar 101 F of 3,800kp (8,380lb) thrust. It first flew on 7 April 1956 and was later fitted with an Atar 101 G-2, which developed a thrust of 4,000kp (8,820lb) in afterburning

The 01 prototype of the Mystère IV B, powered by a Rolls-Royce Avon RA.7R turbojet with afterburner. This was the first European aircraft to exceed Mach 1.0 in level flight. Philip Jarrett

The SFECMAS N.1402 A Gerfaut 1A research aircraft, with very thin delta wings and an Atar 101 C turbojet. This aircraft (H) was the first European aircraft to exceed Mach 1.0 in level flight without the augmentation of an afterburner or rocket. Philip Jarrett

The SNCAN N.1500-02 Griffon II, powered by an Atar 101 E-3 turbojet mounted inside its ramjet duct. This research aircraft reached Mach 2.19 on 13 October 1959. Philip Jarrett

mode. In this form the Gerfaut II was used in 1958 to develop airborne radar and, flown by André Turcat, set up a new world record by attaining 15,000m (49,200ft) in 3 minutes 35 seconds.

Encouraged by initial tests of the Gerfaut 1A, SNCAN built the 1500-01 Griffon research aircraft in order to flight test an aircraft with combined turbojet and ramjet power units. This aircraft had a thin delta wing, swept back 60 degrees on the leading edge, and a large swept-back vertical fin. There was no tailplane but the wings had elevon controls and there were fixed foreplanes at the nose of the aircraft. The air intake for the turbojet was circular and located beneath the forward fuselage. Forward of this intake, the fuselage tapered finely into a needle-like nose. The Griffon ('X') first flew on 20 September 1955, powered by an Atar 101 G-2 turbojet with afterburner, later changed to an Atar 101

F without afterburner. The Griffon was then extensively modified to have a Nord ramjet built integrally with the fuselage. An Atar 101 E-3 turbojet of 3,500kp (7,720lb) thrust was mounted inside the ramjet duct, just forward of its burners. The turbojet was used for take-off, landing and to push the aircraft up to ramjet operating speed, at which point the turbojet was shut down. Thus modified, this aircraft was redesignated N.1500-02 Griffon II and made its first flight on 23 January 1957. The Griffon II made more than 200 flights and attained a speed of Mach 2.19 on 13 October 1959 before its highly successful research programme was concluded.

Another very interesting delta research aircraft was the SNCASE S.E. 212 Durandal, intended to lead to a lightweight interceptor. It was powered by an Atar 101 G-3 of 4,500kp (9,920lb) thrust, which could be augmented by the 825kp (1,820lb)

thrust of a SEPR 65 rocket motor. The Durandal first flew on 20 April 1956, but its programme was shut down in 1957 after only two prototypes were built, since the Mirage III was preferred instead. The Grognard attack aircraft from SNCASE has already been mentioned. The company also began development of the unusual S.E. 5000 Baroudeur jet fighter intended to operate from grass fields instead of hard runways. To this end, it took off on a wheeled trolley, which could be rocket powered, and landed on three retractable skids. It also had a braking parachute for use when landing. All its flying surfaces were swept back and there was a pointed nose. Wing-root intakes fed air to the single 2,800kp (6,175lb) thrust Atar 101 C. Other features of the Baroudeur fighter included the mounting of the tailplane high up on the vertical fin, wing leading edge slots and two stabilizing fins set at an angle below the rear fuselage. The Baroudeur prototype made its first flight on 1 August 1953. A second prototype flew on 12 May 1954, and this machine later went supersonic in a shallow dive. Three pre-production S.E. 5003s followed, powered by the Atar 101 D, but no production contract was received.

In 1956 the Leduc 0.22 appeared as another step in René Leduc's ramjet experiments. It was intended as a Mach 2.0 successor to his 0.21 ramjet aircraft and incorporated an Atar 101 D turbojet within the athodyd fuselage to enable the aircraft to take off under its own power and then accelerate to ramjet operating speed. Flown for the first time on turbojet power on 26 December 1956, the Leduc 0.22 made more than thirty flights, but the ramjet was not tested owing to the withdrawal of government support under general cutbacks.

Atar 8 axial turbojet

During 1954 SNECMA went ahead with work on a new generation of turbojet designated the Atar 8. A new nine-stage axial compressor delivering an air mass flow of 68kg/sec (149.94lb/sec) and a pressure ratio of 5.5:1 at 8,400rpm was designed. To drive it, a smaller but two-stage turbine was provided. Construction of this engine was generally improved over the 101 series and the Atar 8 B-3 produced a static thrust of 4,310kp (9,500lb). For the high-performance fighters envisaged for this engine an afterburner was considered essential, and so the Atar 8 was developed with a new afterburner as the Atar 9. Its

The Sud-Aviation S.E. 212 Durandal lightweight interceptor prototype, powered by an Atar 101 G-3 turbojet, seen landing. Philip Jarrett

afterburner had two flameholders, two fuel injection rows and a short duct with clamshell flaps to vary the exit area. The compressor had a drum rotor formed from discs and a casing of ZRE-1 magnesium alloy. In January 1957 the Atar 9 was tested at a thrust of 5,600kp (12,350lb). After adjustments to the regulation system, a second test run produced a thrust of 6,000kp (13,230lb).

The first test flight of the Atar 9 was made in November 1957 with the engine suspended beneath the port wing of the Armagnac flying test-bed. An Atar 9B, regulated to a thrust of 5,800kp (12,790lb) in afterburner mode, was then test flown in the Super Mystère B4-01 in February 1958, enabling the aircraft to climb to 12,200m (40,000ft) in 4 minutes 37 seconds and attain Mach 2.2 in a dive. The afterburner soon exhibited problems with vibration and screeching, but these had been solved by April 1958 by redesign. Equipped with its new afterburner, the Atar 9B passed a five-hour test and was first test flown in May 1958 in the Mirage III A-001.

Trials began with a new afterburner for the Atar 9 in November 1958. It had an eighteen-flap exhaust nozzle. At the same time, another afterburner duct of increased volume was built and this housed three integral burners with flameholders and two fuel injector rows with upstream-directed burners. This was successfully tested in December 1959 on the Atar 9C with a mechanical pump to give a thrust of 6,200kp (13,670lb). The Atar 9C was

certificated at 6,000kp (13,230lb) in May 1960 and was allowed to overspeed to 8,700rpm at Mach 1.40. This engine had a gas turbine starter from Microturbo, later a successful producer of very small gas turbine machines. In the Atar 9D, the compressor was made largely of titanium for sustained Mach 2.0 flight. Development of this engine produced the Atar 9K with an improved combustion chamber, turbine cooling and an afterburner contributing to a thrust of 6,570kp (14,490lb). The 9K was the last model in the Atar series to have an afterburner.

Dassault Étendard

While the Atar 8 and 9 were being developed, the design of two important Dassault jet aircraft, the Mystère IV fighter and the Étendard carrier-based strike fighter, was proceeding. In July 1953 the Armée de l'Air issued a requirement for a simple, light, strike fighter and this was strongly influenced by a contemporary NATO competition for a similar aircraft. Dassault's first design to meet the requirement was for an aircraft powered by two small Turboméca Gabizo turbojets of 1,100kp (2,425lb) thrust each. This design, known as the Étendard II, was abandoned (as was the Gabizo engine) in favour of the Étendard IV, which was to be powered by a single Atar 101 engine. The single-seat Étendard first flew on 24 July 1956 on the power of an Atar 101 E-3 of 3,500kp (7,720lb) thrust. It then became of much greater interest to the French navy, which was awaiting the

construction of two new aircraft carriers. The navy ordered a semi-navalized version, designated Étendard IV M, the prototypes of which first flew on 21 May 1958 with a 4,400kp (9,700lb) thrust Atar 8 engine. Six fully navalized examples then followed, to develop interceptor and close-support versions.

The Étendard IV M was of all-metal, semi-monocoque construction with sharply swept-back wings (45 degrees at the quarter-chord position) and a broad, swept-back vertical fin supporting a swept-back tailplane. The low-mounted wing featured a two-spar torsion-box structure with stressed skin and integral stiffeners. It had powered, perforated spoilers, double-slotted flaps, powered ailerons with artificial feel and powered, drooping, outboard leading edge flaps; the outer wing panels folded for stowage. The wing flaps enabled a stalling speed of 200km/h (124mph) to be achieved. The fuselage was waisted in accordance with the Area Rule and had a cockpit canopy well forward to give an excellent view. Flanking the cockpit were two semicircular air intakes, each with a large boundary layer splitter plate and housing a DEFA 30mm cannon in the bottom. The short nose housed radar and avionic equipment and, on top, a retractable, hinging refuelling probe. The pilot was provided with a pressurized cockpit and an H-S built Martin-Baker ejection seat. Beneath the fuselage were port and starboard air brakes and an arrester hook. Fuel, carried in the wings, could be supplemented by underwing drop tanks.

A Dassault Étendard IV M strike fighter powered by a SNECMA Atar 8 B turbojet. Aircraft of this type served on board the French aircraft carriers *Clemenceau* and *Foch*, beginning in January 1962. Note the extended air brakes beneath the fuselage. Philip Jarrett

Also underwing could be carried various munitions including rockets, missiles and bombs.

On 2 December 1959 an Étendard IV M ('03') was first flown with blown flaps, using a 5,000kp (11,025lb) thrust R-R Avon R.A.24 turbojet, but this development was not put into production. Series production commenced with the Étendard IV M powered by the Atar 8 B of 4,200kp (9,260lb) thrust, the first such flying in July 1961. Dassault manufactured sixty-nine Étendard IV Ms plus twenty-one of the photographic reconnaissance version, the IV P. Beginning in January 1962, these served on the aircraft carriers *Clemenceau* and *Foch* but it was not until the introduction of the Super Étendard in 1974, way beyond this history's timeline, that any action was seen with them. With a wingspan of 9.60m (31ft 5½in) and a length of 14.40m (47ft 3in), the Étendard IV M could reach Mach 1.02 at an altitude of 11,000m (36,000ft).

Super Mystère B2 fighter

Following a small batch of Mystère IV Bs with R-R Avon or Atar 101 G-1 afterburning engines, Dassault developed the Super Mystère B1, the sole prototype flying for the first time on 2 March 1955 with a R-R Avon engine. This prototype soon exceeded Mach 1.20 in level flight but later crashed. The prototype of the production version, the Super Mystère B2, first flew on 15 May 1956 and this version was powered

The prototype of the Super Mystère B2 fighter, powered by an Atar 101 G turbojet with afterburner. Philip Jarrett

Dassault Super Mystère B2			
Span		10.52m	(34ft 6in)
Length		13.90m	(45ft 7¼ in)
Wing area		35.0sq m	(376.75sq ft)
Height		4.55m	(14ft 11in)
Empty weight		6,932kg	(15,282lb)
Maximum take-off weight		10,000kg	(22,046lb)
Maximum speed	at 12,000m (39,370ft)	1,195km/h or about Mach 1.02	(743mph)
Initial climb rate		5,335m/min	(17,505ft/min)
Service ceiling		17,000m	(55,775ft)
Normal range		870km	(540 miles)

by the Atar 101 G, which produced a thrust of 4,400kp (9,700lb) in afterburner mode. The production version first flew on 26 February 1957 and was reminiscent of the North American F-100 Super Sabre, especially with regard to the oval air intake at the nose. The two exhaust nozzle clamshell flaps of the Atar engine were visible at the end of the fuselage. The order for 370 Super Mystère B2s for the Armée de l'Air was later cut back to 180 in view of the even greater promise of the Dassault Mirage III. The last Super Mystère was to be the B4 version with the Atar 9 engine, of which only two prototypes were built. Most action was seen by the B2 version in Israeli air force service.

Mirage III fighter and Mach 2.0

The main employment for the Atar 9 turbojet was to power Dassault's very successful Mirage III series of fighters, aimed at speeds of Mach 2.0 and more. When studies for such an aircraft began in the mid-1950s it was already known that, beyond Mach 2.50, it would be impractical to use conventional aluminium alloys in the airframe due to adverse heating effects. Therefore, it was reasoned, the new fighter needed to be exceptionally good since it could be around for a long time before it

was superseded. In designing for Mach 2.0, Lockheed chose the very small, unswept wing for their F-104 Starfighter while English Electric chose the highly swept-back wing for their Lightning. Dassault went for yet another solution for their Mirage III – the 60-degree swept delta wing – and the layout of the airframe was very similar to that of Britain's record-breaking Fairey F.D.2.

The unarmed and sparsely equipped prototype Dassault MD 453 Mirage III ('001') made its first flight on 17 November 1956, actually on the power of an Atar 101 G with afterburner. Then, with the addition of a SEPR 66 rocket of 1,500kp (3,307lb) thrust, it reached a speed of Mach 1.80 in level flight on 27 January 1957. This aircraft was later redesigned (almost completely) as the Mirage III A with a new, thinner wing, a more powerful Atar 9B engine of 6,000kp (13,228lb) thrust and a SEPR 841 rocket of 1,680kp (3,704lb) thrust. The previous plain air inlets now had half-cone centre bodies. Ten such aircraft were built for general development and to turn it into a combat machine, the first flying on 12 May 1958.

The Mirage III A's wing, though thin, still provided space for fuel and stowage of the retracted main gear of the undercarriage. An inboard and outboard elevon was fitted

to each wing trailing edge and there was a tall, swept-back vertical fin. Airbrakes were fitted to the upper and lower wing surfaces, at the roots towards the leading edges. The fuselage was waisted, in accordance with the Area Rule, and had a cockpit canopy near to the pointed nose and blended back into the fuselage. Flanking the forward fuselage were semicircular air intakes, each with a boundary layer fence and a translating half-cone centre body for pressure recovery through shock waves. Just before the wing leading edge, in the fuselage sides, were auxiliary air intake doors that opened during taxiing. Extending just beyond the rear end of the fuselage were the variable-area clamshell flaps of the Atar 9 engine and above this, at the base of the fin, was a housing for a braking parachute. The pressurized cockpit was provided with an H-S built Martin-Baker ejection seat and the avionics were extensive. As for armament, this encompassed a whole range of possible underwing missile ordnance plus a ventral fuselage cannon pack and bombs.

The prototype of the Dassault MD 453 Mirage III fighter, powered by an afterburning Atar 101 G and a SEPR 66 rocket, reached Mach 1.80 in level flight in January 1957. Philip Jarrett

Dassault Mirage III A with Atar 9 B turbojet and SEPR 66 rocket		
Span	8.21m	(26ft 11½in)
Length	14.73m	(48ft 4in)
Wing area	34.88sq m	(375sq ft)
Height	4.25m	(13ft 11½in)
Empty weight	5,840kg	(12,880lb)
Loaded weight	9,500kg	(20,944lb)
Maximum speed	Mach 2.20	
Service ceiling	18,300m	(60,025ft)

On 24 October 1958 the Mirage III A-01 attained Mach 2.0 in level flight, without rocket assistance, and in 1959 a Mirage III A reached Mach 2.17 in level flight. The first of the production Mirage III Cs made its maiden flight on 9 October 1959 and the first of the two-seat Mirage III B trainers first flew on 21 October 1959. A number of other derivatives followed, stretching well beyond this history. In addition to service in the Armée de l'Air, the Mirage III was exported to many countries, beginning with Israel and South Africa. Successful and fast, the Mirage III later outclassed Arab-flown MiGs in the Arab-Israeli wars but its weak point, in dog fighting, was its poor turning performance. This was due to the penalty of the drag induced by the large elevons of its delta wing.

During 1956 SNECMA began looking into designs of engines to replace the apparently outdated Atar 101 turbojet. By that time the afterburning Atar 101 G-4 was producing a thrust of 4,700kp (10,360lb) compared to the thrust of 800kp (1,764lb) of its original ancestor, the BMW 109-003A. This impressive increase in performance had been brought about by incremental and meticulous detail development. A Super Atar engine, designated the M.56, in the 9,000kp (19,845lb) class, was designed with a single shaft, variable compressor stators and an afterburner. However, after discussions with the Ministère de l'Air and Dassault, SNECMA decided to import foreign technology and manufacturing licences. Working agreements were made with both Rolls-Royce and Pratt & Whitney, and also later with General Electric. SNECMA and General Electric later became equal partners in the creation of CFM International, SA, the CFM 56 becoming a notable product of this partnership.

S.E. 210 Caravelle jet airliner

No discussion of turbojet development in France during this period would be complete without mentioning the pioneering Caravelle jet airliner, even though it was powered with R-R Avon turbojets. This airliner had its origins in 1951, when the official French civil aviation agency (SGACC) issued a basic specification for a short-haul airliner. The requirements included a range of up to 1,800km (1,120 miles) at 620km/h (385mph) with a payload of between 6 and 7 tonnes. A number of companies submitted proposals for aircraft powered by all types of engine, but the competition was won by SNCASE. Since it was desired to use a French turbojet to power the new airliner (other forms of power had been considered), the only choice was the Atar 101. To obtain the necessary power, three of these engines were needed and so this led to an arrangement of the engines at the rear of the fuselage. This 'Tri-Atar' project, however, was later abandoned in favour of using only two, more powerful, R-R Avon turbojets owing to their longer service record and more development potential.

The project was designated X 210 and an order for four prototypes was placed in 1952. The airliner had a low-mounted wing, swept back 20 degrees at the quarter chord position. The tail empennage was also swept back, the tailplane being mounted on the vertical fin, and the two Avon engines were each enclosed in a nacelle on either side of the rear fuselage, before the tail position. Construction began at the SNCASE (later Sud-Aviation) factory in Toulouse and the first prototype (F-WHHH) made its maiden flight on 25 May 1955, piloted by Pierre Nadot. The first production aircraft, known as Caravelle Is, were delivered to Air France and Scandinavian Airlines Systems (SAS), the latter making the first commercial flight with the Caravelle from Copenhagen to the Middle East on 26 April 1959, much to the chagrin of the French. The Caravelle was not the first aircraft projected with rear engines but it was the first so built, and this arrangement provided a quiet cabin environment for its fifty-two passengers (more in later stretched versions). In its day, the Caravelle was the most successful European short-haul jet airliner and, altogether, more than 280 were built and used by 35 original operators in 27 countries.

Super Atar supersonic turbojet project

In 1955 the government began directing manufacturers towards the development of aircraft capable of speeds up to Mach 3.0. Therefore, during 1956, SNECMA began studies for a high-Mach turbojet under the designation of M.26. Using the Atar compressor as a starting point, the M.26 was planned with an all-steel nine-stage compressor, a central casing also of steel and, in order to keep the weight down, a

Sud-Aviation Caravelle III with R-R Avon 257 turbojets (of 5,170kp/11,400lb static thrust each)		
Span	34.29m	(112ft 6in)
Length	32.0m	(105ft 0in)
Wing area	146.85sq m	(1,579sq ft)
Height	8.71m	(28ft 7in)
Empty weight	27,070kg	(59,686lb)
Maximum take-off weight	46,000kg	(101,413lb)
Cruising speed	765km/h	(475mph)
Approach speed	230km/h	(143mph)
Still air range with maximum payload	2,520km	(1,565 miles)

Two SE-210 Sud-Aviation Caravelle jet airliners, the prototype (F-WHHI) in the foreground and F-BHHH beyond. Each was powered by two Rolls-Royce Avon RA.29 turbojets. Philip Jarrett

single-stage turbine with cooled blades of the type first used in the first prototypes of the Atar engine. This engine was also to have an afterburner. A demonstration prototype, built from a late version Atar but without an afterburner, was run on the bench in May 1957 and gave a thrust of 4,700kp (10,364lb). At the end of 1958 a complete engine commenced an endurance run at the maximum thrust of 6,800kp (14,994lb) with reheat.

The new version, designated the M.28, consisted of an engine with a transonic all-steel compressor of the same technology as the M.26. With slightly improved aerodynamics, the M.28 was tested on the bench in September 1958 at a thrust of 5,200kp (11,466lb) without reheat. Four prototypes of the M.28 were built, including a version with the two-stage turbine of the Atar 9, with the aim of developing the type up to a thrust of 7,000kp (15,435lb). These developments were to lead the way to the development of a definitive Super Atar turbojet that was to produce 8,500kp (18,743lb) of thrust with reheat, for a weight of 1,520kg (3,352lb). The Super Atar was to have a compressor with variable stators, a convergent-divergent exhaust nozzle and a compartment for refrigeration equipment. It was envisaged as powering the turbojet-ramjet Super Griffon M.3. This aircraft, however, did not move beyond the project stage, and following its closure SNECMA terminated the Super Atar project at the end of 1960.

VTOL and the Coléoptère

During 1955, when the prototype Caravelle was making its first flight, SNECMA at Sèvres embarked on a programme to develop a manned ramjet interceptor that would take off vertically and climb rapidly to a high altitude to intercept enemy bombers. It was thought that such an interceptor could take off under turbojet power and accelerate to ramjet operating speed, the ramjet being part of an annular wing. Considering the major developmental problems that needed solving, this was a very bold project to undertake.

The first step was to gain some data on jet-powered VTOL flight and this was done by flying remotely controlled models indoors, one of which was powered by a pulsejet. Next came the full-size C400 P1 Atar Volant (Flying Atar), which comprised an Atar 101 DV, fuel tanks and control systems mounted vertically in a framework. Beginning in 1955, more than 250 flights were made with the P1 under remote control while it was tethered beneath a gantry.

The success of these tests led to the C400 P2, which was ready in March 1957. This had a pilot's ejector seat and controls added to the top of the Atar, making the pilot some 4.5m (15ft) above the ground. Before piloted tests were made, however, the P2 was tested remotely, tethered beneath a gantry. Finally, test pilot Auguste Morel made the first free flight on 14 May 1957 at Melun-Villaroche. Since this machine weighed 2,640kg (5,821lb) and the thrust of the Atar 101 was 2,900kp (6,395lb), there was little margin for errors such as descending too fast or deviating too far from the vertical. The P2 could hover hands-off under the control of the auto-stabilization system and the pilot's view was excellent. Control of the turbojet's exhaust was by means of blasting it with right-angled jets of compressed air tapped from the third stage of the compressor, control of these air jets being by means of electromagnetic relays and valves.

Following further study and tests, a most curious but very interesting VTOL aircraft, the C450 Coléoptère, was designed and built with the aim of achieving both vertical and aerodynamic horizontal flight. The cockpit section of the Coléoptère, equipped with a swivelling ejector seat, was flanked by two air intakes that led back to an Atar 101 E5 turbojet of 3,700kp (8,159lb) thrust. Its rear fuselage section was connected to an annular wing by four swept-back, radial struts, the annular wing itself being based on the work of Prof. Helmut von Zborowski. Four small stabilizing fins were attached to the rear of the annular wing, which also had four shock-absorbing legs with castoring wheels. Control in vertical flight was by means of small swivelling vanes (later found to be inadequate) operating in the Atar's exhaust. Also, the aircraft's nose had two small control surfaces that could be extended to assist in the pitching up from horizontal to vertical transition.

The first tethered hovering of the Coléoptère was made on 17 April 1959. This was followed by the first free hovering flight on 5 May 1959, the pilot being Auguste Morel. Subsequently, partial transitional flights were made but on 25 July 1959, on the ninth flight, disaster struck. The aircraft took off vertically, tilted, flew at constant altitude, tilted up and climbed again to about 1,000m (3,280ft). Then, despite the use of full power, it began to sink too fast and tilted to an angle that further reduced its vertical thrust component. Morel had to eject at very low altitude and he was injured when his parachute failed to deploy correctly. The Coléoptère then accelerated horizontally at an angle of about fifty degrees and almost made a transition to horizontal flight. It then crashed at a speed of about 320km/h (200mph) and was

The sole and unique C450 Coléoptère VTOL research aircraft on its hydraulic erecting transporter. Inside its annular wing was an Atar 101 E5 turbojet. Philip Jarrett

destroyed. With the destruction of the sole prototype, this unique programme was brought to a close. In any case, by now, ground-to-air missiles were beginning to do the job envisaged for the fast-climbing interceptor. The Coléoptère had a diameter of 3.20m (10ft 6in), a length of 6.70m (22ft) and had a maximum take-off weight of 3,000kg (6,615lb).

SNECMA was the principal French company in the turbojet field, but the country's other engine companies will now be discussed.

Avions Marcel Dassault

Already noted for its famous jet fighters, beginning with the MD. 450 Ouragan of 1949, the Avions Marcel Dessault obtained a licence in 1953 to manufacture the Armstrong Siddeley ASV 5 Viper long-life turbojet. Considerable detail redesign was carried out by the Dassault engineers at the Saint-Cloud plant, including the substitution of magnesium for the compressor casing, the use of French accessories and, later, the development of a Dassault afterburner that was intended to become a standard feature on future fighters. The revised turbojet was designated the MD 30 and, although of low thrust, the company's interest in it was to power lightweight fighters.

The MD 30 had a seven-stage axial compressor having an air mass flow of 14kg/sec (30.86lb/sec) at a pressure ratio of 3.5:1. This was followed by an annular combustion chamber with ten burners, and a single-stage axial turbine. The first bench tests were carried out in 1954 and one year later, when the afterburner was developed and used, a thrust of 1,000kp (2,205lb) was obtained. With the afterburner, the engine's weight was 288kg (635lb). Flight trials began in September 1955 with the MD 30 suspended beneath a Bloch 161 Languedoc flying test-bed.

Initially the MD 30 powered the MD 550 Mystère-Delta, which was renamed the Mirage I. The MD 30 also powered the S.O. 9000 Trident I and the S.O. 9050 Trident Is, there being one turbojet at each wingtip in each case. Using its rocket motor and the turbojets, the S.O. 9000 reached a speed in excess of Mach 1.5. On 2 May 1958 one of the pre-production S.O. 9050s reached a record altitude of 24,217m (79,452ft), using both rocket motor and turbojets. In order to have available a more powerful

version, Dassault developed the Viper 10 turbojet under the designation R.7 Farandole, which gave a thrust of 1,410kp (3,109lb) on the test bench in 1956. The R.7 was also to have an afterburner, but the project was terminated in 1959, due to a lack of suitable airframes, and only one prototype was built. Its characteristics included an air mass flow of 25kg/sec (55lb/sec) at a pressure ratio of 3.8:1 and a total weight of 354kg (780lb).

Between 1948 and 1952 Dassault also drew up proposals for a number of civilian jet aircraft, including the MD 500 airliner powered by four R-R Nene turbojets. With wings and tail surfaces similar in planform to the MD 450 fighter, and with a loaded weight 40 tonnes, it was to have transported sixty passengers over a range of 2,000km (1,242 miles). Another proposal was the MD 800, comparable in size to the Vickers Viscount and to have been powered by four R-R Dart turboprops. At a loaded weight of 24 tonnes, it was to have carried forty to sixty passengers, also over a range of 2,000km (1,242 miles). These projects remained on the drawing board.

Société Rateau

Auguste Rateau (1863–1930) established a factory at La Courneuve near Paris in the early 1900s to produce steam turbines and, from 1917, his famous pioneering turbochargers for piston aero-engines and turbocompressors for diesel engines. From September 1940, during the Occupation, the company began secret turbojet research that followed on from Auguste's long interest in gas turbines. Alfred Lafond was commissioned to design the company's first turbojet, designated GTS 65 (alias A 65), and a full-scale mock-up was built at the end of 1940. Later designated the SRA-1 Idole, this represented France's first axial, bypass turbojet engine.

The SRA-1 had a welded steel casing built in three sections and reinforced by three sheet formers. It had a four-stage axial fan followed by a twelve-stage axial compressor, nine reverse-flow combustion chambers arranged around the compressor section and a two-stage axial turbine. The fan and compressor together gave a pressure ratio of only 4.0:1, the flow from the fan largely bypassing around the compressor. The temperature before the turbine was about 700°C. An alloy known as Sural, containing tungsten, was used for the

turbine but was later replaced with the somewhat better Rateau ASR alloy. The complete rotor was mounted on only two bearing points. The bypass air was partially added to the hot gases leaving the turbine, further combustion inside the exhaust duct being possible by the injection of more fuel.

Some component testing and blade cascade tests were carried out and, between 1941 and 1943, all necessary wind tunnel and thermodynamic tests were made and the principal raw materials were sourced. The aircraft designer Marcel Riffard, who as early as 1912 had begun construction of an all-metal monoplane (at about the same time that Hugo Junkers was engaged on the world's first airworthy all-metal aircraft, the J1 Blechesel), was also commissioned to design a twin-engined jet aircraft, reminiscent of the Gloster Meteor.

Once France was liberated, the building of the SRA-1 began. In its first tests, a temperature of only 550°C before the turbine was attained, resulting in a disappointing thrust of only 750kp (1,655lb) at 6,000rpm. By December 1946 static thrust had risen to 1,000kp (2,205lb) at 7,500rpm, rising to 1,400kp (3,087lb) with additional fuel injection into the exhaust duct. The SRA-1 was intended to power the country's first jet aircraft, the SNCASO S.O. 6000 Triton, but was not ready in time (a captured Junkers engine was used). It was eventually certified in June 1947, seven months after the Triton first flew, at a thrust of 1,100kp (2,425lb) at 7,500rpm. Nevertheless, this was a worthy effort when one considers the early date of the engine's conception and the lack of more suitable heat-resisting alloys. SNCAN, in designing its N.1600 in 1945, had hoped to use two SRA-1 (Rateau B-120) engines, each of 1,700kp (3,750lb) thrust, but this was not to be. By 1948 the SRA-1 project had been terminated after only two prototypes had been built. Its salient data included a weight of 1,040kg (2,293lb), an air mass flow of 28kg/sec (61.74lb/sec), a diameter of 1.12m (3ft 8in) and a length of 2.05m (6ft 8¼in).

In 1946 Rateau planned a turboprop derivative of the SRA-1, designated the SRA-1 VG, by adding another turbine to drive contra-rotating airscrews through reduction gearing. This turboprop was expected to give 6,100eshp, using a turbine entry temperature of 880°C, but was not built. Its design was undertaken by the engineers Mission and Alfred Lafond, who later worked for SNECMA.

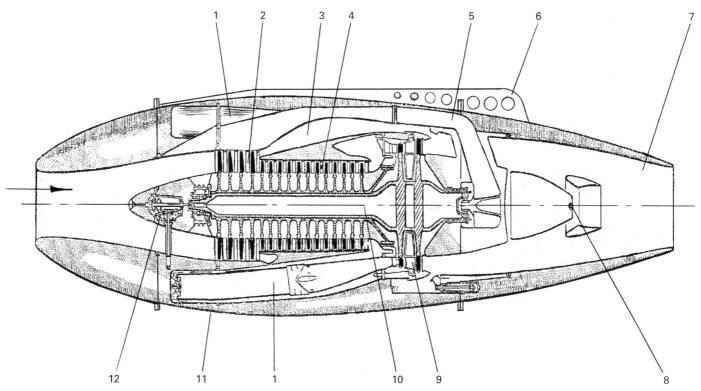

Rateau A 65 (SRA-1 Idole) bypass turbojet: (1) nine reverse-flow, interconnected combustion chambers; (2) four-stage axial fan; (3) bypass air ducts (between combustion chambers); (4) twelve-stage axial compressor; (5) atmospheric air duct for turbine bearing cooling; (6) three sheet steel formers for reinforcing and mounting; (7) fixed-area exhaust nozzle; (8) nozzle for injecting extra fuel; (9) two-stage turbine; (10) drum-type rotor, with two bearing points; (11) welded steel casing; (12) bevel gears and shafts for driving auxiliaries.

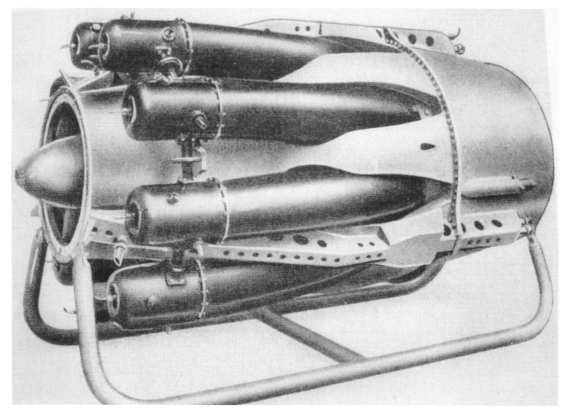

Rateau SRA-1 Idole turbojet, without intake or exhaust ducts.

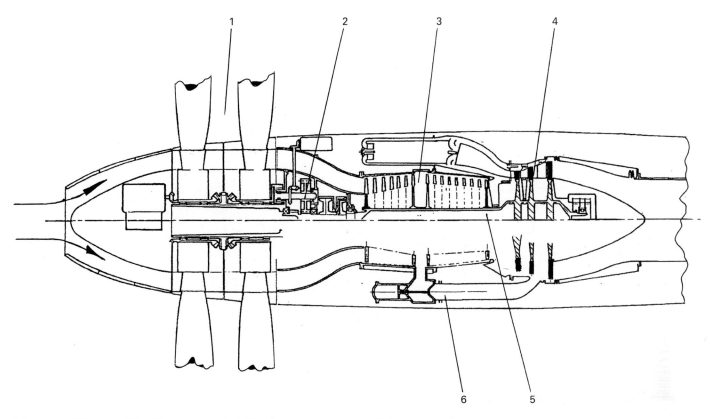

Schematic of 1946 Rateau SRA-1 VG turboprop project: (1) contra-rotating airscrews; (2) airscrew reduction gears; (3) sixteen-stage axial compressor; (4) three-stage turbine; (5) drum-type rotor; (6) valve and cooling air bleed for third turbine.

Collaborative design work between Rateau and SNECMA also resulted, for example, in a project in 1946 for a rear fan bypass turbojet similar in some respects to those worked on by Frank Whittle and Metropolitan-Vickers in England. The French engine featured a centrifugal compressor (preceded by a single row of variable-incidence vanes) followed by a ten-stage axial compressor feeding air to a number of reverse-flow combustion chambers. A two-stage turbine drove the compressors. Following these turbines was a mechanically separate four-stage turbine, the last two stages of which were connected to an external three-stage fan surrounded by an annulus. The cold air flow from the fan did not join the hot gases but had its own annular exhaust nozzle surrounding the hot exhaust nozzle. The area of the cold air exhaust nozzle was to be varied by means of a moving conical ring.

In 1950 the Société Rateau was sponsored to design another turbojet, the SRA-101 Savoie, based on the Rateau-Anxionnaz bypass patents. This was an all-steel engine with, curiously, a divergent ten-stage axial compressor. It also had a twelve-can annular combustion system and a two-stage turbine. First tested in August 1950, it gave a thrust of 3,600kp (7,937lb) at 9,500rpm and 4,000kp (8,820lb) by using methanol-water injection. Its air mass flow was 53kg/sec (116.8lb/sec) at a pressure ratio of 4.3:1. The weight of the SRA-101 was 1,200kg (2,646lb), diameter 1.09m (3ft 7in) and length 3.81m (12ft 6in).

In 1952, while trials continued and some improvements were made, a bypass version of the SRA-101, with afterburning, was designed. Designated the SRA-301 Berry, it had a four-stage fan followed by a twelve-stage axial compressor and a four-stage axial turbine, and was aimed at a thrust of 4,500kp (9,920lb) with afterburning. The weight was now 1,800kg (3,968lb) and the pressure ratio 4.8:1. The combustion chambers were mounted between the fan and the compressor in order to minimize the diameter of the engine. With an optimistically estimated specific fuel consumption of only 0.60 (without afterburning), the SRA-301 was aimed at the civilian transport market, but by 1953 lack of government support forced Rateau to abandon its turbojet work. Most of its team of gas turbine specialists were then employed by SNECMA on its TA 1000 and TB 1000 turboprop projects.

SOCEMA

SOCEMA (Société de Construction et d'Équipements Mécaniques pour l'Aviation) was a subsidiary of the Cie Électro-Mécanique (CEM) located at Le Bourget. In 1941 a team of technicians and specialists in steam and industrial gas turbines at SOCEMA began looking at the possibilities of developing the gas turbine for powering aircraft. Initially this team, led by Paul Destival, head of the technical department working on gas turbines at CEM, was completely isolated from the engineering world by the German Occupation. It is said that they were unaware of the existence of actual German and British work in the aeronautical gas turbine field, although they were aware of patents such as those of Frank Whittle and Brown Boveri. In fact, the SOCEMA engineers had considered aeronautical use of the gas turbine well before war broke out and, in particular, a turboprop engine was seen as the most likely way forward.

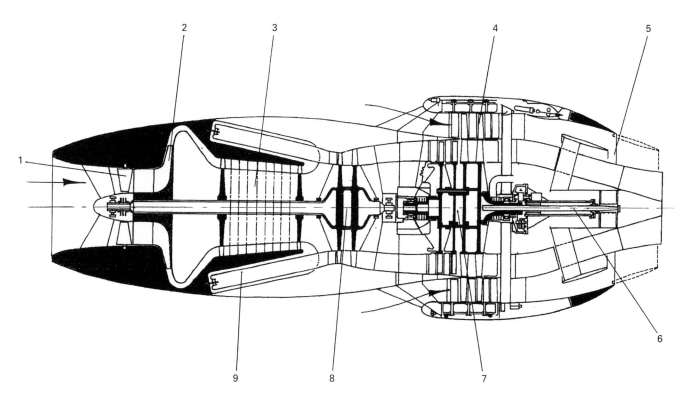

A 1946 joint SNECMA/Rateau project for a turbojet with rear bypass fan: (1) variable-incidence inlet vanes; (2) centrifugal compressor; (3) 10-stage axial compressor; (4) 3-stage fan in annular duct; (5) variable-area cold air annular nozzle; (6) mechanism to move conical ring to vary nozzle area; (7) 4-stage turbine (last two stages connected to fan rotor blades); (8) 2-stage turbine driving compressors; (9) reverse-flow, interconnected combustion chambers.

TGA axial turboprop

With the agreement and help of the Service Technique du Ministère de l'Air, then in Vichy France, SOCEMA was encouraged to pursue a project for a turboprop engine in 1941. In order to conceal the work's purpose from the Germans, this engine was designated the TGA, which could stand for Turbo-Groupe d'Autorail (Railcar Turbo-Unit), but secretly stood for Turbo-Groupe d'Air. To make the link with railways more credible, the contract for the work was issued via the French Railway Authority.

The TGA 1 turboprop was based on a 1939 patent of the Brown Boveri company and was initially laid out with an axial compressor, annular combustion chamber and axial turbines, a surprisingly modern layout adopted by a team in isolation. The main developmental difficulties ahead were seen as combustion and engineering problems and the need to make an engine sufficiently light for the purpose, all this being based on manufacturing techniques and materials current in 1939. Therefore, some conservatism was observed in choosing a low compression ratio and an

air mass flow of 30kg/sec (66lb) for the compressor and a temperature before the turbine of only 600°C at maximum power (or 550°C in the cruise). To assist in keep_ing the diameter of the TGA 1 to barely more than the depth of an aircraft wing, it was planned to fit the accessories into the wing leading edge and drive them from the engine via shafts and bevel gears. It was designed to produce 2,500shp plus 450kp (992lb) of residual thrust at 6,550rpm. As of 1945, the weight of the TGA 1 turboprop was 1,800kg (3,968lb), but three years later this had risen to 2,100kg (4,630lb).

Simplicity and ease of manufacture were aimed for in the design of the TGA: the rotor, for example, was carried on only two bearing points. The compressor was of the fifteen-stage axial type with its blades fitted to a drum-type rotor, the first stages of the blades being in steel and the rest in alloy. It was designed for a compression ratio of 3.6:1. Because the SOCEMA engineers had some experience of compressors with 50 per cent reaction blading, they chose to design a reaction type axial compressor, although with a reaction of almost 100 per cent for

the first stage of blades, gradually reducing to 50 per cent reaction at the last stage of blades. Two reasons for employing this unusual arrangement were that constant geometry could be used for all moving stages and that only two types of blade profile were needed; this approach was necessitated by the incomplete knowledge that SOCEMA had on axial compressors. The combustion system was of the cannular type using ten cans. The turbine was of the four-stage type and the auxiliaries were driven by bevel gears and radial shafts at the rear of the engine. In front of the compressor was a gearbox, its case being supported by struts in the annular air intake. Using epicyclic gears to give a reduction of 5.77:1 to the airscrew shaft, a Ratier three-bladed airscrew of 4.25m (13ft 11¼in) was to be driven.

The main structural member of the engine was the outer, shaped casing, the two halves of which were bolted together longitudinally. This outer casing was, in turn, bolted to the rear of the annular intake casting, which carried the gearbox and front bearing, and to the front of the rear exhaust casting, which supported the rear bearing

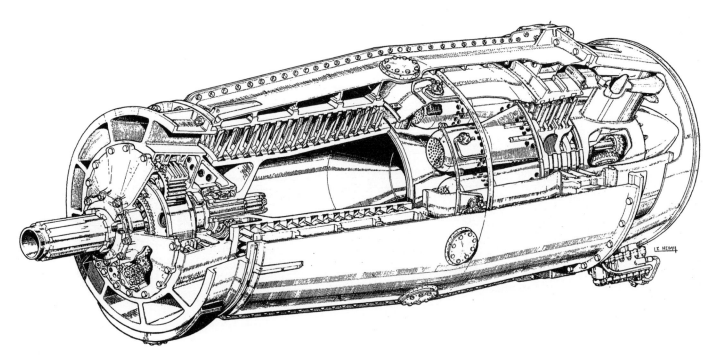

SOCEMA TGA 1 turboprop with a 15-stage axial compressor, ten combustion chambers and a four-stage turbine.

via struts. The outer casing was also bolted at its middle to four stanchions cast integrally with a central ring; this ring formed a diffuser section after the compressor and supported the outlet end of the compressor casing and the forward end of the combustion chamber. The exhaust nozzle had a central bullet and was of the fixed-area type. Four mounting points were provided at the rear of the engine. The TGA was designed to give 3,000eshp at sea level, to have a weight of 2,250kg (4,960lb), a maximum diameter of 1.15m (3ft 9¼in) and a length of 3.05m (10ft).

To gain an idea of the requirements of the TGA turboprop, M. Girondin, the Engineering Director and airframe designer, worked out the design of a suitable twin-engined aircraft in 1941, with an estimated weight of 24,000kg (52,900lb). This aircraft was to have a range of 1,700km (1,060 miles) at a speed of 500km/h (310mph) at sea level, the range increasing to 4,600km (2,860 miles) at 10,000 m (32,800ft). Apparently, and encouragingly, this was better than could be obtained with piston engines at the time. Construction of the TGA began in 1944, before the war ended.

The unusual compressor actually gave little trouble and had an 85 per cent efficiency rate. However, as was usual in turbojet development, the combustion chamber caused many problems. What evolved was a vaporizing fuel system

whereby a coil carrying the fuel surrounded the combustion chamber, the resulting vaporized fuel being fed to each burner by collectors, which were unfortunately heavy and cumbersome. The SOCEMA system was quite different to the Armstrong Siddeley vaporization system in Britain but, from 1946, SOCEMA had a satisfactory vaporizing system.

Beginning in 1943, several examples of the TGA 1 turboprop were run and improvements were introduced in 1945

with the TGA 1 bis. In this, the fuel vaporizing coil and burners were replaced by ten flame tubes. The engine turned at 6,350rpm and the airscrew was to turn at 1,100rpm, the reduction being effected through a single-stage epicyclic gear with three planet gears; this gearing weighed 240kg (529lb) and transmitted some 2,560shp. Two prototypes were built, the first running on the bench at the end of 1947, but no engine was run with an airscrew, which was to be a three-bladed

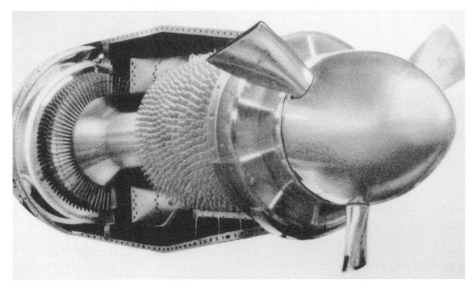

SOCEMA TGA 1 turboprop mock-up with the right side of its casing unbolted.

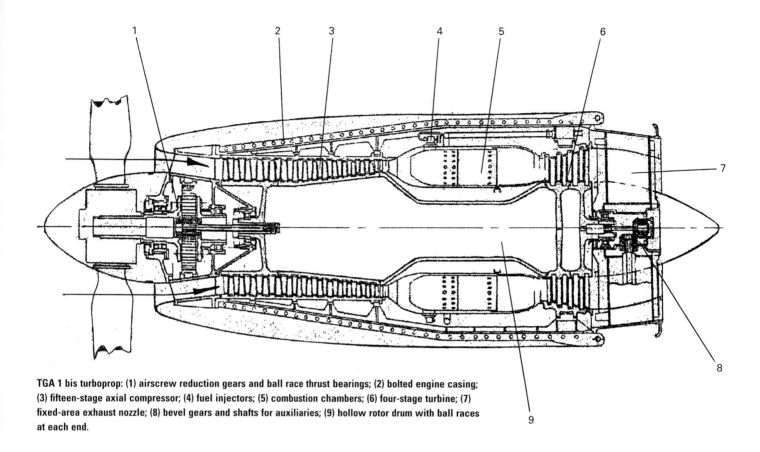

TGA 1 bis turboprop: (1) airscrew reduction gears and ball race thrust bearings; (2) bolted engine casing; (3) fifteen-stage axial compressor; (4) fuel injectors; (5) combustion chambers; (6) four-stage turbine; (7) fixed-area exhaust nozzle; (8) bevel gears and shafts for auxiliaries; (9) hollow rotor drum with ball races at each end.

4.24m (13.9ft) diameter one from Société Rateau. This turboprop achieved an output of about 2,350shp plus 500kp (1,103lb) of residual thrust at 6,350rpm, its weight being 2,100kg (4,630lb), but it was not test flown. With its concept and working cycle superseded, it was abandoned.

TGAR 1008 axial turbojet

In January 1944 the BBC broadcast the fact that British aircraft were flying without airscrews, but of course no technical information was given. There were also rumours of German jet aircraft and actual examples of German turbojet engines began to turn up after the Liberation in August 1944. The first of these were Junkers 109-004B engines found in a machine-gunned and burnt-out truck near Orléans. Naturally these were of great interest to the French engineers. The SNCASE aircraft company then asked SOCEMA to design a turbojet for a fighter-bomber that it was designing. After consultations, it was decided to aim for a static thrust of 1,900kp (4,190lb) and a diameter of about 1.0m (3ft 3¼in). The project study indicated that this could be realized with an engine weighing 1,200kg

(2,646lb) and having a minimum specific fuel consumption of 1.18, these characteristics comparing favourably with the Junkers 109-004B engine. Paul Destival tells us that they were lucky in not knowing anything about the Rolls-Royce Nene turbojet, since they would have been disheartened and perhaps would not have started on their own project.

The new turbojet, designated the TGAR 1008, was conservatively designed for speed of manufacture and reliability, at some expense in performance. In autumn 1945 the optimistic schedule proposed that the TGAR 1008 would be on the test stand by December 1946. In designing the eight-stage axial compressor for this turbojet, the engineers decided to follow that of the Junkers engine, since its compressor was deemed very good. In any case, as with the work on the TGA's compressor, there was no power source available at SOCEMA sufficient to drive a compressor in separate tests. The compressor could only be tested in the actual engine and so using the Junkers design gave some assurance of early success. On the other hand, SOCEMA was not impressed with the Junkers combustion chambers, which had a very short life. At

first a coil vaporizing combustion system was used, as for the TGA engine, but this proved to be unsatisfactory. The development of an annular combustion chamber with an atomizing fuel system and separate, cylindrical flame tubes, was therefore undertaken. The combustion system had to be designed to fit between the compressor and turbine (as already laid out for the earlier combustion system) and comprised a total of twenty cans, in which ten inner cans were enclosed in ten outer ones.

The single-stage turbine of the TGAR 1008 was of special interest in view of the cooling method used. For the turbine inlet guide vanes, a surrounding boundary layer of cooling air was used, the air entering each hollow vane at the inner end and then out through slots near the leading edge to cool the under surfaces, and also out at the tip to cool the outer surface wall. This method, developed by M. Darrieus, Chief Engineer at CEM, allowed the vanes to work at a temperature 250°C lower than the transiting hot gases. The turbine blades were made from Jacob Holtzer's Sirius HT austenitic steel, the stator blades being hollow and made from sheet, and the rotor blades being machined from solid stampings.

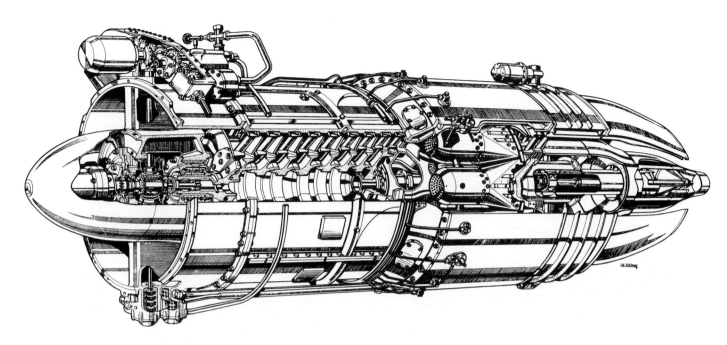

The **SOCEMA TGAR 1008** turbojet, with an eight-stage axial compressor, cannular combustion chamber and a single-stage turbine.

Four bearing points were used, two fore and aft of the compressor and two fore and aft of the turbine. A mechanically operated exhaust bullet was used to vary the nozzle area and a starter motor was enclosed in the air intake bullet. The regulator was based on the Junkers hydro-mechanical design. On 30 April 1948 the TGAR 1008 prototype successfully completed a preliminary 2-hour run at 1,500kp (3,307lb) thrust at 5,500rpm. It was the first of nine prototypes under construction at Bourget and was eventually expected to produce a thrust of 2,500kp (5,512lb). By 1949 the TGAR 1008 was developing a thrust of 2,200kp (4,850lb) at 6,600rpm for a dry weight of 1,250kg (2,755lb). It had good acceleration, going from idle to full power in 7 or 8 seconds. Tests of this engine gave efficiencies of 85 per cent for the compressor, 96 per cent for the combustion system and 88 per cent for the turbine, and it passed a 150-hour type test at a thrust of 2,100kp (4,630lb). However, it was never test flown. The TGAR 1008 had a pressure ratio of 3.7:1, an air mass flow of 45kg/sec (99.2lb/sec) and a specific fuel consumption of 1.18. Its diameter was 1.03 m (3ft 4½in) and its length 2.80m (9ft 2¼in).

A Languedoc flying test-bed was prepared to allow either a turboprop or turbojet engine to be mounted in a nacelle above the fuselage. Construction of nine prototypes was begun and flight tests took place with the Languedoc. However, despite its remarkable achievements without special alloys or much outside assistance, SOCEMA's turboprop and turbojet work was closed down in 1950.

Finally, two turboprop studies by SOCEMA, designated the TP.1 and TP.2, were derived from the TGAR 1008. The TP.1 was designed to produce 3,200shp

This TGAR 1008 axial turbojet, on a SOCEMA exhibition stand, appears somewhat massive and heavy. Musée de l'Air

plus 510kp (1,124lb) of residual thrust. The TP.2 was designed as a more efficient turboprop and was to produce 3,750shp plus 550kp (1,213lb) of residual thrust, the estimated weight being 1,540kg (3,395lb). Neither made it beyond the design stage.

Société Hispano-Suiza

The Société Hispano-Suiza (Spanish-Swiss or H-S) was founded by the Swiss Marc Birkigt in 1904 when he established a factory in Barcelona, mainly to build quality automobiles. In April 1914 Birkigt set up another plant at Levallois-Perret in Paris. This factory was soon moved to Bois-Colombes on the Seine and became larger than the Spanish factory. By 1915 H-S was building aero-engines and its 150hp water-cooled V-8 aero-engines were used world-wide. After the First World War H-S continued to make aero-engines and superchargers, and took out a licence to manufacture Wright radial engines.

From 1940, during the years of the Occupation, H-S had a hostile attitude towards the Germans and this resulted in the systematic looting of the company's machine tools. This, coupled with bombing, meant there was no possibility of design or development from the beginning of the war. By its end the company found itself with a damaged factory, worn equipment and inadequate testing facilities. However, close and friendly relationships existed between Hispano-Suiza and Rolls-Royce, and so about a dozen of the staff were sent to England to study the turbojet engine, notably the Nene.

Licence-built Nene centrifugal turbojet

An agreement was reached between the two companies whereby H-S was to build the Nene under licence. Drawings and other documents from England arrived at Bois-Colombes from July to December 1946. In order for parts to be interchangeable worldwide, the French decided to work to Imperial measurements, rather than convert the drawings to metric standards. (On the other hand, the reader will recall, the Americans converted the drawings to US standards to produce their version of the Nene, the J 42). Despite this, the H-S engineers still had to translate the terms on the drawings and also make drawings of the tools required, which then had to be

adapted to the machines in their factory. This phase was almost complete by July 1947, the cost of preparing to manufacture the Nene amounting to over 300 million French francs.

While production of the Nene began at Bois-Colombes, test benches were set up in the country near Saint-Cyr to avoid disturbance in residential areas. The production of heat-resisting steels and alloys equivalent to British types required the establishment of production facilities in France at great cost. In fact, a whole range of new companies and facilities had to be established to meet the demands of the turbojet, including the production of auxiliary accessories. In preparing to produce the Nene, H-S aquainted itself with many new techniques, including the use of the lost-wax process to precision cast turbine inlet nozzles, and the building of special machines, such as for milling, became necessary. Test flying of the Nene was made using an S.O.30 Bretagne (F-WAYB), first flown with these engines on 15 March 1951.

Hispano-Suiza built the Nene in large numbers, including the Mks. 101, 102, 104 and 105. A major use of the engine was to power Vampires built by SNCASE as the S.E.535 Mistral. Other uses included the Arsenal VG 90 carrier-based fighter designed to compete with the Aérocentre N.C.1080 and the SNCAN 2200 for an Aéronavale order. The first of two VG 90s (F-WFOE) flew on 27 September 1949 but later crashed and no order was received.

An afterburner was developed for the Nene 102 B. For this, Hispano-Suiza investigated various methods of thrust augmentation and, with little outside information, its engineers had to start from scratch. They soon discovered that there was more involved than merely injecting extra fuel into an extended tail pipe and expecting it to burn and create extra thrust. The two main problems encountered were how to protect the tail pipe from excessive heat and how to achieve stable burning in the engine's exhaust, which approached a speed of Mach 1.0. The solution was found in enlarging the diameter of the afterburner, about halfway along, so that the exhaust gases expanded and lost some of their velocity. At that point the extra fuel was injected into a cross of six air-cooled tubes with holes, the area downstream of these tubes having eddies of lower velocity where flame propagation could occur. Towards the exit of the afterburner, the diameter of

the pipe was reduced to create a venturi effect and increase the velocity of the gas through the exit nozzle. Here there were hydraulically operated eyelid or clamshell flaps to vary the nozzle exit area. Ignition was started by using two igniter plugs and the pump for the afterburner fuel was of the air turbine type, driven by air tapped from the compressor. This pump required less than 0.5 per cent of the 41.95kg/sec (92.5lb/sec) of the compressor's air mass flow. The Nene 102 B's maximum thrust of 2,268kp (5,000lb) was increased by 680kp (1,500lb) using the afterburner.

Hispano-Suiza then developed the R-300 centrifugal turbojet from the Nene, with air-cooled turbine stator blades and giving a static thrust of 2,700kp (5,955lb), but this was abandoned in 1951 in favour of licence-building the R-R Tay 250 of 2,850kp (6,285lb) thrust. A prototype only of an afterburning Tay 250R of 3,850kp (8,490lb) thrust was not proceeded with. The final version of the Nene developed by H-S was the Verdon 350, which was first flown in a Mystère in August 1953. Further increases in air mass flow, speed and temperature led to the Verdon giving a thrust of 3,500kp (7,720lb) at 11,100rpm for a weight of 935kg (2,060lb).

R.800 and other small axial turbojets

During 1953 Hispano-Suiza competed in a programme to develop a small turbojet in the 1,000kp (2,205lb) thrust class to power the lightweight fighters that the government was then interested in. The new engine was to be an axial turbojet, designated the R.800. As we have seen, the company had quite a lot of experience in the manufacture of British centrifugal turbojets but no experience with axial compressors. The R.800 was originally intended to use a six-stage axial compressor but tests showed that, in order to obtain the required pressure ratio of 5.0:1, another stage needed to be added. This seven-stage compressor was then tested at Rolls-Royce because H-S did not have the facilities needed.

At the beginning of 1955 the R.800 prototype began bench running and produced a thrust of 1,200kp ((2,646lb). In 1956 the R.800 successfully completed a contractual 10-hour run at 1,420kp (3,131lb) thrust at 12,100rpm, and a new version, the R.804, was certified at a thrust of 1,500kp (3,308lb) in March 1957. This engine had a seven-stage axial compressor, an annular combustion chamber and a single-stage turbine. The compressor had an air mass flow of 26kg/sec (57.33lb/sec) at a pressure ratio of 4.8:1. The engine weighed 308kg (679lb) and had a specific fuel consumption of 1.09. For unknown reasons, the Service Technique stopped the funding of this turbojet but H-S carried on financing the development itself; altogether three prototypes were built. Another proposed version, designated the R.854, was expected to produce a thrust of 2,000kp (4,410lb) with afterburning. H-S also envisaged a civilian version of the R.854 of 2,200kp (4,851lb) thrust. H-S did not succeed in getting its small turbojets into production, but the experience gained in the work was put to good use in the development of the company's family of THM 1000 industrial gas turbines.

Other work carried out by Hispano-Suiza included licensed production of the R-R Tyne turboprop, production of the SEPR 844 rocket engine (for the Mirage III) and responsibility for fitting the R-R Avon turbojets to the Caravelle airliner and Dassault fighters. In December 1968 the Société Hispano-Suiza was absorbed into SNECMA.

ONERA

The Office National d'Études et de Recherches Aéronautiques (ONERA) 240 small turboprop engine was designed to produce 240shp at 36,000rpm for a weight of 72.5kg (160lb). It had a single-stage compressor, five combustion cans and a single-stage turbine, with reduction gearing for the airscrew. It was abandoned in 1948, probably because of a lack of funding and the success of Turboméca's small turboprops.

Société Turboméca

This company was formed by Joseph R. Szydlowski and André Planiol in 1938 in Billancourt, Paris, to develop blowers, compressors and turbines. Its first major task was the large-scale manufacture of turbocompressors for Hispano-Suiza piston engines. In June 1940 the factory was moved to Bordes in the Pyrenees, where the Germans looted its machines and equipment. Up to that time, Turboméca had manufactured turbochargers.

In 1945 the company was once again working in the gas turbine field, their small engines being intended for aircraft propulsion and for auxiliary power production. In June 1946 some 125 German technicians converged on Pau in the Basses Pyrenées, led by Dr Siegfried Decher, formerly Chief Technician of Junkers turbojet work in Dessau. Formed into a team, these technicians began work in provisional offices in Nay, some 10km south of the Turboméca plant in Bordes. Their task was to develop a 7,000kp (15,432lb) thrust turbojet, designated the B-701, which had been ordered by the Ministére de l'Air to be used in clusters to power a transocean aircraft. This was to carry another aircraft, itself powered by four turboprops, each of 2,500shp. This B-701 project appears to have followed on from the Daimler-Benz projects that Fritz Nallinger and a team from that company brought to Pau. It had an eight-stage axial compressor, an annular combustion chamber and a two-stage axial turbine. Other characteristics included a pressure ratio of 5.0:1, a weight of 4,000kg (9,820lb), a diameter of 1.60m (5ft 3in) and a length of 5.5m (18ft ½in). A model of the B-701 was exhibited at the Paris Aero Salon of 1946 and a model compressor was run on the test bench, but, needless to say, this project was over-ambitious and not realizable. Consequently the project was closed down at the end of 1947 and most of the German engineers returned home in 1948.

Joseph Szydlowski, the presiding genius of Turboméca, now decided to tackle the other end of the gas turbine power scale and to concentrate on developing small engines. He contracted a group of about a dozen of the remaining German engineers under Dr-Ing. Bruno Eckert, a former thermodynamics expert at the LFA. Szydlowski's first small gas turbine was of 60hp and featured a radial compressor, annular combustion chamber and a single-stage turbine. Its simple combustion chamber was of a novel type with rotating fuel injection jets and was developed under Dr Glammann and Hans Hagedorn. It became a standard feature of most Turboméca gas turbines. This first small gas turbine was a success and resulted in the company receiving a contract in 1947 to develop a gas turbine of 100shp to drive a generator. First run in 1948, this engine was designated the TT 782.

Further development of the TT 782 resulted in the 160shp Orédon, which went into series production but did not propel an aircraft. This was followed in 1951 by the Marboré turbojet and the Artouste and Palouste gas turbines. Georg Oberländer was the chief designer of these and other engines, while Dr Heinrich Kühl played a significant role in their development. Other German development engineers who worked at Turboméca alongside their French colleagues included W. Syring, O. Engel, G. Sporer, G. Hagedorn (combustion) and J. Ziegler (regulation).

Only this prototype of a Rolls-Royce afterburning Tay 250R was built by Hispano-Suiza.

Piméné, Turboméca's first turbojet to fly

The first Marboré turbojet engine to be flown was the TR.011 Piméné, which was also the first small turbojet in the world to be built in quantity. It had a single-sided centrifugal compressor driven by a single-stage axial turbine, the blades of the latter being integral with its disc. A perforated ring rotating with the main compressor drive shaft sprayed fuel under centrifugal force, the fuel being vaporized in the combustion chamber. The drive shaft was sufficiently rigid to allow only two bearing points, a ball bearing in front of the compressor and a self-aligning roller bearing behind the turbine. The turbine inlet guide vanes were of fabricated sheet and were internally cooled by compressor bleed air. The Piméné's compressor gave an air mass flow of 2kg/sec (4.41lb/sec) and a pressure ratio of 4:1. The engine delivered a thrust of 110kp (243lb) at 36,000rpm, for a weight of 54kg (119lb), and its specific fuel consumption was remarkably good for a small engine at 1.05. The diameter of the Piméné was 0.40m (1ft 3¾in) and its length 0.80m (2ft 7½in). In 1950 this turbojet had a price tag of about £1,500.

The first flight of the Piméné turbojet took place on 14 July 1949 when one powered a Fouga CM.8R-13 Sylphe. This single-seat aircraft was essentially a sailplane (Fouga's speciality) with a butterfly or vee tail empennage and with the turbojet fitted above and just behind the cockpit. A more refined version of this aircraft, the CM.8R-9.8 Cyclope, was first flown on 31 January 1951. This was powered by a 230kp (507lb) thrust Palas turbojet, scaled up from the Piméné, and many Cyclope aircraft were built. In 1950 the Piméné passed an official 150-hour type test at the Centre d'Essais des Moteurs et Hélices at Chalais-Meudon, an experimental establishment of the Ministère de l'Air.

Marboré turbojets

Then, to provide a flying test-bed for Turboméca turbojets, Fouga constructed a 'Twin Cyclope' aircraft, in which two such airframes were joined by a new centre wing section and by a new, very thin, horizontal surface between the rear fuselages, the inboard tips of the butterfly tail being shortened and joined together. This test aircraft, designated the CM.88-R Gémeaux I, was first flown on 6 March 1951, with a

A Turboméca Piméné, the first small turbojet to be built in quantity. Musée de l'Air

110kp (243lb) thrust Piméné engine above each fuselage. The maximum level speed of the Gémeaux I was 285km/h (177mph). Four other variants were built, designated Gémeaux II to IV, to test the Marboré I, Marboré II, Aspin I and Aspin II engines, respectively. In the case of these larger engines, just one was fitted above the wing centre section, its jet efflux passing below the inner tail surfaces. Test flying of Turboméca turbojets was also carried out under the wings of an S.O.30 Bretagne.

The Marboré turbojet was developed as a further enlargement of the Piméné/Palas series to give more power. This turbojet was destined to become a big seller. At its maximum speed of 22,600rpm, the production Marboré's compressor gave an air mass flow of 7.60kg/sec (16.75lb/sec) at a pressure ratio of 3.9:1 and a take-off thrust of 400kp (882lb). Other data included a dry weight of 140kg (309lb), a diameter of

0.567m (22.3in), a length of 1.093m (3ft 7in) without jet pipe and a specific fuel consumption of 1.07. The Marboré I, of only 275kp (606lb) thrust, was first flown on 16 June 1951, one being fitted above the wing centre section of the Gémeaux II (F-WEPJ). A Marboré II turbojet of 350kp (772lb) thrust was first flown on 25 August 1951 on the Gémeaux III and finally, on 2 January 1952, a production Marboré II of 880kp (1,940lb) thrust was first flown using the same aircraft.

Fouga Magister, the world's first jet trainer

The Marboré turbojet powered the world's first basic jet trainer, the Fouga Magister. Previously jet trainers had been conversions of existing jet fighters, with consequent high running costs. Even before its experience with sailplanes powered by Turboméca

The small Turboméca Marboré turbojet sold in great numbers. Musée de l'Air

turbojets, the Fouga company approached the Ministère de l'Air with a proposal for a basic (*ab initio*) jet trainer, powered by two Palas turbojets. An enlarged version, powered by two Marboré engines and designated C.M.170R, was then designed by Pierre Mauboussin and proposed as more suitable for military training; Fouga received a contract for three prototypes in December 1950. This was a brave step for a company used to building wooden sailplanes and now proposing an all-metal aircraft, and it entailed a large capital outlay for new tooling and equipment.

In fact, the C.M.170R Magister had something of the look of the sailplane about it, encouraged by the extremely short tricycle undercarriage, the high aspect ratio wings and the typical Fouga butterfly tail. There was a long canopy to enclose the two crew in tandem and two small, wing-root air intakes to feed the two Marboré turbojets that flanked the rear fuselage and exhausted below the tail surfaces. Fuel was carried in the fuselage, just aft of the cockpit, and there were airbrakes top and bottom of the wings. The view from the front (student's) seat was excellent, but because the rear (instructor's) seat was on the same level, unlike today's trainers, the view was not so good and the instructor was provided with forward vision periscopes.

The prototype Magister made its first flight on 22 July 1952, powered by two Marboré engines of 400kp (882lb) thrust each. This was followed by a second prototype with wingtip fuel tanks and a third prototype, which had a conventional tail empennage purely for comparison with the butterfly tail. Development was rapid and almost trouble-free and the Magister was liked by all who flew it. In June 1953 a pre-production batch of ten aircraft was ordered, all to be simply armed with two nose-mounted machine guns. Full production began in Fouga's new plant at Toulouse-Blagnac, the first of hundreds of Magisters entering into Armée de l'Air service early in 1957. The Magister was also developed as the CM.175 Zéphyr for use by the French Aéronavale as a basic jet trainer, including carrier training. For this the aircraft was semi-navalized with an arrester hook, naval equipment and a certain amount of anti-

Fouga C.M.170 Magister			
Span		12.15m	(39ft 10in)
Length		10.06m	(33ft 0in)
Wing area		17.30sq m	(186.1sq ft)
Height		2.80m	(9ft 2in)
Empty weight		2,150kg	(4,740lb)
Loaded weight		3,200kg	(7,055lb)
Maximum speed	at 9,000m (29,520ft)	715km/h	(444mph)
Initial climb rate		1,020m/min	(3,346ft/min)
Service ceiling		11,000m	(36,090ft)
Range		925km	(575 miles)

corrosion protection. Perhaps the most celebrated use of the Magister was by the national aerobatic team, La Patrouille de France. The trainer was exported to many air forces around the world and was also made under licence by West Germany, Finland and Israel. The first aircraft ever assembled in Israel was, in fact, a Magister. Altogether, some 930 production examples were built.

Utilization of the Marboré

Other aircraft manufacturers also used the Marboré and this engine was built under licence by the Continental Motor Corporation (as the Marboré 352 or J69) and by Blackburn and General Aircraft. One of the most exotic uses of the engine was where two Marboré I's were fitted to the wingtips of the Leduc 0.16 experimental ramjet aircraft, first flown on 8 February 1951. Another experimental aircraft using wingtip-mounted Marboré turbojets (of 400kp/882lb thrust) was the SNCASO S.O.

9000 Trident, which was also designed to have a fuselage-mounted rocket motor. Studies for this aircraft were begun in October 1948. It was the ultimate French example of the 'manned missile', designed to streak skywards and shoot down high-flying bombers. Its competitors were the Mirage I, SNCAN Gerfaut and Griffon and the SNCASE S.E.212 Durandal. The Trident had a perfectly streamlined, needle-nosed fuselage with a small cockpit canopy, short, straight wings and a tail empennage that included a tailplane with pronounced anhedral. Its first flight was made on 2 March 1953, piloted by Jacques Guignard, but without the rocket motor. An SEPR rocket motor of 4,500kp (9,921lb) thrust was later fitted and speeds of up to Mach 1.6 were attained. In the Trident II, or S.O. 9050, the wingtip engines were Gabizo II turbojets of 1,100kp (2,425lb) thrust each and the rocket motor was a two-chambered SEPR of 5,450kp (12,015lb) thrust. This version of the Trident first flew in July 1955, but by this time the aircraft was regarded as a

The SNCASO S.O. 9000 Trident interceptor was powered by two wingtip Marboré turbojets. It also had provision for fitting an SEPR rocket motor in the rear fuselage. Philip Jarrett

research machine: its maximum speed was Mach 1.95 at 10,600m (34,768ft).

The Morane-Saulnier company also utilized the Marboré in January 1953 for the first flight of the prototype of its two-seat jet trainer, the M.S. 755 Fleuret. This twin jet was a competitor to Fouga's Magister and, although it lost this competition, it formed the basis of the M.S. 760 Paris small executive jet transport. The Paris, powered by two Marboré II engines, first flew on 29 July 1954 and achieved a speed of 650km/h (405mph) at sea level. It was ordered by the French forces, as well as by foreign air forces and civilian operators, and some 165 were built.

The Marboré was the ideal engine to power a small research aircraft such as the Italian Ambrosini Sagittario (Archer), designed by Sergio Stefanutti. Flying for the first time on 5 January 1953, the Sagittario was largely made of wood and was used for research into transonic flight using a swept-back wing, preparatory to the design of a larger fighter. A much more prolific use was then found for the Marboré in the USA, where Americanized versions, designated the Continental J69, were used to power the successful Cessna T-37 (Model 318) side-by-side jet trainer, the prototype of which first flew on 12 October 1954. This very neat aircraft had the air intakes and two engines buried in the wing roots and fillets to exhaust either side of the fuselage and below the tailplane located halfway up the tail fin. It went into service with the USAF in 1957 as the T-37A after considerable development to ensure its suitability for training. The T-37A's top speed was 684km/h (425mph) and some 535 were built.

Spain's first turbojet aircraft, the HA-200 Saeta (Arrow), first flew on 16 August 1955 and was powered by two Marboré II engines. This aircraft was designed by the famous Willy Messerschmitt as a tandem two-seat jet trainer and had straight wings, a long canopy and a tricycle undercarriage. Some thirty were built for the Spanish air force. Armed versions were then developed for training and ground attack. Production continued under licence in Egypt, most going to the Spanish air force. Counting all versions, 250 were built. The HA-200E Super Saeta, powered by more powerful Marboré VI engines and armed with underwing weapons for ground attack, had a wingspan of 10.41m (34ft 1¼in) and a maximum speed of 690km/h (428mph) at 3,000m (9,840ft).

Another trainer, this time using a single Marboré turbojet, was the private-venture, all-metal Miles M.100 Student, the prototype of which (G-APLK) first flew on 15 May 1957. It had side-by-side seating and was a useful enough aircraft but the hoped-for RAF production contract went to Percival's Jet Provost.

The foregoing examples indicate the utility of the Marboré, its general employment around the world and its great success for Turboméca. In Britain, however, the Blackburn company did not enjoy the same success with its licence-built versions of Turboméca's engines, which it considerably redesigned. Blackburn did find a market for the Turmo as a free turbine or turboshaft engine that was developed from the Artouste I in 1950 by the addition of an extra, single-stage, power turbine and gearbox. It was mainly used to drive generators, pumps and similar applications. The Turmo was developed in many versions, beginning with the 400shp Turmo II of 1954 and going on to the Turmo IV of 1,610shp.

Artouste and helicopters

Meanwhile, Turboméca developed the Ossau turbojet of 800kp (1,764lb) thrust, but then abandoned it in 1952. However, success attended their Artouste engine as the power unit in various small helicopters of the 1950s. This engine was originally used to supply air and/or hot gas to the rotors of helicopters to provide a simple drive, but the penalty of high fuel consumption and great noise gradually brought about the use of the engine as a turboshaft driving the rotor through a gearbox. During the war Doblhoff in Germany had already demonstrated the WNF 342 helicopter, which used a piston engine to provide a fuel/air mixture to simple jets at the rotor tips. In April 1951 a similar system was used in the SNCASO S.O. 1120 Ariel III three-seat helicopter (F-WFUY), but a 240shp Artouste gas turbine was the power source; this machine, with a fully loaded weight of 1,200kg (2,646lb), had a maximum speed of 180km/h (112mph), a ceiling of 3,600m (11,800ft) and a range of 250km (155 miles). The very neat Ariel III had no tail rotor but used a tubular tail boom with deflector vanes to direct the engine's exhaust as required for yaw control. This foreshadowed the method used in today's NOTAR (no tail rotor) when using a gas turbine in a helicopter.

The world's first mass-produced jet helicopter, the SNCASO experimental S.O. 1220 Djinn (F-WGVD), made its first flight on 2 January 1953, followed by the two-seater S.O. 1221 Djinn on 16 December 1953. In this helicopter, no fuel was burnt at the rotor tips, but instead a Palouste gas turbine drove a compressor that delivered compressed air to the rotor tips. A rudder working in the engine's exhaust efflux gave directional control. The fuselage was extremely light and simply comprised welded steel tubing. The two-seat Djinn weighed only 800kg (1,764lb), had a maximum speed of 130km/h (81mph) and a range of 180km (112 miles). Early in 1957, one of them set a new world altitude record for helicopters by reaching a height of 8,458m (27,742ft).

In May 1953 the SNCASO S.O. 1310 Farfadet (F-WBGD) made its first flight. This was France's first convertiplane, whereby a rotor was used for take-off but a normal airscrew was used for forward flight when the rotor autorotated. It had a well-streamlined fuselage, short wings to partially unload the rotor in forward flight and could seat three people. Two Turboméca gas turbines were fitted: an Artouste II to drive a nose-mounted airscrew and exhausting below the nose, and an Arrius II (enlarged Palouste) in the rear fuselage to drive a compressor providing compressed air for the rotor tips. The exhaust from the Arrius II was ducted to the tail for steering. Weighing 1,500kg (3,308lb) fully loaded, the Farfadet could cruise at 155km/h (96mph) as a helicopter or at 250km/h (155mph) as an autogyro, and had a maximum range of 400km (248 miles).

In 1954 Sikorsky in the USA decided to use the Artouste II as a turboshaft with a gearbox to power its four-seat S 59 (H39), successor to the S 52, for the US Army. The engine and gearbox formed a very compact unit above the cabin and also drove a tail rotor. The whole machine was well streamlined and had a retractable undercarriage. On 26 August 1954, Billy Wester piloted an S 59 to a new world helicopter speed record when he reached 251.067km/h (155.91mph). Fully loaded the S 59 weighed 1,633kg (3,600lb), had a ceiling of 7,470m (24,500ft) and a range of 400km (248 miles).

Following Sikorsky's lead, SNCASE also used the Artouste II as a turboshaft engine to power its S.E. 3130 Alouette (Lark) II helicopter, which first flew on 12 March 1955. This five-seat helicopter was aimed

at both military and civilian use and was mass produced. On 6 June 1955, not long after its maiden flight, the Alouette II was flown to a new world helicopter altitude record (without payload) of 8,209m (26,925ft) by Jean Boulet. Its success led to Republic Aviation building it under licence in the USA from 1957. Fully loaded the Alouette II weighed 1,500kg (3,308lb), had a cruising speed of 170km/h (106mph) and a range of 550km (342 miles). In 1957 a streamlined, less utility version of the Alouette appeared, known as the Gouverneur (Govenor), and this could cruise at 195km/h (121mph).

Back in Britain, 1955 saw the appearance of the Fairey Ultra-Light two-seat utility helicopter for the British Army. It used a Palouste gas turbine with an oversized compressor to supply air, mixed with fuel, to burn in rotor-tip jets of its torqueless rotor. This helicopter, as with all similar schemes, was doomed to failure by its high fuel consumption and high noise level.

In Spain, home of Juan de La Cierva, inventor of the autogyro, the Aerotecnica company produced the AC 13 three-seat helicopter in 1955. Two prototypes were actually built by SNCAN (as the Nord 1750) in France, one being tested there and the other in Spain. The AC 13 used a 260shp Artouste I as a turboshaft for the rotor and used deflected exhaust gas at the tail instead of a tail rotor. It was further developed as the AC 14 with a 360shp Artouste II, this version having a maximum speed of 170km/h (106mph) and a range of 470km (292 miles).

Aspin turbofan

While Turboméca was developing its gas turbines and turbojets, Joseph Szydlowski decided at an early stage to study the turbofan engine. Rateau and Whittle had already patented their ideas on such engines, while Metropolitan-Vickers had run its F2/3 turbofan in Britain in 1943, but Turboméca's Aspin I turbofan was the first in the world to fly, when one was fitted above the centre wing of the Fouga Gémeaux IV and flown on 2 January 1952. This first Aspin had a thrust of only 200kp (441lb) but the Aspin II, flown in June 1952, had a thrust of 350kp (772lb). In the same year an Aspin I was used to power the somewhat ugly Dorand DH 011 experimental helicopter. The mixed hot and cold gases (140°C) from the Aspin were ducted to drive the rotor and also to the rear to give controlled, horizontal anti-torque jets.

The Aspin was along the lines of other Turboméca turbojets, having a single-sided, centrifugal compressor, centrifugal fuel injection and an annular combustion chamber, but it had a two-stage turbine. To this was added reduction gearing to drive a single-stage fan, the output from which was divided partly into the compressor inlet and partly to bypass the engine and mix with the hot exhaust gases in the exit nozzle. In front of the fan was a single row of variable-incidence vanes, the purpose of these being to vary the amount of power absorbed by the fan and compressor (and thus altering the thrust) without altering

the engine's speed. Changes in compressor load could therefore be immediately altered without having to overcome the inertia of the rotor.

From an early stage in its development, the Aspin showed great promise. In 1950 the Aspin I completed a 1,000-hour type test under the control of the Ministère de l'Air, running at between 33,500 and 36,500rpm for more than 820 hours during this test. At the conclusion, the engine's performance had not changed and inspection of its components showed them to be in excellent condition.

Gabizo mixed-compressor turbojet

The first French turbojet to have a centrifugal compressor supplemented by an axial stage compressor was the Turboméca Gabizo. It was also the first of this company's turbojets to have an afterburner. The Gabizo featured a single-stage axial compressor followed by a centrifugal compressor, an annular combustion chamber, a single-stage turbine and a variable-area exhaust nozzle regulated with shutters. Its compressor system gave an air mass flow of 20.5kg/sec at a pressure ratio of 5.2:1. Initial trials began in December 1954 and a thrust of 900kp (1,985lb) was produced. By 1956 the Gabizo's thrust had risen to 1,500kp (3,308lb) and it passed a 150-hour endurance test in 1957.

Although the Gabizo never went into series production, it was used to power a number of experimental aircraft. Its main use was to power the S.O. 9000 Trident

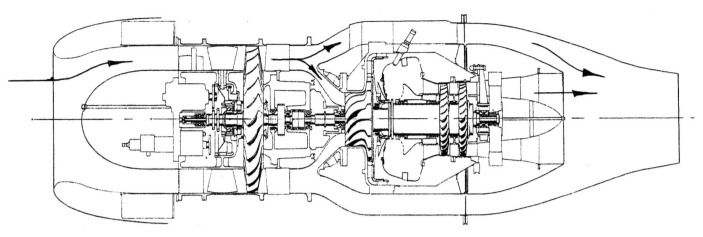

Turboméca Aspin I small bypass turbojet.

interceptor, one engine being fitted to each wingtip, supplemented by two SEPR rockets. The S.O. 9000 Trident 04 established altitude and climbing records in April and May 1958 but, with the cancellation of this interceptor, the Gabizo programme was also cancelled.

An axial/centrifugal compressor system was also used in the Bastan turboprop of 1957, which began at 650shp plus 78kp (172lb) of residual thrust and went on to a long development and production life.

Turboméca has continued to the present day as the world's premier producer of small gas turbines in all its forms. In due course it went on to concentrate on turboshaft engines, largely to power helicopters, but did not neglect the small turbojet and turboprop engines, the Astazou being the best selling of the latter variety.

Canada

Canada has always been seen as living in the shadow of its giant neighbour, the USA, but despite this a country with only a fraction of the defence budget of the USA, Great Britain or the Soviet Union managed to develop in a short time a highly creditable and promising advanced turbojet and aircraft programme. This post-war programme was compressed into only fifteen years and yet from it came a world-beating, two-spool, supersonic turbojet engine and an advanced aircraft to be powered by it. Only cancellation by the Canadian government, for misguided reasons, brought this programme to a close.

After details of Frank Whittle's work in England reached Canada, the country's National Research Council (NRC) decided to investigate the new form of power and a visit to England was arranged at the instigation of the RCAF's Air Vice Marshal E.W. Stedman. This was not too difficult to arrange, since Canada, as part of the British Commonwealth, was making a large contribution to the prosecution of the war against Germany. Ties between the two countries in matters of aeronautics (and much else) were strong. As war raged in Europe, many British pilots were trained in unmolested conditions in Canada. Manufacture of existing designs of aircraft was undertaken at Malton, Ontario, by the company known by 1945 as the Victory Aircraft Company. There was also the Rolls-Royce of Canada company in Montreal, which manufactured spare parts for the Merlin piston engines and carried out servicing on the same. (After the war, this company built R-R Nene turbojets using British components. These engines were to power the CL-30 Silver Star jet trainers being manufactured by Canadair. In fact, most of the Nenes were built by R-R in Derby, but those from Montreal were designated the Nene 10 and could be identified by a projecting electric starter. Canadair built 656 CL-30s, their version of the Lockheed T-33.)

The first visit to England to see Frank Whittle and the Power Jets company was made late in 1942 by Dr J.J. Greene and Malcolm Kuhring of the NRC. Following their report, the Department of Munitions and Supply (DMS) arranged for a technical mission to gain as much knowledge as possible from Power Jets concerning the then very secret turbojet work. Accordingly, the mission left for England early in 1943, its members including Dr Ken Tupper and Paul D. Dilworth of the NRC and C.A. Banks of the DMS. On its return to Canada the technical mission made two key recommendations: that the turbojet was of such importance that Canada should set up its own research and development organization, and that this should investigate how the turbojet would perform under the extremely cold conditions that prevail during the Canadian winter.

Within a short time, under the leadership of Paul Dilworth and the NRC, the Cold Weather Experimental Station (CWES) was set up in Winnipeg. The British Government provided the first engine for testing there, a Whittle W.1, and this made its first run at the CWES on 4 January 1944. As the war came to a close, captured German turbojets also became available for tests under cold conditions, the Junkers 109-004B-1 being tested in simulated icing conditions. For such tests, a duct of about 6.0m (20ft) and 1.52m (5ft) diameter was connected by a flexible seal to the inlet of the engine. Water spray nozzles were positioned at various distances inside the duct. Most runs were made at low outside temperatures, with the Junkers engine running at 7,600rpm and with its exhaust duct bullet locked in the open or starting position. The effects of the ingestion of ice into the 109-004B-1 was to double the exhaust gas temperature (EGT) in about 30 minutes, double the specific fuel consumption and reduce the thrust by up to 20 per cent.

Turbo Research Ltd

During 1944, while the CWES was being established, the government-owned company Turbo Research Ltd was formed on 1 July 1944 at Leaside, Ontario, with the aim of directing all gas turbine work in Canada and taking over the CWES from the NRC. Using the facilities of another government company, Research Enterprises Ltd, Turbo Research gradually built up its research and design staff under the leadership of Brig. F. Wallace and design studies of turbojet engines were soon begun.

These design studies, led by Paul Dilworth and in which the RCAF collaborated, were designated 'TR' for Turbo Research and included the TR-1, TR-2 and TR-3 centrifugal engines. Following these studies, the TR-4 was designed as an axial engine for a twin-engined fighter and this was to become the Chinook, a turbojet of about 1,180kp (2,600lb) static thrust named after a warm wind that blows down the Rockies. It was designed specifically as a research engine to develop engineering and manufacturing skills, but without any plans for series production.

During 1945 and 1946 a number of notable engineers joined Paul Dilworth at Turbo Research, including Winnett Boyd, Joe Purvis, Burt Avery and, from Power Jets, F.H. (Harry) Keast. The British Hawker Siddeley Group bought the Victory Aircraft Company from the Canadian government and renamed it A.V. Roe Canada or Avro Canada, established on 1 December 1945. On 4 May 1946 Avro Canada took over Turbo Research as its Gas Turbine Division and moved the organization to Malton, near Toronto, where conditions were, at first, less than ideal.

Design work on the TR-4 Chinook was then completed in the first part of 1947. It had a nine-stage axial compressor that produced an air mass flow of 19kg/sec (41.9lb/sec) with a compression ratio

The Chinook axial turbojet, only three of which were made.

of 4.5:1. This compressor had discs of aluminium alloy (except for the ninth stage, which was of steel) and rotor blades of aluminium alloy (except for the first two stages, which were of stainless steel). There were six straight-through, interconnected combustion chambers and a single-stage turbine, the temperature at the jetpipe being 650°C. The Chinook weighed 567kg (1,250lb) and had a diameter of 0.81m (2ft 8in) and a length of 3.09m (10ft 1½in). The Chinook first ran on 17 March 1948 and gave a thrust of 1,180kp (2,600lb) at 10,000rpm, an amazing result from the team's first attempt at an indigenous turbojet. Only six sets of parts were made and, from these, only three engines and one test compressor were built. By October 1949 some 1,000 hours of test-bed running had been made with these engines and each achieved a thrust of 1,360kp (3,000lb).

only after much deliberation and project studies and discussions with Canada's airline, TCA. Two Sapphire engines had been preferred to power the aircraft but the designers were told that no civilian use was foreseen for this military engine and so, from the autumn of 1947, the four-jet configuration had to be used. The Derwents were first run in the prototype (CF-EJD-X) on 24 June 1949. The maiden flight took place on 10 August 1949, the pilot being Jimmy Orrell, the co-pilot Don Rogers and the flight engineer Bill Baker. Soon afterwards, however, the C-102 was badly damaged on 16 August when its undercarriage failed during landing.

Once repaired and fitted with later marks of Derwent engines, the Jetliner went on a sales tour in 1950. It was flown by several American pilots and the US Navy and Air Force expressed an interest in it. On the civilian side, a considerable number of

airlines became interested in the Jetliner, including National, United, American, Eastern, TWA, Swissair, Air France, Sabena and SAS. In July and August 1950 investigations were made into making the aircraft more attractive for airlines in the USA, including the use of J-47, J-33 and Nene engines in order to carry up to sixty passengers at a higher gross weight. Discussions also took place with TWA regarding the fitting of all types of other turbojets. In October 1950 a second C-102 prototype was planned, to be completed with J-33 turbojets, but work on it ceased in February 1951. By the end of January 1951, the sole Jetliner had accumulated more than 200 hours on 150 flights; its highest speed reached was 845km/h (525mph) with a tailwind. In the end, however, the C-102 failed to elicit any orders in spite of its excellent performance, this failure being engendered by the fact

Avro Canada C-102 Jetliner

In 1946, even before work began on the Chinook, Avro Canada began the design of a thirty-seat (later fifty-seat), medium-range jet airliner, with a crew of two, designated the C-102 Jetliner. It was similar in configuration to a typical piston-engined airliner of the day but was powered by four Rolls-Royce Derwent 5 turbojets of 1,633kp (3,600lb) thrust each. It also featured a tall, angular vertical fin, with the tailplane mounted halfway up it, and a tricycle undercarriage. The engines were inside nacelles, closely paired and built integral with the wings. This point was reached

Avro Canada C-102 Jetliner with Derwent 5 turbojets		
Span	29.90m	(98ft 1in)
Length	25.12m	(82ft 5in)
Wing area	107.49sq m	(1,157sq ft)
Empty weight	16,738kg	(37,000lb)
Maximum take-off weight	29,484kg	(65,000lb)
Maximum speed at 9,150m (30,000ft)	737km/h	(458mph)
Maximum cruising speed at 9,150m (30,000ft)	725km/h	(450mph)
Service ceiling	9,150m	(30,000ft)
Maximum still-air range	2,415km	(1,500 miles)

that Canada's own airline, TCA, had not ordered the airliner. By this time it was already outclassed by the DH Comet and the Bristol Britannia, but nevertheless it is of great interest as Canada's first indigenous jet aircraft.

During November 1946 the Gas Turbine Division was moved to the Nobel Test Establishment of Defense Industries Ltd, which had been making explosives and ammunition during the war. The location was on the shores of Georgian Bay, Ontario, just north of Parry Sound, where there were a 4,700hp steam turbine (driving an alternator), five 500hp air compressors and a machine shop, all left by Defense Industries. Apart from this section, the previous establishment had all been burned down for reasons of safety. The remaining facilities were gradually developed into an excellent engine development establishment and some 6,000 personnel worked there by 1955. The steam turbine drove a compressor test rig and, by pushing its boilers to their short-life limit, 6,500hp could be obtained at 3,600rpm; through gearing, the compressor under test could be driven up to 10,800rpm. Later, by means of a closed circuit, altitudes up to 21,335m (70,000ft) could be simulated. Another test rig used a Chinook turbine to drive single stages of compressors. There were a considerable number of other test rigs, including a blade cascade wind tunnel, combustion rigs, an afterburning rig, a water tunnel and a turbine cooling test rig. Housing and other facilities were provided in the old village of Nobel for the personnel, most of whom were very happy with their work and conditions.

Orenda turbojet

Prior to this move, in summer 1946 Avro Canada received an order from the government to design an all-weather fighter for the RCAF. This aircraft was to become the CF-100 Canuck and its engines were to be developed by the Gas Turbine Division. Project work on the engine, designated TR-5, was began under Winnett Boyd in autumn 1946 and detail design was put in hand by the end of the year. The actual contract for the engine, known as the Orenda (the name of an Iroquois Indian spirit), was received in April 1947 and drawings were completed by 15 January 1948. It was specified that the engine should be more powerful than any other turbojet then available in the West.

Being short of experience, much reliance was laid upon external suppliers for components. Avro and other Canadian companies also bought expertise and licences to manufacture from other countries, such as the USA and Great Britain. The Joseph Lucas company in England, for example, was commissioned to design the combustion system and its recommendation that longer combustion chambers should be used delayed the design of the Orenda. Apart from anything else, this meant redesigning the rear components of the engine to accommodate the longer chambers. Many Canadian companies, eventually as many as 1,200, became familiar with new manufacturing techniques and processes thanks to their involvement with turbojet development: Light Alloys Ltd of Renfrew, Ontario, for example, learned to make large magnesium alloy castings and Shawinigan Chemicals Ltd of Montreal learned to produce stainless steel castings. Other companies developed skills and facilities for making precision forged blades and high-quality gears, and many other new industries came into being.

The first Orenda 1 turbojet had a ten-stage axial compressor, six combustion chambers and a single-stage turbine. It was delivered to the test-bed on 8 February 1949 and made its first run two days later. There was enough confidence in the engine to make this first run before the highest officials from the government, the RCAF and Avro, this considerable official interest being engendered by the fact that a great deal depended on the success of the new industry. Nerves were tested by an electrical

An Orenda axial turbojet, Canada's first into production. Below and near the front is the engine's oil tank.

short-circuit needing correction before the engine would start. Notwithstanding this glitch, this first test was a resounding success and, in the short space of two months, the engine achieved 100 hours of running. On 10 May 1949 the Orenda 1 delivered its design thrust of 2,720kp (6,000lb) for the first time. This engine weighed 1,225kg (2,700lb) and had a maximum diameter of 1.14m (3ft 9in).

By 21 July 1949 the Orenda 1 prototype had achieved 500 hours of running, 477 hours being made before it was rebuilt. It was on its way to clocking up 1,000 hours in September 1949 when an unfortunate accident, amusing in retrospect, occurred. A technician, intent on topping up the engine's oil tank, which was close to the engine's air intake, had his loose lab coat sucked off him. In the pocket of his coat was a packet of razor blades, which caused enough damage to stop the engine. Luckily the careless technician was not hurt. Owing to this accident, later engines had a debris guard consisting of multiple, concentric rings in the intake.

The repaired prototype Orenda was joined by two other examples and the three together built up some 2,000 hours of running by 10 February 1950. At this point,

A comparison of the sizes of the 2,720kp (6,000lb) thrust Orenda turbojet (left) and the 1,360kp (3,000lb) thrust Chinook.

all engines were developing fatigue cracks in the blades of the seventh and eighth stages of their compressors. After much hard work, a solution was found by thickening the troubled blades. By July 1950 the Orenda engines had reached a total running time of 3,000 hours.

It was now time to flight test the Orenda. For initial flight tests, a Lancaster bomber (FM209) was converted and its two outboard Merlin piston engines were replaced with two Orenda 1 turbojets. Thus equipped, this Lancaster first flew on 13 July 1950, piloted by Don Rogers, for a duration of thirty minutes. Altogether the Lancaster flew 500 hours of engine tests until it was destroyed in a hangar fire at Malton. Then, the high-altitude, high-speed characteristics of the Orenda were explored using a North American F-86A Sabre (49-1069) flying from Edwards AFB in California. For this work, an Orenda 2 was specially modified as the Orenda 3 to fit the Sabre mountings and an Orenda team went to the Los Angeles plant of North American to carry out the fitting.

The Orenda 2 was the first production engine. It was designed for a thrust of 2,755kp (6,075lb) and it passed its qualification test at this design thrust in February 1952. Fatigue cracks then appeared in the ninth stage compressor blades and this problem was solved in a similar manner to the previous failures. During May 1951

erection of a new production and development facility was begun at Georgian Bay and this new facility was opened on 29 September 1952 amid celebrations and a flypast that included CF-100s.

CF-100 Canuck all-weather fighter

While the Orenda was being developed up to production status, work was going forward on the CF-100 all-weather fighter. Design work began in October 1946 and, to ensure success with Canada's first jet fighter, a straightforward layout was chosen. The CF-100 had a low, unswept wing, equally tapered on leading and trailing edges and the tailplane and elevators were mounted halfway up an angular vertical fin. Alongside the fuselage at each side was a long engine nacelle that extended considerably fore and aft of the wing. A long canopy enclosed the pressurized cockpit, giving accommodation to the crew of two seated in tandem. The undercarriage was of the tricycle type, each main leg having twin wheels. The CF-100 was to have radar and be armed with machine guns and unguided missiles. To pilot the CF-100 on its maiden flight and initial trials, it was decided to engage Canadian-born Bill Waterton from the Gloster company in England, since no Canadian pilot had any

experience of high-performance fighters. He arrived in Canada in December 1949 and taxiing trials began on 17 January 1950. Waterton flew the first of two unarmed Mk 1 prototypes (18101) on its maiden flight on 19 January 1950. Because the Orenda engines were not ready, both this and the second prototype (18102) were powered by Rolls-Royce Avon RA 3 turbojets of 2,948kp (6,500lb) thrust. Following the successful tests with the Mk 1, ten pre-production CF-100 Mk 2s, also unarmed, were ordered, each to be powered by two Orenda 2 engines. The flight of the first of these (18102), on 20 June 1951, marked the advent of the first all-Canadian built jet fighter.

One of these pre-production aircraft went into RCAF service on 17 October 1951 and another was fitted out as a dual-control trainer and was designated CF-100 Mk 2T. This was not the RCAF's first experience with jet aircraft, since two Gloster Meteor F-3s (EE311 and EE361) were shipped out to Montreal from England, the first (EE311) arriving in mid-1945 just after the end of the war in Europe. Even earlier, the Canadian pilot F/Lt W.H. McKenzie had flown a Meteor at Farnborough on 1 June 1944. On 1 September 1945 EE311 made the first jet aircraft flight in Canada and subsequently flew around Ontario and in winter tests. Both Meteors crashed in 1946, however, EE311 because of a fuel problem and EE361 because of loss of control during a dive. In January 1947 an RAF Vampire (TG372) was used to carry on the winter trials.

For RCAF service, the CF-100 was ordered into production as the Mk 3,

The unarmed prototype of the Avro Canada CF-100 Canuck (18101) all-weather fighter. This and the second prototype were each powered by two Rolls-Royce Avon RA.3 turbojets, but production fighters were powered by two Orenda 8 turbojets. Philip Jarrett

In service with the RCAF, the CF-100 Canuck was nicknamed the 'Clunk'. Note the anti-icing alcohol spinner in the port intake.

powered by two Orenda 8 engines. The first of these made its maiden flight early in September 1952 and the type entered service soon after. Armament consisted of eight 0.50in machine guns in a ventral pack, the nose enclosing radar equipment. The Orenda 8 was similar to the Orenda 2 but was made in left- and right-handed versions especially for the CF-100. More importantly, it had an improved compressor to give better acceleration characteristics. Its maximum thrust was 2,883kp (6,355lb) at 7,800rpm and its weight was 2,277kg (5,020lb).

Seventy CF-100 Mk 3 fighters were built, fifty of which were later converted as dual-control trainers, and it was followed into service by the CF-100 Mk 4 (later designated the Mk 4A), first flown on 11 October 1952. In service the CF-100 Canuck was known by its crews as the 'Clunk'. Apart from structural redesign, the Mk 4A. first flown on 4 October 1953, had new radar and was armed with unguided rockets in wingtip pods. Also, the ventral machine gun pack could be replaced with one containing more rockets. Power was provided by Orenda 9 engines, which were an unhanded version of the Orenda 8 and had a distinctive anti-icing alcohol spinner. The alcohol tank was mounted on the port side of the engine and an oil tank was mounted on the starboard side. On 18 December 1952 a CF-100 exceeded Mach 1.0 in a dive.

Orenda 10 and 11 turbojets

The Orenda 10 engine of 2,883kp (6,355lb) take-off thrust was built for the Canadair Sabre 5 fighter (see below). This engine is now described as typical of the developed series before the final models. The compressor was of the ten-stage axial type with a pressure ratio of 5.5:1 and an air mass flow of 48kg/sec (106lb/sec) at 7,800rpm. The compressor casing was formed from two horizontally bolted castings of magnesium-zirconium. This casing was machined internally with 'T' grooves to accept alloy half-rings carrying the stator blades. Bolted to the front of the compressor casing was the intake casting, which carried at its centre a section for the front roller bearing, the gears to drive the auxiliaries and an electric starter that also doubled as a generator once the engine was running. Hollow, streamlined inlet vanes enclosed the drive shafts for the auxiliaries. The

intake nose bullet, enclosing the starter/generator, was curved downwards to match the centreline of the Sabre's upswept air intake duct. Although the engine was delivered with an intake debris guard, this was removed when the engine was fitted into the Sabre.

The compressor rotor comprised a three-piece alloy drum on which nine alloy discs were mounted, the tenth stage being in steel and bolted to the end of the drum. The stator blades were of aluminium alloy except for the tenth stage, for which stainless steel was used. Stainless steel was also used for the first three and the last rows of the rotor blades, the rest being of aluminium alloy.

A centre casting of aluminium alloy formed an annular manifold to receive the compressed air. From there, it was divided into six diffuser passages for the same number of combustion chambers. The main structural member of the engine was formed by a magnesium alloy casting, this joining the centre casting and a turbine nozzle box. The rear end of this structural member extended to an inner flange to carry the rear ball bearing assembly for the turbine. Each of the six combustion chambers was attached at the front end to the centre casting diffuser flanges by only two bolts and sealed with an 'O' ring. Of exceptionally large diameter, the combustion chambers were made of nickel-alloy and had their torch igniters fitted into two of the six interconnecting tubes. Duplex 3 downstream fuel injectors were used.

The turbine wheel was forged from an austenitic alloy, complete with an integral stub shaft and labyrinth seal. Solid turbine blades were precision forged from Iconel X nickel-chromium alloy and were mounted on their wheel with fir-tree roots. Air tapped

from the fifth compressor stage was used to cool the front face of the turbine wheel. The exhaust cone and the central bullet, with its support fairings, were formed by welding sheet-metal pressings. The connection between the turbine and compressor rotors was by a splined and flexible coupling, in front of which was a centre bearing of the self-aligning, ball type. Axial loads from the compressor and turbine were taken by the centre bearing. Air, tapped from the compressor's second stage, was used to cool the centre bearing, rear bearing and the inner cone of the nozzle box. Air tapped from the compressor's tenth stage was used to cool the rear face of the turbine wheel. The Orenda 10 had an automatic starting system. The dimensions of the Orenda 10 included a diameter of 1.067m (3ft 6in) and a length of 3.086m (10ft 1½in). Its dry weight was 1,141kg (2,515lb) and specific fuel consumption was 1.12.

With the introduction of the CF-100 Mk 4B, more powerful Orenda 11 engines of 3,355kp (7,400lb) thrust were fitted. This version of the Orenda had an improved ten-stage compressor with a higher compression ratio and air mass flow and, to drive this, a new two-stage turbine. It retained the alcohol spinner but was unhanded. With its improvements, the thrust of the Orenda 11 was 3,357kp (7,400lb) and its weight was 1,114kg (2,455lb). The Orenda 17, of which a few were made, combined the compressor of the Orenda 9 with the turbine of the Orenda 11 and had a simplified afterburner. Using the afterburner, the Orenda 17 had a thrust of about 3,850kp (8,490lb).

To improve the altitude performance of the CF-100, its wingspan was increased by 1.83m (6ft) and a larger tailplane was fitted. The engines were Orenda 11s or the similar Orenda 14s. First flown in September 1954,

Avro Canada CF-100 Mk 5 Canuck			
Span		17.68m	(58ft 0in)
Length		16.48m	(54ft 1in)
Wing area		54.90sq m	(591sq ft)
Height		4.74m	(15ft 6½in)
Empty weight		10,478kg	(23,103lb)
Maximum take-off weight		16,783kg	(37,007lb)
Maximum speed	at 3,050m (10,000ft)	1,046km/h	(650mph)
Service ceiling		16,460m	(54,000ft)
Radius of action		1,046km	(650 miles)
Maximum range		3,220km	(2,000 miles)

the CF-100 Mk 5 became the most prolific of the type and it served in the Belgian air force as well as the RCAF. The extended wingtips were not used on the final CF-100 versions, the Mk 5C and D, which were used in the electronic countermeasures role.

There was a proposal, as late as June 1959, for a CF-100 Mk 8 long-range missile version, the missile to be a Mach 3 Bendix Eagle. The Mk 8 was to have a new thin wing and Orenda engines apparently modified by Bristol Engines as BE 61s. Mention should also be made of the CF-100 (100760) that was used as a flying test-bed for the P&W JT15 turbojet; from its first flight on 22 August 1951 to its last in January 1981, this flew 850 hours in about 400 flights. About 680 CF-100s of all versions were built and the type served the RCAF well for thirty years.

Canadair built various versions of the North American F-86 Sabre jet fighter for the RCAF and RAF. Illustrated is the Sabre 6 version, powered by an Orenda 14 turbojet. It was the fastest of all Sabres.
Philip Jarrett

Canadair Sabres

In 1954 the Hawker Siddeley Group in Canada was reorganized and A.V. Roe Canada Ltd became the holding company of the two divisions, actually separate companies, known as Orenda Engines Ltd and Avro Aircraft Ltd. A third subsidiary, Canadian Steel Improvement Ltd, special-ized in steel, light alloy and titanium products. For RCAF Sabres based in Europe, Orenda turbojets were serviced by Brock-worth Engineering in England, the company set up to manufacture Sapphire turbojets.

While the CF-100s were flying with the RCAF, arrangements were made under the Mutual Defense Assistance Program (MDAP) to introduce the more potent, but shorter range, F-86 Sabre from the USA. Canada, of course, was a vital component of the North American Air Defense Command (NORAD), which, particularly in the menacing early days of the Cold War, needed to be in a condition of top battle-readiness. NORAD's prime concern was the possibility of air attack by the Soviet Union over the Arctic wastes. The Sabre selected for RCAF service was the F-86E with its very important all-flying tailplane. Canadair Ltd at Montreal pro-duced sixty F-86Es, in various sub-types, and then continued to produce it in modified form as the Canadair Sabre 2.

One Sabre 3 was then built and tested with an Orenda 3 engine prior to the production of the Sabre 5, which was powered with the Orenda 10 engine of 2,883kp (6,355lb) thrust. Canadair also built 438 Sabre 4s, with General Electric J47 engines, for delivery to the RAF. Considered as the best Sabre, the Sabre 6 was produced with the Orenda 14 engine of 3,300kp (7,275lb) thrust, this being similar to the Orenda 11. Having more power than American-built Sabres, the Orenda-powered Sabres set a number of records. Jaqueline Cochran set various speed records at Muroc, California, the fastest being 1,078km/h (670mph) over a 15km (9.3 miles) course on 3 June 1953. Amongst other records, Sqn Ldr R. Christie of the RCAF flew Ottawa–Montreal–Ottawa (296km or 184 miles) at an average speed of 1,178.8km/h (732.5mph) in an unofficial record on 12 June 1954.

Altogether, Canadair built 1,754 Sabres and, in addition to those for the RAF, exported about 640 of them to West Germany, South Africa and Colombia. On 18 February 1954 the thousandth Orenda engine was completed and, exactly one year later, another one thousand Orendas had been built. By the end of 1958 the TBO of the Orenda had been extended to 400 hours and it had flown some 600,000 hours in the CF-100 and 400,000 hours in the Sabre.

Pilots of the RCAF's No.2 Fighter Wing in France, who had previously flown the Sabre 2 with the GE J47 engine, found the Orenda-powered Sabre generally better. The Sabre 5, for example, had a higher cruising speed, cruising altitude and service ceiling (more than 13,700m or 45,000ft), only the range remaining about the same. Pilots also found that, should they need to overshoot from a landing, the Orenda's acceleration was very rapid, maximum rpm from about half speed being obtained in four or five seconds. Altogether, the success of the Orenda was all the more remarkable, coming as it did from a new team in such a short time.

Iroquois turbojet

In 1951 and 1952, Orenda tried, without success, to interest the RCAF in the development of a new turbojet in the 5,500kp (12,128lb) thrust class. This failure decided Orenda's management to plan the development of a much more ambitious engine (later known as PS-13) that would, after a lengthy gestation period, be competitive with later, large American and British turbojets. During 1953, when production of the CF-100 fighter and the Orenda engine was well under way, the DDP and the RCAF decided that Canada's future home defence could best be met by a new supersonic, long-range interceptor, later to be known as the CF-105 Arrow. This interceptor was to have a maximum speed of Mach 1.5 at 15,250m (50,000ft). Naturally, it was foreseen that a turbojet of far greater power than the Orenda would be needed and so, by the autumn of 1953, the Gas Turbine Division of Avro Canada had produced Project Study 13, or PS-13, for a large, supersonic engine. This project, for which huge capital outlay was required for research and development, was given the green light by the Hawker Siddeley Group Design Council and the Group provided funds sufficient for initial development costs. These funds amounted to $8 million and were sufficient to take the project up to and including the first prototype. (Today, it would be unheard of for a company to tackle such an advanced project without government backing and without other companies to share the development costs.) The work was led by Chief Engineer Charles A. Grinyer, who had arrived in April 1952 from Bristol Engines in England.

On 13 January 1954 Orenda Engines, as they now were, received the official Instruction to Proceed from the DDP and the PS-13 became known as the Iroquois turbojet. While this project was secret, there were rumours in the press that a large engine was being developed under the name of Super Orenda or Waconda. It was accepted that the CF-105 would fly most of its mission above Mach 1.0 and so the engine was designed for maximum efficiency in supersonic flight. Since there was to be no variable geometry used in the compressor or turbine, this meant a less than optimum subsonic performance. Another part of the engine's specification required that, from a cold start on the ground, the aircraft was to be airborne in one minute. It was decided that all requirements could be met with a twin-spool turbojet having a thrust-to-weight ratio of 5:1, a sea level thrust of 8,732kp (19,250lb) and a thrust of 11,794kp (26,000lb) in afterburner mode.

The Iroquois had a three-stage low-pressure axial compressor driven by a single-stage turbine and, in between these, a seven-stage axial compressor driven by a two-stage turbine. The compressors were designed to give a total air mass flow of 136kg/sec (300lb/sec). There were no inlet guide vanes, the first stage of the low-pressure compressor being transonic, this being a unique feature at the time. The combustion chamber was of the annular type and the afterburner was designed integral with the engine from the start. In the drive for minimum weight, it was decided to use as much titanium as possible and this eventually amounted to about 20 per cent of the engine's weight. Titanium Ti-140, used for discs, spacers and blades in the compressor, required the solution of many difficult manufacturing problems and Orenda was forewarned of this by titanium

The advanced, two-spool, Iroquois turbojet, as first revealed to the world's press. It was designed to give a thrust of 11,794kp (26,000lb) in afterburner mode. Its slender shape and high fineness ratio are apparent. The circular devices on the left are simply cable reels for the electric overhead hoists.

problems at Pratt & Whitney. The first problem was that the three titanium ingots, purchased earlier, had a hydrogen content of over 100 parts in a million (0.01%) and it was necessary to find a way of reducing this to a maximum of 20 parts in a million (0.002%) if hydrogen embrittlement was to be avoided after manufacture of the parts. Following laboratory experimentation, it was found that satisfactory hydrogen reduction could be obtained by heating and de-gassing the titanium at a moderate temperature in a vacuum furnace. The only such furnace available to Orenda was one

with a capacity of about 16kg (35lb) but, nevertheless, this was used to get the job done.

The larger compressor blades, the first four stages, were forged from titanium and then machined, while smaller blades in titanium were precision cast. The Canadian Steel Improvement company later perfected its precision casting of titanium so that all the compressor's titanium blades were so made. Only in the final, very hot, stages of the high-pressure compressor were steel blades used. Apart from weight saving, other benefits accrued from the use of titanium, including the use of lighter supporting structures and fewer bearing problems, due to the lighter rotating masses.

The casing for the low-pressure compressor was split into two halves, joined longitudinally, but the casing for the high-pressure compressor was fabricated as a single unit to ease the problems of sealing. Aft of the high-pressure casing was the mid-frame that led into the combustion chamber and shrouded the burners. The mid-frame also acted as a main structural member to carry major engine loads. A vaporizing fuel system, having thirty-two burners with upstream injection, was used. Forged turbine blades were used at first, but Orenda favoured cast turbine blades, without internal cooling, and, after investigating all available heat resisting alloys, chose for the blades Iconel 700 and 713, which had been developed by the International Nickel Company. With the success of these alloys, the programme to research and develop air-cooled blades was closed down. Each of the two rotors was supported by only two bearing support points, the low-pressure compressor having its bearing at a mid-rotor point.

Because the CF-105 interceptor was to have fixed geometry air intakes, intake gills adjacent to the engine's compressor inlet opened up at a speed greater than Mach 0.5. This allowed excess air to bypass around the engine for cooling purposes and also minimized air spillage drag at the aircraft's air intakes at high speeds. The bypassed air was used to cool the walls of the engine compartments and the afterburner duct. Because of this need to have a bypassed airflow through the engine compartments, it was not possible to use transverse firewalls. Therefore, the fuel system and other accessories were enclosed in a box through which the ventilating airflow was restricted to a level, which permitted the use of sufficient fire suppressant gas.

A fully variable, convergent exhaust nozzle with sixty segments mounted on rollers in cam tracks was used and was operated by four hydraulic actuators through a unison ring. The Iroquois 2 had an automatic starting and acceleration control system of a hydro-mechanical type, the pilot having a single-lever master control. The engine starter was an air turbine type, from AiResearch, and this was mounted on an external gearbox. Each of the two spools had an overspeed governor. Two Lucas-Rotax air turbine

driven centrifugal pumps were provided for the fuel system and the circulated oil passed through a fuel-cooled heat exchanger.

The prototype Iroquois (X 101) went to the test-bed at Malton on 5 December 1954 and made its first run at 4.24 pm on 19 December, only fifteen months after the project was begun. One year later, in a sustained, maximum speed run, the Iroquois was giving a static thrust of 8,618kp (19,000lb). On 24 June 1956 the first official 50-hour PFRT was successfully run (firstly with a Lucas fuel system and later with a Bendix system), and on 3 July the first run with the afterburner was made. By 19 September 1956 the Iroquois had achieved 1,000 hours of running and arrangements were being made to flight test it at high speed.

However, this point was not reached without some major problems, mainly concerning the use of titanium. There were several fires and some engines were destroyed. In the first, a compressor blade failed, became trapped and tore off the other blades. Because titanium is a very poor conductor of heat, the resulting friction caused parts to heat up to incandescence and air pressure blew a hole in the compressor casing. A torch effect then followed, which set the whole engine on fire, and which could not be extinguished with water. Consequently new methods of fire control had to be developed. These engine failures, attributable to titanium, were costly experiences and Chief Engineer Grinyer decided to replace titanium in the stator rings and compressor casing with steel. This modification had a weight penalty of 135kg (298lb).

Another problem found in the development of the Iroquois was that if one of the coaxial shafts vibrated, its vibration was transferred to the other. Rig tests eventually showed that this vibration coupling problem could be avoided if the bearings of each shaft were arranged in the same plane. This meant that the bearings of the inner shaft were mounted directly inside the positions of the bearings of the outer shaft. Once all these major modifications had been incorporated, an Iroquois was run on the test bench in April 1957 at a dry thrust of 8,165kp (18,000lb) and this was increased to 9,070kp (20,000lb) by the end of the year. Later, afterburner tests were carried out on test rigs, not only at Malton, but also by the Marquardt company in California.

Avro Canada CF-105 Arrow interceptor

Meanwhile, Avro Canada was proceeding with the development of the CF-105 Arrow two-seat, all-weather, long-range interceptor, which was to be powered by two Iroquois engines. This large aircraft had a pointed nose, closely followed by the cockpit. The fuselage was flanked by two rectangular air intakes to feed the two engines, which were installed side-by-side and exhausted either side of a tail cone. The large delta wing, with 'saw tooth' leading edges, was shoulder mounted and there was a single, large vertical fin and rudder. Each main leg of the tricycle undercarriage had a twin-wheel bogie. Five developmental Arrow 1s were put in hand, each to be powered by two Pratt & Whitney J75-P-3 turbojets of 10,659kp (23,500lb) thrust in afterburner mode. These were to be followed by the Arrow 2, powered by two Iroquois engines and armed with eight Sparrow air-to-air missiles carried in an internal weapons bay.

The J75-powered prototype (RL-201) made its first flight on 25 March 1958 and it was then joined by the four other Arrow 1s in the testing and development programme. To flight test the Iroquois, it was decided that the most suitable aircraft to use as a test-bed was the Boeing B-47 Stratojet bomber. The B-47 was chosen because it was the only aircraft that could approach Mach 1.0, fly the Iroquois at full power and at high altitude, and could also carry the large amount of data measuring and recording equipment needed. Analysis of the results was aided by the use of early IBM computers. A B-47 was loaned to Orenda by the USAF, together with the necessary servicing equipment. A crew of three was trained at the SAC Training Base in Wichita and they emerged fully qualified to combat status on the B-47 after ten weeks. Meanwhile, a SAC crew from Wichita delivered a B-47 to Canadair in Montreal for modification as the flying test-bed. This work entailed the mounting of a large nacelle for an Iroquois engine under the tailplane on the starboard side of the aircraft, the nacelle measuring 1.83m (6ft) diameter by 9.14m (30ft) long. The balance of the B-47 was maintained by the appropriate installation and positioning of the test and control equipment in the bomb bay. Once modified, the B-47, with a dummy test nacelle, was flown from Canadair's

The Boeing B-47 Stratojet bomber used as a flying test-bed for the Iroquois turbojet. The huge nacelle for the test engine is seen on the right of the fuselage under the tail.

Cartierville airfield to Orenda at Malton, where an Iroquois engine was fitted.

The first high-altitude flight of the Iroquois on the B-47 was made on 13 November 1957 and flying this test-bed had its share of hairy moments. On one occasion, there was a large explosion in the Iroquois, shaking the aircraft, and pieces of turbine blade pierced the nacelle and the aircraft's fuselage. This occurred during a climb and the only time that the Iroquois was opened up to full power in flight. Fire was avoided by prompt use of the fire extinguisher system and, trailing much smoke, the aircraft was quickly flown back to Malton. During take-off, to help

balance the asymmetric thrust of the Iroquois on the aircraft, one of the B-47's port engines was kept running while another was kept running to provide hydraulic and electrical power. However, once airborne, the normal procedure was to run the B-47's six normal engines throttled right back and limit the thrust of the Iroquois to 7,250kp (15,985lb), thereby remaining within the B-47's speed and altitude limits. During landing, another precaution had to be observed since considerable ground effect from the Iroquois's nacelle tended to lift the tail of the B-47. The high-altitude tests progressed well, its acceleration was excellent and the Iroquois

showed no tendency to stall or any reluctance to relight after a flame-out.

While test flying was proceeding, ground tests of the Iroquois continued as a major part of the development programme. One of the problems that came up during ground running was air intake distortion and this could be a major factor in putting the engine off-design. The need grew for more test facilities and so three very large test-beds, a high-altitude test cell and an afterburner test rig were commissioned at Malton. While waiting for these to come on stream it was arranged to use the NACA's laboratories in Cleveland, Ohio, and it was there that an Iroquois was successfully run in simulated altitude, speed and temperature conditions in January 1958, one test being a two-hour run in an air temperature of 115°C, with a peak of 176°C, which was equivalent to Mach 2.3. During these tests, amounting to just over 100 hours of running, the Iroquois demonstrated successful relights at high Mach numbers and at altitudes of up to 18,288m (60,000ft). Additional cold tests were carried out at the CWES facility in Winnipeg. By this time, the Iroquois was giving a thrust of 8,777kp (19,350lb) dry, or 11,612kp (25,600lb) with afterburner on, for a weight of about 2,040kg (4,500lb).

The second prototype (RL-202) of the advanced Avro Canada CF-105 Arrow all-weather, long-range interceptor flying over Malton, air brakes extended. The four prototypes were each powered by two Pratt & Whitney J75 turbojets, but production Arrow 2 aircraft were to use the Iroquois engine. The Arrow suffered the same fate as Britain's very advanced TSR-2. Philip Jarrett

It seemed clear that the Iroquois, designed for Mach 2.0, could have been readily developed for flight at Mach 2.5.

During December 1958 the first two pre-production Iroquois 2 engines were delivered to Avro Canada for fitting into the first of the five Arrow 2s (CL-206) under construction. As the fitting of the engines was about to begin, the government cancelled the CF-105 Arrow on 20 February 1959, and with it the Iroquois engine. To say that this was a bitter blow to the Canadian aeronautical industry would be an understatement. Following the lead of British politicians who cancelled the very advanced TSR-2 strike aircraft (and much else besides), the Canadian government mistakenly believed that the days of manned combat aircraft were numbered and that guided missiles would soon replace them. It is said that the money saved by cancelling the Arrow was used to subsidise Canadian farmers. As with the TSR-2, all CF-105 airframes were ordered to be cut up for scrap. Later, when the Soviet pilot Victor Balenko defected to Japan with a MiG-25, this interceptor was found to have many similarities with the CF-105 and it transpired that Soviet intelligence had infiltrated the Avro Canada plant.

By the time of its cancellation on 20 February 1959, the Iroquois had accumulated a total of 7,000 hours running, of which 31 hours were in flight on the B-47. Final data for the Iroquois 2 included a take-off thrust of 10,430kp (23,000lb), or 13,600kp (30,000lb) with afterburner on, for a weight of 2,110kg (4,650lb). Its compressor gave an air mass flow of 158.76kg/sec (350lb/sec) and a pressure ratio of 8.0:1. The specific fuel consumption was 0.85, rising to 1.80 in afterburner mode. Dimensions for the Iroquois 2 included a diameter of 1.07m (3ft 6¼in) at the intake end, a diameter of 1.19m (3ft 11in) at the exhaust nozzle and a length of 5.89m (19ft 4in).

With the cancellation of the CF-105 programme, Canada was obliged to turn to the USA for air defence equipment. The role of the CF-100 Canuck was superseded by McDonnell F-101 Voodoo interceptors and Bomarc ground-to-air missiles in the mid-1960s, equipment that was a very poor substitute for the CF-105. Orenda went on to build American turbojets under licence, including the P&W J57 for the Voodoo and the P&W J79 for Canadian-built CF-104s. By 1966 Orenda Ltd., as it was renamed, was owned 60/40 by Hawker and United Aircraft.

Avro Canada CF-105 Arrow 1 with P&W J75 engines		
Span	15.24m	(50ft 0in)
Length	23.72m	(77ft 9¾in)
Wing area	113.80sq m	(1,225sq ft)
Height	6.48m	(21ft 3in)
Empty weight	22,244kg	(49,040lb)
Take-off weight	25,855kg	(57,000lb)
Maximum speed during trials Mach 2.3		

Following the cancellation of the CF-105 Arrow, Canada was forced to rely for defence on American aircraft, such as the F-101 Voodoo and, illustrated, Canadian-built Lockheed CF-104 Starfighters. The latter was powered by the P&W J79 turbojet, built under licence by Orenda. Philip Jarrett

Another American aircraft built under licence in Canada for the RCAF was the Lockheed T-33 jet trainer. Philip Jarrett

 # CHAPTER THIRTY

Sweden

Sweden, a country of high technical and engineering expertise, was technically well placed to develop a gas turbine for aeronautical use, but, with a population that remains less than that of a city such as New York or London, it ultimately found the cost of development too high, especially in the face of engines readily available from Britain. Nevertheless, Sweden did develop an excellent aircraft industry to supply most of its needs in defence and the efforts made to develop its own turbojet engine industry are of historical interest. Although Sweden was traditionally a neutral country, during the Second World War it continued to trade with Nazi Germany, much to the chagrin of the Allies, and, in particular, continued to export iron ore to that country.

One of the country's earliest pioneers of consequence was Alfred J.R. Lysholm, chief engineer of the Aktiebolaget Ljungströms Angturbin (Ljungström Steam Turbine Company) of Stockholm. Lysholm worked on all types of steam turbine for the company and, beginning in 1928, began investigating the gas turbine. The Bofors company, famous for its guns and armaments, began construction of Lysholm's turbines from 1932, and later also built and tested various types and sizes of compressors for him. In 1934 Bofors built and tested a small turbojet that used a multi-stage compressor consisting of several centrifugal compressors in series. This engine was later intended to be converted into a turboprop, but the compressor suffered from severe surging, to the extent that a reversed flow

sometimes occurred; it had been abandoned by 1935.

Following this failure, Lysholm carried out experiments with other types of compressor. Deciding that a positive displacement type was the way to proceed, he devised a modified Roots compressor. This curious compressor was of a helical lobe or coarse screw pattern and an example was under construction before the outbreak of war, and later tested. The Ljungström company designed a turbojet, based on Lysholm's ideas, that employed two helical compressors, geared together and driven, through the gears, by a multi-stage turbine. Air from the compressors passed down the length of the engine and then reversed direction inwards into the combustion chamber, the hot gases from which reversed

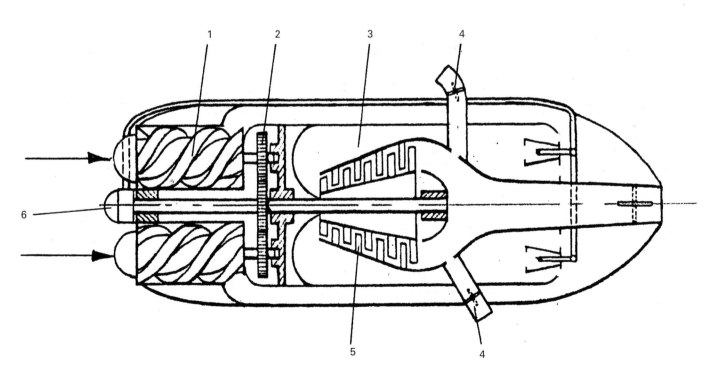

The Ljungström turbojet scheme: (1) two helical compressors; (2) 1:1 gearing between compressors and rotor; (3) reverse-flow, annular combustion chamber; (4) valves venting to atmosphere; (5) five-stage axial turbine; (6) fuel pump.

flow to enter the turbine and then exit through an exhaust nozzle.

Another curious feature of this design, apart from the compressors, was for the purpose of promoting rapid acceleration of the engine. To achieve this, it was proposed that valves could be opened to divert the gases from just behind the turbine into the open air and that this would result in a reduction of back pressure and a temperature increase and pressure drop in the turbine. The turbine would then add extra energy to the compressor. An experimental gas turbine along these lines was built by the Elliot Corporation for the US Navy, but was not a success and so the scheme was abandoned in 1945. Lysholm's ideas were encompassed in US Patent 2,085,761 (15 February 1933) and UK Patent 472,650 (21 April 1936).

Development of Lysholm's ideas by the Milo and Bofors companies

The Milo Aktiebolaget of Stockholm also designed turbojets and turboprops based on Lysholm's ideas, but these were not built.

One of these, a turbojet, featured a four-stage centrifugal compressor and an annular combustion chamber surrounding a seven-stage axial turbine. Air from the compressor was to be pre-heated by passing around the outer wall of the combustion chamber and then entering the latter by reversing its direction. The hot gases from the combustion chamber were then to reverse direction to enter the turbine. The turbine needed seven stages since it was small enough in diameter to fit inside the inner walls of the combustion chamber.

During 1936 Lysholm studied the use of an exhaust gas turbine on a piston engine, the turbine driving either an airscrew or, for a turbojet, a compressor. A unit with a six-stage turbine and compressor was built and tested on a piston-driven aircraft by the Flygvapen (Swedish Air Force) during July and August of 1942.

Having assisted Lysholm with his ideas, the Bofors company took sufficient interest in aeronautical gas turbines to work up more of his ideas into design studies, but none of these were built apart from the small engine built and tested in 1934. The company's first design study, in 1933, was for a turbojet with a four-stage centrifugal

compressor, can-type combustors (or perhaps annular) and a seven-stage axial turbine (Swiss Patent 174,257). This was followed by another 1933 design study for a turboprop having a six-stage centrifugal compressor, can-type combustors and an eleven-stage axial turbine. A study was also made of a heat exchanger for the turboprop.

A more elaborate design, this time for a turbojet, was also made in 1933. It comprised two two-stage centrifugal compressors with radial turbines in between and a large combustion chamber at the rear. The first, low-pressure, compressor fed compressed air (around the turbine casing) to the second, high-pressure, compressor, the two compressors revolving in opposite directions. Air from the high-pressure compressor passed around the outer casing of the bell-shaped combustion chamber and then reversed direction to enter the chamber at its smaller end, passing through a burner nozzle. The resultant hot gases then left the chamber at its large end via pipes and were fed into the radial turbines, which had opposing vanes, thereby driving the compressors in opposite directions. Thrust was to be produced by the exhaust gases leaving the engine at its largest diameter

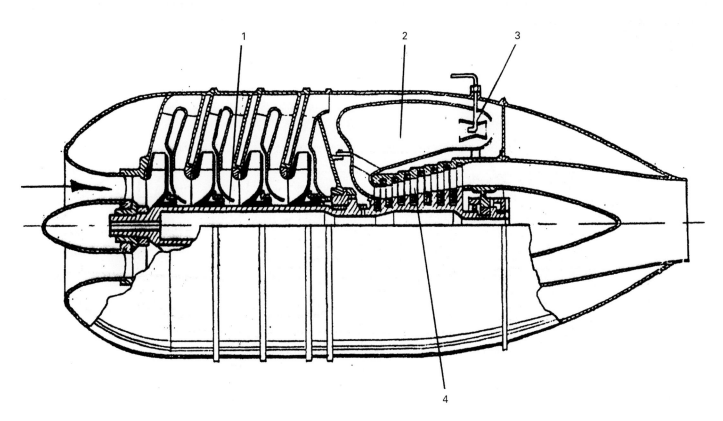

The Milo centrifugal turbojet scheme: (1) four centrifugal compressors in series; (2) reverse-flow, annular combustion chamber; (3) fuel injector; (4) seven-stage axial turbine.

(approximately at the middle) through circumferential ejector pipes. This design was covered by Swiss Patent 170,667. Finally, 1936 saw a design study for a turboprop with two helical screw compressors, an annular combustion chamber and a ten-stage axial turbine; this turboprop was planned for more than 1,200eshp and a diameter of 0.85m (2ft 9¾in).

Svenska Flygmotor AB

During the war Lysholm became the chief designer of Svenska Flygmotor AB (SFA). Based in its underground plant at Trollhättan, he continued to work on layouts of turbojets and turboprops, in collaboration with G.A. Dalhammar. One of these, designated the P/15-54, had a two-stage single-sided centrifugal compressor, an annular, reverse-flow combustion chamber and a four-stage axial turbine. The P/15-54 (R.201), of 1944 vintage, was built and tested post-war by SFA and was said to have delivered about 1,800kp (3,969lb) of thrust. It had a specific fuel consumption of 0.95, a weight of 1,300kg (2,866lb) and a diameter of about 0.910m (3ft).

The post-war work of SFA centred around building British turbojets under licence, namely the DH Goblin 3 (RM1) and Ghost (RM2B) and the Rolls-Royce Avon (RM6). The DH-built Goblin 2 engines of 1,406kp (3,100lb) thrust powered the 70 Vampire I jet fighters ordered in 1946 as well as initial prototypes of the Saab J21RA. The 1,500kp (3,300lb) thrust Goblin 3 (RM1) powered the Swedish-built Vampire VII (similar to the RAF's Vampire 3) and the Saab J21RB production aircraft.

As early as 1945 the Flygvapen Commander Bengt Nordenskjold had decided that all of its future fighters should be jet propelled. No doubt this view was encouraged by some knowledge of German and British jet fighters. This led to work by SFA on the turbojet with centrifugal compressor, while the experienced turbine manufacturer STAL developed a rival axial turbojet, the Skuten.

Saab J21R fighter

The J21R was Sweden's first jet fighter and was based on SAAB's earlier rear-engined J21 fighter, which had twin tailbooms and, in between, a pusher airscrew. The SAAB company had been formed on 2 April 1937 by combining the Svenska Järnvagsverkstäderna AB (ASJA) aircraft manufacturer with Svenska Flygmotor AB to produce a company making both aircraft and aero-engines. The plan was to manufacture indigenous aircraft rather than import foreign machines as before and the first product was the Saab-17 two-seat reconnaissance aircraft, first flown on 18 May 1940.

To adapt the J21 to have a turbojet engine instead of its piston engine seemed, at first, to be a straightforward job but actually entailed a fair amount of work, including the strengthening of the airframe to meet an increase in speed of 160km/h (100mph). The rear of the fuselage also needed widening and lengthening to accept the DH Goblin 3 turbojet of 1,500kp (3,300lb) thrust, this being fed from two air intakes flanking the fuselage aft of the cockpit. The twin fins were given a squarer shape and the tailplane was moved to the top of these fins in order to clear the jet exhaust. Finally, the tricycle undercarriage was shortened with advantage, there no longer being an airscrew to give ground clearance to.

The J21R prototype made its maiden flight on 10 March 1947 but, owing to protracted development, the first production aircraft were not delivered until February 1949: owing to this delay only half of the 120 examples ordered were built, since the more advanced J29 was already in development. Half of the J21Rs (J21RAs) had British-built Goblin 2 engines, while the others (J21RBs) had SFA-built Goblin 3s. Soon after entering service, these first jet fighters were converted for the ground attack role and armed with underwing rocket missiles. In the interim, the Flygvapen had decided in 1946 to adopt as its front-line jet fighter the DH Vampire (designated J28) and acquired some 400 of them.

The Saab J21R, Sweden's first jet fighter, was derived from an airscrew-driven fighter. It was powered by a de Havilland Goblin 3 turbojet and went into Royal Swedish Air Force service in 1949.
Philip Jarrett

Saab J21RB fighter		
Span	11.60m	(38ft 0¾in)
Length	10.45m	(34ft 3½in)
Wing area	22.20sq m	(238.97sq ft)
Height	2.95m	(9ft 8in)
Maximum take-off weight	4,990kg	(11,003lb)
Maximum speed at 8,000m (26,250ft)	800km/h	(497mph)
Service ceiling	12,000m	(39,370ft)
Range	720km	(447 miles)

Saab J29 Tunnan fighter

The first Swedish jet fighter to be designed for this role from the outset was the Saab J29, later nicknamed the Tunnan (Barrel) because of its portliness. SAAB's original intention had been to produce a conventional monoplane, powered by a DH Goblin turbojet. Data on swept-back wings released from Germany at the end of the war, however, and the availability, at about the same time, of the more powerful DH Ghost engine sent the whole project back into the melting pot. Initially a swept-back wing was tested on a Saab 91 Safir (Sapphire) four-seat light aircraft in order to obtain low-speed data. Then the Saab fighter was redesigned to have shoulder-mounted, swept-back wings, the leading edge sweep-back decreasing on its outer panels. The rotund fuselage had a pressurized cockpit set well forward in the nose and was equipped with a bubble canopy and an ejector seat. A nose intake supplied air to an SFA-built Ghost engine (RM2B) of 2,800kp (6,173lb) thrust that was mounted in the lower fuselage and exhausted beneath the short tail boom. The tail empennage was swept back on its leading edges and there was a retractable tricycle undercarriage. Armament comprised four 20mm cannon in the lower nose and underwing munitions.

The first of four Saab-29 prototypes first flew from Linköping on 1 September 1948, piloted by Bob Moore, but it was not until 1951 that production J29A fighters began to enter Flygvapen service. Its barrel shape belied its good performance. A total of 660 J29s, including ground attack and reconnaissance versions, was built and the last remained in service until 1963, being gradually replaced by J32s. Perhaps the finest hour of the J29 was with the Flygvapen in the Congo, where nine J29Bs and two reconnaissance J29Cs undertook ground attack and reconnaissance sorties. In January 1963 the J29s of Flygflottilj 22 (Volunteers) attacked the base at Kolwezi with precision and destroyed almost the whole of the Katangese air force. Surplus J29s were then sold on to Austria.

STAL

The steam turbine company of Svenska Turbinfabriks AB Lungström of Finspång, not far from the SAAB plant at Linköping, began the development of turbojets immediately after the end of the war. In this it was encouraged, along with SFA, by the Flygstaben (Air Board). Each company was to produce rival, experimental turbojets: the SFA produced a centrifugal engine (see above) but STAL designed an axial engine, designated the Skuten (named, like all its turbojets, after a nearby lake). It had an eight-stage compressor, can-type combustors and a single-stage axial turbine. The Skuten, which reached the stage of bench running in 1947, produced 1,450kp (3,200lb) thrust, weighed 780kg (1,720lb) and served as a research engine for the later Dovern. At that point, however, the Goblin became available for licence manufacture and so attention switched to that task.

The SAAB J29 Tunnan was Sweden's first jet fighter designed from the outset as such. Its power was provided by a de Havilland Ghost turbojet. Philip Jarrett

Saab J29F fighter		
Span	11.0m	(36ft 1in)
Length	10.13m	(33ft 2¾in)
Wing area	24.0sq ft	(258.34sq ft)
Height	3.73m	(12ft 3¾in)
Empty weight	4,300kg	(9,480lb)
Maximum take-off weight	8,000kg	(17,637lb)
Maximum speed at 1,550m (5,100ft)	1,060km/h	(658mph)
Service ceiling	15,500 m	(51,000ft)
Range	2,700km	(1,678 miles)

The STAL Skuten axial turbojet of 1947 served as a research engine for the Dovern.

Dovern axial turbojet

Both STAL and SFA continued to work on designs for larger engines in the 3,000kp (6,615lb) thrust class. The much larger turbojet named the Dovern was designed using STAL's experience with the Skuten. Chief designer of the Dovern was Curt R. Nicolin (also Vice Chairman of STAL), his chief collaborators being Eric Oestmar (Chief Engineer of the gas development section) and G. Stener (head of the gas turbine section).

The Dovern IIB (RM4) had a nine-stage axial compressor giving an air mass flow of 55kg/sec (121lb/sec) and a pressure ratio of 5.2:1. Its rotor, blades and casing were all of steel and there were four blow-off valves fitted to ease starting. British influence was evidenced by the nine tubular combustion chambers having flame tubes of Nimonic alloy and the fuel control system being by Lucas. The single-stage turbine used British Jessop H46 steel for its disc. Other British components included a Rotax electrical starter (or a BTH cartridge-type turbo-starter) in the nose intake bullet, Rotax high-energy igniters and Lodge plugs. In the Dovern IIB, de-icing of the air intake,

supporting struts and nose bullet was performed by hot air tapped from the compressor. The Dovern IIC was to be equipped with an afterburner.

As usual in the development of a new engine, numerous problems needed solving but development was slowed by constantly having to compete with SFA's centrifugal engine for official funds. Two serious breakdowns occurred during bench tests: in one a turbine blade broke off due to resonance vibration and, in the second breakdown, a turbine bearing failed. The blade failure was solved by using blades of more rigid design, while the turbine bearing failure was solved by modifying its cooling and lubrication system. Almost all the engine's vital parts were modified or improved at different times, but all the problems (including compressor surging) were eventually solved and, after thousands of changes, the Dovern was ready for flight testing by July 1952. This was carried out by mounting the turbojet beneath the fuselage of an Avro Lancaster (80001) flying test-bed (known as the Tp-80 in the Flygvapen). The test engine was neatly cowled in a streamlined nacelle having an oval air intake.

In mid-1949 the Flygstaben decided to sponsor development of STAL's axial Dovern rather than SFA's R201 centrifugal engine, since there were insufficient funds to do both. Furthermore, SFA was ordered by the Flygstaben to collaborate with its former competitor, STAL, in the development of the Dovern and other turbojets that might come later. Maj.-Gen. Nils Söderberg then left the Flygstaben in order to coordinate the development work between the two companies and also SFA's production work on British engines. The Dovern II was then chosen as the powerplant for SAAB's projected A32 Lansen (Lance) two-seat, all-weather, jet attack aircraft. SAAB had originally projected this aircraft in the late 1940s to provide the Flygvapen with an all-weather attack aircraft powered by two DH Goblin turbojets, but the promise of a Swedish engine initiated a redesign using such an indigenous turbojet.

Unfortunately, after the Dovern had been run for more than 4,000 hours, including 300 hours under the Lancaster, and was nearing production status, it was unexpectedly cancelled. At the time of its cancellation, the engine was said to be developing 3,300kp (7,277lb) of static thrust at 7,200rpm but it is not known how close it came to its originally specified weight of 1,200kg (2,646lb) or specific fuel consumption of 0.92. Its diameter was 1.095m (3ft 7in) and length 3.85m (12ft 8in). The Dovern IIC was to be fitted with an afterburner developed by SFA and intended to increase the thrust by 40 per cent to 4,620kp (10,185lb). The reason for the cancellation was that the Rolls-Royce 100 series Avon turbojet was to be built under licence by the SFA: the 3,400kp (7,500lb) thrust RA.7 as the RM5, the afterburning version of 4,700kp (10,360lb) thrust as the RM5A, and the Avon 200-series as the RM6 (to power the A32 Lansen). Another factor in the cancellation of the Dovern was budgetary constraints.

Saab A32 Lansen

The A32 Lansen (Lance) was a two-seat aircraft with a low-mounted, 35-degree swept-back wing and swept tail empennage. The two crew were accommodated in tandem beneath a bubble canopy, their cockpit being pressurized and fitted with ejection seats. All controls were powered and there was a retractable tricycle undercarriage. The engine was fed by air from intakes flanking the fuselage, above the wings. The Lansen's first flight was made on 3 November 1952, powered by an imported R-R RA.7R turbojet, but production aircraft had SFA RM6A engines with an afterburning thrust of 6,900kp (15,212lb). Production began in 1953 and deliveries to four wings of the Flygvapen began late in 1955. On 7 January 1957 an all-weather, night-fighter version, the J32B, first flew and this was followed by the S32C reconnaissance version. Altogether, about 450 SAAB 32s were built for the Flygvapen.

Saab J35 Draken

In 1949, when development of the Dovern turbojet was begun, the Flygstaben issued a specification for a Mach 1.5, radar-equipped fighter for the defence of Sweden. This fighter was later designated the J35 Draken (Dragon). A special project team, headed by Erik Bratt and his chief engineer Hans Palme, was formed at SAAB to undertake design proposals. Utilizing data gained from a small experimental double-delta aircraft, the Saab 210 (first flown on 21 January 1952), an aircraft was evolved with a unique double-delta wing, with 80 degrees sweep

The Saab A32 Lansen two-seat, all-weather, attack aircraft went into service in 1955. It was powered by a Rolls-Royce Avon RA.7 turbojet. Philip Jarrett

Saab J32B fighter		
Span	13.0m	(42ft 7¾in)
Length	14.90m	(48ft 11in)
Wing area	37.40sq m	(402.58sq ft)
Height	4.65m	(15ft 3in)
Empty weight	8,000kg	(17,637lb)
Maximum take-off weight	13,500kg	(29,762lb)
Maximum speed	1,145km/h	(711mph)
Service ceiling	16,000m	(52,495ft)
Range	2,000km	(1,242 miles)

on the inboard sections and 57 degrees on the outboard panels, and a thickness/chord ratio of only 5 per cent. Due to the long chord of this wing, there was still plenty of depth for the stowage of equipment. The long inboard sections of the wings had, at their front, oval plain air inlets to feed the single turbojet. There was a broad, swept-back vertical fin, a cockpit set well forward at the nose and a tricycle undercarriage. Liberal use was made of bonded honeycomb structure. In many technical respects, the aircraft was ahead of the world's fighters at that time. Items such as radar and the autopilot were of foreign origin and the initial armament comprised two 30mm Aden cannon in the inboard wings.

The prototype of the Draken was first flown on 25 October 1955, the pilot being Bengt Olow. This and the next two prototypes were powered by imported R-R Avon engines. Power for subsequent aircraft was provided by SFA-produced RM6B versions of the Avon, with SFA-developed afterburners. The first J35As were delivered

to the Flygvapen (wing F13) on 8 March 1960. The type was developed in reconnaissance and trainer versions and later could be equipped with drop tanks, Sidewinder missiles and a braking parachute. Some 606 of all versions combined were produced.

Glan two-spool turbojet project

The cancellation of the Dovern brought an end to all of STAL's work on turbojets, including that on the two-spool Glan. This engine was aimed at a dry thrust of 5,000kp (11,025lb), or 7,000kp (15,435lb) in afterburner mode, and had reached the stage of component manufacture by 1952. All was not lost for the Glan, however, because from it was developed the successful GT 35 stationary gas turbine of 13,400hp (10,000kW), which was exported to several countries.

The Glan turbojet was intended for a planned supersonic fighter. As early as May 1952 the Saab designers, led by project

Saab J35 Draken fighters, each powered by an SFA-built RM65 turbojet with afterburner, based on the Rolls-Royce Avon. These aircraft can reach speeds approaching Mach 2.0. Philip Jarrett

Another example of the Saab J35 Draken. Author

manager Erik Bratt, began exhaustive studies for a replacement for the J35 Draken. The System 36 (or future J36), one of more than a hundred designs, was well into the design stage before it was cancelled in 1958, but it was to lead to the J37 Viggen. In November 1952 the Flygstaben announced the cancellation of the entire Swedish turbojet programme. This decision was influenced by Rolls-Royce offering the Avon. SFA continued to build foreign turbojets under licence. The company was taken over by its majority shareholder, the Volvo car company, in 1970 and renamed Volvo Flygmotor. Swedish jet aircraft continued to be produced by SAAB, examples being the J35 Draken and J37 Viggen (Thunderbolt) interceptors, powered by licence-built Rolls-Royce and P&W engines respectively.

SAAB J35 Draken fighter			
Span		9.40m	(30ft 10in)
Length		15.34m	(50ft 4in)
Wing area		50.03sq m	(538sq ft)
Height		3.90m	(12ft 9½in)
Empty weight		6,335kg	(13,970lb)
Loaded weight		8,255kg	(18,200lb)
Maximum speed	at 11,000m (36,080ft)	1,910km/h or Mach 1.79	(1,186mph)
Initial climb rate		9,450m/min	(31,000ft/min)
Service ceiling		17,300 m	(56,750ft)
Normal range		1,300km	(807 miles)

A Volvo RM8 axial turbojet under test. It is based on the Pratt & Whitney JT8D engine and is used to power the Saab J37 Viggen interceptor. Volvo Flygmotor AB

CHAPTER THIRTY-ONE

Switzerland

A small but industrialized country, although with almost no raw materials of its own, Switzerland was scientifically and technically well equipped to develop jet aircraft. Having the industrial capacity to meet its defence needs, it relied on exporting machinery, watches, chemicals and pharmaceuticals and its special banking services for foreigners. However, like Sweden, after making a good start on various aeronautical projects, most, if not all, of these were closed down by the politicians on the grounds of unsustainable economics. Again, like Sweden, Switzerland was traditionally neutral in time of war. During the Second World War, however, despite its status as the most important neutral country in Europe, it carried on trade with foreign countries, especially Germany. Indeed, every major German industry had links with Switzerland, to the extent that some 100,000 Germans were resident there. Swiss exports to Germany included aircraft parts, radio equipment, ammunition, fuses, diesel engines and chemicals. In addition, the Swiss railway system and Alpine tunnels were at Germany's disposal, ensuring an indispensable link with that country's Axis partner, Italy. For its part, Germany supplied Switzerland with coal and steel. It should be remembered that the neutral countries could easily have been conquered had this suited Hitler's purpose and they had little choice but to carry on as the Germans required.

Since 1905 Brown Boveri & Cie (BBC) had been pre-eminent in the development of gas turbines that used waste heat to drive turbo-blowers to supply compressed air to blast furnaces. In BBC's first schemes, furnace gases were burned in a combustion chamber and the ensuing hot gases were used to drive a turbine that drove the compressor. BBC's equipment was being sold even before 1910 and was subsequently built in many other countries. In this, and later more elaborate schemes, can be seen the precursors of aeronautical gas turbines

and Brown Boveri's experience, covering the manufacture of steam turbines, centrifugal compressors, centrifugal turbosuperchargers (for diesel engines), and geared centrifugal superchargers for aero-engines (during the First World War) put it in an excellent position to develop the gas turbine and turbojet. For other pioneers, BBC built the multi-stage centrifugal compressor for the Armengaud-Lemale turbine and also a number of explosion turbines for Hans Holzwarth. In the end, however, as we shall see, BBC failed to enter the turbojet field in any major way but continued to prosper in the industrial field.

Prof. Jakob Ackeret

Jacob Ackeret was a first-rate physicist and theoretician who trained under Prof. Ludwig Prandtl at the Aerodynamische Versuchanstalt (AVA), Göttingen, as did future key physicists such as W. Encke, Albert Betz and Theodore von Kármán. Prandtl's work, including his aerofoil theory of 1918, had influenced others to investigate the axial compressor and turbine by 1926, notably, in chronological order, A.A. Griffith (England), Ackeret (Switzerland), and Betz and Encke (Germany). Their investigations had a great influence on the development of the axial turbojet.

In 1925 Ackeret published his first comprehensive theoretical analysis of supersonic lift and drag for an aerofoil and qualified as a Doctor of Engineering. By 1927 he had moved back to Switzerland, where he headed the Institute for Aerodynamics from its creation in 1931 at the Eidgenössische Technische Hochschule (Federal Institute of Technology) in Zürich. This institute became the foremost centre of the country's aeronautical research and, thanks to Prof. Ackeret's work and guidance, aerodynamics in Switzerland was raised to an international calibre. In 1933 Ackeret designed and oversaw the

construction there of the world's first supersonic wind tunnel, capable of speeds up to Mach 2.0. For this, he designed a thirteen-stage axial blower that gave a pressure ratio of just over 2:1 at an efficiency of 80 per cent. This was built by BBC, which was already investigating axial blowers and compressors and had built single and two-stage axial blowers as cooling fans. It had also carried out thorough wind tunnel work on single-stage units. The company's previous work had included building a small experimental four-stage compressor in 1927 after the discovery of free vortex blading by the French engineer Georges Jean-Marie Darrieus.

Although Ackeret's tunnel was used for aeronautical research, its primary purpose was to investigate the phenomena of aerofoil compressibility to provide data useful in the design and construction of large steam turbines and turbocompressors. This wind tunnel was of the closed-circuit type and it became the forerunner of other supersonic wind tunnels, including one built in 1935/6 for the Italians at Guidonia and several in Germany. Among the latter was the BMW wind tunnel at Oberweisenfeld/Munich used for high-altitude engine testing, the finest in the world at that time. Ackeret was also involved in the development of a closed-cycle gas turbine in the late 1930s. By then BBC had developed turbine wheels and axial-flow compressors with high efficiencies, around 85 per cent, although these were for industrial uses such as the Houdry process in the oil industry and Velox boilers in the steel industry. By 1939 BBC had produced a 4,000hp gas turbine to drive a stand-by electrical generator for the city of Neuchâtel and to drive a locomotive on the Swiss Federal Railways. Meanwhile, in 1938, Prof. Ackeret wrote an article proposing the use of the gas turbine to power aircraft.

Switzerland's second centre for aeronautical research was the Federal Aircraft

Works (EFW) at Emmen military airfield near Lucerne. The EFW had various wind tunnels and was controlled by the KTA of the Defence Department. Work was begun on the facility in 1944 and completed in 1947. It was directed by Dipl.-Ing. W. Haussmann and its chief work involved applied research, aeronautical development and engineering work on airframes and engines.

Escher, Wyss AG

The Escher, Wyss (EW) company was founded in Zürich in 1805. Its main business was the engineering of hydraulic turbo-machinery for water power generation, especially important in a country lacking coal but possessing plentiful mountain water. Among its other engineering activities, EW developed marine propellers and textile machinery. The first hydraulically operated, controllable pitch propeller in the world was built by EW for the passenger vessel *Etzel*.

The company's first work in the aeronautical sphere was the development of high-performance, variable-pitch airscrews.

Between 1936 and 1938 the EW Research Department developed the world's first variable-pitch airscrew that, by using negative pitch, could be used for braking purposes during landing. This department, headed by Dr C. Keller, later worked out design proposals for turbojet engines and jet aircraft, all for civilian use.

On 25 April 1945, just before the end of the war, a Messerschmitt Me 262 jet fighter from Germany landed at Dübendorf, causing general astonishment and creating the impetus, if any were needed, to develop jet aircraft in Switzerland. The Kriegstechnische Abteilung (KTA) commissioned the companies of BBC, Sulzer and Escher, Wyss to examine one of the Junkers 109-004B turbojets from the Me 262. This was carried out in EW's workshops and the engineers concluded that, as far as the axial compressor was concerned, Swiss work was already in advance of the German.

Work in the EW Research Department principally encompassed a Campini-type jet engine with a piston engine, examination of all the different circulatory systems possible for jet engines, jet propulsion systems for multi-engined aircraft, a general proposal for a ZTL two-circuit turbojet, a

proposal for a 10,000eshp turboprop engine and a proposal for a Turboliner commercial aircraft.

From this programme, the most important EW project was that for the ZTL turbojet, which envisaged features only later realized in modern turbojets. The ZTL turbojet (EW used no designation) had a four-stage low-pressure compressor, about half the airflow from which passed into an outer or secondary annular combustion chamber, the resultant hot gases accelerating out through an annular exhaust nozzle surrounding the inner nozzle. The other part of the airflow entered a five-stage high-pressure axial compressor and then a central or primary annular combustion chamber. Hot gases from this chamber entered a single-stage turbine, which drove both compressors on the same rotor, and then exhausted through a variable-area, central nozzle. The rotor was carried on three bearing points, a roller bearing in front of the low-pressure compressor and a ball bearing at the rear of the high-pressure compressor, and a ball bearing in front of the turbine – leaving this overhung. Load bearing and thrust arms led from the ball bearing journals and out of the engine to

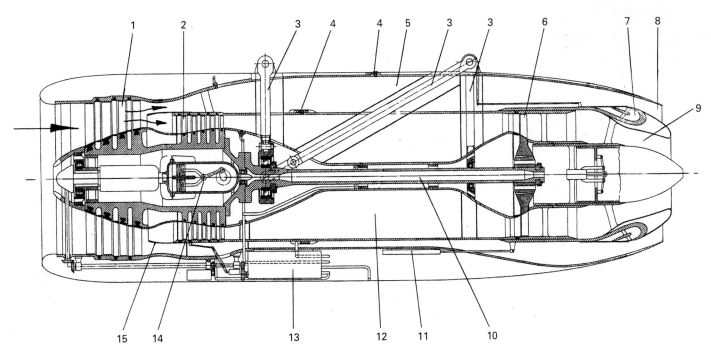

The Escher Wyss projected ZTL two-circuit turbojet: (1) four-stage axial LP compressor; (2) five-stage axial HP compressor; (3) load-bearing and thrust arms; (4) fuel injection nozzles; (5) outer, secondary, annular combustion chamber; (6) single-stage turbine; (7) reverse-thrust deflector ring (uncovered when moved fully aft); (8) variable-area annular exhaust nozzle; (9) variable-area central exhaust nozzle; (10) single rotor, with three bearing points; (11) servo/s for variable-area and reverse-thrust systems; (12) inner, annular combustion chamber; (13) injection pump and governor; (14) mechanism (in fixed housing) to adjust air inlet guide ring; (15) movable guide ring, varying area of air inlet to HP compressor.

mounting points. The overall pressure ratio of the compressor system was said to be rather low for the time.

There were some particularly novel features in this engine, concerning a variable-area inlet system, variable-area of both exhaust nozzles and a reverse-thrust system. Variation of the entry area also altered the 'bypass' ratio (of primary or main air to secondary air). A movable bullet and a movable shroud (between the inner and outer exhaust systems) altered the area of the inner and outer exhaust nozzles. A control system for regulating the entry and exhaust cross-sectional areas and also the rate of fuel flow was being studied.

If the shroud was moved fully aft, a recessed, built-in deflector ring was uncovered and this, by impingement, reversed the direction of the outer, secondary exhaust gases to give reversed thrust during landing. The reverse thrust system was to be coupled to the aircraft's main undercarriage so that it was activated immediately upon touch down. With the activation of reverse thrust, the high-pressure section of the engine was to be throttled back to produce less positive thrust.

Escher, Wyss worked out its ZTL design in the three sizes of 1,500, 3,000 and 4,500 thrust hp, at 700km/h (435mph) at 6,000m (19,680ft) altitude. The largest of these was planned to give a static thrust of 3,200kp (7,056lb) and an overload (with reheat) thrust of 4,500kp (9,923lb), with a best specific fuel consumption of 0.77. Its diameter was 1.40m (4ft 7in) and length 4.50m (14ft 9in). Due to the voluminous and long combustion chambers, the estimated weight was somewhat high at 2,400kg (5,292lb). The ZTL turbojet reached the stage of a completely designed compressor system and the testing of its combustion chambers.

In April 1945 EW proposed a turboprop engine of 5,000 shp, or alternatively 10,000 shp. This engine was to drive four-bladed, variable-pitch, contra-rotating airscrews (doubtless, made by EW). By mid-1945 a 7,500shp version of this engine was proposed, to power a twin-engined, Swiss-built airliner called the Turboliner. This aircraft was to weigh about 50 tonnes and transport sixty-five passengers 3,500km (2,173 miles) at 600km/h (373mph). The industrialist J. Schmidheiny was proposed by EW to assume commercial leadership of this project but, as with the ZTL turbojet, the scheme foundered because of financing problems.

In 1946 the variable-pitch airscrew department of Escher Wyss was closed, apparently owing to the lack of orders for Swiss-built piston aircraft. Work on the company's gas turbine projects was gradually reduced, due to the lack of sponsorship, and was finally terminated in 1947. In 1969 Escher Wyss merged with Sulzer Bros to form a high technology corporation with worldwide interests.

Sulzer Bros Ltd

Sulzer was founded as an iron foundry and manufacturing business in Winterthur as early as 1834, and by 1878 the company had expanded into the fields of refrigeration, compressors and steam engines, the latter being gradually replaced from 1898 by the manufacture of diesel engines. Between 1909 and 1912 Dr Alfred J. Buchi of the company's Research Department developed the first exhaust-driven supercharger, principally for diesel engines. His ideas gained little following at the time, but Sulzer opened an experimental turbocharging plant in 1911. In due time, of course, turbo-superchargers were developed worldwide, especially for piston aero-engines.

In April 1945 the EFW requested interested Swiss companies to produce studies for powerful aero-engines. This project interested the Sulzer company and its engineers made studies for the turbojet, the two-circuit turbojet and the turboprop types of engine in July 1945. From this work, Sulzer proposed the design of a turboprop of 1,500shp, but then decided to concentrate on a turbojet design to achieve higher speeds.

Sulzer joined forces with the BBC and Escher Wyss companies to work out a scheme whereby two main turbojets partially fed air to eight secondary propulsive units. Only Sulzer, however, completed this scheme to the detail design stage. Known as Scheme A, it was to use two main turbojets, each with a bypass airflow that was fed to the smaller, secondary propulsive engines. In each of these engines, the air was used to support combustion, the gases from which drove a radial turbine, which in turn drove a centrifugal compressor giving a bypass airflow. This bypassed air mixed with the hot exhaust gases in a propulsive nozzle that could also be used as an afterburner by the injection of extra fuel. The two main turbojets provided the main forward thrust,

while the secondary engines could give forward thrust, boosting and jet lift, as required. Scheme A promised excellent lift coefficients and the advantageous use of jet flaps over the entire wing span, combined with a higher load capability through the use of auxiliary combustion in the secondary propulsive engines. Although many years later similar systems were proposed again for STOL and VTOL aircraft, in 1946 they were deemed to be too complex.

The aim of Sulzer's endeavours was to provide power for the projected N-20 fighter aircraft (see below). In November 1946 powerplant Scheme B was proposed whereby a turbojet was to be housed in each wing root. The turbojet proposed was of a coaxial, two-circuit type (ZTL). This engine was designed for a static thrust of 1,800kp (3,970lb) at 4,000rpm and a specific fuel consumption of only 0.64. By the end of 1946 the EFW at Emmen decided that the N-20 fighter should be powered by two coaxial ZTL engines, installed in the wing centre section at each side. Sulzer produced proposals at the end of March 1947 for two engines of this type, under the designation of DZ-45 (the figure was the diameter of the combustion chamber in centimetres). Because Sulzer had experience of only heavy industrial gas turbines, where weight was of minor consequence, a new Jet Engine Development Group was formed, headed by Ing. H. Egli. Development of a small, lightweight engine, and with a small but intense combustion system, was completely new ground to Sulzer.

The DZ-45 turbojet featured a two-stage, low-pressure axial compressor driven by a single-stage turbine. In between, there was a seven-stage high-pressure axial compressor driven by a single-stage turbine through a separate, coaxial shaft. A portion of the air after the low-pressure compressor was to be diverted into a tubular diffuser duct to supply secondary combustion chambers, or afterburners, brought in as required to increase thrust. The main airflow from the two compressors passed through an annular combustion chamber, the two turbines and out through a fixed-area exhaust nozzle. The DZ-45 was designed for a static thrust of 1,054kp (2,325lb) for a weight of 450kg (993lb) and a specific fuel consumption of 0.82. Its maximum diameter (over the LP compressor section) was 0.66m (2ft 2in), maximum width (across the diffuser duct and accessories) 1.04m (3ft 5in) and length 2.10m (6ft 10in).

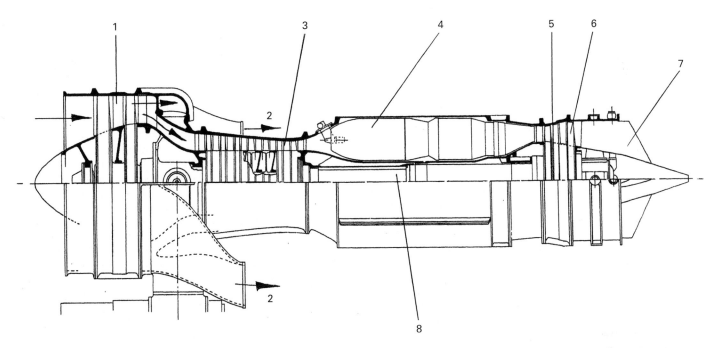

Sulzer DZ-45 two-shaft ZTL two-circuit turbojet: (1) two-stage LP axial compressor; (2) LP air to secondary combustion chambers; (3) seven-stage HP axial compressor; (4) annular combustion chamber; (5) two-stage HP turbine; (6) single-stage LP turbine; (7) fixed-area exhaust nozzle; (8) coaxial rotor shafts.

Unfortunately, the major funds needed to develop the DZ-45 were not forthcoming from the government. The same applied to a variant known as the DK-45, which was to have concentric but completely separate main and secondary air streams producing thrusts of 462kp (1,020lb) and 478kp (1,055lb), respectively. Realization of the coaxial turbojet had to await the appearance of the Rolls-Royce Conway engine in the early 1950s.

Instead, in 1948, the order was given for the production of two D-45 turbojet prototypes. The D-45 was planned as a lightweight engine in the 700kp (1,545lb) thrust class. As a straightforward axial turbojet, this was considered an easier development prospect than the previous projects. It had a nine-stage axial compressor, six can-type combustion chambers, a single-stage turbine and a variable-area exhaust nozzle with a translating central cone. There were four main bearing points. The first prototype, D-45.01, was purely for bench testing. Development work up to 1949 was performed on components such as burners, combustion chambers, the compressor, turbine, accessories and the regulation system.

The first runs with the D-45.01 commenced at the beginning of July 1950 and some 140 hours of running had been accumulated by January 1951, by when the compressor had also been tested for 85 hours, up to its maximum speed. These tests gave generally satisfactory results, the compressor performance being especially good and showing a higher efficiency than those in the German Junkers turbojets. The D-45.01 gave a static thrust of 752kp (1,660lb) at 16,000rpm for a weight of 263kg (580lb), without accessories, and a specific fuel consumption of 1.05.

The second prototype, the D-45.04, was similar to the first prototype, but an extra compressor stage was added and air was bled off from the compressor to operate a blow-off valve to ease starting. Improved

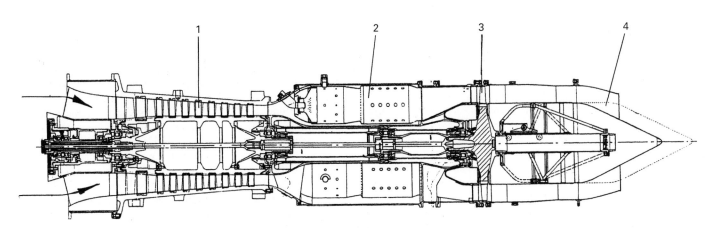

Sulzer D-45.01 axial turbojet: (1) nine-stage axial compressor; (2) six combustion chambers; (3) single-stage turbine; (4) variable-area exhaust nozzle.

combustion chambers were also fitted. Main components were generally of lighter construction in order to produce an engine with at least limited flight capability. Already, however, the Kommission für militärische Flugzeugbeschaffung (KMF) had turned down financing of the D-45 turbojet in its session of 15 July 1949 and the aircraft planned as a flying test-bed was not built. On its own initiative, therefore, Sulzer continued to develop accessories for the engine and carried out bench tests until 1955. Several larger versions of the D-45 were proposed, such as the D-70 of 1,800kp (4,960lb) thrust and the D-90 (DX) of 3,000kp (6,615lb) thrust, but Federal funds were not available for any more work. The government had expended SwFr3 million on the D-45 alone and more funds were spent by Sulzer. With abandonment of its turbojet programme, the company found that some of the experience gained could be utilized in its development of industrial gas turbines and so some good came from it.

Brown, Boveri & Cie

The Brown Boveri company's pioneering work, from 1905 to the late 1930s, in industrial gas turbines, blowers and axial compressors for wind tunnels has already been noted. As early as 1940 Brown Boveri & Cie (BBC) proposed the use of the gas turbine as an aircraft powerplant in the patent application (221,503) by Dr Claude Seippel. In the same year a proposal for a turboprop was patented (214,256) and, in 1944, a turboprop engine had been drawn up by Dr H. Pfenniger. This turboprop was planned to give 2,000eshp at 8,600rpm. It featured a long, eighteen-stage axial compressor with a low pressure ratio, the rotor blades being fitted to a drum-type rotor with conical ends to allow for expansion. This was followed by a relatively short combustion system (probably annular), a four-stage turbine and a fixed-area exhaust nozzle. The rotor was supported at three bearing points, the bearing aft of the turbines being cooled by air tapped from the centre of the compressor. The airscrew was to be driven at 1,200rpm via a planetary gearbox mounted in a hub at the centre of the annular air intake. The maximum diameter was 0.99m (3ft 3in) and the length (without airscrew) was 3.490m (11ft 5¼in). BBC's turboprop did not progress beyond the drawing stage. The company did not participate in the KTA competition for a powerplant for the new Swiss jet fighter (see above) and so did not work out any proposals for a turbo-jet.

On the experimental front, BBC built a small three-stage, high-speed axial compressor of an interesting design in which the rotor blade angles of attack could be varied between zero and 45 degrees while running. The company also designed a new two-stage LP compressor for the Swiss-Mamba SM-03 turbojet and designed a new three-stage turbine for the projected SM-05 turbojet. No other aeronautical gas turbine work by BBC in Switzerland is known, but the Mannheim branch of the company worked on a new compressor (the Hermso project) for BMW's 109-003D turbojet. There seems to be no question that BBC was quite capable of developing turbojets and turboprops, and the fact that it failed to become more than peripherally involved was due to its concentration on the equally important field of industrial gas turbines and processing systems.

Switzerland's first jet aircraft

At the end of the war, the Swiss Flugwaffe was operating ageing Messerschmitt Bf 109E fighters and a low-cost jet fighter was sought

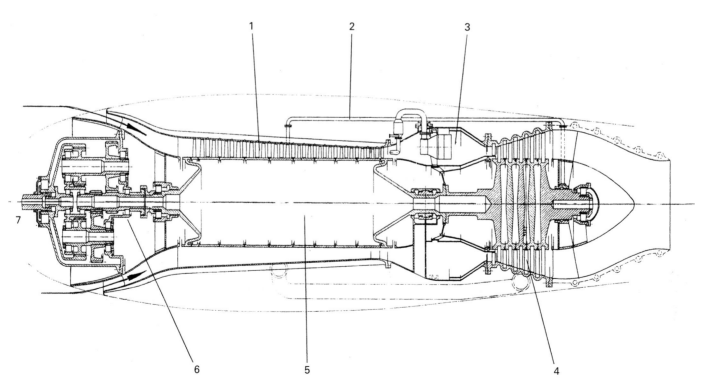

Projected 1944 Brown Boveri 2,000eshp turboprop: (1) eighteen-stage axial compressor; (2) pipe for cooling air to turbine bearing; (3) annular combustion chamber; (3) four-stage axial turbine; (5) drum-type rotor; (6) planetary reduction gears for airscrew shaft; (7) airscrew shaft.

as a replacement. The DH Vampire Mk 6 was found to be ideal, as it was in so many countries, and was ordered in 1948: seventy-five were built in England and a further hundred were built in Switzerland by a consortium of EFW, Pilatus and Doflug. During 1952 the DH Venom was chosen as a successor to the Vampire. The Venoms were built under licence by a consortium of EFW at Emmen, Flug- und Fahrzeugwerke (FFA) at Altenrhein and Pilatus at Stans: 100 were built as Venom FB. Mk 1s and 150 as Venom FB. Mk 4s. The DH Ghost 48 Mk 1 turbojet for the Venoms was built under licence as the Ghost 103 in Italy by Fiat, and in Switzerland by Sulzer in Winterthur and by Service Technique Militaire. These Venoms went on to serve as fighter bombers and as trainers at the Fliegerschule into the 1980s. Thus, British aircraft and engines took the Swiss into the jet age.

Even before the Vampires were ordered, however, the EFW at Emmen had begun studies for an indigenous jet fighter, particularly tailored to the country's needs. The design requirements arrived at were the attainment of a critical Mach number of 0.90, a good climb rate (2 minutes from 1,000m to 10,000m) and a high combat ceiling of 15,000m (49,000ft). Because of the mountainous nature of the country, the take-off and landing was to be made in a fraction of the length of the available runways: instead of the then-usual 900m (2,950ft), take-off was to be made within 200m (660ft) and landing within 250m (820ft). Flying characteristics were, above all, to include excellent manoeuvrability near the ground. The basic armament was to comprise two 20mm cannon and up to 800kg (1,764lb) of bombs for short-range missions.

In August 1952 the government placed development contracts with the EFW Emmen factory and with FFA at Altenrhein to build competing prototypes to fulfil the above specification. These two aircraft were designated the EFW N-20 and the FFA P-16. The former was to be powered by a Swiss-developed turbojet version of the Armstrong Siddeley (AS) Mamba turbo-prop (see below) and the latter by the AS Sapphire turbojet.

The EFW N-20, named the Aiguillon (Sting), was an all-wing single-seat interceptor and ground attack aircraft. Its wing was swept back on the leading edges in two stages and was thick enough to accommodate four Swiss-Mamba SM-01 turbojets,

each of 635kp (1,400lb) static thrust. There was a single, swept-back, vertical surface and the air-conditioned cockpit, enclosed by a bubble canopy, was positioned well forward in the nose. In an emergency, the cockpit section was detached from the aircraft and had its own parachute, the pilot then baling out once the speed and altitude were low enough. Each Mamba engine, in addition to providing forward thrust, diverted some of the air from its low-pressure compressor to ducts either side of the engine. These ducts (built into the wings) could be used as afterburners to provide extra thrust for take-off or could provide cold air blown through slots in the wings to provide extra lift and reverse thrust during landing. The only other controls were large ailerons and a rudder. Armament for the N-20 was to be carried in a streamlined ventral container that was interchangeable.

Before building the N-20 prototype, two 60 per cent scale aircraft were constructed to carry out flight tests. The first was an all-wood glider with a retractable undercarriage and, in addition to the pilot, a cramped, glazed position for an observer in the centre of the fuselage where the engine would normally be. It was flown in 1950. The second model was powered by four very small Turboméca Piméné turbojets, each of 110kp (242lb) thrust, mounted above and below the wings, and first flew on 16 November 1951. After these test aircraft had satisfactorily tested the layout, the N-20.10 prototype was built and made some

test hops in April 1952. However, when it was found that the Swiss-Mamba turbojets gave insufficient thrust, a full flight was not attempted. Improved SM-03 engines were fitted to the N-20.11 prototype but performance was still inadequate; government sponsorship was cancelled and further development of this interesting aircraft was curtailed. The competition against the rival P-16 therefore vanished.

The competing P-16 aircraft, designed under the leadership of Dr Hans-Luzius Studer, was of a completely different concept and no doubt had a better chance of early development to operational status. Unlike its competitor, the P-16 was designed to be powered by a single AS Sapphire Sa.6 turbojet of 3,269kp (8,000lb) static thrust. It had a low-mounted, straight wing of low aspect ratio, fitted with leading edge and trailing edge flaps and permanently attached wingtip fuel tanks to supplement the fuselage tankage. A swept-back vertical fin had a long strake in front of it and supported the tailplane about halfway up. Air intakes flanked the fuselage just aft of the cockpit and there was a large airbrake either side of the rear fuselage. The single cockpit was enclosed by a bubble canopy and was provided with a Martin Baker ejector seat. All members of the tricycle undercarriage had twin wheels to aid operation from grass and there was a braking parachute to minimize the landing run. Armament comprised two 30mm cannon in the lower fuselage plus underwing bombs and rockets for ground support missions, and

EFW N-20 Aiguillon all-wing, single-seat interceptor. It was powered by four Swiss-Mamba SM-01 turbojets. In addition, secondary air from these engines supplied extra combustion chambers in the wings and also cold air through slots in the wings for extra lift and reverse thrust during landing. Philip Jarrett

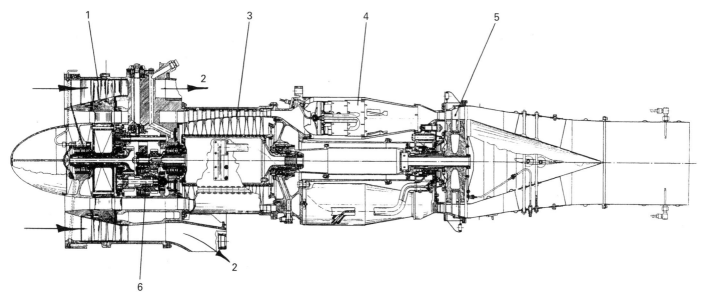

EFW Swiss-Mamba SM-01 bypass turbojet: (1) two-stage LP axial compressor; (2) LP air to secondary combustion chambers and cold-air wing slots; (3) ten-stage HP axial compressor; (4) six combustion chambers; (5) two-stage turbine; (6) reduction gears for LP compressor.

EFW N-20.10 Aiguillon		
Span	12.6m	(41ft 4in)
Length	12.5m	(41ft)
Wing area	54sq m	(581sq ft)
Height	3.13m	(10ft 3¼in)
Empty weight	6,550kg	(14,440lb)
Loaded weight	9,000kg	(19,842lb)
Estimated maximum speed	1,000km/h	(621mph)
Estimated minimum speed	150km/h	(93mph)
Estimated service ceiling	11,000m	(36,080ft)
Estimated range	500km	(310 miles)

Generally improved performances were expected with the N-20.15 Aiguillon and the N-20.20 Harpon, the latter with two Sapphire engines.

a radar gunsight was fitted. In addition, vertical magazines of Matra rockets were fitted within the fuselage, behind the cockpit section, and these fired from below the fuselage.

The prototype P-16-01 (J-3001) was first flown on 25 April 1955 and soon exhibited the requisite short take-off and landing performance. Its overall flight characteristics, however, were found to be less than satisfactory when evaluated by Flugwaffe pilots between 28 February and 12 March 1956. Despite this the P-16 possessed many good features and so its development was persevered with, even though the prototype crashed into Lake Constance on 22 March 1956, following the fracture of a fuel line, the pilot ejecting to safety.

It was not until 16 June 1956 that the P-16-02 (J-3002) prototype could make its first flight; this aircraft went supersonic in a dive on 15 August 1956. The P-16-03 first flew on 4 April 1957 and had an improved performance thanks to the use of a more powerful engine, the Sapphire Sa.7 of 5,000kp (11,025lb) dry thrust, or 7,000kp (15,435lb) in afterburner mode. On the strength of the 03's performance, the government ordered 100 P-16 Mk IIIs in

The prototype FFA P-16-01 fighter bomber (J-3001), powered by an AS Sapphire turbojet, competed against the N-20. Both aircraft were designed to operate from airfields surrounded by mountains, but offered completely different solutions to the problem. Philip Jarrett

FFA P-16 fighter/bomber with Sapphire Sa.7 engine			
Span		11.0m	(36ft 1in)
Length		14.00m	(45ft 11in)
Wing area		27.0sq m	(290.5sq ft)
Height		7.0m	(22ft 11½in)
Empty weight		6,000kg	(13,230lb)
Take-off weight (fighter)		8,120kg	(17,905lb)
(ground support)		9,320kg	(20,550lb)
Minimum take-off roll	(fighter)	470m	(1,540ft)
Minimum landing roll	(using parachute)	550 m	(1,800ft)
Maximum speed at low level		Mach 1.2	
	Ceiling	16,000 m	(52,500ft)
	Range	800km	(497 miles)

March 1958, but this prototype also crashed into Lake Constance only a week later. This time the crash was caused by a failure in the hydraulically powered controls. Once again the pilot ejected to safety. Following this accident the government rescinded the order. Despite some redesign of the control system and, at FFA's expense, the construction of two more prototypes by March 1960, the government would not change its mind. This promising aircraft then faded into obscurity, despite the fact that the modified aircraft were tested using only one of the hydraulic systems or the manual system at a time and were found to be fully satisfactory.

This project was not a complete loss, however, since the design of the wing, including the wingtip tanks, was used in the famous Learjet designed under Dr Studer. This high-speed, twin-engined, executive jet aircraft was originally designed as the SAAC-23, but later designated the Lear Jet 23. A company was set up in 1960 by the industrialist William P. Lear and was known as the Swiss American Aviation Corporation (SAAC). It was to manufacture the Learjet at Altenrhein, beginning with two prototypes, but the venture eventually became an all-American one and the aircraft were built by the Lear Jet Corporation in Wichita, Kansas.

Swiss-Mamba turbojets

At a meeting of the KMF on 29 June 1948, the Federal Aircraft Works (EFW) proposed an alternative turbojet development for the N-20 fighter. This followed the withdrawal of government support for Sulzer's complex DZ-45 turbojet. EFW proposed that Armstrong Siddeley's Mamba turboprop engine be developed as a bypass turbojet. This idea was accepted and a series order was awarded.

The 1,135eshp Mamba 1 (AS Ma.1), already described in the British section, needed considerable modification to turn it into a turbojet and more work was needed to enable it to be slid on rollers into the wings of the N-20. This meant reducing the engine's diameter by rearranging the combustion chambers. The intake portion of the Mamba with airscrew drive gearbox was replaced with a two-stage low-pressure compressor and new reduction gearing, the latter being necessary (because of the high 15,000rpm speed of the engine) to prevent the low-pressure compressor blades becoming supersonic. The low-pressure compressor had a pressure ratio of 1.58:1.

Two Swiss Mamba turbojets were to be designed into each wing of the N-20 fighter, the engines and the wings, with internal ducts and flaps, forming an integrated system to provide not only thrust but extra lift and braking as well. The secondary airflow from the engines, kept separate from the primary flow, was fed into the wing ducts. This air was used to either support auxiliary combustion or was used as a cold airstream. In either case, the auxiliary hot or cold air could provide extra thrust from the wing trailing edge slots or could be diverted from forward-facing wing surface slots to provide extra lift during high-incidence approaches or a braking effect. Manipulation of the flow from the wings was made by the use of built-in flaps acting as valves in the ducts; diversion of the flow to the bottom slots of the wing increased

lift, while diversion to both top and bottom slots gave a braking effect. About half of each wing's trailing edge was taken up with the two engine exhaust nozzles flanked by auxiliary air/combustion exhaust slots. The forward-facing slots on the top and bottom of the wings were likewise spread across the inner half of each wing. Another benefit of ejecting hot gases and air from the wing trailing edges was that, because of the ejector effect, the external airflow on the wing was less likely to break away.

This secondary airflow and combustion system entailed some difficult development work, which was led by Ing. E. Munzinger. The main problem was caused by the fact that the secondary air flow was fast flowing but of low compression, and was therefore relatively cold. Its temperature had to be raised to 1,150°C for the combustion of large amounts of fuel. Initially, very long flame lengths resulted from the injection of fuel, but a solution was eventually found by developing vaporizing combustion chambers that vaporized aviation petrol in two stages by the use of radiation.

Although EFW was an aircraft plant, it carried out the development work at Emmen, aided by Armstrong Siddeley, and designed new parts: only the high-pressure compressor and turbines were taken over from the original Mamba turboprop design. Most new parts were manufactured by Maas, Bührle and Sauer, but assembly was carried out at the Emmen works.

During 1949 an original Mamba engine, without the new low-pressure compressor, was tested, but the manufacturer's quoted performance could not be obtained due to poor turbine efficiency. Consequently, thrust reductions had to be accepted. On 12 January 1950 the SM-01 (Swiss-Mamba 01 prototype) was first run on the EFW test stand and 600kp (1,323lb) of thrust was measured. Unfortunately, below 10,000rpm the engine could not be accelerated. Although the Emmen-built LP compressor slightly exceeded its design performance, the rest of the Mamba engine behind it did not develop the requisite power. Therefore, a considerable amount of power was needed to start the engine. Other problems included a reduction in thrust down to 500kp (1,103lb) once the engine was installed in the wing (due to intake and exhaust duct losses) and blade vibration in the LP compressor. Finally, after much work, the SM-01 completed a 50-hour run in September 1952 and delivered a maximum thrust of 750kp (1,655lb).

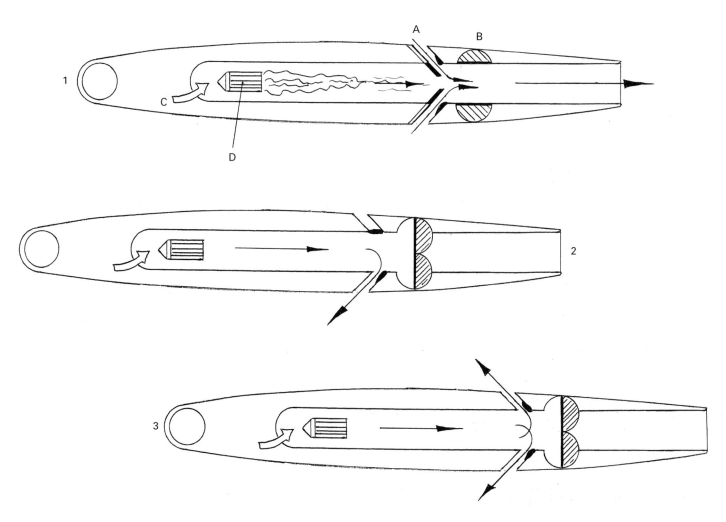

Schematic wing sections of the N-20 Aiguillon, showing the effects of the flow diversion system. In each of the eight secondary air side-flow channels in each wing are two hinged flaps plus sliding ramps (A) for the wing slots and two rotating flaps (B). The secondary air (C) is supplied by the low-pressure compressors of the Swiss-Mamba SM-01 turbojets. (D) is a secondary combustion chamber. The different modes of operation are:

(1) For normal flight, the rotating flaps and the hinged flaps are all closed. For extra thrust, secondary combustion is used with the injection of extra fuel to combustion chambers (D). During combustion, all flaps are open but small sliding ramps are moved to vary the exhaust nozzle area; extra air is drawn in through the wing slots. The hot gas efflux is from the wing trailing edge.

(2) For increased lift during high angle of attack landing approaches, both rotating flaps and the top hinged flap are closed and a cold air jet is directed downwards to augment lift.

(3) For braking by flow reversal of cold-air jets, both rotating flaps are closed and both hinged flaps are open.

Flight trials then began on 7 October 1952, using a DH Mosquito that had landed in Switzerland during the war and been impounded. The SM-01 was suspended beneath the Mosquito's fuselage and was flanked by aerodynamic fairings. Flight tests were made up to 8,000m (26,250ft) altitude without problems, these being the first flight tests with a two-circuit engine.

As already related, when the SM-01 engines were used in 1952 to power the N-20.10 prototype on its first test hops, they were shown to develop insufficient thrust. In the SM-03 engine, an improved low-pressure compressor, designed by BBC, was fitted and this engine was tested in 1952/3. Its performance, however, was still not sufficient to improve the N-20.11 prototype enough.

Other versions of the Swiss-Mamba were projected. The SM-04 had an LP compressor in which the secondary air and the primary air were to be compressed with a common blade arrangement. As before, the LP compressor was driven via reduction gearing. In the SM-05 there were to be contra-rotating turbines, designed by BBC, giving separate drives for each compressor. There was no reduction gearing for the LP compressor and so the blade tips would be supersonic. This and a new seven-stage HP axial compressor (replacing the previous ten-stage type) were designed by EFW. The SM-05 was also to have an annular combustion chamber instead of the previous six can-type combustors. The SM-05's maximum overload thrust was to be 1,660kp (3,660lb), its combustion chamber temperature being 1,000°C compared with the

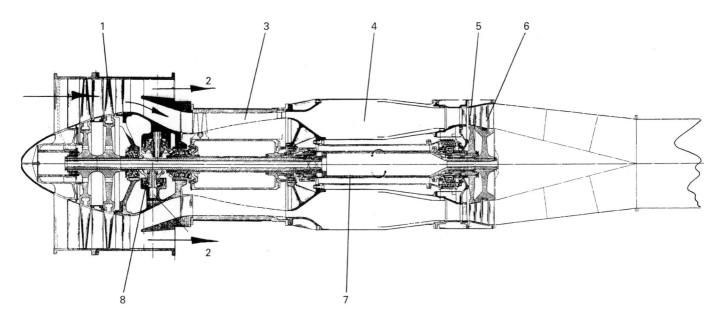

EFW SM-05 coaxial, bypass, axial turbojet: (1) two-stage axial LP compressor; (2) LP air to secondary combustion chambers and cold-air wing slots; (3) ten-stage axial HP compressor; (4) annular combustion chamber; (5) single-stage HP turbine; (6) two-stage LP turbine; (7) coaxial, hollow rotor shafts; (8) reduction gears for LP compressor.

800°C of previous engines. For the SM-06, the layout was to be similar to the SM-04 but without reduction gearing for the LP compressor, which would have been supersonic. All the Swiss-Mamba turbojet designs were of a similar size, their diameter being 0.65m (2ft 1½in), length 2.60m (8ft 6½in) and weight around 500kg (1,103lb).

The SM-05 design was eventually preferred, since the SM-04 and 06 designs had too many unknowns. Interestingly, the SM-05 coaxial engine corresponded roughly with the DZ-45 turbojet proposed by Sulzer in 1947. As we have seen, the compact coaxial turbojet was soon developed elsewhere, especially in Britain, the USA and the Soviet Union. On 14 March 1952 the government decided to stop all funding of indigenous turbojet development. Thus, development of the Mamba turbojet at EFW came to an end after the praiseworthy work carried out with scant resources and personnel.

With the cancellation of the FFA P-16, the Flugwaffe only had its ageing Vampires and was therefore facing a first-line fighter gap. It therefore began evaluating the fighters of other countries that were available from both East and West: these included the Dassault Mystère IVA, the Saab J-29, the S-102 (Czech-built MiG-15) and the Hawker Hunter F.6. In summer 1957, two Hunters were sent to Switzerland and subjected to the most rigorous of tests, especially regarding turning radius and combat manoeuvres needed for the narrow confines of Swiss valleys and terrain. The results of the tests were highly satisfactory and led to the Swiss government ordering 100 Hunters, designated the Mk 58, in January 1958.

CHAPTER THIRTY-TWO

Italy

Italy, fully industrialized and technically capable, was keen to promote itself in the field of aviation, as was shown by its regular participation and certain victories in the Schneider Cup air races in the years between 1913 and 1931. The speed records of the pilots de Bernardi and Agello and the altitude records of Donati and Pezzi are examples of the country's aeronautical progress. The country was, therefore, in a good position to develop the turbojet in the early years, but Italian engineers instead chose to pioneer a dead-end motor jet in which a piston engine carried out the work of air compression before an 'afterburner'. Following the Fascist dictator Benito Mussolini's disastrous decision to enter the war, even this development was more or less abandoned, but not before the great publicity of its motor jet flights had inspired similar developments in Germany, the USSR, the USA, Japan and other countries. The publicity given to these flights in 1940 was all the more sensational because wartime secrecy prevented announcements of Allied progress in the jet propulsion field until January 1944. Despite Italy's thriving aircraft industry, the country's contribution to jet propulsion was only meagre. Indeed, it did not even mass-produce the turbo-supercharger for its piston engines during the Second World War and was the only major belligerent not to do so.

The first Italian aircraft to fly with a ducted airscrew, although not of course a jet, was that of Antonio Mattioni of Savona, who had studied the ducted airscrew idea from 1910. His aircraft was powered by an 80hp Gnôme engine and had two crew members accommodated side-by-side in open cockpits beneath a large-diameter, hollow fuselage frame. It flew for the first time on 22 December 1923, piloted by Maj. Vasco Magrini at Campo di Marte in Florence. Between 1923 and 1931 Prof. Dott.-Ing. Gaetano Arturo Crocco published articles on the possibilities of flight at high altitudes and at speeds up to

supersonic, and also theoreticially about ramjets. Between 1927 and 1935 Crocco carried out secret experiments with both solid and liquid rockets.

Secondo Campini and Gianni Caproni

In the late 1920s Secondo Campini realized quite correctly that aircraft ought to be capable of much higher speeds and that the major obstacle to such speeds was the airscrew. By 1928 Campini had earned a civil engineering degree and he published studies on jet thrust in the journal *L'Aeronautica* in 1930. In the same year he also patented a jet system in which a ducted fan inside an annular fuselage was followed by the combustion of fuel to increase the thrust. The fan was to be of the multi-stage type and driven by a piston engine or a turbine engine.

In January 1931 Campini met with Count Dott.-Ing. Gianni Caproni, the founder and owner of Aeroplani Caproni, Italy's oldest aircraft company, and outlined his jet propulsion ideas to him. He also sent a paper to the Ministerio dell'Aeronautica detailing his ideas on a new powerplant and its promise of very high speeds and altitudes. Caproni must have been encouraging, because later in the year Campini formed the VENAR company, with a design office in Milan. Early in 1932 the VENAR hydrojet boat, built by the Costruzioni Meccaniche Riva company, was tested in the Venetian lagoon; this boat was propelled by two water jets flanking the hull above the water line, the pump being driven by an aero-engine, but its performance was about the same as a similarly powered boat with a conventional propeller. On the aeronautical side, Campini filed two jet aircraft patents, in January 1931 and July 1932.

The next aircraft to use the much simpler hollow fuselage concept was that designed by Dott.-Ing. Luigi Stipa. His aircraft, built

by the Caproni company at Taliedo airfield, Milan, was a two-seat monoplane in which the crew was accommodated in tandem in open cockpits above a barrel-like fuselage. Extremely ugly, the Stipa-Caproni was powered by a 120hp de Havilland Gipsy III engine and it made a number of successful flights from Linate and Guidonia in 1932, but was destroyed in a crash in 1933. In 1935 Stipa applied for a jet propulsion patent for an engine that appeared to be a cross between a pulsejet and a ramjet.

No doubt encouraged by Secundo Campini's propulsion concept, Gianni Caproni similarly applied for jet propulsion schemes of his own from September 1931, his French patent 767,816, for example, being applied for on 30 January 1934 and granted on 7 May 1934. This patent envisaged two schemes. In the first of these, a nose piston engine and airscrew (or a gas turbine) was flanked by an annular intake through which additional air was drawn in ahead of the wingroot leading edge and fed to the extended central exhaust nozzle aft of the main engine. The combined cold and hot flows then exhausted towards the fuselage tail within the large-diameter hollow fuselage duct to provide an additional reaction thrust. The second scheme provided for the combined efflux of gases to exhaust in the form of an annular ring over the surface of the fuselage just aft of the wing trailing edge. Neither of these schemes was put into practice by Caproni.

Campini jet system and the N.1

On 5 February 1934 the Regia Aeronautica (Royal Italian Air Force) signed a contract with VENAR and paid 4.5 million lire for the delivery of a test fuselage and two aircraft powered by the Campini jet system, for delivery by 31 December 1936. Considering that the design of the aircraft had only been roughly outlined at that stage, the delivery date was over-optimistic, but the gravest error lay in the decision to power the aircraft with a piston engine rather than develop a gas turbine for the purpose. This fateful decision was made in order to avoid the metallurgical research needed to develop such a turbine to drive the ducted fan. (In England, Frank Whittle had, unknown to Campini, already calculated that using a piston engine in a Campini-type jet system was not superior to a piston engine and airscrew combination, and that the piston engine was far too heavy. Consequently he rejected the idea.)

Campini's next move was to enlist the Aeroplani Caproni company to build the aircraft and the innovative Caproni was pleased to oblige. Therefore, in 1934 the

Centro Sperimentale Campini (Campini Experimental Centre) was formed within Caproni's Taliedo factory, on the east side of Milan, and work on the two aircraft, designated the N.1, began late that year. In May 1935 the Regia Aeronautica supplied an Isotta Fraschini Asso 750R aero-engine, which was then used for ground tests during 1936. By summer 1937 it was obvious that the project was going to overrun both the deadline and the budget, and so the delivery date was moved to December 1938 and more funds were provided. The new deadline and budget also proved to be optimistic, but Caproni supported the project with the company's technical and financial resources far exceeding his contractual remit.

While construction of the prototypes was proceeding, Campini busied himself with designing other projects: for example, on 17 December 1935 he patented in the USA a more ambitious design of an aircraft with two centrifugal compressors in series, driven by a radial engine, all followed by an 'afterburner'. The afterburner consisted of an annulus with venturii just before the throat of which the fuel burners were to be positioned. The exhaust nozzle had a central, movable cone for the purpose of altering the exit area. There was also a means of swivelling this exhaust cone in order to alter the direction of the exhaust, and Campini seems to have been the first person to have thought of jet deflection, an idea that did not come to fruition for

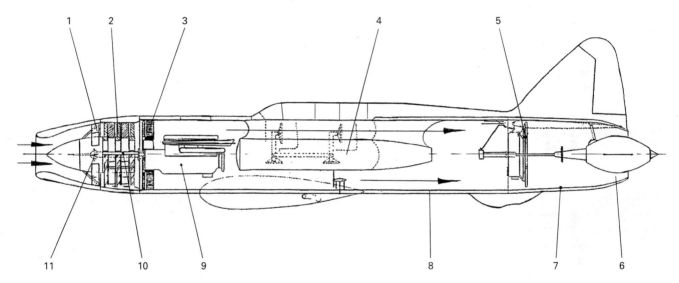

Schematic of the Campini-Caproni N.1 experimental motorjet-powered aircraft: (1) fixed inlet guide vanes; (2) three-stage fan, stator blades pitch variable in flight, rotor blades pitch variable on the ground; (3) annular radiator and coolant tank; (4) sealed well for pressurised cockpit (in air and exhaust flow); (5) vaporizing fuel and flame holder grid (see photo below); (6) variable-area exhaust nozzle with hydraulically movable bullet; (7) final inner section of fuselage with extra steel lining; (8) double-skinned fuselage wall (inner skin corrugated); (9) twelve-cylinder 900hp piston engine; (10) fan drive shaft; (11) hydraulics for stator blade pitch change.

With the tail unit and exhaust nozzle removed, this partially built Campini-Caproni N.1 experimental aircraft is undergoing a burner test.

another fifty years. This scheme envisaged a shoulder-mounted wing, a conical nose section for the crew of two and an annular air intake, surrounding which was a cylindrical casing that could be moved forward to enable dynamic compression to take place at transonic speeds. Campini had the expectation that this aircraft would be at least transonic, if not supersonic, even though the N.1 aircraft under construction had not been tested. However this may be, his design certainly envisaged advanced features such as jet deflection and the variable-geometry intake.

The two N.1 aircraft under construction at Taliedo were numbered 1 and 2 for Campini, 4849 and 4850 respectively for Caproni, and MM.487 and MM.488 respectively for the Regia Aeronautica. Each was of all-metal construction with a circular-section, parallel-sided fuselage that only tapered slightly at the extremities. The fuselage was double-skinned in aluminium alloy, the inner skin being corrugated and the outer skin smooth, circular formers and stringers supporting the skins. Four sections made up the fuselage and these were the air intake section, the fan and duct section, the central section with piston engine and pressurized cockpit and, finally, the tail

section with combustion chamber and exhaust nozzle with its movable bullet. To resist the heat of combustion, the final section was lined with steel. The low-mounted wing was built in one piece and had an elliptical planform and a thick, almost symmetrical, aerofoil section; two main spars were used and there were four-section trailing edge flaps. Large wing root fillets were used to meet the fuselage and the aircraft's fuel was contained in the wing.

Accommodation comprised two independent cockpits in tandem, with dual controls, each accessed by two removable, curved ladders. Individual rearward-sliding hoods were provided, the line of the hoods continuing back to a fairing that met the base of the rounded vertical fin. A similarly shaped, two-spar tailplane was mounted at the base of the vertical fin. An undercarriage of the tailwheel type was fully retractable and had air-operated brakes. Drawing air from the nose intake, a three-stage fan was preceded by fixed guide vanes and driven by the piston engine. The three stator stages of the fan, each with fifteen vanes, were pitch variable in flight, the hydraulic mechanism for this being housed in the large spinner inside the intake. The three rotor stages of the fan, each with

sixteen vanes, could have their pitch altered on the ground. Behind the fan there was a large annular radiator, at the centre of which was a semicircular coolant tank. At the point where the tailwheel was (and where the tail section could be removed) there was a circular grid supporting the fuel injectors and flameholders, making a crude form of afterburner. Heated air and gases were accelerated out of the exhaust nozzle, inside which was an hydraulically operated bullet, moved to vary the nozzle area. This bullet was supported by three streamlined struts.

During construction of the N.1 airframes, the designed empty weight of 1,200kg (2,646lb) had risen alarmingly by February 1940 to 3,500kg (7,718lb) and the aircraft finished up roughly twice as heavy as the first turbojet aircraft of Germany and Britain. Also, as requested by the Ministerio dell'Aeronautica, several design changes were made to the tail empennage during construction. In March 1940 two 900hp Isotta-Fraschini Asso L.121 RC40 V-12 piston engines were delivered to Taliedo for installation in the N.1 airframes and engine runs were begun on 28 June 1940. Initial tests showed that the three-stage fan absorbed about 700hp from the engine to produce a thrust of about 700kp (1,544lb)

LEFT: The large circular radiator used to cool the piston engine of the N.1 aircraft. In the centre is the semicircular coolant tank.
RIGHT: A view looking towards the tail, showing the exhaust nozzle bullet.

without burning extra fuel. Afterburner tests were made on the ground and, for these, the complete rear section of the fuselage was removed by crane to reveal the flameholder grid.

By July 1940 the completed aircraft, which had been built side-by-side, were ready for testing and Mario de Bernardi, a good friend of Caproni and the winner of the 1926 Schneider Cup, was nominated as the test pilot. Taxiing tests began with No.1 aircraft at Linate airfield, east of Milan, on 8 August 1940. During the second taxiing test, on 27 August 1940, Bernardi took off for a ten-minute flight at 7.35pm. This was Italy's first 'jet' aircraft flight, although the 'afterburner' was not lit, and was made exactly one year after Germany's Heinkel He 178 made the world's first turbojet aircraft flight. (Bernardi claimed that he had already flown the aircraft on 30 April 1940, but this date does not fit in with the sequence of events mentioned above.)

In any event, Bernardi's reminiscences of his first flight are of interest:

That afternoon, going as usual to the airfield to continue the aeroplane's ground testing, I unexpectedly found there many people including Regia Aeronautica officers, well-known engineers and famous pilots. Rumours thrived and everyone wanted information. I confess that at first I was taken aback, but perhaps it was just the gazing crowd that stung my pride. I climbed aboard and throttled the engine; the aeroplane moved (and certainly not one of the onlookers believed that heavy machine with its high-pitched whine could lift itself off the ground, while I was certain of it). I slowly increased the speed. I was careful to keep the aircraft under control by moving the stick ever so gently. I felt it lighten, but the trees around the field's perimeter rushed towards me with what I saw as undue haste. I admit my heart was thumping loud. Finally, the aircraft came unstuck, cleared the tree tops and climbed away. The dream of us all – designers, builders, workers who tracked me anxiously – had come true.

What Bernardi does not mention at that time was the fact that the badly under-powered aircraft had an initial climb rate of only 42m (138ft) per minute, and so whether or not it was going to clear the trees after take-off must have been a serious concern.

Due to a tendency for the N.1 to dive, the tailplane incidence was decreased before the first official contract flight on 16 September 1940. After Bernardi broke a heel in a fall, flight testing could not recommence until 11 April 1941, just over one month before the maiden flight of Britain's first turbojet aircaft, the Gloster E.28/39. Finally, on 5 May 1941, the N.1 made its first take-off with the afterburner on, but the piston engine suffered from backfiring and vibration and had to be replaced that summer. On 7 July 1941 the N.1's seventh flight was made, of one hour's duration, during which the afterburner was lit for fifteen minutes and performed satisfactorily. Comparing the dates of these first flights is of some historical interest, but the N.1 could in no way be compared technically to the E.28/39 or even the He 178.

Unfortunately the replacement engine also gave trouble and had to be removed for a complete overhaul. Once this was done, Bernardi was permitted to carry the world's first jet aircraft passengers, beginning with engineer Pedace on 5 November 1941 in a one-hour flight. This was followed on 30 November 1941 by a delivery flight from Linate to Guidonia (with a bad-weather diversion, without landing, to Pisa), this being made at an average speed of 217km/h (135mph) over 475km (295 miles). This flight became the first official FAI record for a jet aircraft and was made the subject of worldwide publicity.

Guidonia airfield, east of Rome, was the location of the main aeronautical experimental establishment in Italy, equivalent to Farnborough or Wright Field. Its facilities included six wind tunnels (one small, supersonic type), laboratories, workshops and a seaplane and torpedo testing gallery. The testing and examination of captured Allied aircraft was carried out at Guidonia. The head of this test centre, Col Torre, described Campini as a keen academic engineer having little practical experience. However, the establishment made only a few flights of the first N.1 aircraft, enough to establish its poor performance.

On the other hand, a great furore was made about the aircraft in the Italian press and thorough photographic coverage was spread around the world after the aircraft was paraded at ceremonies and before foreign visitors. In particular, the flight from Milan to Guidonia (passing over Rome at the request of the enthusiastic 'Il Duce') created a sensation on 30 November 1941, but the aircraft consumed 675 ltr (149 gal) of its 800 ltr (176 gal) fuel load to cover some 525km (326 miles). The only accident with the first N.1 was on 9 April 1942 when Bernardi was obliged to land on only one of the main wheels, following the partial retraction of the right side one. Thanks to his skill, damage was minimized and the aircraft was back in the air by 10 June 1942. Little did the world realize that this aircraft was a failure, although many were aware by 1943 that Campini's motor jet had no hope of competing with the turbojet engine. The N.1 was too inefficient and had too much drag and too little thrust to give a worthwhile performance.

As for the second N.1 prototype (MM.488), this was used for static tests and not rolled out of the Taliedo workshop until 1941. It was used for ground tests and only one contract flight, on 31 August 1941, was made. Thus it survived the war in good condition and finished up in Rome's Vigna di Valle museum. A different fate befell the first aircraft (MM.487), which was badly damaged at Guidonia as the Germans retreated. German forces, embittered when

This view of a completed N.1 illustrates the central bullet used to vary the exhaust nozzle area.

Underpowered and thirsty, the Campini-Caproni N.1 on its flight from Milan to Guidonia, during which de Bernardi flew the aircraft over Rome at the request of Benito Mussolini.

Italy signed the Armistice with the Allies and declared war on Germany in October 1943, destroyed everything at Guidonia that they did not take away. The small supersonic wind tunnel was one piece of equipment that was removed to Germany.

When the British came across the N.1 (MM.487) at Guidonia in June 1944 they found that the fuselage was damaged in a few places by shrapnel, all glazing was broken and the instrument panel was slightly damaged. The one-piece wing was separated from the fuselage, its skin cut open by looters over the wheel wells and the tyres removed. The nose section, containing the three-stage fan, was detached and its intake cowling was damaged by shrapnel. Although detached and in three sections, the tail empennage

was complete. Taken to RAE Farnborough in October 1944, the wreck of this historic aircraft was found to be so corroded that it was scrapped in 1949.

Other Campini designs

Campini had a number of other designs on the drawing board for aircraft using his jet system. In March 1939 he submitted to the Direzione Generale delle Costruzioni Aeronautiche (DGCA or Construction Directorate) two three-engined, high-altitude bomber designs, the CS.3 and CS.4, followed in 1940 by his CS.5 and CS.6 jet helicopter designs, but, in view of the fact that the N.1 prototypes had not yet flown, he did not receive a favourable response.

Undeterred, in February 1942, he submitted further proposals to the DGCA for three single-seat variants of a twin-jet fighter (with different cockpit locations), which each resembled the Gloster Meteor in overall layout. However, the similarity was superficial only because his fighter was planned to have a piston engine in the fuselage driving wing-mounted compressors in nacelles having afterburners. Campini also proposed two similar aircraft tailored for the bombing role. Examining these bomber designs, the Air Ministry concluded that an equal or better performance could be realized by a conventional bomber such as the Breda BZ 301 or CANT Z.1018, and suggested that Campini contact these companies to see if the performance of their aircraft could be improved with Campini powerplant.

In 1942, when contracts had been awarded for two single-crew, jet-propelled miniature submarines of Campini design (to be built at Riva del Garda for the Navy), the DGCA placed an order for the construction of two examples of Campini's 'No.2 Turbine', which was in fact a turbo-prop engine. This turboprop was aimed at 3,500shp and was to have an eight-stage centrifugal compressor with intercooling for the last two stages, can-type combustors and a nine-stage centrifugal turbine, the first three stages of which drove the compressor. The airscrews were to be driven at 1,400rpm via reduction gearing from the final six turbine stages. By the date of the Armistice in September 1943, only a few components of this engine had been built and, following the disappointing performance of Campini's N.1 jet aircraft, the authorities had little faith in his expectations for the turboprop.

Also in 1942, the Air Ministry carried out independent studies to convert the standard Reggiane Re.2005 Sagittario, Italy's finest fighter of the war, into a high-performance, mixed-power variant. In addition to the normal nose-mounted piston engine, the fighter was to have an auxiliary Fiat A.20 engine housed in a widened rear fuselage and exhausting beneath the tail surfaces. The A.20 engine was to drive two centrifugal superchargers, one to supercharge the nose engine and the other to supply compressed air to a combustion chamber and exhaust nozzle in the tail. Weight and performance calculations were made for two distinct variants, one designated the Re.2005 R (for Reazione) and the other the Re.2005 SF (named after the project officers, Majors

Campini-Caproni N.1 experimental aircraft			
Span		14.63m	(48ft)
Fuselage length	with bullet in normal	11.824m	(38ft 9½in)
	protruding position	12.664m	(41ft 6½in)
Wing area		36.0sq m	(387.36sq ft)
Height		4.70m	(15ft 5in)
Empty weight		3,640kg	(8,026lb)
Take-off weight		4,409kg	(9,722lb)
Take-off run		800m	(2,624ft) with burners off
Climbing time	to 4,000m (13,120ft)	53 minutes	
Maximum speed	at 3,000m (9,840ft)	325km/h	(202mph) without combustion
		375km/h	(233mph) with combustion
Cruising speed	(Milan to Rome)	217km/h	(135mph)
Range		600km	(373 miles)

Sarracino and Ferri). The Re.2005 R's maximum speed was estimated at 730km/h (454mph); although it reached the final drawing board stage in July 1943, it was never completed.

Another mixed-power fighter should also be mentioned. This was the Caproni Ca 183bis, which was to be powered by a Daimler-Benz DB605 engine driving contra-rotating airscrews in the fuselage nose ahead of the cockpit and supplemented by a Fiat A.30 motor in the rear fuselage driving three centrifugal blowers, one to supercharge the front DB 605 engine and two to supply compressed air to a two-stage Campini-type compressor fan in the rear fuselage duct for the jet propulsion unit with an afterburner. This was to be a high-altitude fighter having a ceiling of perhaps 18,000m (59,000ft) and a prototype was under construction in 1943 but never completed.

Post-war developments

With the end of the war in Europe in May 1945, Campini re-established his design office in Milan and still had the loyal support of Caproni. Among his work was a design for an industrial gas turbine. In 1950 the Aeroplani Caproni organization went bankrupt and this also ended Campini's work. The Caproni organization, however, had comprised many companies and one of the few survivors was Aeroplane Caproni Trento at Gardolo, Trento. This company was mainly an aircraft repair and maintenance concern but in 1951, under the design leadership of Dott.-Ing. Stelio Frati, it built Italy's first post-war light-weight jet aircraft. This took the form of the Caproni Trento F-5, a low-wing, all-wood, tandem two-seat trainer and touring aircraft with dual controls. It was powered by two 150kp (331lb) thrust Turboméca Palas turbojets, with air intakes above the wings at the wingroots and exhausting below the rear fuselage, and had a retrac-table, tricycle undercarriage. Flown for the first time on 20 May 1952, the F-5 weighed only 750kg (1,655lb) at take-off, had a wing span of 7.85m (25ft 9in) and a maximum speed at sea level of 360km/h (224mph). Unfortunately it failed to save Caproni.

After the Allied post-war restrictions on a resurgence of military aviation in Italy were lifted, an early example of the country's post-war jet aircraft was the Fiat G.80 two-seat jet trainer, which first flew on 9 December 1951. This was powered by a

3,500lb thrust de Havilland Goblin turbojet and was followed by two production prototypes, each of which was powered by a 5,000lb thrust R-R Nene. Soon Fiat was building the de Havilland Ghost engine under licence (as the Ghost 48 Mk 1) and had a maintenance contract for the Allison J35 turbojet powering NATO Republic F-84G Thunderjet fighters. This experience doubtless encouraged the Fiat SpA, Divisione Aviazione, in Turin to embark on a number of turbojets of its own design.

The first of these to be built was the Fiat 4002, which was an attempt to develop a simple, cheap and easily maintained turbojet suitable for use in military trainers, targets and missiles. It had a single-sided centrifugal compressor, a reverse-flow annular combustion chamber with twelve fuel injectors and a single-stage turbine. The compressor gave an air mass flow of 6.3kg/sec (13.89lb/sec) at a pressure ratio of 4.0:1. Bench testing of this engine commenced early in 1955 but it is not known to have flown. Its static thrust was 250kp (551lb) at 25,000rpm with a specific fuel consumption of 1.25 and a weight of 88kg (194lb). The diameter was 0.572m (1ft 10½in) and length 1.030m (3ft 4½in). A turboshaft derivative of the 4002 for helicopter use was also planned.

Fiat also projected two more-powerful turbojets of the axial type. The Fiat 4032, designed for a static thrust of 3,000kp (6,614lb), had a nine-stage axial compressor, an annular combustion chamber and a single-stage turbine. The smaller Fiat 4033 was designed for a static thrust of 1,000kp (2,205lb) at 12,700rpm.

Meanwhile, at the Ambrosini company, the designer Sergio Stefanutti was working on designs for swept-wing jet aircraft. Initial data was obtained by fitting 45-degree swept-back wings to an otherwise standard piston-engined Ambrosini S.7 trainer, this experimental aircraft being dubbed the Freccia (Arrow). Stefanutti then designed

the Sagittario (Archer) for research into transonic compressibility: this swept-wing aircraft was built largely of wood and was powered by a 400kp (882lb) thrust Turboméca Marboré turbojet exhausting below the fuselage. It had a low-mounted wing, swept flying surfaces, a nose intake and a tricycle undercarriage. The Sagittario flew for the first time on 5 January 1953 and provided information useful in the design of the Sagittario II, which was an all-metal, swept-wing aircraft powered by a R-R Derwent of 1,633kp (3,600lb) thrust. First flown on 19 May 1956, the Sagittario II became the first supersonic Italian aircraft when it attained Mach 1.1 in a dive on 4 December 1956.

The next development stage was the Aerfer Ariete (Battering Ram), which was generally similar in appearance to the Sagittario II but was built by the Industrie Aeronautiche Meridionali-Aerfer as a mixed-power research aircraft. This was to be the final step before the projected Leone (Lion) mixed-power light interceptor, which was financed by the US government. The Ariete was powered by a Derwent turbojet, exhausting beneath the centre fuselage, and, for boosting, a 821kp (1,810lb) R-R Soar R.Sr 2 auxiliary turbojet mounted in the tail. The Derwent was fed from a nose intake and the Soar from a retractable dorsal intake. The Ariete prototype (MM 568) made its first flight on 27 March 1958, but in due course this research project was terminated.

The first really successful Italian jet aircraft was the Fiat G.91 light fighter and tactical support aircraft, modelled on the overall design of the North American F-86 Sabre fighter and first flown on 9 August 1956. It was powered by a Bristol Orpheus turbojet and won a NATO order against stiff competition. It went on to obtain orders both at home and abroad and equipped the air forces of Italy, West Germany and Portugal.

Ambrosini Sagittario II		
Span	7.50m	(24ft 7¼in)
Length	8.50m	(31ft 2in)
Wing area	14.73sq m	(158.56sq ft)
Height	2.02m	(6ft 7½in)
Maximum take-off weight	3,293kg	(7,260lb)
Maximum speed	1,006km/h	(625mph)
Service ceiling	14,000m	(45,930ft)

CHAPTER THIRTY-THREE

Czechoslovakia

Following the collapse of the Habsburg empire towards the end of the First World War, the Czechoslovak Republic was declared in Prague on 28 October 1918 and confirmed by the Treaty of Saint-Germain-en-Laye on 10 September 1919. During the 1930s the country began the process of building up respected, indigenous industries, the products of which included cars, aircraft, aero-engines, armaments and other equipment. Prominent in these industries was the Skoda works in Pilsen, which became the main supplier of arms to the Soviet Union from 1936. A high proportion of the country's population consisted of ethnic Germans, so-called 'Sudeten' Germans, and this gave Hitler a pretext to march his troops into the Sudetenland on 1 October 1938 and exert control over the rest of the country, with Slovakia seceding from the former joint republic in March 1939.

Once occupied by German forces, the widespread aviation industry in the 'Reich Protectorate of Bohemia and Moravia' came under the control of the RLM (German Air Ministry) in Berlin. Indigenous aircraft, aero-engines and associated equipment that were wanted by Germany continued in production but, increasingly, Czech factories were obliged to manufacture German products. Led by eight major aircraft companies and other engine companies, Czech industry was capable of manufacturing all German aircraft types and the main aero-engines.

By 1944, when Allied bombing and strafing of Germany had made manufacturing increasingly difficult, the production of the latest jet aircraft and engines began dispersal to safer locations in the Protectorate. The first step in this process was the production of forward fuselage sections and other parts for the Messerschmitt Me 262A fighter at the Avia plant in Letnany and parts for its Junkers 109-004 B turbojets at CKD in Prague. The first Luftwaffe units then moved with their

Me 262s on 13 November 1944 to Ruzyne and Kbely airports outside Prague. At these airports, construction of long concrete runways, ideal for the jets, and well-equipped maintenance and servicing facilities had been commenced before the war. Luftwaffe units based in the Protectorate were directed to attack the Allied bomber streams flying over the Reich.

At the end of the war, there was a total of at least 110 Me 262s, and possibly as many as 130, located on bases in Prague-Ruzyne and Kbely, Pilsen, Latec, Cheb, Písek and Ceské Budéjovice, but massive attacks by USAAF P-47 Thunderbolt and P-51 Mustang fighters devastated the jets on the airfields at Ruzyne, Kbely, Letnany and Cakovice. In one account, on a single day, around 100 aircraft, comprising Ju 88s, Fw 200s and Me 262s, were parked at Ruzyne airport. In the chaos that existed, there was no more J2 fuel for the jets at Cheb, Kbely and Zatec on 22 April 1945 and only a miniscule amount at Ruzyne. More J2 fuel was transported from Germany from 24 April and some was eventually available at Ruzyne and Zatec. As many as fifty Me 262s were stationed at Ruzyne by 4 May 1945, but many were destroyed by Soviet artillery. However, the episode had a sequel in that this experience with the Me 262 was instrumental in launching the country into the jet age.

Of the 100 or more Me 262s that were based in Czechoslovakia by May 1945, a small number were flown back by their pilots to Germany in the closing days of the war. Several of the remainder, mainly those aircraft stationed outside Prague and elsewhere, were damaged by artillery shells fired by units of the Russian Vlasov Army. This army had fought on the side of the Nazis in the hope of liberating the country from Stalinist terror, but when it became apparent that Germany had all but lost the war the Vlasov Army changed its allegiance on 5 May 1945 and declared for the Allied

cause in the hope of avoiding later Soviet reprisals.

S-92 and CS-92

What remained of the Me 262 airframes and engines at the end of the war appeared sufficient to assemble some eighteen aircraft at the former Avia plant in Cakovice. Testing of the Junkers 109-004B turbojets and the Rheinmetall-Borsig RI-502 solid-fuelled RATO units was conducted at Podmokly, where a turbojet test stand had been erected. The first post-war Czech-built Me 262, designated the S-92 (S for Stíhac or fighter), was completed in 1945 but examples of the 109-004B-1 turbojets, built at the former Praga plant at Karlín, only became available for installation in June 1946. Prior to the first flight of the S-92.1 Turbina (Turbine) prototype, numerous problems were experienced. One of these was the lack of J2 fuel, since existing stocks were rather low and its German production at Leuna and elsewhere had ceased with the capitulation. The Czech LRX equivalent of J2 was intended to be useable at a temperature as low as −20°C but was found to freeze at only −8°C. This made it useless for winter operations but it was later made suitable for use by the addition of substitutes.

Another problem was that there were no maintenance or flight manuals and no operating instructions for the turbojet either. Also, no Czech pilots had any flight experience with jet aircraft. The experienced Avia test pilot Antonín Krauss therefore volunteered to fly the S-92.1 and continued to flight-test subsequent prototypes (at least the next nine) until others were ready to take over. Meanwhile, the 109-004B-1 turbojet was modified and put into production at Malesice as the M-04, the first example commencing test-bed runs on 5 March 1946. By 9 April 1946 the first M-04 was ready for installation in the S-92. Detail differences between Czech-built turbojets and the German originals are unknown, other than that the fuel system was altered to suit Czech-produced fuel.

The S-92.1 prototype first flew on 27 August 1946, piloted by Krauss, and this was followed by the first flights of a second prototype on 24 October and a two-seat trainer on 10 December. Only one S-92 was completed and flown in 1947, probably because of the political upheaval that existed in the country that year. All of the East European countries that came within the Soviet sphere of control were being increasingly put under pressure, on the direct orders of Joseph Stalin, to install 'Soviet-friendly' governments. However, during 1948 and 1949, further examples of S-92s were rolled out, complete with Czech-built 30mm MK 108 cannon and FuG 16ZY and FuG 25A radio equipment.

It was fortunate that Antonín Krauss was such a skilful pilot since there were a number of mishaps with the aircraft that he tested. On the sixth flight with the S-92.1 prototype on 5 September 1946, a speed of 960km/h (596mph) was attained in a dive from 4,000m (13,120ft), but, following an engine flameout, Krauss had to make an emergency landing at 230km/h (143mph) and the aircraft was written off. On 24 October 1946 the S-92.2 second prototype also suffered a flameout but Krauss made a safe landing. During a flight of the first two-seater, the S-92.3, Krauss was again the pilot, together with V. Svoboda in the rear seat, when the port engine failed due to the LRX fuel blocking the feed lines. Despite losing all hydraulic power, he executed a safe landing. Early in 1949 Krauss took the third two-seater, the CS-92.7, up on a test flight but once again had to make an emergency landing following an engine flameout. This aircraft had been re-engined by Avia with two M-03 turbojets (Czech-built BMW 109-003As), but the plan to use these engines was scrapped following this accident. It had been hoped that the normal thrust of the BMW 109-003A could be increased from 800kp (1,764lb) to 900kp (1,984lb), and even 930kp (2,050lb) in the M-03.

Visually, there were no external differences between the S-92 and the Me 262A-1. However, the appearance of the two-seat CS-92 differed from that of its Me 262B-1

counterpart in that the four transparent panels of the hood were made flat from the fixed front windscreen to the rear cockpit fairing, thereby interrupting the smooth curve used on the German original. CS-92s also had their gun ports faired over. The summer of 1950 saw S-92 aircraft being delivered to the 5th Fighter Squadron (5 stíhachi letka) of the Czechoslovak Air Force. Five S-92s and one CS-92 took part in the flypast on 9 May 1951, the sixth anniversary of the entry of Soviet forces into Prague (the flypast planned on the previous May having been cancelled due to bad weather). The S-92s were not long in Czech service before being replaced by licence-built MiG-15s and all were scrapped, except for an S-92 and a CS-92 sent to the Military Museum at Prague-Kbely airport.

The only country that evinced interest in buying S-92s from Czechoslovakia was Yugoslavia, which was already a customer for aircraft in the immediate post-war years. On 23 May 1947 a delegation of Yugoslav Air Force officials witnessed a demonstration of the S-92.2 and the two-seat CS-92.3. Maj. Jiří Manák piloted the CS-92.3, with Yugoslav Maj. Zelenika in the rear seat. Following this demonstration, Yugoslavia placed an order for two aircraft and six turbojets in 1947 and a number of Yugoslav personnel underwent ground and flight training until mid-1948. However, political events in Czechoslovakia delayed delivery and so, in 1951, Yugoslavia commenced the design of its first single-seat, twin-jet, experimental aircraft, the M-451M. The prototype of this machine first flew in 1952 and was powered by two Turboméca Palas turbojets. Another Yugoslav design was the swept-wing, single-seat M-452M built by Ikarus at Zemin, near

Belgrade. It too was powered by two Palas turbojets and was first flown on 24 July 1953. These aircraft were planned as lightweight ground-attack and high-speed liaison aircraft, but neither type went into production.

Letov L.52 fighter

In spring 1947 the Letov company at Letnany commenced work on a design of a jet fighter intended to be a more advanced replacement for the S-92 and to use components of the Me 262. Designated the L.52, the fighter had a pressurized cockpit and a compressed air-operated ejection seat (copied from that of the Heinkel He 219). This fighter was to have used the wings, tail empennage and undercarriage from the Me 262 and its armament was to consist of MG 151/20 or MK 108 cannon plus air-to-air rockets. However, the big difference was that this fighter was to be powered by a single Rolls-Royce Nene turbojet of 2,268kp (5,000lb) static thrust. A model of the L.52 was tested in a Soviet wind tunnel and strength tests on the wings were carried out. An order for two prototypes was placed and a two-seat trainer version was contemplated, but these and a further development, the L.152, never came to fruition.

Letov also had a project for a new airliner, the L.103, designed to carry thirty passengers and a crew of six. It was to be powered by two conventional piston engines, but a more interesting version was to be powered by two Bristol Theseus turboprops, which at the time were producing about 2,400shp. However, the L.103 did not go forward.

Letov L.52 fighter		
Span	12.50m	(41ft 0in)
Length	12.0m	(39ft 4½in)
Empty weight	3,314kg	(7,306lb)
Loaded weight	5,670kg	(12,500lb)
Estimated maximum speed	920km/h	(571mph)
Planned range	1,000km	(621 miles)

CHAPTER THIRTY-FOUR

Hungary

In Hungary, a technologically well-developed country, early efforts to produce an aeronautical gas turbine engine centred upon the work of Dipl.-Ing. György Jendrassik (1898–1954). He took his mechanical engineering degree at the Joseph Technical University in Budapest and was first employed in 1922 by the Danubius machine, wagon and ship works of the Ganz company (established 1844). Jendrassik worked to great effect in improving the diesel engine and the first Ganz-Jendrassik engines were built for locomotives in 1927. This work brought him worldwide fame and some 550 Ganz-Jendrassik locomotives were delivered all over the world, from Argentina to Egypt, before the Second World War.

Jendrassik's first experimental gas turbine installation

Jendrassik's interest in the gas turbine led, in 1938, to the company producing his design for the world's first low-output gas turbine installation with a separate combustion chamber. The eventual failure of Hans Holzwarth's explosion gas turbines was already known about (initially these had seemed highly promising, but the cooling and ventilation losses for the turbine wheel were so great that there was practically no balance of useful work left). Jendrassik's gas turbine was of the constant-pressure, not explosion, type but was also intended, like Holzwarth's, for industrial use. It was constructed by K. Arpay with the financial assistance of the Royal Hungarian Ministry for Industrial Affairs and developed about 100hp at 16,400rpm.

The compressor was a ten-stage axial type and was connected to two large, vertical air ducts, one to draw in air for compression and the other to deliver it to a large, box-shaped heat exchanger. Driving the compressor was a seven-stage axial turbine that received hot gases from an oil-burning, cylindrical, vertical combustion chamber and exhausted into the heat exchanger to heat the air from the compressor. The turbine blades were made from heat-resisting steel and the compressor blades were of aluminium alloy. Starting was by means of an electric motor and accessories, driven via a worm gear from the compressor rotor, included a speed governor, a Bosch fuel pump and a lubrication pump. Ignition was by means of a spark igniter positioned near to the fuel final injection nozzle, and a water brake was used to measure the power developed.

On 7 January 1939 the Royal Hungarian Institute for Technology and Material Evaluation conducted measurements on Jendrassik's experimental gas turbine installation and found the following values: the power was 98.5hp at a speed of 16,400rpm, with a fuel consumption of 28.5kg/h (62.84lb/h) and an overall efficiency of 21.2 per cent. The compression ratio was 2.183:1 and the temperature before the turbine was 475°C.

However, these unimpressive figures do not tell the whole story by any means, and Jendrassik claimed that much higher efficiencies could have been obtained for the following reasons. The large heat exchanger used metal sheets welded together, between which the hot gases passed in a contra-flow manner. Unfortunately, the welding method showed some deficiencies that were at the expense of a deterioration of the throughflow and, thereby, the efficiency. Further heat losses occurred due to poor insulation of the ducts and all these circumstances had an adverse effect on the overall efficiency of the installation. Despite this, the fact that the equipment worked at all was due to the excellent efficiencies of the compressor and turbine. Apparently the turbine efficiency was of the order of 84 to 85 per cent and that of the compressor 85 per cent, these being outstanding values for the time. Furthermore, lower than possible combustion temperatures were chosen in order to demonstrate usability of the installation at low temperatures, but it was thought that the then-current technology (some heat-resisting steels were available) would allow a temperature of 600°C at the turbine. Thus, at such a temperature and with all the defects corrected, it was considered that the gas turbine would rival other forms of powerplant.

Cs-1 turboprop

Much valuable experience was gained from this experiment, and the axial compressor and axial turbine had proved especially successful. It is assumed that the design of these had roots in steam turbine practice. Jendrassik's thoughts now turned to the possibility of an aeronautical gas turbine and work began in July 1939 on a project for a turboprop engine. Designated the Cs-1, this featured a fifteen-stage axial compressor, an annular reverse-flow combustion chamber, an eleven-stage axial turbine and a fixed-area exhaust nozzle. It was aimed at an initial rating of 1,000shp at 13,500rpm. Its rotor was mounted on only two bearings and there was an airscrew reduction gearbox mounted in front of the annular air intake.

Jendrassik's innovative method of keeping the temperature of the turbine blades within acceptable limits was to isolate them from their discs as far as possible and not rely on special heat-resisting metals. In order to provide an efficient turbine, blades of narrow profile were considered necessary and such blades had little room for cooling air holes of sufficient size. Therefore, he patented a design whereby the blades were connected to their discs by legs, contrived so as to isolate the blades sufficiently from their discs. It was then only necessary to air cool between the discs and, by this means, the

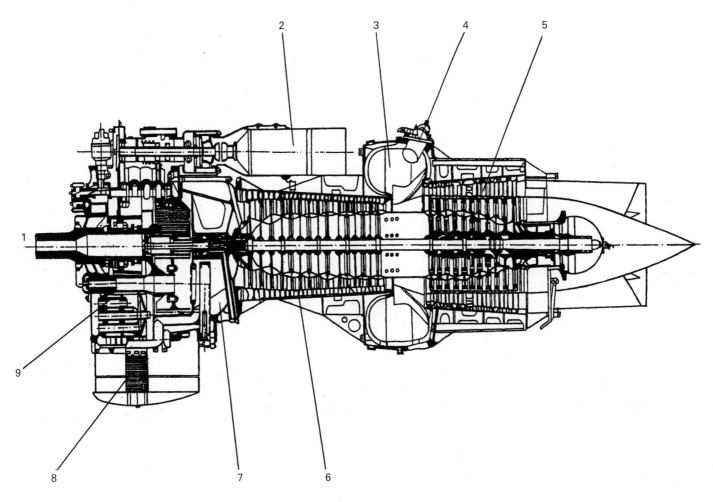

Jendrassik's Cs-1 axial turboprop: (1) airscrew shaft; (2) starter motor; (3) annular, reverse-flow combustion chamber; (4) six fuel injectors; (5) eleven-stage axial turbine; (6) fifteen-stage axial compressor; (7) annular air intake; (8) radiator; (9) airscrew reduction gears.

discs were kept at a temperature of about 100°C lower than that of the blades and the abstration of large quantities of air was avoided. Thus, the discs ran at a temperature of not more than 500°C and could be made of simple metal, while the blades were kept below 600°C and used heat-resisting metal.

RMI 1 (X/H) turboprop fighter-bomber

Such was the enthusiasm for the neat Cs-1 that, even before it was bench tested, the design of a fighter-bomber powered by a pair of the turboprops was begun. The design of this aircraft was headed by László Varga at the Repülö Müszaki Intézet (RMI or Technical Institute for Aviation) and the prototype was built at the Sóstó Repair Works. Designated the RMI 1 and the X/H,

this aircraft was a low-wing monoplane of all-metal, stressed skin monocoque construction, suitable for stresses up to the dive-bombing role, and it accommodated two or three crew. It had a fully glazed nose and a long, glazed, framed canopy over the cockpit. The wing had a rectangular centre section, supporting two Cs-1 turboprops below it and projecting slightly forward of the nose, and had tapered, dihedralled outer panels. There was a conventional tail empennage and a tailwheel undercarriage.

During 1940 bench tests of the Cs-1 engine began, but combustion problems, the stumbling block of so many pioneers, limited its power output to about 400shp. Unfortunately work on the engine was then halted because the decision was taken to manufacture the Daimler-Benz DB 605 piston engine and the Messerschmitt Me 210 fighter-bomber in Hungary. This followed on from the signing of the

German-Hungarian Mutual Armament Programme in June 1941. Sadly, what was probably the world's first turboprop, the Cs-1, never took to the air. It seems strange that the Germans apparently took no interest in the Cs-1 and did not encourage its further development.

As for the RMI 1, its airframe was completed with great difficulty in 1941 (the Hungarians being unfamiliar with metal monocoque construction at the time) and it was then stored at Sóstó pending the acquisition of engines of sufficient power. Taxiing trials began in September 1943, using two Jumo 210E engines. Then, in December 1943, the aircraft was taxied with Daimler-Benz DB 605B engines, but flight testing planned for June 1944 was delayed after the failure of an undercarriage leg. Around May 1944, however, the RMI 1 was destroyed in a USAAF bombing attack.

Two views of Jendrassik's Cs-1 turboprop of 1940, under restoration at the Közlekedési Múzeum in Budapest. It has the appearance of a solidly built, well-engineered machine, remarkable for the early days of the aeronautical gas turbine: TOP: view from the front, showing the annular air intake; BOTTOM: view from the rear with the exhaust nozzle removed. Three of the fuel injectors and the housing for the starter motor can be seen.

One of the turbine wheels from the Cs-1 turboprop. Dr Jendrassik devised a special way of attaching the blades to the wheel to combat heating.

RMI 1 fighter-bomber with Cs-1 turboprops			
Span		15.70m	(51ft 6in)
Length		12.56m	(41ft 2¼in)
Empty weight		4,500kg	(9,923lb)
Loaded weight		6,500kg	(14,333lb)
Estimated maximum speed	at 4,000m (13,100ft)	540km/h	(335mph)
No other details known			

Jendrassik, a great engineer and gas turbine pioneer, became the Chief Executive of the Ganz company in 1942. He settled in Argentina in 1947 and later moved to London. By the time of his death, in 1954, he had seventy-seven patents registered in Hungary and twenty other countries.

APPENDIX

Engine Data Tables

These tables are not exhaustive but, in 286 entries, they give representative examples of the turbojet, turboprop and turboshaft engines, more details of which are to be found in the text. Regarding the data, it is not always possible to be exact since an engine may be in a prototype or developmental stage, or else exact data is simply not available. Fuel consumption for turboprops is given as lb/eshp/hr, turboprop weights are without the airscrew and thrust is dry. Space precludes exact definitions.

ABBREVIATIONS

Headings

Comp.	compressor
Comb.	combustion chamber/s type
sfc	specific fuel consumption
eshp	equivalent shaft horsepower
L	length
D	diameter
Wt	weight

Tables

A	axial compressor
Ann	annular combustion chamber

BP	bypass turbojet
C	can-type or cannular combustion chamber/s
C	centrifugal compressor (single- or double-sided)
D	diagonal-flow compressor
D	duct
DF	ducted fan turbojet
F	fan
GP	gas producer
P	turboprop
T	turbojet
TF	turbofan
TS	turboshaft

Engine designation	Type	Comp.	Stages	Comb.	Turbine stages	Thrust or eshp	sfc	L	D	Wt.	Date	Remarks
						The Soviet Union						
Lyul'ka RD-1	T	A	6	C	1	525					1941	Insufficient backing
Lyul'ka S-18	T	A	8	Ann	1						1945	Development engine
Lyul'ka TR-1	T	A	8	Ann	1	1,300	1.27			840	1946	Small production
Lyul'ka TR-1A	T	A	8	Ann	1	1,600					1946	Small production
RD-20F	T	A	7	Ann	1	1,000					1946	Soviet BMW 109-003A
RD-10A	T	A	8	C	1	1,000					1946	Soviet Junkers 109-004B
Lyul'ka TR-3	T	A	7	Ann	1	4,600	1.1			1,900	1947	
Lyul'ka AL-5	T	A		Ann		5,000					1950	
Lyul'ka AL-7	T	A	9	Ann		6,500					1954	In production
Kuznyetsov												
NK-12	P	A	14	C	5	11,834	0.57	6	1.15	2,300	1955	Largest turboprop
NK-12M	P	A	14	C	5	15,000		6	1.15		1957	Largest turboprop
NK-4	P	A	6	C	3	4,000				1,050	1957	
AI-20	P	A	10	Ann	3	4,000					1956	Ivchyenko. In production
Lotarev D-36	TS	A				5,600						Three-shaft engine
RD-500	T	C	1	C	1	1,590	1.4	2.11	1.09	581	1947	Soviet R-R Derwent
RD-45	T	C	1	C	1	2,300	1.06	2.46	1.26	800	1947	Soviet R-R Nene
Klimov												
VK-1	T	C	1	C	1	2,700				900	1947	Nene based. Large numbers
VK-3	T	A+A	2+8			5,730					1952	2-shaft engine. Abandoned
VK-7	T	C	2	C		4,200					1952	Nene based. No production
Mikulin												
AMTKRD-01	T	A	8	A	1	3,300			1.365	1,720	1947	Experimental
AMTKRD-02	T	A	9	C	1	3,850		3.6	1.38	1,675	1949	Experimental
AM-3	T	A	8	A	2	6,750			1.4		1950	Major production as RD-3
AM-5	T	A				2,000		2.77	0.67	445	1953	No production
AM-9	T	A	9	A	2	2,150		5.56	0.66	700	1954	Production as RD-9

Engine designation	Type	Comp.	Stages	Comb.	Turbine stages	Thrust or eshp	sfc	L	D	Wt.	Date	Remarks
AM-11	T	A+A	3+5	A	2	4,000				1,040	1953	2-shaft. Production as R-11
Soloviev												
D-20P	BP	F+A	3+8	C	2+1	5,400				1,468		1st Soviet prod. Turbofan
D-25V	TS	A	9	C	1+2	5,500				1,325	1954	1st Soviet helicopter GT

The United States of America

Engine designation	Type	Comp.	Stages	Comb.	Turbine stages	Thrust or eshp	sfc	L	D	Wt.	Date	Remarks
Lockheed												
L-1000 (XJ35)	T	A+A	16+16	C	1+3	2,000?		3.73	0.635	735	1946	Experimental
XT 35	P	A+A	16+16	C	1+3						1946	Turboprop version of XJ 37
Northrop												
Turbodyne	P	A	18	Ann	3	3,800					1944	Experimental
XT37	P	A				10,000					1947	
General Electric												
Type I-A	T	C	1	C	1	590	1.1	1.79	1.12	354	1942	First US-built turbojet
I-14B	T	C	1	C	1	635					1943	Small production
I-16	T	C	1	C	1	647	1.23	1.83	1.05	365	1943	Small production, as J31
I-20	T	C	1	C	1	908	1.2	1.83	1.05	409	1944	
J33 (I-40)	T	C	1	C	1	1,816	1.19	2.62	1.22	839	1944	Large production by Allison
J35 (TG-180)	T	A	11	C	1	1,816	1.08	4.22	0.95	1,088	1944	Large production by Allison
T31 (TG-100)	P	A	14	C	1	1,380		2.92	0.89	885	1943	First US turboprop
T31 (TG-100B)	P	A	14	C	1	2,750		2.87	0.94	907	1946	Few made
J47 (TG-190)	T	A	12	C	1	2,200	0.9	3.91	1		1947	Prototype
J47-GE-15	T	A	12	C	1	2,358	1.03	3.66	1	1,145	1948	2,720 with water injection
J47-GE-17	T	A	12	C	1	2,449		5.74	1	1,480		Reheat version giving 3,400
J47-GE-25	T	A	12	C	1	2,720	1	3.66	1			3,265 with water injection
J47-GE-27	T	A	12	C	1	2,766	0.9	3.91	1			3,129 with water injection
XJ53	T	A	13	C	2	8,150				2,950	1951	Experimental. Too heavy
J73	T	A	12	C	2	3,550		3.74	0.94	1,655	1952	Only used by F-86H fighter
J79-GE-17	T	A	17	C	3	5,040	0.81	5.3	0.99	1,740	1959	Variable stators
CJ-805	T	A	17	C	3	5,290					1958	Civilian version of J79
CJ-805-23	DF	A+F	17+1	C	3+1	7,310					1960	Few built
X 104	T	A	6	Ann	2	1,135					1954	Decoy engine. Not built
J85-GE-21	T	A	9	Ann	2	1,590	0.99	2.94	0.51	310	1959	2,270kp with reheat
T58-GE-10	TS	A	10	Ann	1+2	1,500	0.61	1.49	0.51	156	1956	Many built
T64	TS	A	14	Ann	2+2	1,850					1959	Prototype
T64-GE-419	TS	A	14	Ann	2+2	4,230		2	0.83	342	1959	Also in turboprop version
Pratt & Whitney												
T34 (PT-2)	P	A	13	C	3	5,375		2	0.83	1,210	1949	
J42 T-Wasp	T	C	1	C	1	2,268	1.09	2.62	1.26	778	1948	Licence-built R-R Nene
J48 (JT-7)	T	C	1	C	1	2,838	1	2.71	1.27	908	1949	Licence-built R-R Tay
J57 (JT3)	T	A+A	9+7	C	3+2	4,150	0.82	6.78	1.03	2,195	1950	First US 2-spool turbojet
TF33 (JT3D)	TF	A+A	8+7	Ann	1+3	6,575	0.505	3.46	1.35	1,771	1958	Derived from J57
J75 (JT4)	T	A+A	9+7	C	3+2	6,490	0.77	6.59	1	2,698	1,960	2-spool engine
Allis-Chalmers												
J36	T	C	1	C	1	1,225					1946	US-built Goblin. Cancelled
Westinghouse												
19A Yankee	T	A	6	C	1	545					1943	First US-designed turbojet
J30 (19XB)	T	A	10	Ann	1	613	1.27	2.66	0.66	332	1944	
J34 (24C)	T	A	11	Ann	2	1,200	1.05	3.1	0.61	570	1945	In production
J40	T	A	10	Ann	2	2,724	2.2	7.62	1.02	1,587	1948	Cancelled

Engine designation	Type	Comp.	Stages	Comb.	Turbine stages	Thrust or eshp	sfc	L	D	Wt.	Date	Remarks
J46	T	A	10	Ann	2						1952	Cancelled
XJ54	T	A	16	Ann	2	2,815	0.85	3.6	0.89	680	1955	Based on Avon. No production
XJ81	T	A	8	Ann	2	790		1.06	0.508	138	1956	R-R Soar turbojet
Allison												
T38 (501)	P	A	19	C	4	2,250	0.63	2.13	0.51	556	1947	No production
T40 (500)	P	2xA	2x17	C	2x4	4,000	0.6	4.62	0.99	1,134	1948	Coupled T38A
T56	P	A	14	Ann	4	3,460	0.52	3.71	0.69	836	1953	In production
J71	T	A	16	Ann	3	3,670	0.88	4.86	1	1,855	1950	In production
Wright Aeronautical												
J65-W-20	T	A	13	Ann	2	3,356	0.93	2.87	1.02	1,268	1951	Americanized AS Sapphire
T49	P	A	13	Ann	4?	8,000					1952	Turboprop version of J65
J67	T	A+A	5+7	C	1+1	7,260		3.16	1.02		1956	Americanized BS Olympus
Avco Lycoming												
T53	TS	A+C	5+1	Ann	1+1	1,000	0.69	1.21	0.6	228	1955	Large production
T55	TS	A+C	7+1	Ann	2+2	2,500		1.12	0.62	263	1956	Large production
Boeing												
Model 502	P	C	1	C	2	160	1.5	1.19	0.69	64	1947	In production
Model 520	TS	C	1	C	1+1	550	0.65				1955	Turboprop version also
Fairchild												
J44	T	A+C	1+1	Ann	1	455	1.55		0.56	127	1948	Expendable engine
J83	T	A	7	Ann	2	1,112	0.94			165	1957	Decoy engine. Cancelled
Teledyne												
J69	T	A+C	1+1	Ann	1	870	1.1	1.14	0.57	159	1952	Drone engine
T51	P					130	1	1.38	0.59			Based on Artouste
Fladder												
J55	T	A	1	Ann	1	500	1.6	2	0.4			Supersonic compressor
Japan												
TR-12	T	A+C	4+1		1	300				350	1943	Abandoned
TR-12B	T	A+C	4+1		1	320		1.8	0.86	315	1944	Abandoned
Ne 130	T	A+C		C	1	900		3.85	0.85	900	1944	Based on Junkers 109-004B
Ne 230	T	A		Ann	1	885		3.43	0.76	870	1944	Based on BMW 109-003
Ne 330	T					1,300		4	0.88		1944	Maybe based on 109-011
Ne 20	T	A	8	Ann	1	475	1.5	2.7	0.62	470	1945	Powered Japan's first jet aircraft
Fuji Jo-1	T	A	8	C	1	1,000	1.01	2.8	0.68	450	1954	Based on Ne 20
Fuji Jo-3	T	A	8	Ann	1	1,200	1.08					Project
Fuji Ji-1	T	A	12	C	2	3,000						Project
IHI J3-7	T	A	8	Ann	1	1,400	1.05	2.0	0.62	430	1956	Booster for P-2J Neptune
France												
de Lavaud	T	C	1	Ann	1	100		1.127	0.265	50	1939?	Experimental
SNECMA												
TA 1000	P	A	10	C	2	5,800?				3,900	1947	Abandoned
TB 1000	P	A	9	C	2	1,500	0.68	2.75	0.7	480	1950	Abandoned
Atar 101 V1	T	A	7	Ann	1	1,680					1948	Based on BMW 109-003
Atar 101 B	T	A	7	Ann	1	2,400	1.1	2.84	0.906	850	1951	Development engine
Atar 101 B-2	T	A	7	Ann	1	2,395					1952	Developed version
Atar 101 C	T	A	7	Ann	1	2,800	1.05	3.68	0.89	940	1952	First production series

Engine designation	Type	Comp.	Stages	Comb.	Turbine stages	Thrust or eshp	sfc	L	D	Wt.	Date	Remarks
Atar 101 E	T	A	8	Ann	1	3,310		3.684	0.89	925	1955	Water-injection version
Atar 101 F	T	A	7	Ann	1	*3,800	2	5.23	0.89	1,090		*Thrust with reheat
Atar 101 G	T	A	8	Ann	1	4,200				1,240	1956	Reheat version of 101 E
Atar 8	T	A	9	Ann	2	4,400				1,100	1959	New generation
Atar 9B	T	A	9	Ann	2	4,400				1,350	1957	5,800kp in afterburner
R.104 Vulcain	T	A	7	Ann	1	4,500		3.235	1.16	1,525	1952	Prototypes only
R.105 Vesta	T	A	8	Ann	1	1,250	1.1			290	1954	Prototypes only
Avions Marcel Dassault												
MD 30 Viper	T	A	7	Ann	1	744	1.09	1.67	0.62	288	1953	Licence-built AS Viper
R.7 Farandole	T	A	7?	Ann	1	1,410				354	1956	Licence-built AS Viper 10
Société Rateau												
SRA-1 Idole	BP	F+A	4+12	C	2	1,000	1	2.05	1.12	1,040	1946	Prototypes only. Aka A.65
SRA 101	T	A	10	C	2	3,600	0.86	3.81	1.09	1,200	1950	Prototypes only. Aka Savoie
SRA 301 Berry	BP	F+A	4+12	C	4	4,500					1952	Project based on SRA 101
SOCEMA												
TGA 1	P	A	15	C	4	2,915	0.57	3.05	1.15	2,250	1945	Prototypes only
TGA 1 bis	P	A	15	C	4	2,350				2,100	1947	Prototypes only
TGAR 1008	T	A	8	Ann	1	2,200	1.18	2.8	1.03	1,250	1948	Prototypes only
TP.1	P	A	8	Ann	2?	3,200					1949	} Projects based on
TP.2	P	A	8	Ann	2?	3,750				1,540	1949	}TGAR 1008
Hispano-Suiza												
Nene 104	T	C	1	C	1	2,300	1	2.44	1.26	800	1947	Others made under licence
Tay 250A	T	C	1	C	1	2,835	1.06	2.53	1.27		1951	Licence-built R-R Tay
R.450 Verdon	T	C	1	C	1	3,500	1.1	2.62	1.27	935		Developed from R-R Nene
R.800	T	A	7	Ann	1	1,800			0.692	300	1954	Abandoned
R.804	T	A	7	Ann	1	1,500	1.09			308	1955	Prototypes only
ONERA												
ONERA 240	P	C	1	C	1	240					1947	Abandoned
Société Turboméca												
Piméné	T	C	1		1	110	1.05	0.8	0.4	54	1949	Large production
Palas	T	C	1		1	160	1.17			72	1950	
Marboré	T	C	1	Ann	1	300	1.1			130	1950	
Aspin I	TF	F+C	1+1	Ann	2	200	0.64			127	1949	First turbofan to fly
Gabizo	T	A+C	1+1	Ann	1	900				265	1954	No series production
Canada												
TR-4 Chinook	T	A	9	C	1	1,180	1	3.18	0.813	567	1948	Research engine
Orenda 1	T	A	10	C	1	2,720	1	3.351	1.14	1,225	1949	
Orenda 10	T	A	10	C	1	2,883	1.12	3.086	1.067	1,141		
Iroquois 2	T	A+A	3+7	Ann	1+2	10,430	0.85	5.89	1.07	2,110	1954	Twin-spool engine
Sweden												
P/15-54 (R201)	T	C	1	Ann	4	1,800	0.95		0.91	1,300	1944	
Ghost 50	T	C	1	C	1	2,268	1.07	3.43	1.35			Licence-built as RM2B
STAL												
Skuten	T	A	8	C	1	1,450					1947	Research engine for Dovern
Dovern IIA	T	A	9	C	1	3,300	0.92	3.85	1.1		1949	
Dovern IIB	T	A	9	C	1	3,300	0.92	3.85	1.1	1,200		With de-icing. Aka RM4
Dovern IIC	T	A	9	C	1	*4,626						*To have afterburner

Engine designation	Type	Comp.	Stages	Comb.	Turbine stages	Thrust or eshp	sfc	L	D	Wt.	Date	Remarks
Glan	T	A+A				5,000					1952	Two-spool engine

Switzerland

Engine designation	Type	Comp.	Stages	Comb.	Turbine stages	Thrust or eshp	sfc	L	D	Wt.	Date	Remarks
Escher, Wyss												
ZTL	T	A+A	4+?	2xAnn	1	3,200	0.77	4.5	1.4	2,400	1945	Projected 2-circuit engine
Sulzer												
DZ-45	T	A+A	2+7	Ann	1+1	1,054	0.82	2.1	0.66	450	1945	Projected coaxial, 2-circuit
D-45.01	T	A	9	C	1	752	1.05			263	1950	Prototype
Brown-Boveri												
Pfenniger	P	A	18	Ann?	4	2,000		3.49	0.99		1944	Project
EFW												
SM-01	BP	A+A	2+10	C	2	750		2.6	0.65	500	1950	Based on Mamba. Tested
SM-05	BP	A+A	2+10	Ann	1+1	1,660		2.6	0.65	500	1951	Coaxial engine. Project

Italy

Engine designation	Type	Comp.	Stages	Comb.	Turbine stages	Thrust or eshp	sfc	L	D	Wt.	Date	Remarks
Campini No.2	P	C	8	C	9	3,500					1943	Construction begun
Fiat												
4002	T	C	1	Ann	1	250	1.25	1.03	0.572	88	1955	Tested. For missiles etc.
4032	T	A	9	Ann	1	3,000						Project
4033	T					1,000						Project

Hungary

Engine designation	Type	Comp.	Stages	Comb.	Turbine stages	Thrust or eshp	sfc	L	D	Wt.	Date	Remarks
Jendrassik Cs1	P	A	15	Ann	11	400		2.31	0.775		1940	Earliest turboprop. Tested

Abbreviations
and Acronyms

AS	Armstrong Siddeley
AB	Aktiebolaget (Joint-stock Company Ltd)
AVA	Aerodynamische Versuchsanstalt, Göttingen
BBC	Brown Boveri & Cie
CAHI (or TsAGI)	Central Aerodynamics and Hydrodynamics Institute, Zhukovskii
CALTEC	California Institute of Technology
CEM	Compagnie Electro-Mécanique (a subsidiary of SOCEMA), Le Bourget
CIAM (or TsIAM)	Central Institute of Aviation Motors
CWES	Cold Weather Experimental Station, Winnipeg
DDP	Department of Defence Production
DGCA	Direzione Generale delle Costruzioni Aeronautiche (Construction Directorate)
DH	de Havilland
DMS	Department of Munitions and Supply
EFW	Eidg. [Eidgenössische] Flugzeugwerke Emmen (Federal Aircraft Works, Emmen)
EGT	exhaust gas temperature
FFA	Flug- und Fahrzeugwerke AG, Altenrhein (formerly Dornier Altenrhein)
GAZ	State Aviation Factory
GE	General Electric
GKO	State Defence Committee
Gosplan	State plan
GTPR	Gas Turbine Propeller Rocket (turboprop)
GU NKAP	Chief Administration of NKAP
GUAP	Chief Administration of the Aviation Industry
GVF	Civil Air Fleet (Aeroflot), which could be used by the military, if needed
H-S	Hispano-Suiza
IHI	Ishikawajima-Harima Heavy Industries Co. Ltd
IJA	Imperial Japanese Army
IJN	Imperial Japanese Navy
JJE	Japanese Jet Engine Company
JASDF	Japanese Air Self Defence Force
KB	Constructor Bureau or design office. Construction work then given to an OKB or GAZ

KhAI	Kharkov Aviation Institute
KMF	Kommission für militärische Flugzeugbeschaffung
Kogisho	Naval Air Arsenal (at Yokosuka)
KTA	Kriegstechnische Abteilung (Military Engineering Division of the Defence Department)
LII	Flight Research Institute, attached to CAHI
MD	Avions Marcel Dassault
MIT	Massachusetts Institute of Technology
MQT	Model Qualification Test (150-hour)
MVTV	Moscow Higher Technical School
NACA	National Advisory Committee for Aeronautics (USA)
NAS	National Academy of Sciences
NATO	North Atlantic Treaty Organisation
Ne	Nensho (combustion rocket)
NII	Scientific Test Institute (there were about thirty, eg NII V-VS)
NKAP	State Commissariat for Aviation Industry
NKOP	Inventors' Department
NRC	National Research Council
OGK	Chief Designer's Department
OKB	Experimental Construction (and design) Bureau
PFRT	Preliminary Flight Rating Test (fifty-hour) Pre-Flight Rating Test
RCAF	Royal Canadian Air Force
R-R	Rolls-Royce
SAAB	Svenska Aeroplan Aktiebolaget
SAC	Strategic Air Command
SEPR	Société d'Etude de la Propulsion par Réaction
SFA	Svenska Flygmotor AB
SKB	Special Design Bureau
SNCA	Société Nationale de Construction Aéronautique
SNECMA	Société Nationale d'Etudes et de Construction de Moteurs d'Aviation
SNK	Sovnarkom (Council of People's Commissars)
SOCEMA	Société de Construction et d'Equipements Mécaniques pour l'Aviation
STA	Service Technique Aéronautique

STAL	Svenska Turbinfabrik AB Ljungström	VTOL	vertical take-off and landing
STO	Council of Labour and Defence	V-VS	Soviet Air Force. From 1946 it consisted of five Commands:
TBO	time between overhauls	DA	Long-range Aviation
TIU	Tokyo Imperial University	IA-PVO	Fighter Aviation of the Air Defence Forces
TR	turbine rocket	FA	Frontal Aviation
USAAF	United States Army Air Force (USAF from September 1947)	A-VMF	Naval Aviation
USAF	United States Air Force	A-VDV	Aviation of the Airborne Troops (of the V-VS)
USSR	Union of Soviet Socialist Republics		
VENAR	Velivoli e Natanti a Reazione (Jet Aircraft and Boats (company))	ZTL	Zweikreisturbinen-Luftstrahltriebwerk (two-circuit turbojet engine)

Bibliography and Further Reading

Many of the following titles have been consulted during the creation of this book, and others have been listed to provide further relevant reading. In addition, many articles from periodicals and journals, plus other papers and reports too numerous to mention, were read. Various issues of *The Aeroplane, Aeroplane Spotter, Air International, Air Pictorial, Aerofan, Engineer, Flight, Flug Revue, Flying Review, Flypast, Interavia, Jet & Prop, Luftfahrt International, RAeS Journal, Wings, Airpower* and *Aero Magazine* were consulted.

SOVIET UNION

Berne, L.P., et al: *Otechestvennye Aviatgionnye Dvigeteli XX Vek* (Avico Press, 2003) [in Russian]

Chehuiko, V.M., et al: *Aviadvigatelestroenie* (Aviamir, 1999) [in Russian]

Geust, C.F.: *German Aircraft of the Soviet Union: Red Stars*, 2 vols (Apali Oy, 1998)

——: *Under the Red Star: Luftwaffe Aircraft in the Soviet Airforce* (Airlife, 1993)

Gordon, Yefim, and Bill Gunston: *Soviet X-Planes* (Midland, 2000)

Goryelov, A.I.: *Moi Vospominaniya* (Salut, 2002) [in Russian]

Gunston, Bill: *Encyclopedia of Russian Aircraft* (Osprey, 1995)

Kotelnikov, Vladimir, and Tony Buttler: *Early Russian Jet Engines*, Historical Series no. 33 (Rolls-Royce Heritage Trust)

Nemecek, V.: *The History of Soviet Aircraft from 1918* (Willow Books, 1986)

Shustov, I.G.: *Aviagateli* (AKS Konversalt, 2000) [in Russian]

Sobolew, Dimitri A.: *Deutsche Spuren in der sowjetischen Luftfahrtgeschichte* (Verlag E.S. Mittler, 2000)

Various contributors from NPO Saturn: *Aviadvigateli Saturna* (Polygon Press, 2003) [in Russian]

Various contributors: *MMMP Salut Strantis Istorii* (Salut, 2002) [in Russian]

Various contributors: *Motorostriotelnoe Proizdstvennoe Obedinenie* (UMPO, 2000) [in Russian]

Various contributors: *Put Dlinou v Zhehikhni* (Gonchar, 2002) [in Russian]

Zrelov, V.A., and G.G. Kartashov: *Avigateli NK* (Samara, 1999) [in Russian]

USA

Allward, Maurice: *F-86 Sabre* (Ian Allan, 1978)

Bower, Tom: *The Paperclip Conspiracy* (Michael Joseph, 1987)

Bowers, Peter M.: *Boeing Aircraft since 1916* (Putnam, 1966)

Constant II, Edward W.: *The Origins of the Turbojet Revolution* (Johns Hopkins University Press, 1980)

Dorr, R.F, Jon Lake and Warren Thompson: *Korean War Aces* (Osprey, 1995)

Dorr, Robert F.: *US Jet Fighters since 1945* (Blandford Press, 1988)

General Electric: *Seven Decades of Progress* (Aero Publishers, 1979)

Hallion, Richard P.: *Supersonic Flight* (Smithsonian Institution, 1972)

Leyes II, Richard A., and William A. Fleming: *The History of North American Small Gas Turbine Aircraft Engines* (AIAA and The Smithsonian Institution, 1999)

MacCloskey, Brig. General Monro: *The United States Air Force* (Frederick A. Praeger, 1967)

Miller, Jay: *The X-Planes: X-1 to X-45* (Midland, 2001)

Neville, Leslie E., and Nathaniel F. Silsbee: *Jet Propulsion Progress* (McGraw-Hill, 1948)

Pratt & Whitney: *The Pratt & Whitney Aircraft Story* (Pratt & Whitney Aircraft Division, 1950)

Sonnenburg, P., and A. Schoneberger: *Allison, Power of Excellence, 1915–1990* (Coastline Publishers, 1990)

St Peter, James J.: *The Memoirs of Ernest C. Simpson* (Air Force Wright Aeronautical Laboratories, 1987)

——: *The History of Aircraft Gas Turbine Engine Development in the United States* (The American Society of Mechanical Engineers, 1999)

Yeager, Chuck, and Leo Janos: *Yeager* (Century, 1985)

JAPAN

'Airevue': *General View of Japanese Military Aircraft in the Pacific War* (Kanto-Sha Co., 1958)

Francillon, R.J.: *Japanese Aircraft of the Pacific War* (Putnam, 1970)

Anon: *Japanese Aircraft Industry in WW2 – USAF 1946 Report* (ISO Publications, 1996)

Mikesh, Robert C.: *Kikka*, Close-Up 19 (Monogram Aviation Publications, 1979)

FRANCE

Bodemer, Alfred, and Robert Laugier: *L'ATAR et tous les autres moteurs à réaction français* (Editions J.D. Reber, 1996)

Cuny, Jean: *Les chasseurs Dassault: Ouragans, Mystères et Super-Mystères*, Collection DOCAVIA, 13 (Editions Larivière, 1980)

Jane's All The World's Aircraft 1945/46 (Jane's Publishing, 1946)

Kalnin, A., and M. Laborie: *Le turboréacteur et autres moteurs à réaction* (Dunod, 1958)

Lacroze, Jean, and Philippe Ricco: *René Leduc, un pionnier de la propulsion à réaction* (Editions Larivière, n.d.)

Noettinger, Jacques: *Histoire de l'Aéronautique Français, hommes et événements, 1940–1980* (Editions France-Empire, 1983)

——: *Histoire de l'Aéronautique Français, l'épopée 1940–1960* (Editions France-Empire, 1978)

Opdycke, Leonard E.: *French Aeroplanes before the Great War* (Schiffer, 1999)

CANADA

Floyd, Jim: *The Avro Canada C102 Jetliner* (The Boston Mills Press, 1986)

Milberry, Larry: *The Avro CF-100* (CANAV Books, 1981)

Organ, Richard, Ron Page, D. Watson and L. Wilkinson: *Avro Arrow* (The Boston Mills Press, 1980)

Page, Ron: *Avro Canuck – CF-100 Fighter* (The Boston Mills Press, 1981)

Peden, Murray: *Fall of an Arrow* (Stoddart Publishing, 1987)

Zuuring, Peter: *The Arrow Scrapbook* (Arrow Alliance Press, 1999)

SWEDEN

Andersson, Hans G.: *Saab Aircraft* (Putnam, 1989)

Dorr, Robert F.: *Saab Viggen* (Ian Allan, 1985)

Gohlke, Werner: 'Thermal Air Jet Propulsion', *Aircraft Engineering*, 14 (February 1942), p. 33

SWITZERLAND

Bridel, Georges: *Schweizerische Strahlflugzeuge und Strahltriebwerke*, Sonderveröffentlichung Nr 2 (Verkehrshaus der Schweiz, 1979)

Jackson, Robert: *Hawker Hunter* (Airlife, 1989)

ITALY

Alegi, Gregory: *Campini-Caproni*, Ali d'Italia, Serie 5 Mini (La Bancarella Aeronautica, 2000)

Marcozzi, G., and R. Bettiolo: *Il primo aviogetto italiano* (Aerofax No. 5, 1988)

CZECHOSLOVAKIA

Author consortium: *Messerschmitt Me 262* (MBI/Sagitta, Prague, 1992)

Balous, Miroslav, and Jirí Rajlich: *Messerschmitt Me 262* (MBI Publishing House, 1995)

Fleischer, Seweryn, and Marek Rys: *Me 262 Schwalbe, part 2*, Aircraft Monograph no. 9 (AJ Press, Warsaw, 1988)

Kroklikiewicz, Tadeusz: *Messerschmitt Me 262* (Warsaw, 1999) [in Polish]

HUNGARY

Gunston, Bill: *World Encyclopaedia of Aero Engines* (Patrick Stephens, 1986)

——: Jet and Turbine Engines (Patrick Stephens, 1997)

Jendrassik, György: 'Communications on the Combustion Gas Turbine', *Proceedings of the Institute of Mechanical Engineers*, CXLII/4 (February 1940)

——: 'Versuche an einer neuen Gasturbine', *VDI Zeitschrift*, lxxxvi/26 (July 1939)

EGYPT AND SPAIN

Brandner, Ferdinand: *Ein Leben zwischen Fronten* (Verlag Welsermuhl, 1973)

Gersdorf, Kyrill von, Kurt Grasman and Helmut Schubert: *Flugmotoren und Strahltriebwerke* (Bernard & Graefe Verlag, 1995)

Index

For convenience, this Index has been divided into **General, Aircraft and Engine** sections.

Aircraft

Engines